MANHATTAN PREP

GMAT Foundations of Verbal

GMAT Strategy Guide Supplement

This supplemental guide provides in-depth and easy-to-follow explanations of the fundamental verbal skills necessary for a strong performance on the GMAT.

GMAT Foundations of Verbal, 6th Edition

10-digit International Standard Book Number: 1-941234-53-4
13-digit International Standard Book Number: 978-1-941234-53-2
eISBN: 978-1-941234-55-6

Layout Design: Cathy Huang
Production Manager: Derek Frankhouser
Cover Design: Frank Callaghan
Cover Photography: Kate Espada

STRATEGY GUIDES

0 GMAT Roadmap

1 Fractions, Decimals, & Percents

2 Algebra

3 Word Problems

4 Geometry

5 Number Properties

6 Critical Reasoning

7 Reading Comprehension

8 Sentence Correction

9 Integrated Reasoning & Essay

STRATEGY GUIDE SUPPLEMENTS

Quant Supplement Guides

Foundations of GMAT Math

GMAT Advanced Quant

Official Guide Companion

Verbal Supplement Guides

GMAT Foundations of Verbal

Official Guide Companion for Sentence Correction

December 1st, 2015

Dear Student,

Thank you for picking up a copy of *GMAT Foundations of Verbal*. I hope this book provides just the guidance you need to get the most out of your studies.

At Manhattan Prep, we continually aspire to provide the best instructors and study resources possible. We hope that you will find our commitment manifest in this book. If you have any questions or comments, please email us at gmat@manhattanprep.com. Our Student Services and curriculum teams are very interested to hear what you have to say.

Many people were involved in the creation of this book. First and foremost is Zeke Vanderhoek, the founder of Manhattan Prep. Zeke was a lone tutor in New York when he started the company in 2000. Now, a decade and a half later, the company serves the needs of thousands of students each year.

Our books are based on the continuing experiences of our instructors and students. Stacey Koprince led the rewriting of *GMAT Foundations of Verbal*, resulting in the new edition you hold in your hands. Additional contributions were made by Mary Adkins, Chelsey Cooley, Dmitry Farber, Whitney Garner, Rina Goldfield, Andrea Pawliczek, and Emily Meredith Sledge. We should note that Jennifer Dziura drove the creation of the first edition, to which Stacey and Tommy Wallach contributed significantly.

Meanwhile, Cathy Huang provided her production and design expertise to make the book sing off the page. Derek Frankhouser made sure all the moving pieces came together at just the right time.

At Manhattan Prep, we are proud of this book and of the people who have worked hard to make it for you.

Thanks again for trusting us to help you prepare for the GMAT. Best of luck!

Sincerely,

Chris Ryan
Vice President of Academics
Manhattan Prep

www.manhattanprep.com/gmat 138 West 25th Street, 7th Floor, New York, NY 10001 Tel: 212-721-7400 Fax: 646-514-7425

HOW TO ACCESS YOUR ONLINE RESOURCES

IF YOU ARE A REGISTERED MANHATTAN PREP STUDENT

and have received this book as part of your course materials, you have *automatic* access to *all* of our online resources. This includes all practice exams, Question Banks, and online updates to this book. To access these resources, follow the instructions in the Welcome Guide provided to you at the start of your program.

IF YOU PURCHASED THIS BOOK FROM MANHATTANPREP.COM OR AT ONE OF OUR CENTERS

1. Go to: **www.manhattanprep.com/gmat/studentcenter**
2. Log in with the username and password you chose when setting up your account.

IF YOU PURCHASED THIS BOOK AT A RETAIL LOCATION

1. Create an account with Manhattan Prep at this website: **www.manhattanprep.com/gmat/register**
2. Follow the instructions on the screen.

Your one year of online access begins on the day that you register your book at the above URL.

You only need to register your product *once* at the above URL. To use your online resources any time *after* you have completed the registration process, log in at the following URL: **www.manhattanprep.com/gmat/studentcenter**

Please note that online access is nontransferable. This means that only *new* and *unregistered* copies of the book will grant you online access. Previously used books will not provide any online resources.

IF YOU PURCHASED AN EBOOK VERSION OF THIS BOOK

1. Create an account with Manhattan Prep at this website: **www.manhattanprep.com/gmat/register**
2. Email a copy of your purchase receipt to **gmat@manhattanprep.com** to activate your resources. Please be sure to use the same email address to create an account that you used to purchase the eBook.

Email **gmat@manhattanprep.com** or call **800-576-4628** with any questions.

Please refer to the following page for a description of the online resources that come with this book.

YOUR ONLINE RESOURCES

YOUR PURCHASE INCLUDES ONLINE ACCESS TO THE FOLLOWING:

GMAT FOUNDATIONS OF VERBAL QUESTION BANK

This bank consists of extra practice questions (with detailed explanations) that test the variety of foundational verbal concepts and skills covered in this book. These questions provide you with extra practice beyond the problem sets contained in this book. You may use our online timer to practice your pacing by setting time limits for each question in the bank.

5 FREE INTERACT™ LESSONS

Interact™ is a comprehensive self-study program that is fun, intuitive, and directed by you. Each interactive video lesson is taught by an expert Manhattan Prep instructor and includes dozens of individual branching points. The choices you make define the content you see. This book comes with access to the *first five lessons* of GMAT Interact. Lessons are available on your computer or iPad so you can prep where you are, when you want. For more information on the full version of this program, visit **www.manhattanprep.com/gmat/interact**.

ONLINE UPDATES TO THE CONTENT IN THIS BOOK

The content presented in this book is updated periodically to ensure that it reflects the GMAT's most current trends. You may view all updates, including any known errors or changes, upon registering for online access.

The above resources can be found in your Student Center at manhattanprep.com/gmat/studentcenter

TABLE *of* CONTENTS

Introduction

Welcome to *GMAT Foundations of Verbal*!

This book will improve your English for the rest of your life.

This guide will also help you with the GMAT, of course, but its usefulness isn't limited to the GMAT. You'll learn how sentences work, how arguments are constructed, and how written English is used and understood in business contexts.

The vast majority of this guide is helpful for both native and non-native speakers, though the section on vocabulary in Reading Comprehension is primarily oriented toward English language learners.

Either way, this book will open your eyes:

- You may discover that words you thought you knew can be used in ways you weren't aware of. (Did you know that *qualified* can mean *limited*?)
- You may also discover that passages you thought you understood actually have additional meaning that you missed on a first reading.
- And you may discover that the way even educated native speakers communicate in spoken English is not actually considered correct in written English. (Did you know that *I have done more studying than has he* is correct, and *Everyone who attended the meeting bought their own snacks* is incorrect? The word *their* should be *his or her*.)

This is certainly not the only book you will need in order to succeed on the GMAT. You will also need the latest ***The Official Guide for GMAT® Review***, a book filled with past official GMAT questions via which you are going to practice.

Getting Started

We also recommend that you "graduate" from this book to the *Manhattan Prep GMAT Strategy Guide Series,* which includes individual guides to *Sentence Correction* (SC), *Critical Reasoning* (CR), and *Reading Comprehension* (RC), as well as additional books on the Quantitative (Quant), Integrated Reasoning (IR), and Analytical Writing Assessment (AWA) sections of the GMAT.

All right, let's talk about how to get the most out of this strategy guide.

If you've never been sure exactly how to identify the subject of a sentence, if Quant is your natural strength and you dislike the Verbal section, or if you're a non-native speaker who feels that you could use some additional instruction on the fundamentals, then you'll likely want to work through this guide.

If you fall into one of the categories above, you may need only one or two of the major sections in this book before you feel ready to move on to the individual (and more advanced) *Sentence Correction, Critical Reasoning,* and *Reading Comprehension Strategy Guides.* Alternatively, you may want to work through this book thoroughly before you move to the Strategy Guides.

If you generally feel comfortable with your language, reading, and reasoning skills, then you can move straight to the main Strategy Guides, but use this *Foundations* guide as a reference whenever needed. You can look up adverbs here to remind yourself what they do. If you are struggling to find assumptions on CR or to articulate the main idea of a reading passage, flip open this book to drill your foundational skills.

If you aren't sure whether you need the material in this book, try a few end-of-chapter problems to see how you do. If you struggle with any of the material, then make time to work through the relevant exercises in the body of the chapter.

Finally, if you are planning to take a class, we recommend that you work through any needed material in the *GMAT Foundations of Verbal* or *Foundations of GMAT Math* Strategy Guides before starting your course, if at all possible.

Let's get started!

Chapter 1
of

GMAT Foundations of Verbal

Part 1: **Sentence Correction**

Words & Sentences

In This Chapter...

Chapter 1

Words & Sentences

A GMAT Sentence Correction problem looks something like this:

> In order to improve profit margins, the hospital adopted a number of measures, <u>to eliminate some administrative personnel and raising</u> fees for certain elective services.
>
> (A) to eliminate some administrative personnel and raising
> (B) to eliminate some administrative personnel and rising
> (C) eliminating some administrative personnel and raising
> (D) by eliminating some administrative personnel and the rise of
> (E) eliminated some administrative personnel and raising

The answer choices represent possible replacements for the underlined portion of the original sentence. Choice (A) is a repeat of the original. Choices (B) through (E) contain at least one difference.

What Is Tested

Sentence Correction tests **grammar** and **meaning**—and these two things are sometimes intertwined. It does not test every little rule—for instance, you are not evaluated directly on comma placement, and no one cares whether you end a sentence with a preposition.

You do need to know the main rules of English grammar (though you don't need to know the technical names) and you do have to think about logical and unambiguous meaning.

Here's the good news:

> If you can read this simple sentence, you already know tons of grammar.

You just don't know how much you already know! If you learn what is necessary to construct a "legal" sentence, as well as what roles the different words fill, then you can learn how to tackle Sentence Correction.

Here is the same sentence again, with the words in alphabetical order:

> already can grammar. If know of read sentence, simple this tons you you

You know the meaning of each word, but the new "sentence" is nonsense!

Whether English is your first or your fifth language, you are reading and understanding this sentence right now. As you read normal grammatical sentences, your brain is doing much more than looking up concepts in your mental dictionary. On the fly, your brain is assembling those concepts into complete thoughts.

Guess what? **A grammatical sentence is a complete thought.** Grammar and logic (or meaning) are what let you construct and understand these complete thoughts.

Of course, if everyone's internal grammar genie worked perfectly all the time, Sentence Correction would be very easy. The genie is fallible. In particular, you may be awesome at understanding *spoken* language, but you can be more easily fooled by *written* text, especially when the text uses constructions that are totally legal but rarely heard.

In fact, you are actually *too* smart for the GMAT! You already automatically decode garbled messages and figure out what people actually meant to say. Unfortunately, this skill can make it harder to spot subtle flaws in SC questions on the GMAT.

You're going to need to refine your intuitive knowledge of grammar. Work to **articulate the rules explicitly**. Consider this example again:

> If you can read this simple sentence, you already know tons of grammar.

Look at the words one after another. How would you classify each one grammatically?

If you started to think of terms such as "nouns" and "verbs," you're on the right track. Here are the words, classified by their **part of speech** in this sentence:

Noun:	sentence, tons, grammar	**Verb:**	can, read, know
Pronoun:	you	**Adverb:**	already
Adjective:	this, simple	**Conjunction:**	if
Preposition:	of		

The next few chapters will focus on these seven parts of speech. You will learn their characteristics, as well as commonly associated errors. You will practice spotting these parts of speech and associated errors in simple sentences.

Some languages clearly indicate the part of speech right on the word itself. For instance, the ending *-skii* on a Russian word practically shouts, "I'm an adjective!"

If you are not a native speaker, be aware that English doesn't often do this. What part of speech is *believe*? It's a verb, but you just have to know that. Don't worry: in a pinch, you can make up a simple test sentence, as you'll see later.

It gets trickier to pin down words such as *light* and *sound*, which can easily take on more than one part of speech. The choice depends on context. In other words, it depends on the other words in the sentence:

Noun:	There's no *light* in here, and I can't hear a *sound*.
Verb:	Can you *light* a match? Wait, what does that *sound* like to you?
Adjective:	My head feels *light*. I hope we get out of here safe and *sound*.

Even when you know the part of speech of every word in a sentence, there's still more to do. Read the following two sentences and think about the meaning that each one conveys:

1. Mary tickled Joe, who sat still and frowned quietly.

2. Joe tickled Mary, who sat still and frowned quietly.

Word order matters immensely in English. It tells you who did what to whom.

In the first sentence, the noun *Mary* is in front of the verb *tickled*, so *Mary* is the **subject** of *tickled*. Who did the tickling? Mary. Meanwhile, *Joe* is the **object** of *tickled*. Who was tickled? Joe. In addition, *Joe* is the effective subject of *sat* and *frowned*. Who sat still and frowned quietly? Joe.

The second sentence reverses the grammatical roles of the nouns *Mary* and *Joe* by swapping their positions. As a result, the real-life roles of Mary and Joe are also reversed. The sentences describe different situations.

Word order is one aspect of **sentence structure**, which is an incredibly important part of grammar. In later chapters, you will practice spotting errors related to sentence structure.

In addition to testing grammar, GMAT Sentence Correction also tests your ability to pick an answer choice that makes the most sense. You must ensure that the intended **meaning** comes through clearly. Even grammatically perfect sentences can have ambiguous or illogical meanings. For example:

> The spill has greatly affected the Gulf of Mexico, where thousands of office workers toil despite the pollution.

This perfectly grammatical sentence implies that thousands of office workers work *in* the Gulf of Mexico, which is a body of water! While it's possible that some people do work in this body of water, *office* workers wouldn't. When the original sentence is illogical, pick an answer that fixes the problem. For instance, the correct answer might say that the office workers work in the *area surrounding the Gulf of Mexico.*

Finally, be careful about the concept of concision. While it is generally true that it is better to say things concisely, you must first ensure that the sentence is grammatically correct and has a logical meaning.

Use concision only as a tiebreaker: if you still have two or more answers left after examining everything else, then one possible path forward is to guess the most concise answer.

Listening to Your Ear versus Learning Grammar

Your ear already tells you whether something sounds right or wrong, so it can be a valuable tool. There's a hitch, though: many common errors have crept so far into the spoken language that these errors now sound correct to people who are reading casually. The test writers exploit this situation, writing such errors into some incorrect answer choices.

In other words, your ear is likely causing you to fall into traps on the GMAT. Your task is to *retrain* your ear based on the proper rules so that you no longer fall into these traps.

For instance, according to GMAT rules, the following sentence contains *five* mistakes:

> I credited the counselor for the astute observation that each of the students differ from their friends in ways that affect their development, which is crucial to understand when counseling each one.

Your ear might tell you that the sentence above sounds funny, but your ear will probably tell you that the correct version sounds funny, too:

> I credited the counselor WITH the astute observation that each of the students DIFFERS from HIS OR HER friends in ways that affect HIS OR HER development, AN IDEA crucial to understand when counseling each one.

Don't worry right now about the particular issues going on in the examples above; you'll learn all about these issues as you work through this book. For now, just be aware that you can't fully rely on your ear as it stands; you are going to need to learn the rules and retrain your ear regarding what is right or wrong.

The Answer to the Question

Did you solve the question at the beginning of the chapter? If not, turn back to it, then return with your answer.

Here is the original sentence again:

> In order to improve profit margins, the hospital adopted a number of measures, to eliminate some administrative personnel and raising fees for certain elective services.

And here is the corrected version:

> (C) In order to improve profit margins, the hospital adopted a number of measures, eliminating some administrative personnel and raising fees for certain elective services.

The word *and* is a conjunction: a word that connects two parts of a sentence. (The official grammar term for this issue is **parallelism**.) When you see *and*, ask yourself, "What is the sentence trying to connect?" In the incorrect sentence, *and* is connecting *to eliminate . . . and raising fees.*

There are two things to manage when trying to connect two (or more) parts of a sentence. First, the two parts have to be logically comparable; that is, both *eliminating* and *raising* provide information about the types of measures the hospital adopted.

Second, the two words have to have the same form; that is, they have to be structurally comparable. *To eliminate* is not the same form as *raising.* Among the given answer choices, only answer (C) offers a pair in the same form: *eliminating* and *raising.*

Therefore, answer choice (C) is the only one that is properly parallel.

In later chapters, you'll learn about these issues in more depth. For now, let's get started with nouns, pronouns, and adjectives.

Chapter 2

of

GMAT Foundations of Verbal

Part 1: **Sentence Correction**

Nouns, Pronouns, & Adjectives

In This Chapter...

Nouns
Categories of Nouns
Singular and Plural
Nouns Wrap-Up
Pronouns
Antecedents
A Special Note About the Pronoun "One"
Pronouns Wrap-Up
Making Flash Cards
Adjectives
Nouns, Pronouns, and Adjectives Wrap-Up
Answers to Pop Quizzes
Answers to Drill Sets

Chapter 2

Nouns, Pronouns, & Adjectives

Nouns

A noun is a word for a thing, a place, a person, an animal, an action, or an idea. These words are nouns or can be nouns:

kitchen	case study	love	Tuesday	product	stop
children	cleanliness	Afghanistan	fluidity	the rich	cry
removal	division	water	finding	production	administration

A few of these words are commonly found as other parts of speech. For instance, *love, stop,* and *cry* can all be verbs:

Used as nouns:	Can you feel the **love**?	This is my **stop**.	I want to let out a **cry** of joy.
Used as verbs:	Wait, you don't **love** me?	**Stop**!	I **cry** when I cut onions.

How to Spot Nouns

How can you tell when a word is being used as a noun?

First, ask yourself whether the word is being used to describe a thing. It could be an abstract thing, such as an emotion (*love*), an event (*discussion*), a quality (*cleanliness*), an action (*removal*), or a result of an action (*production*). Try putting the word *a* or *the* before the potential noun. These little words tell you that a noun is coming . . . eventually. For example:

> *a* **discussion** *the* **cleanliness** *the* popular and heartwarming **production** of *Annie*

As a last resort, try inserting a silly noun in place of the word in question. You'll probably get a silly sentence, but that sentence will be grammatical if the original word is a noun. Try inserting the word *cheese* in the previous example:

Replace with *cheese*: the popular and heartwarming **cheese** of *Annie*

This sounds a little weird, but it is possible that Annie's *cheese* is popular, since cheese is an actual thing—a noun! However, look what happens if you replace some of the verb forms listed earlier with the word *cheese*:

Original words used as verbs: Wait, you don't **cheese** me?

I **cheese** when I cut onions.

These examples aren't just weird; they don't actually make any sense. Since they fail the cheese test, you know that in the original versions, *love* and *cry* were not being used as nouns.

Categories of Nouns

You may have noticed some unusual nouns on the list above. There are several different kinds of nouns, which are discussed here.

It's not necessary for you to memorize the grammatical terms below. Rather, your goal is to be able to recognize that all of these strange nouns really are nouns.

Notice that some nouns seem to be made from simpler words. *Cleanliness* and *fluidity* are made from the adjectives *clean* and *fluid.* Most nouns made from adjectives are **qualities**. Sometimes, an adjective with a *the* in front (*the rich*) can function as a noun: *The rich love these nice cars.* Here, *the rich* is really just a short version of *rich people.*

Nouns can also be made from verbs. *Removal* comes from *remove. Discussion* comes from *discuss.* Both *product* and *production* come from *produce.*

Many of these nouns made from verbs represent **actions** or the results of actions. Be careful! Verbs represent actions, too. The difference is that in the noun form, the action is a *thing*, even if abstract, so the action can play the role of a noun in a sentence.

Try putting *the* or *this* in front of an action noun. Write short sentences to see how action nouns work as subjects or objects. For example:

The **removal** was great. The **discussion** inspired me. I like this **product.**
I like this **production**.

Some nouns (*Tuesday, Afghanistan*) are spelled with capital letters. These nouns are proper nouns, nouns that name specific items. All other nouns are common nouns. Some words can be used as proper or common nouns, as in *Harvard University* and *all universities*. When *university* is used as part of a proper noun, it is capitalized. When it is used as a common noun, it is lowercase. You don't need to memorize capitalization rules for Sentence Correction; simply recognize that both proper and common nouns are perfectly good nouns.

Some nouns (*case study, post office, dog collar*) contain more than one word. These are compound nouns. Some compound nouns are hyphenated (*gun-carriage, attorney-at-law*), and others have been welded into one word (*landlord, bookkeeper*). When you see two nouns in a row, the first noun is usually modifying the second noun, and together they form a compound noun. In essence, the first noun becomes an adjective. The second noun stays a noun. For example:

kitchen sink = a kind of *sink*
love poem = a kind of *poem*
dog collar = a kind of *collar*

Collective nouns refer to groups composed of members (*administration, jury, society*). In American English, collective nouns are singular: *The army IS advancing* (not *ARE advancing*). In British English, these same nouns are typically plural, as in *The family ARE on holiday* or *Manchester United HAVE scored again*. So which is correct on the GMAT?

When the test writers want to test this issue, they will always give you a clue in the non-underlined portion of the sentence that will tell you whether they want this collective noun to be singular or plural. Your task is to find the clue. For example:

> The team of <u>players from the local high school (is / are) comprised</u> entirely of first-year students and includes both boys and girls.

This sentence contains two verbs to go with the subject *team*: The *team* (*is / are*) *comprised* . . . and *includes* boys and girls. The second verb, *includes*, is not underlined and it is singular, so the noun *team* is intended to be singular. Therefore, *the team is comprised . . . and includes boys and girls.*

The GMAT also tests gerunds, or *-ing* forms of verbs that function as nouns. For example, *studying* is a gerund, from the verb to study:

> Studying is important if you want to do well on the test.

In the example sentence above, the word *studying* is acting as a noun; in fact, it is the subject of the sentence. You'll learn more about gerunds in the Verbs section of this guide.

Drill 2.1 — Find the Nouns

Circle all of the nouns in the following sentences. Most sentences contain more than one noun.

2

1. Companies in the European Union receive certain protections from imports.

2. Jane Austen wrote *Pride and Prejudice,* a novel that in 2005 was adapted into a film starring Keira Knightley.

3. The primary purpose of the passage is to present an alternative explanation for a well-known fact.

4. A recent study has provided additional support for a particular theory about the origin of the fruit bat.

5. I am only happy if you are happy; my happiness depends on yours.

Answers are on page 41.

Singular and Plural

Dog by itself refers to one dog. You'll often see *a* or *the* in front of *dog*, as in these examples: *I saw a dog walking down the street. The dog was a cocker spaniel.* Either way, the noun *dog* is **singular**.

To talk about more than one dog, make the noun *dog* **plural** by adding an *-s*. For instance: *I have three dogs.*

Some languages do not emphasize the difference between singular and plural, so if your native language does not distinguish singular and plural, pay close attention. Even native English speakers can get tripped up on this issue, and the GMAT loves to exploit tricky cases.

First of all, in English you can count some things but not others. Countable nouns have a singular form when you have just one of them and a plural form when you have two or more of them. Most plural forms add an *-s*: *one pencil, two pencils, seven pencils.* You talk about how much you have of a countable noun by using numbers or other words (*many, few, more, fewer*).

Some things, such as bread or water, can't be counted directly without adding a word such as *slice* or *cup*: *one slice of bread, two slices of bread; one cup of water, two cups of water.*

MEMORIZE IT!

Use *amount* for something you can't count and *number* for something you can count. For example: "A great *number* of friends have shown me a great *amount* of kindness."

Less and *fewer* work the same way. Use *less* for something you can't count (*I have less stress this term than last*) and *fewer* for something you can count (*This express lane is only for people with 10 items or fewer*).

This means that most grocery stores are incorrect. Virtually all of their signs say "10 items *or less*." Since items are countable, *less* should be *fewer*.

In this case, you're really counting the *slices* or the *cups*. These nouns don't have a plural form (*I have many breads?*). You talk about how much you have of an uncountable noun by counting units (*pieces* or *cups*) or by using *much, little, more,* or *less*.

Some abstract nouns are uncountable (*fluidity*), while others are countable (*concept*). You can usually use common sense to tell whether the noun is countable: try to count the actual word! One concept, two concepts, three concepts? Yes, it is possible to have several different concepts. One fluidity, two fluidities, three fluidities? Nope, that doesn't work.

Nouns Wrap-Up

Throughout this book, you will see a summary, or wrap-up, at the end of each section. Ideally, try to come up with your own takeaways before you read ours.

✓ Nouns can describe all of the following:
- Physical things
- Abstract things
- Actions
- Events
- Emotions
- Qualities

✓ If you can place *a* or *the* before a word and it makes sense, then that word is a noun.

✓ Nouns can be singular or plural; the GMAT will test you on subject–verb agreement and noun–pronoun agreement.

Pop Quiz!

True or False: The sentence, "I have a great amount of homework and a great amount of deadlines," is correct.

Answer is on page 40.

Pronouns

A pronoun is a word used in place of a noun or noun phrase. All of these are pronouns:

he	his	it	they	myself	their
who	those	everyone	somebody	each	its

Unlike nouns, there simply aren't that many pronouns in existence. The bad news is that pronouns are so common and so unassuming that readers often blow right past them. By their very nature, pronouns do not call attention to themselves! They're stand-ins, substitutes, the unobtrusive words in a sentence. For this reason, on a GMAT problem, they're often the most important words around.

Categories of Pronouns

As with nouns, you absolutely do *not* need to memorize the grammatical terms for these types of pronouns. However, you should be able to recognize all the different kinds of pronouns *as pronouns.*

Personal pronouns are what most people think of when they think of pronouns. You use personal pronouns such as she or them because it sounds silly to say, "Cory did Cory's homework in Cory's room" rather than "Cory did his homework in his room." Personal pronouns can be divided into three subcategories:

1. Subject pronouns: **I you he she it we they**

Subject pronouns are used as the subjects of sentences or clauses (sets of words containing a subject and a verb). Subject pronouns perform actions, represented by verbs. Examples: ***He** ate. The rain fell as **they** continued practicing.*

2. Object pronouns: **me you him her it us you them**

Object pronouns serve as the object of a verb. That is, actions (represented by verbs) get done to them. *The boss gave **her** a raise.* Object pronouns can also be the objects of prepositions: *What do you think of **it**? Give this to **her**. I see through **them**.*

3. Possessive pronouns: **mine yours his hers its ours theirs**

These pronouns indicate ownership: *The car is **hers**. The dog loves **its** chew toy.* Don't confuse the possessive pronoun *its* with the contraction *it's*. "Its" indicates that something belongs to whatever "it" is; the *chew toy* belongs to the *dog*. "It's" always means "it is."

You might be wondering, where are *my, your, her, our,* and *their*? These possessive adjectives are a kind of cross between pronouns and adjectives. They're technically adjectives because they modify nouns (*my sheep, your water*). They don't stand in place of nouns, as real pronouns do.

However, like the true possessive pronouns, possessive adjectives have to refer back to a noun—the person or thing doing the possessing. Pay particular attention to *its* and *theirs.*

2

The noun that a personal pronoun stands in for should be clear. This is also true of possessive adjectives. For instance, *The Senator and the lobbyist had a heated disagreement about* ***her*** *agenda.* Whose agenda? The Senator's or the lobbyist's? It's ambiguous, and ambiguity makes for a bad sentence.

Reflexive pronouns: **myself ourselves itself etc.**

These pronouns are formed by adding *-self* to the end of possessive pronouns or adjectives and are used to reflect back on the noun. Example: *The executives rewarded* ***themselves*** *with bonuses.*

Use a reflexive pronoun when the person doing the action and the person receiving the action are the same, as in *He hit himself in the head* or *The dog groomed itself.* The other correct use is to provide emphasis, as in *I made this gift myself.*

Interrogative pronouns: **who whom whose which**

These pronouns can be used to ask questions. They can also introduce modifiers, which you'll learn more about later in this book.

Demonstrative pronouns: **this that these those**

These pronouns are used to point out, or to demonstrate, a specific thing: *Are* ***those*** *my shoes?* ***That*** *is my car right over there.* These same words can be used as adjectives: ***that*** *car,* ***those*** *shoes.*

Indefinite pronouns are very important on the GMAT. They take the place of nouns, but do not refer to specific people, places, or things. For instance, instead of saying, "All people have an inherent sense of justice," you could say, "*Everyone* has an inherent sense of justice." *Everyone* is an indefinite pronoun.

Notice in the example above that when the sentence was changed from using *All people* as the subject to using *Everyone,* the verb was changed as well—from *All people* ***have*** to *Everyone* ***has.***

This is because **most indefinite pronouns are singular**, including *everyone,* even though that word sounds plural. In some languages, the typical way you refer to *everyone* is with a plural pronoun. Not in English!

Here is a list of indefinite pronouns:

everyone	someone	no one	anyone		
everybody	somebody	nobody	anybody		
everything	something	anything	nothing		
all	many	more	most	much	
several	some	few	both	one	none
each	either	neither			
another	any	other			

The most commonly used of these pronouns are the "-ones" (*everyone, someone,* etc.), *each,* and *either.*

One of those pronouns needs to be called out specially because so many people fall into this trap: ***Each* is always singular.** It may at times *seem* plural, but it is not.

MEMORIZE IT!

If the pronoun ends with *-one, -thing,* or *-body* (*anybody, everyone, something,* etc.), it's singular. In addition, the word *each* is singular.

Drill 2.2 — Find the Pronouns

Circle all of the pronouns in the following sentences. Include possessive adjectives.

1. It is clear to everyone that Chairman Frankel will have to resign his position.

2. If one wants to drive over rugged terrain, one will need a vehicle far more powerful than mine.

3. Everybody at the comics convention is hoping for a chance to get an autograph from each of the celebrities.

4. While Steve isn't a good enough athlete to play soccer professionally, he is certainly better than most people.

5. Who just saw me spill soup all over myself?

Answers are on page 41.

Antecedents

An *antecedent* is the word or group of words that a pronoun refers to. In the sentence, *The company was forced to cut staff so that it could avoid going out of business entirely,* the pronoun is *it* and the antecedent is *the company.*

Not all pronouns have antecedents:

- An indefinite pronoun such as *anyone* will not have an antecedent.
- The pronoun *you* is often used without an antecedent, both in reference to a specific person (*Will you please take out the trash?*) and in reference to "the reader" or people in general (*You should learn about pronouns if you want to do well on the GMAT*).
- In a few circumstances, the pronoun *it* doesn't need an antecedent, as in *It's raining* or *It is hoped that taxpayers will use these refund checks to stimulate the economy.* In these cases, the word *it* is acting as a placeholder for a general state of being or idea, not a specific noun. If you see *it* used in the same way as the pronoun is used in the sentence *It's raining*, you don't need to find an antecedent.

However, take a look at this sentence:

> They say that the grass is greener on the other side of the fence.

Who are *they*? This sentence is considered incorrect. The pronoun *they* always needs a clear antecedent. The same is true of *them, their, it* (except for the exception mentioned earlier), and *its.* When you see one of these pronouns, **find its antecedent**. If the antecedent is missing or unclear, there is a problem.

The sentence above could be rephrased correctly—and more informatively—in this way:

> CORRECT: An old proverb says that the grass is greener on the other side of the fence.

In real-life speech and writing, an antecedent is often in a different sentence than the pronoun: *I'd like you to meet my brother.* ***He*** *is an anesthesiologist.* The pronoun *He* has the antecedent *my brother.* This sort of English is perfectly fine, as long as it's clear what the pronoun refers to.

However, no Sentence Correction question contains more than one sentence. So, on the GMAT, you need to match pronouns with antecedents in the same sentence.

It is possible to have the pronoun come before the antecedent:

> CORRECT: Having finally put the pain behind her, Shilpa decided it was time to have a little fun.

The pronoun *her* occurs before the antecedent, *Shilpa.* This is perfectly acceptable as long as it's clear who *she* is.

Pop Quiz!

True or False: *You* and *it* can be both subject and object pronouns.

Answer is on page 40.

Drill 2.3 — Connect Pronouns with Antecedents

For each sentence, circle each pronoun or possessive adjective and make an arrow pointing to its antecedent, if it has one.

> Example: (Everyone) sacrificed to get the job done, so when Ellen attributed the project's success to (herself,) (she) lost a lot of friends.

1. The report is due today; can you finish it?

2. All of the cake was gone before we had a chance to try it.

3. Marina joked about our security badges while ceremonially turning in hers—she said she would be certain to enjoy the fact that retired people no longer have to wear nametags.

4. As soon as Davis saw his colleague working on her project, he started plotting to take credit for it.

5. It is clear that the dog loves the new toy that Joey bought for it, so much so that Joey is glad he didn't spend the money on himself.

Answers are on page 41–42.

A Special Note about the Pronoun "One"

Sometimes, *one* simply means "one of the things I just mentioned."

> CORRECT: Of all the corporate "green" policies, this is the **one** I find most disingenuous.

Here, *one* refers back to *policies* and means "one of the policies."

One can also mean *everyone* or *everyone in a certain group* or *the average person*:

> CORRECT: **One** will benefit immensely from increasing **one's** verbal skills prior to taking the GMAT.

This usage is very common in British English. In American English, it is correct, but can sound formal or excessively fancy, especially when *one* is used multiple times (*If one wants to do well, one should do one's homework).*

In many situations in which *one* is used, *you* would also work:

CORRECT: If **you** want to do well, **you** should do **your** homework.

However, it is wrong to switch between *one* and *you:*

INCORRECT: **One** must be careful to account for all sources of income on **your** tax return.

In the sentence above, *one* and *one* would be fine, and *you* and *you* would also be fine, but don't mix and match. *One* also doesn't mix with nouns that require the pronouns *he, they,* etc.:

INCORRECT: **People** who want to become politicians should keep **one's** reputation spotless.

Just as you would normally refer back to *people* with *they* or *their* (as in *People should pay their taxes*), you must do the same here.

The reflexive form of *one* is *oneself:*

CORRECT: Learning does not have to stop at graduation; **one** can educate **oneself** throughout life.

Drill 2.4 — Mixed Practice

First, circle the pronouns and, where appropriate, draw arrows to the antecedents. Then determine whether the sentence has an error and circle "Correct" or "Incorrect."

1. Each of the dogs is masterfully trained to detect when someone is about to suffer an epileptic seizure. CORRECT/INCORRECT

2. Firefighters should always secure one's safety gear before rushing into a fire. CORRECT/INCORRECT

3. It is important for employers to show appreciation when an employee puts forth extra effort, lest they become disgruntled and decide to look for a new job. CORRECT/INCORRECT

4. Sally was so impatient to learn whether the school had accepted her that she called the admissions office every day, annoying everyone who worked there. CORRECT/INCORRECT

5. The data contained in the report by the outside auditor establish unequivocally that the CEO committed fraud; in fact, it is so damning that he has agreed to resign and repay the money immediately. CORRECT/INCORRECT

Answers are on page 42–43.

Pronouns Wrap-Up

✓ Training yourself to spot pronouns and check their antecedents will help you improve your SC game. Most pronouns will need to match a specific noun somewhere in the sentence, with a few exceptions (indefinite pronouns, such as *anyone*, the pronouns *you* and *one*, and the placeholder *it*). If a required antecedent is missing, you've found an incorrect answer.

✓ If there is a singular–plural mismatch, you can knock out that answer choice.

Making Flash Cards

Now is a good time to introduce the idea of flash cards.

Taking notes as you work through this book is also a fine strategy, of course. Flash cards are good because when you later review your cards, it will be very clear that you're supposed to *do* something with them. When people review notes, they tend to smile and nod (or maybe just nod). When people review flash cards, they actually start thinking in a more GMAT-like way.

Sometimes, you'll put an entire sentence or drill on a flash card:

Firefighters should always secure one's safety gear before rushing into a fire.

FoV book page 33

INCORRECT

The pronoun "one" does not match the plural "firefighters" (correct pronoun is "their").

The example includes a source on the front of the flash card ("FoV," for *GMAT Foundations of Verbal*, plus a page number). You may wish to later make flash cards from *The Official Guide* books, the *Manhattan Prep GMAT Strategy Guides*, and practice exams from Manhattan Prep or from www.mba.com. It's helpful to note the source of the problem in case you want to look it up again later.

On other flash cards, you might list key words that you want to recognize on one side and information about those key words on the other. For example:

Everyone, Somebody, Anything

Each

Either, Neither

> Indefinite pronouns. Don't need to refer to a specific noun in the sentence.
>
> Singular. Everyone. Somebody. Anything. Each of the dogs = each one.
>
> Either option works for me. (Either ONE = singular)

Buy larger index cards (4 inches by 6 inches) to ensure that you have plenty of space to add notes and examples. Later, you may wish to make flash cards for entire Sentence Correction, Critical Reasoning, or Quantitative questions from the *Official Guide* and online exams, so using larger index cards is a good idea.

Adjectives

Adjectives describe or modify nouns or pronouns. They answer questions such as "What kind is it?", "Which one?", and "How many are there?" All of these are adjectives or can be used as adjectives:

red	annoying	75	third	happy	studious
patterned	utter	your	10-minute	unique	French

Categories of Adjectives

Nouns can sometimes act as adjectives, as the word *kitchen* in the phrase *kitchen floor.* (A "phrase" is just a group of words, by the way.) Similarly, the word *diamond* by itself is a noun, but in *diamond mine,* it is an adjective. A *diamond mine* is a kind of *mine.*

> **ADVANCED TIP**
>
> Remember *compound nouns* from the section on nouns? Some would say that *diamond mine* is a compound noun rather than an adjective and then a noun. Grammar experts could argue about this all day (the more common a two-word phrase is, the more likely that experts would consider it a compound noun), but this distinction is not important for the GMAT. Here, the key point is that in the phrase *diamond mine,* the main noun is *mine.*

Proper adjectives are formed from proper nouns. Proper adjectives include *Japanese, Keynesian,* and *United Nations* (when used to describe nouns, as in the phrase *United Nations representative*).

Numbers are usually adjectives. *The school has 250 first-year students.* Here, *250* is an adjective that answers the question, "How many first-year students?"

Compound adjectives (such as *first-year* in the previous sentence) contain more than one word and sometimes have hyphens. For example, a *twenty-minute workout* or an *egg-shaped jewel.* Many compound adjectives are hyphenated when placed before nouns, but not when on their own; for instance, *I am broken hearted* does not have a hyphen, but *She is a broken-hearted Justin Bieber fan* does. The hyphen in these cases makes the meaning clear. A *blue, striped dress* (a dress that is blue and has stripes of some unspecified color) is not the same as a *blue-striped dress* (a dress that has blue stripes).

GMAT questions are not going to test you on hyphen placement within compound adjectives. Don't automatically cross off an answer that contains *an all-too-common refrain* or even *left- and right-handed people.*

ADVANCED TIP

Hyphens are also used in other cases where the meaning would be ambiguous without them. Is a *smelly cheese salesman* someone who sells smelly cheese or someone who sells regular cheese but doesn't shower? *Smelly-cheese salesman* makes it clear that the man sells pungent dairy products.

You already saw possessive adjectives in the section on pronouns (***his*** *car,* ***its*** *prey*). Several other pronouns—*whose, which, this, that, these, those, all, both, some*—can also be used as adjectives. Again, memorizing grammatical terms is not important for the GMAT. Just know that there is some overlap between adjectives and the "weird" pronouns. In general on the GMAT, don't stress over exactly what part of speech a word is. Focus on the specific job the word is doing in the sentence.

Pop Quiz!

Is there a difference in meaning between "the economic factors are important" and "the economical factors are important"?

Answer is on page 40.

Drill 2.5 — Circle the Adjectives

Circle all of the adjectives in the following sentences.

1. Air pollution is a significant concern in dense, overcrowded cities.
2. She felt that she was an utter failure, but her mother felt that she was a thoroughgoing success.
3. The hockey fans were furious when the opposing team's player slammed into their goalie, leaving visible black and blue marks behind.
4. Danish queen Margrethe II is the first female monarch of Denmark since Margrethe I, who took the throne in 1388.
5. I know that this is a banausic concern, but six is my lucky number, so I am disappointed that I was only able to purchase five tickets for the raffle.

Answers are on page 43.

Absolute Adjectives

Absolute adjectives are adjectives that are **not** capable of being intensified. To *intensify* an adjective is to turn *intelligent* into *more intelligent* or *tall* into *taller* (*intelligent* and *tall* are not examples of absolute adjectives).

By contrast, *dead* **is** an absolute adjective. You're either dead or you aren't. There is no such word as *deader. More dead* is also incorrect because it is illogical.

Other absolute adjectives include *square, essential, universal, immortal,* and the word *absolute* itself.

Traditionally, *unique* has been considered an absolute adjective, because it means "one-of-a-kind." Something is either one-of-a-kind or it isn't. The expression *more unique* is now common in everyday speech (many people simply use *unique* to mean *special*), but *more unique* should be avoided in formal English.

Similarly, *circular* is an absolute adjective. People might casually describe one oval as *more circular* than another, but in formal speech, *more nearly circular* would be preferable. The logic here is that *circular* indicates a 100% match with being a circle, and you can't go above 100%—thus, *more circular* is illogical. But *more nearly circular* means "closer to being a perfect circle than something else is." If two things are less than 100%, one can be closer to 100% than the other one.

So you might read that one disease is *more likely fatal* than another, for instance. Maybe one of them is fatal 0.01% of the time, and the other one is fatal 0.0001% of the time!

More likely fatal is correct. *More fatal* is not, because *fatal* is absolute. Remember, do not just go for the shorter answer! Sometimes, these little "extra words" (such as *likely* in this case) are not extra at all.

Drill 2.6 — Find the Errors

Determine whether the sentence has an error and circle "Correct" or "Incorrect."

1. The chefs taught us to make delicious Chinese food, and they were always very nice about answering questions. CORRECT/INCORRECT

2. The Chinese army is the largest military force in the world; they have approximately 3 million members. CORRECT/INCORRECT

3. This liquor is a fifteen-year-old Scotch. CORRECT/INCORRECT

4. Each of the college administrators believe that the college needs a budget increase in order to continue operating in the new year. CORRECT/INCORRECT

5. That professor never gives anyone an A, but he did tell me that my paper was more nearly perfect than any of my classmates' papers. CORRECT/INCORRECT

Answers are on page 44.

Nouns, Pronouns, & Adjectives Wrap-Up

You've now covered three very important parts of speech—*Nouns, Pronouns,* and *Adjectives.*

✓ In later chapters, you'll learn more about the core parts of sentence structure; the first main part is the subject of the sentence. The subjects of sentences are nouns:

- People
- Places
- Things
- Actions
- Events
- Emotions
- And more

✓ Pronouns take the place of nouns (also called antecedents) and could be the subjects of sentences themselves. The most commonly tested pronouns on the GMAT are:

- Subject: it, they
- Object: it, them
- Possessive: its, their
- Demonstrative: this, that
- Indefinite: one, each, ending in *-one*, ending in *-body*

✓ Both nouns and pronouns come in singular and plural forms; you'll need to match pronouns and their antecedents accordingly. (You'll also need to match subjects with verbs; more on this in the next chapter.)

✓ Adjectives need to attach clearly to a specific noun and make logical sense in the sentence.

Answers to Pop Quizzes

Nouns, page 27

The sentence, "I have a great amount of homework and a great amount of deadlines," is correct.

FALSE! *Homework* is not countable, so the first *amount* is correct. But *deadlines* are countable, so the second part of the sentence should read *a great NUMBER of deadlines* or *many deadlines.*

Pronouns, page 31

You and *it* can be both subject and object pronouns.

TRUE! Most pronouns have different forms for the subject and object versions; for example: "*She* threw the ball to *him*." *She* is a subject pronoun (the corresponding object pronoun is *her*). *Him* is an object pronoun (the corresponding subject pronoun is *he*). In the case of *you* and *it,* however, there is no "other version"—both *you* and *it* can go in either spot. *You* gave *it* a cat toy. *It* gave *you* a nasty bite on the arm.

Adjectives, page 37

Is there a difference in meaning between "the economic factors are important" and "the economical factors are important"?

Yes! The words *economic* and *economical* are both adjectives but they do not convey the same meaning.

Economic refers to the economy or broad financial matters. *Economical* refers to the act of using money efficiently or operating efficiently in general. Someone might suggest, for example, that the company improve profit margins by cutting unnecessary expenditures, an *economical* way of operating.

2

Answers to Drill Sets

Answers to Drill 2.1 — Find the Nouns

1. Companies in the European Union receive certain protections from imports.

2. Jane Austen wrote *Pride and Prejudice*, a novel that in 2005 was adapted into a film starring Keira Knightley.

3. The primary purpose of the passage is to present an alternative explanation for a well-known fact.

4. A recent study has provided additional support for a particular theory about the origin of the fruit bat.

5. I am only happy if you are happy; my happiness depends on yours.

Answers to Drill 2.2 — Find the Pronouns

1. It is clear to everyone that Chairman Frankel will have to resign his position.

2. If one wants to drive over rugged terrain, one will need a vehicle far more powerful than mine.

3. Everybody at the comics convention is hoping for a chance to get an autograph from each of the celebrities.

4. While Steve isn't a good enough athlete to play soccer professionally, he is certainly better than most people.

5. Who just saw me spill soup all over myself?

Answers to Drill 2.3 — Connect Pronouns with Antecedents

1. The report is due today; can you finish it?

2. All of the cake was gone before we had a chance to try it.

3. Marina joked about our security badges while ceremonially turning in hers—she said she would be certain to enjoy the fact that retired people no longer have to wear nametags.

4. As soon as Davis saw his colleague working on her project, he started plotting to take credit for it.

5. It is clear that the dog loves the new toy that Joey bought for it so much so that Joey is glad he didn't spend the money on himself.

Answers to Drill 2.4 — Mixed Practice

1. CORRECT. The word *each* refers to the *dogs* but is singular: *each dog.*

Each of the dogs is masterfully trained to detect when someone is about to suffer an epileptic seizure.

2. INCORRECT. *Firefighters* is plural and cannot mix with *one's.* A correct version would say *their safety gear.*

Firefighters should always secure one's safety gear before rushing into a fire.

3. INCORRECT. The plural pronoun *they* would need to refer to a plural noun, such as *employers*, but logically, it is the *employee* (singular) who might become disgruntled and look for a new job. A correct version might say *lest she become disgruntled.*

It is important for employers to show appreciation when an employee puts forth extra effort, lest they become disgruntled and decide to look for a new job.

4. CORRECT. The word *her* correctly refers to *Sally.* The pronoun *everyone* does not need to have an explicit antecedent.

Sally was so impatient to learn whether the school had accepted her that she called the admissions office every day, annoying everyone who worked there.

5. INCORRECT. This is a tricky one. The word data can be singular or plural. The verb paired with data is plural (*the data establish*), so in this case, the sentence is intending *data* to be plural. The pronoun *it*, then, is incorrect; it should be plural (*they are so damning*).

The data contained in the report by the outside auditor establish unequivocally that the CEO committed fraud; in fact, it is so damning that he has agreed to resign and repay the money immediately.

Answers to Drill 2.5 — Circle the Adjectives

1. Air pollution is a significant concern in dense, overcrowded cities.

Note that *air* is usually a noun (*The air is refreshing),* but here it is an adjective because it is modifying *pollution*. Remember, you can test whether a word is an adjective by trying to replace it with other adjectives—*bad* pollution, *smelly* pollution, etc.

2. She felt that she was an utter failure, but her mother felt that she was a thoroughgoing success.

Thoroughgoing is an adjective that means "thorough, complete." Even when you do not know the meaning of a word, you may be able to tell its part of speech by substituting other words—in this case, adjectives—to see whether they fit (*big success, minor success).*

3. The hockey fans were furious when the opposing team's player slammed into their goalie, leaving visible black and blue marks behind.

4. Danish queen Margrethe II is the first female monarch of Denmark since Margrethe I, who took the throne in 1388.

5. I know that this is a banausic concern, but six is my lucky number, so I am disappointed that I was only able to purchase five tickets for the raffle.

Here, an extremely obscure word was chosen—*banausic*—that you most likely will never see again in your entire life (and certainly not on the GMAT). The important point is that you don't need to know this word to analyze the sentence—you can still tell that it's an adjective (the *-ic* ending is a good clue) by substituting words you know are adjectives: *small concern, silly concern.* Note that *six* is being used as a noun, but *five* is describing *tickets*, and so it is an adjective.

Answers to Drill 2.6—Find the Errors

1. CORRECT. The pronoun *they* refers back to *chefs*. Both are plural, and the meaning is clear.

2. INCORRECT. The pronoun *they* is attempting to refer back to *army* but the pairing *army is* indicates that *army* is singular. A plural pronoun cannot refer to a singular noun.

3. CORRECT. *Fifteen-year-old* is a hyphenated adjective. The hyphens are appropriate here because the Scotch is not *fifteen*, and *year*, and *old* (the way we would say *tight, shiny pants*). *Fifteen-year-old* is just a single adjective.

4. INCORRECT. The pronoun *each* is always singular: *each one* of the administrators *believes* something.

5. CORRECT. *More nearly perfect* is a good way to describe being closer to perfect than something else. Some language experts say that *perfect* is an absolute adjective (like *dead*) and that it is not possible to be *more perfect*. However, the phrase *more perfect union* appears in the U.S. Constitution, so there is some variation in usage. For the GMAT, just know that *more nearly perfect* is fine.

Chapter 3 of

Verbs & Adverbs

In This Chapter...

Verbs

Gerunds

Infinitives

Subject–Verb Agreement

"Has/Have" Verbs

"Had" Verbs

Verbs Wrap-Up

Adverbs

Adverbs Wrap-Up

Answers to Pop Quizzes

Answers to Drill Sets

Chapter 3

Verbs & Adverbs

Verbs

Verbs are a necessary part of all sentences. They express actions, events, or states of being.

ADVANCED TIP

Did you know that *We left, Joe ran,* and *I do* are all complete sentences? Each has a subject and a verb.

All of the following are verbs:

is	went	decided
accomplishes	forsook	arose

Many verbs occur in combination with one another to express more information. Here are some examples:

will go	has been eating	is writing
had swollen	will have been broken	should have gone

Verbs occur in a variety of **tenses** (past, present, future, and many more complicated ones), **voices** (active and passive), and even **moods** (which have to do with the intention of what's being said). This guide will cover tenses but leave the more complex voices and moods for the primary *Sentence Correction GMAT Strategy Guide.*

The main verb in a sentence is always conjugated: She **is** tall; You **are** tall; He **is** tall; We **are** tall; They **are** tall. In these examples, the verb *to be* is conjugated as either *is* or *are*, depending on the form of the subject.

The main verbs in a sentence are also known as *working verbs*; the rest of this guide will use the term working verbs.

Almost everything in English is in the indicative mood. *Indicative* means "indicating," and of course virtually all sentences indicate something. The imperative mood is for giving commands, as in ***Run** faster!* or ***Consider** the case of the cassowary.*

Categories of Verbs

3

Action verbs (such as *eat, disagreed, go*) express the action performed by a subject. The tense of an action verb (past, present, etc.) gives information about *when* the action was performed.

Linking verbs (such as *is, are, was, become, feel, seem)* "link" the subject to a noun or adjective:

Otto **is** a miniature bulldog. He **seems** nice.

On the GMAT, you do not need to distinguish between action verbs and linking verbs.

Helping verbs (such as *is, was, has, does, will, should, can*) "help" other words to become complete compound verbs:

He **is planning** to attend.

Is is the helping verb. *Planning* is not quite a complete verb (you can't say *He planning to attend* in standard English), but together, *is planning* is a complete verb form.

Notice that *planning* is made out of the verb *to plan. Planning* is an "*-ing*" word. These *-ing* words need helping verbs to become complete compound verbs that could run a sentence:

She **will be leaving** shortly.

In this case, *will* and *be* are helping verbs. *Leaving* is an *-ing* word made out of the verb *leave.* Together, *will be leaving* is a complete verb form.

It's fine to think of a phrase such as *is planning* or *will be leaving* as a single verb. Just keep in mind that sometimes another word (an adverb, a word that modifies the verb) can separate the individual verbs within this kind of verb form:

CORRECT: He **has** frequently **defaced** public property.

Here, you can say that *has defaced* is the verb (*frequently* is an adverb, telling you how often *has defaced* has happened). *Has* is the helping verb, and *defaced* is an "*-ed*" word created from the verb *deface.* Together, they make the verb form *has defaced.*

Careful! You *can* use that *-ed* word as a complete past tense for many verbs, including *deface.* You are allowed to say *He frequently **defaced** public property.* However, this means something a little different from *He **has** frequently **defaced** public property.* A prosecutor would say *has defaced* to imply that the person in question is still doing these actions, or that he still is the type of person who would do them.

A defense attorney would say *He defaced property, but now he has reformed . . .* to put the vandalism clearly in the past.

You'll get to those tense distinctions later—here's the point for now. To catch errors on the GMAT, **don't neglect the *has* if it's there**. If you mistakenly thought that *defaced* by itself was the verb in the example above, this addition to the sentence might sound fine to your ear:

INCORRECT: He **has** frequently **defaced** public property and **went** to jail.

Those who do not catch the error in this sentence are probably imagining that *defaced* and *went* are both in the past tense and therefore match: *He defaced property and went to jail.*

However, *went* should be *gone*. Even though the helping verb *has* is written only once, it actually applies to both *defaced* and *gone*. That is, the two verbs are really *has defaced* and *has gone* (*has went* is never correct):

CORRECT: He **has** frequently **defaced** public property and **gone** to jail.

Making parts of a sentence—especially those in a series or list—"match" is a topic that is discussed at more length in Chapter 6, which includes *parallelism*.

The individual verbs within a multi-word verb form also can be separated from one another when the sentence is a question:

CORRECT: **Will** you **be taking** any leftovers home with you?

Here, the verb form is *will be taking*.

Pop Quiz!

True or False: In the sentence, "When she is finally released from prison in 2034, she will have never so much as touched a cell phone," the main verb form is *have touched*.

Answer is on page 61.

Complex situations can call for complex verb tenses. But you can figure them out—both the situations and the tenses.

CORRECT: By 2019, I will have been working on my Ph.D. for 10 years.

This sentence is totally fine. The *will* expresses moving into the future, to 2019. *Have been working* expresses the action being performed *from the perspective of the speaker in 2019,* implying that, even in 2019, the action will be ongoing. In 2019, the speaker will have started his or her Ph.D. but will not yet have finished it.

For a more in-depth discussion of complex verbs, see the *Sentence Correction GMAT Strategy Guide.*

3

Drill 3.1 — Find the Parts of the Verb

Circle all parts of each verb form.

Example: I (have) always (wanted) to be an astronaut.

1. That rumor has been spreading like wildfire.
2. The pygmy marmoset has typically been found in the rainforest areas of South America.
3. I will run faster, jump higher, and play more aggressively this season.
4. The firm's executives had supported the eco-initiative until the financial crisis struck and they re-evaluated.
5. Are you going?

Answers are on page 62.

Gerunds

Some *-ing* words are not actually verbs. For instance, what part of speech is the word *losing*? Most people would say that the word *losing* is a verb. If so, then what's going on in this sentence?

EXAMPLE: Losing stinks.

While *stinks* is being used in a somewhat slang sense (in this case meaning that losing is no fun, not that it smells bad), this is a complete sentence. Certainly, then, *losing* and *stinks* can't both be verbs in this context. Two verbs in a row without a subject could never be a complete sentence.

As it turns out, *stinks* is the verb. *Losing* is what is performing the action of stinking. Thus, *losing* is the subject of the sentence. Although *losing* looks like a verb, it is acting like a noun. Subjects of sentences are always nouns or constructions such as this one that "act like nouns."

In *Losing stinks,* the word *losing* is called a gerund. A gerund is an *-ing* word used as a noun.

Gerunds can be subjects of sentences (***Overeating*** *causes weight gain)* or objects of verbs or prepositions (*I love* ***dancing****; This is a seminar about* ***writing***).

When looking for the main verb in a sentence, don't let yourself get distracted by gerunds. A good rule is this: **An *-ing* word without a helper verb isn't a real verb.**

If the *-ing* word is a gerund, you should be able to substitute in a noun in its place. For instance, in the sentence *Dating is tricky*, the word *dating* is a gerund. Try substituting a regular noun: *Algebra is* *tricky*. The sentence *I just adore dancing* works the same way: *I just adore cake. I just adore differential calculus.*

Here's how one *-ing* word can be used as three different parts of speech:

> *I am boxing.* The verb form is *am boxing. Am* is the helper verb and *boxing* is part of the verb form.
>
> *I love boxing.* The verb is *love* and *boxing* is a gerund, which effectively functions as a noun. Note that you could easily substitute another noun for *boxing* (*I love dogs* or *I love this book*).
>
> *I wish Christian Bale were my boxing coach.* The adjective *boxing* is describing the noun *coach.* Try substituting an adjective for *boxing* (*I wish Christian Bale were my tall, handsome, famous coach*).

ADVANCED TIP

To determine whether a word ending in *-ing* is a verb, look for helper verbs. If the *-ing* stands alone, it is not a verb.

Pop Quiz!

True or False: In the sentence "I hate smiling," *smiling* is a gerund, but in the sentence "I am smiling as big as I can," *am smiling* is the main verb.

Answer is on page 61.

Identifying gerunds will be an important skill later on when you need to match up a sentence's subject with its verb. A gerund may or may not be the subject, but it is not acting like a verb, so it can't be the main verb of the sentence.

Infinitives

As noted in the last section, identifying verbs can be tricky because some constructions look like verbs, but aren't really. Infinitives are another example.

An infinitive takes the form *to love, to defeat, to go.* These sure look like verbs! The infinitive form is the base form *before* you conjugate the verb; for this reason, **an infinitive is never the main or working verb of a sentence**.

That's not to say that infinitives aren't handy! Like gerunds, they can act like nouns to some degree. Infinitives can be the subjects of sentences or the objects of verbs:

> **To love** is divine.

To love is an infinitive and is the subject of the sentence. What *is divine*? *To love,* in other words, the act of loving.

I hate **to pay** taxes.

To pay is an infinitive and is the object of the verb *hate*. What do I hate? To pay taxes. That is the thing being hated.

You can test whether infinitives are acting like nouns just as you can with gerunds: substitute a regular noun:

Music	asparagus
~~To love~~ is divine.	I hate ~~to pay taxes~~.

Infinitives can also act like adjectives or adverbs. *A friend* ***to call*** *would be nice.* Here, *to call* modifies the noun *friend. I went outside to sing.* Here, *to sing* modifies the verb *went.*

Identifying infinitives will be an important skill later on when you need to match up a sentence's subject with its verb. For now, recognize that an infinitive is not a true verb. It cannot serve as the main verb in a sentence.

Drill 3.2 — Find the Gerunds and Infinitives

Underline any gerunds or infinitives. Circle the main working verb of the sentence.

Example: I (despise) watching television.

1. To be a ballerina is my lifelong dream.

2. The executive has been accused of embezzling funds.

3. Eating, praying, and loving are apparently author Elizabeth Gilbert's favorite activities.

4. To kill is to break the social contract.

5. Recovering from my accident is using all of my energy right now.

Answers are on page 62.

Subject–Verb Agreement

The most basic issue related to verbs on the GMAT is **subject–verb agreement**. Simply put, singular subjects go with singular verbs, and plural subjects go with plural verbs.

It is a bit weird that, in English, singular verbs generally end in *-s*, and plural verbs do not end in *-s*. Of course, some verbs are irregular (for instance, *is / are*):

Singular verbs (for *it, he, she*):	runs	differs	goes	has	is
Plural verbs (for *we, they*):	run	differ	go	have	are

In a short sentence, it's usually pretty easy to tell whether the subject and verb agree (that is, whether singular is matched with singular or plural is matched with plural):

> ***Dogs bark.*** ***It runs*** *well.* ***The students study*** hard.

The GMAT, of course, will offer much more complex sentences. For example:

> The desire of our daughter to learn and the dedication of her teacher (provide/provides) a solid foundation for success.

In this case, the subject is *the desire and the dedication*, a plural subject, so the verb should be plural as well: *The desire and the dedication provide a strong foundation for success.* Even though the individual subjects are singular, the *X and Y* structure mandates that both are counted toward the subject.

If you're having trouble figuring out whether a particular verb form is singular or plural, try the possible verbs with *it* (singular) and *they* (plural):

> It provides a solid foundation for success.
>
> They provide a solid foundation for success.

Now you know that *provides* is singular and *provide* is plural.

Drill 3.3 — Determine Subject–Verb Agreement

In each sentence, the subject is underlined. Find the verb, determine whether the subject and verb agree, and circle "Correct" or "Incorrect."

1. Several new species were added to a list of endangered animals. CORRECT/INCORRECT

2. Companies that offer job-sharing policies or a flexible workday is lauded by *Working Parents* magazine. CORRECT/INCORRECT

3. Every one of our students was accepted to the college of his or her choice. CORRECT/INCORRECT

4. Our nation's legal code deem it illegal to use other people's creative and intellectual work without permission. CORRECT/INCORRECT

5. Rock climbing and hang gliding over the ocean is dangerous but exciting. CORRECT/INCORRECT

Answers are on page 62.

"Has/Have" Verbs

How are these two sentences different in meaning?

Linsu ate an apple. Linsu has eaten an apple.

The first sentence describes a single past event: at some point in the past, Linsu ate an apple.

The second sentence also describes something that took place in the past, but this action is either still true or still occurring in the present. It is true right now that Linsu has eaten apples sometime in the past.

Has or *have* as helping verbs (I/you/we/they *have* danced, he/she/it *has* danced) create verbs in the *present perfect* tense.

Present perfect verbs are used to describe actions that occurred over some period of time before the present. You cannot use the present perfect with past-indicating time expressions (*yesterday, last week,* etc.). The exact time of the action does not matter. What matters is the effect in the present:

I **have danced** the tango.

Google **has become** not just the top search engine, but one of the most important companies in the world.

Scientists **have mapped** the human genome.

In every case, the effect continues or is still true: it is still true that I have danced the tango in the past, Google is still the top search engine and one of the most important companies in the world, and the map of the human genome still exists.

The present perfect can also be used in questions. In many questions, the parts of a compound verb are separated. For instance:

Has she **taken** ballet lessons for a long time?

If you make this question into a statement—*She has taken ballet lessons for a long time*—it is easier to see the present perfect.

"Had" Verbs

The "had" verb is an informal way to refer to a verb preceded by the helper verb *had,* as in *had danced, had eaten, had gone.*

Here's an example. What's wrong with this sentence?

INCORRECT: The jury had delivered a verdict of "guilty."

Had delivered? Why not just say *delivered?*

MEMORIZE IT

Don't use a complicated tense when the simple past tense will do.

The regular past tense verb *delivered* would do the job nicely here. In fact, you can't even use a *had* verb by itself in this context. There has to be another past action that the *had* verb comes before.

"Had" verbs, or *past perfect* verbs, are used to describe situations in which one past event occurred before a different past event. That is, these verbs express the "double past"!

> CORRECT: The judge **had spent** most of the trial convinced of the defendant's guilt, but the DNA test **proved** the defendant's innocence.

Here, two things happened in the past: first, the judge thought that the defendant was guilty and, later, the DNA test proved the defendant was innocent. The sentence correctly assigns the past perfect *had spent* to the first event and the simple past *proved* to the second event.

In a sentence with a "had" verb and a regular past tense verb, the sentence order can change, but that doesn't change which verb gets the *had.* It's the real-life order of events that is important. For instance, in both of the cases below, the *had* creates a compound verb with *eaten:*

> CORRECT: I **had eaten** three pieces of cake when I **learned** that the cake was poisoned.

> CORRECT: By the time I **learned** that the cake was poisoned, I **had** already **eaten** three pieces.

MEMORIZE IT

A verb with the helping verb *had* is used to express "the past of the past."

In both cases, the action that happened first (before something else in the past) gets the *had.*

Past perfect can also be used with a past time marker:

> CORRECT: By 2011, she had traveled to India twice.

The time marker, *2011,* is in the past. Before that past point in time, she went to India, so the past perfect tense is appropriate for the situation.

A good way to check a "had" verb is to ask these questions of two events in the past:

> What happened first? (This one gets a *had.*)
> What happened second? (This one does not get a *had.*)

Interestingly, you aren't *required* to use the past perfect when you have two events that took place at different times in the past. Other language can convey the same information:

> CORRECT: In my college years, I joined the sophomore pledge class at a fraternity and worked on the senior class homecoming float.

CORRECT: After she earned her degree, she spent a year serving with the Peace Corps in Guatemala.

In the first example, the designations *sophomore* and *senior* indicate the time frames. In the second sentence, the sequence of events is conveyed by the word *after*.

The key thing to remember is that you can only legally use past perfect when a sentence is trying to talk about the first past event in a sequence of two (or more) past events. If that circumstance doesn't exist, but the sentence is trying to use past perfect, then that answer choice is incorrect.

Drill 3.4 — Has/Have and Had Verbs

For each sentence, circle "Correct" or "Incorrect." If you circled "Incorrect," cross out the incorrect verbs and write the correct verb.

1. My mother always warns me to stay away from the pet store, reminding me that I had been highly allergic to dogs and cats since childhood. CORRECT/INCORRECT

2. By her 50th birthday, prolific mystery writer Agatha Christie had already written 28 books. CORRECT/INCORRECT

3. As she graded the final exams, the teacher realized that Pat had cheated on the exam. CORRECT/INCORRECT

4. The doctor told me I had a heart attack. CORRECT/INCORRECT

5. I just began working at the circus when a clown stabbed me in the back. CORRECT/INCORRECT

Answers are on page 63.

Verbs Wrap-Up

All sentences contain at least one *main verb*, also known as a *working verb*. Here are some facts about the working verb:

✓ The working verb has to match the subject in number (singular or plural).

✓ An *-ing* word is only part of a main verb if it has a helping verb right before, as in *She is walking*. (An *-ing* word can also function as a noun, as in *Studying every day is exhausting*.)

✓ Infinitives (e.g., to study, to eat) cannot function as the main verb of a sentence.

✓ The present perfect tense is used to talk about something that happened in the past but is still true or still ongoing in the present, as in *She has earned her bachelor of science degree in biology*.

✓ The past perfect tense is used to talk about a past event that occurred prior to another past event or a past time marker, as in *The scientist had thought that his hypothesis was valid until he saw the latest test results.*

Adverbs

Adverbs are primarily used to modify verbs. They can also be used to describe adjectives and other adverbs. What they definitely do *not* do is describe nouns (that's the job of adjectives).

Many people think of adverbs as words that end in *-ly*, such as *slowly* and *suspiciously*. While these words certainly are adverbs, other adverbs do not end in *-ly*. All of the following are adverbs:

shyly	also	favorably	really	quite	economically
truly	agilely	wholly	duly	usually	simply

Also, the following words can be both adjectives and adverbs (there are others):

fast	only	late	hard	high	monthly

Here are some examples:

CORRECT: He eats raisin bran **daily**.

The adverb *daily* answers a question about the verb, *eats*. He eats raisin bran? Well, *when* does he eat it?

CORRECT: "I'm free after the conference," she said **coyly**.

The adverb *coyly* (meaning "in a shy yet flirtatious way") modifies *said* and answers the question, "*How* did she say it?"

NOTE

In India, the word *timely* is used as an adverb, as in *Please do it timely*. In American English, this is NOT correct. While *timely* ends in "*-ly*," it is actually an adjective, so saying *Please do it timely* is incorrect, just as *Please do it quick* and *Please do it cheerful* are wrong. Instead, say *Please do it in a timely manner.* (The Indian way is certainly more concise. Perhaps this usage will make it into American English in the coming decades.)

Adverbs Modifying Adjectives and Other Adverbs

Adverbs can also modify adjectives:

CORRECT: He is **very** tall.

Very is an adverb modifying the adjective *tall.*

CORRECT: You are **quite** correct.

Quite is an adverb modifying the adjective *correct.*

CORRECT: The employee you hired is **wholly** inadequate to the task.

The adverb *wholly* answers a question about the adjective *inadequate.* The employee is inadequate? *How* inadequate?

Finally, adverbs can modify other adverbs:

> CORRECT: The contestant danced **quite** awkwardly.

The verb is *danced. Awkwardly* is an adverb modifying *danced;* it answers the question, "*How* did he dance?" *Quite* is another adverb modifying *awkwardly;* it answers the question, "*How* awkwardly did he dance?"

The situation in which an adverb modifies another adverb is different from the situation in which there are simply two or more adverbs modifying something else:

> CORRECT: The child **drowsily** and **adorably** asked whether naptime had arrived.

Drowsily and *adorably* both modify the verb *asked.*

Pop Quiz!

True or False: Adverbs can modify verbs, adjectives, or nouns.

Answer is on page 61.

Adverb Errors on the GMAT

Few errors on the GMAT are related solely to adverbs. Certainly it is incorrect to modify a verb with an adjective, rather than an adverb:

> INCORRECT: The company needs to move quick if it is to launch its new product before the holiday shopping season.

Quick should be *quickly.* In the corrected version, *quickly* (an adverb) modifies the verb *move.*

Note that *fast* is on the list of adverbs that are also adjectives. That is, you can have a *fast car* (*fast* is an adjective describing the noun *car)* or you can *run fast* (*fast* is an adverb describing the verb *run*).

If you have a word that does not end in *-ly* that is modifying a verb and you want to see whether it is correct, try asking, *Would this word make more sense with -ly on the end?*

> EXAMPLE: The boxer hit his opponent hard.

> TRY IT: The boxer hit his opponent *hardly.*

The original was correct. *Hard* is both an adjective and an adverb. *Hardly* is also a word, but has a different meaning (it means *not at all*, or *almost not*).

By the way, people often say *I feel badly* when what they mean is *I feel bad. Badly* is the adverb form of *bad.* When you say *I feel bad,* then the verb *feel* is a linking verb between the subject *I* and the adjective *bad.* The same pattern exists in *I feel smart* or *I feel pretty,* which of course are correct. *Smart* and *pretty* are adjectives! *I feel bad* matches this pattern and is just fine.

When you say *I feel badly,* the adverb *badly* is modifying the verb *feel,* which then turns into an action verb. *I feel badly* means that you are unskilled at the act of feeling. This would indeed be appropriate if you had burned your hands and no longer had a sense of touch, but this is not typically what people mean when they say *I feel badly.*

Drill 3.5 — Find the Adverb Errors

Determine whether the sentence has an error and circle "Correct" or "Incorrect." If the sentence is correct, circle all adverbs, and draw an arrow from each adverb to the word it modifies. If the sentence is incorrect, try to correct it.

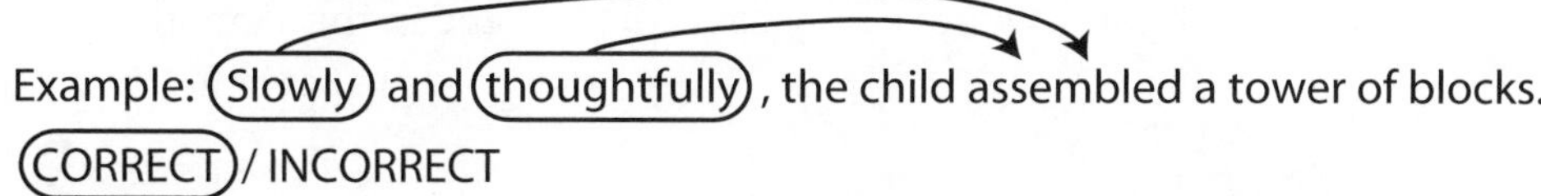

Example: Slowly and thoughtfully, the child assembled a tower of blocks.

CORRECT / INCORRECT

1. The new vendor did the job quite quick. CORRECT/INCORRECT

2. The analyst painstakingly ascertained that the surprisingly promising financial forecast was, indeed, too good to be true. CORRECT/INCORRECT

3. He woke up early and cheerfully did the dishes. CORRECT/INCORRECT

4. The performer danced lively, delighting the children. CORRECT/INCORRECT

5. I feel bad for doing the job so badly. CORRECT/INCORRECT

Answers are on page 63.

Adverbial Phrases

Some adjectives (*timely, friendly, lovely, lively, ugly, silly, holy*) that are *not* also adverbs end in *-ly*. If you want to use *friendly* to modify a verb, you can't say *friendlyly* (that's not a word). Instead, say *in a friendly manner* or *in a friendly way.*

You can use other adjectives in this manner as well—for instance, although the adjective *agile* (meaning "skilled") has an adverb form, *agilely,* many people find *agilely* very awkward to say. There's nothing wrong with saying, *The quarterback moves down the field in such an agile way!*

Sometimes, phrases can do the job of adverbs:

I will take control *quickly.*

I will take control *on Tuesday.*

The adverb *quickly* is answering a question about the verb: *How will the speaker take control?* The phrase *on Tuesday* is also answering a question about the verb: *When will the speaker take control?* The phrase *on Tuesday* is doing the same job as the adverb *quickly.* They're both modifying the verb.

Pop Quiz!

True or False: "Popeye eats only spinach" and "Popeye only eats spinach" mean the same thing.

Answer is on page 61.

Adverbs Wrap-Up

✓ Adverbs provide extra information about something else in a sentence. They can modify any of the following:

- Verbs: He studied *obsessively* for the test.
- Adjectives: The student received an *amazingly* high score on the test.
- Other adverbs: She stated *very* clearly that she wanted a raise.
- Other constructions that you'll learn about in coming chapters.

Answers to Pop Quizzes

Verbs, page **49**

In the sentence, "When she is released from prison in 2034, she will have never so much as touched a cell phone," the verb form is *have touched.*

FALSE! The verb form is *will have touched.* (*Never* is an adverb.) Make sure you catch all the parts of a multi-word verb form!

Verbs, page **51**

In the sentence, "I hate smiling," *smiling* is a gerund, but in the sentence, "*I am smiling* as big as I can," *am smiling* is the main verb.

TRUE! The first use of *smiling* could be replaced with a noun *(I hate pizza),* but the second cannot. Also, the second use of *smiling* has a helper verb.

Adverbs, page **58**

Adverbs can modify verbs, adjectives, or nouns.

FALSE! Adverbs can modify verbs, adjectives, or other adverbs—NOT nouns! Use *adjectives* to modify nouns.

Adverbs, page **60**

"Popeye eats only spinach" and "Popeye only eats spinach" mean the same thing.

FALSE! The word *only* can function as an adjective (modifying a noun) or as an adverb (modifying something other than a noun. In the sentence *Popeye eats only spinach*, the word *only* modifies *spinach*: he eats only one thing and that one thing is spinach. In the sentence Popeye only eats spinach, *only* is now modifying the verb *eats*. In this case, Popeye does nothing else at all besides eating spinach (sounds like a pretty boring life!).

Answers to Drill Sets

Answers to Drill 3.1 — Find the Parts of the Verb

1. That rumor has been spreading like wildfire.

2. The pygmy marmoset has typically been found in the rainforest areas of South America.

3. I will run faster, jump higher, and play more aggressively this season.

4. The firm's executives had supported the eco-initiative until the financial crisis struck and they re-evaluated.

5. Are you going?

Answers to Drill 3.2 — Find the Gerunds and Infinitives

1. To be a ballerina is my lifelong dream.

2. The executive has been accused of embezzling funds.

3. Eating, praying, and loving are apparently author Elizabeth Gilbert's favorite activities.

4. To kill is to break the social contract.

5. Recovering from my accident is using all of my energy right now.

Answers to Drill 3.3 — Determine Subject–Verb Agreement

1. CORRECT. *Species* can be singular or plural, but the word *several* indicates that the word is plural in this sentence. The matching verb is *were.*

2. INCORRECT. The subject *companies* is plural. The verb *is* should be *are.*

3. CORRECT. *Every* is singular. The matching verb is *was.*

4. INCORRECT. *Code* is singular. The verb *deem* is plural and should be *deems.* (To *deem* is to judge or consider.)

5. INCORRECT. The full subject comprises two activities: *rock climbing and hang gliding.* The subject is plural, so the matching verb should be *are.*

Answers to Drill 3.4 — Has/Have and Had Verbs

1. INCORRECT. *Had been* should be *have been.* The speaker is saying that he or she started being allergic in the past and is still allergic.

2. CORRECT. First, Agatha Christie wrote 28 books. Then, the author turned 50. The first past action properly uses past perfect to indicate that the writing took place before the second past action, turning 50.

3. CORRECT. The teacher is in the process of grading the exams, so the students have finished taking the test. Pat cheated before the teacher started grading his or her exam, so it is correct to describe this action using the past perfect tense.

4. INCORRECT. *Had* should be *had had.* The speaker *had had* a heart attack before the doctor *told* him or her about it. You can test *had had* by substituting another verb; here, *had had* means *had suffered.*

5. INCORRECT. *Just began* should be *had just begun.* Two things happened in the past, and *had just begun* happened before *stabbed.*

Answers to Drill 3.5 — Find the Adverb Errors

1. **INCORRECT.** The new vendor did the job quite quickly.

Quick should be *quickly.* In the corrected sentence, *quickly* is an adverb modifying the verb *did,* and the adverb *quite* is modifying *quickly.*

2. **CORRECT.** The analyst painstakingly ascertained that the surprisingly promising financial forecast was, indeed, too good to be true.

3. **CORRECT.** He woke up early and cheerfully did the dishes.

4. **INCORRECT.** The performer danced in a lively manner, delighting the children.

Lively looks like an adverb but is actually an adjective and thus incorrect. Since *livelyly* is not a word, a phrase such as *in a lively manner* could be used, or another word (*spiritedly, enthusiastically*) could be substituted.

5. **CORRECT.** I feel bad for doing the job so badly.

Chapter 4

of

GMAT Foundations of Verbal

Part 1: **Sentence Correction**

Prepositions, Conjunctions, & Mixed Drills

In This Chapter...

Prepositions

Prepositions Wrap-Up

Conjunctions

Conjunctions Wrap-Up

Mixed Drills

Answers to Pop Quizzes

Answers to Drill Sets

Chapter 4

Prepositions, Conjunctions, & Mixed Drills

Prepositions

Prepositions are used to construct modifiers, which provide additional information about something else in the sentence.

There are more than 100 prepositions in English. Here are a few of the most common:

of	in	on
at	to	for

Many words are, or can be, prepositions:

after	against	with	across
among	around	above	at
before	behind	along	beneath
beside	by	as	despite
but	during	below	for
down	in	between	into
from	near	inside	off
on	onto	of	out
outside	over	toward	under
underneath	to	up	upon
about	until	within	without

Study this list. It is important to be able to recognize prepositions immediately when they appear in GMAT sentences. Be careful—the word *to* can also do a few other jobs, such as being the first word in an infinitive. Similarly, the word *but* is usually a conjunction, but is a preposition when used to mean *except,* as in *All developed nations* ***but*** *the U.S. have some form of national health insurance.*

As you can see from the list, many prepositions give information about location. For example, any word you can logically put in the blank in this sentence is a preposition:

The cat hid __________ the house.

Depending on the type of house (and the abilities of the cat), a cat could hide *beneath, inside, beside, above, near, against, on, underneath, around, upon, at, within, behind, below,* or *in* the house. All of these prepositions answer the question, "Where did the cat hide *in relation to* the house?"

Other prepositions give information about time and would fit into the blank in this sentence:

I exercised __________ noon.

Here, you could logically use *after, around, before, until,* or *till* (just a short verison of *until*). These all answer the question, "When did I exercise *in relation to* noon?"

Complex prepositions consist of two or more words, at least one of which is a preposition:

according to	apart from	aside from
as for	in back of	instead of
out of	ahead of	because of
in case of	in front of	in view of
prior to	apart from	by means of
in place of	next to	as of
in addition to	in spite of	on account of

Drill 4.1 — Find the Prepositions

All of the words below are short, but not all of them are prepositions. Circle the words that are (or can be) prepositions, then check your answers.

or	in	out
before	and	new
some	with	into
slow	beside	outside
upon	never	underneath
now	is	about
go	off	

Answers are on page 82.

Prepositional Phrases

A prepositional phrase is a group of words with two major components: the preposition itself and the object attached to it. The object is almost always a noun or something acting like a noun (a pronoun, a gerund, even a clause). Don't worry—that sounds a lot more complicated than it is!

Here are some prepositional phrases:

into the garden

until next Thursday

by committing murder

from him

between a rock and a hard place

under the table

along the rushing river

beyond good and evil

of them

at a gallop

Notice that each phrase begins with one of the words from the list of prepositions in this section of the book. After the preposition, there is some kind of noun (*garden, Thursday*, etc.), pronoun (*him, them*), or gerund (*doing, committing*).

Notice that none of the prepositional phrases contain a main or working verb. Remember, a gerund is an *-ing* word acting as a *noun*, so it doesn't count as a verb.

Moreover, the object in a prepositional phrase is just that: an object. It's a noun, but it cannot be the *subject*. What does all that mean? **You won't find the subject and the verb of a sentence in a prepositional phrase.**

In fact, when reading a GMAT sentence, you know a prepositional phrase is over when you hit a verb or the main subject of the sentence. Here are the prepositional phrases from the list above in context:

She ran **into** the garden, hoping to hide in the bushes.

I'm sorry I couldn't figure out where to put all these cans and bottles—I didn't see your recycling station **under** the table. Maybe I'll take care **of** them myself.

I really don't care about the success of this project, because I'm only employed here **until** next Thursday.

I got a letter—maybe it's **from** him!

The stallions raced **along** the rushing river **at** a gallop.

By committing murder, she lost her chance to win a Nobel Peace Prize.

I find myself caught **between** a rock and a hard place, needing either to lie to a very nice person or to confess that I've been seeing other people.

Nietzsche's book presented a system of ethics that he argued was **beyond** good and evil.

Pop Quiz!

True or False: In the sentence, "He wants to go," the word *to* is not a preposition, but in the sentence, "He went to the store," the word *to* is a preposition.

Answer is on page 81.

Recognizing prepositional phrases is very important. Start by spotting a preposition. In addition, the preposition should have an object, which will be a noun, pronoun, or gerund.

Most prepositional phrases are short, but it is perfectly possible to have more than one prepositional phrase in a row, taking up a lot of real estate in the sentence. You already saw *the horses race **along** the rushing river **at** a gallop*. Here's another example:

I walked **through** the valley **between** the two largest mountain ranges **in** South America.

The three underlined portions represent three prepositional phrases strung together. Valuable meaning is contained in those prepositional phrases, but they do not contain the subject or the verb. Once you recognize the prepositional phrases, you can temporarily ignore them in order to see the **core sentence**: *I walked.*

Drill 4.2 — Find the Prepositional Phrases

Put brackets [around the prepositional phrases]. Then, read the sentence back to yourself without the phrases—there should still be a complete sentence containing at least a subject and a working verb.

1. After a spell in the sun, a spot in the shade sounded delightful.
2. Seventy-five people with asthma marched in the parade.
3. In our club, to play by the rules is crucial.
4. The committee, which meets monthly for the purpose of discussing the fiscal management of the charitable fund, recommends passing the annual budget on Monday.

5. To run with the wolves on thirty consecutive cold winter mornings in Minsk, Belarus, is to truly strengthen your spirit in just one month; to drink nothing but cold mountain water and eat nothing but goat meat for thirty days in any of the former Soviet republics is to truly strengthen your character in a similarly spartan manner.

Answers are on page 82.

Prepositions Separating Subjects and Verbs

Why is it so important to be able to recognize prepositional phrases? So you can temporarily ignore them!

4

Prepositional phrases often separate a subject and a verb, sometimes so much so that it is difficult to tell whether the subject and verb match. When multiple prepositional phrases or other "junk" separates the subject and verb, errors become difficult to find. For instance:

> The pies Mother cooled in the window on Christmas Day in the dead of a bleak winter in the 1990s after a long bout with an insidious form of tropical parasitic infection was delicious.

If you are reading this sentence in small chunks instead of mentally taking in the whole thing at once (a difficult task), then you might think that the core of the sentence is that last bit: *parasitic infection was delicious.* That sounds kind of gross, but not necessarily ungrammatical.

Cross out the prepositional phrases, though. Watch what happens:

> The pies Mother cooled ~~**in** the window **on** Christmas Day **in** the dead **of** a bleak winter **in** the 1990s **after** a long bout **with** an insidious form **of** tropical parasitic infection~~ was delicious.

That was a series of *eight* consecutive prepositional phrases! Wow! You're left with a simple core sentence: *The pies Mother cooled was delicious.* The subject, *the pies,* is plural, while the verb, *was,* is singular. *Was* should be changed to *were.* This was a fairly extreme example, but prepositional phrases are used widely on the GMAT to keep a subject and verb far apart—so far apart that it is hard to match them up mentally.

Pop Quiz!

True or False: Sometimes the main subject of a sentence is located inside a prepositional phrase.

Answer is on page 81.

Drill 4.3 — Strip Out the Prepositional Phrases

Put brackets [around the prepositional phrases] and then determine whether the sentence has an error. Circle "Correct" or "Incorrect" for each sentence.

1. The trolls under the bridge really just want to be understood. CORRECT/INCORRECT

2. The statistics from the study reveals that the populace of the United States is plagued by poor health. CORRECT/INCORRECT

3. Each of the spouses of the company's executives have expressed their wish that the executives would work less and spend more time with family. CORRECT/INCORRECT

4. Each of the runners who chose to run this marathon in polyester is experiencing serious chafing. CORRECT/INCORRECT

5. I ran over the bridge, through the woods, and into your arms. CORRECT/INCORRECT

Answers are on page 83.

Drill 4.4 — Strip Out More Prepositional Phrases

More practice with prepositions. Practice your skills from the previous drill on more GMAT-like sentences. Put brackets [around the prepositional phrases] and then determine whether the sentence has an error. Circle "Correct" or "Incorrect" for each sentence.

1. The editor of the newspaper would later make his reputation as a union firebrand. CORRECT/INCORRECT

2. Construction of the Parthenon, a temple in the Athenian Acropolis, began in 447 B.C. CORRECT/INCORRECT

3. Because provisions of the new international trade agreement specifies that imports must be inspected for drugs, international disputes have already begun over delayed shipments. CORRECT/INCORRECT

4. A company that specializes in the analysis of body language purports, from a one-minute video of a person's speech, to be able to ascertain numerous truths about the person. CORRECT/INCORRECT

5. Because the payment of interest is prohibited under Sharia law, some practicing Muslims in the U.K. and U.S. are able to obtain what is known in modern parlance as an "Islamic mortgage," often an arrangement in which a bank purchases a home outright and rents it to a tenant who pays down principal as he or she accumulates ownership. CORRECT/INCORRECT

Answers are on page 83.

Ending a Sentence with a Preposition

Some people say that it is not acceptable to end a sentence with a preposition. For instance, rather than say, *That is the mat I do yoga* ***on,*** they would like you to say, *That is the mat* ***on which*** *I do yoga.*

However, most grammarians agree that it is fine to end a sentence with a preposition; both versions above are fine. Thus, this issue is not tested on the GMAT.

Do be aware that it is considered correct to say, *This is the colleague* ***with whom*** *I am producing the plans for our next product.* Because people don't typically speak this way, many think that this sentence sounds wrong. It is not wrong; it is correct. The GMAT may try to fool your ear on something similar and get you to fall into a trap.

While you should not use prepositions that don't add any meaning (for instance, *That is the house she went inside* ***of*** is more awkward than *That is the house she went inside*), it is often perfectly appropriate to end a sentence with a preposition. For instance, say you bumped into something in the dark and heard a crash, you could very reasonably ask, "What did I just knock *over*?"

As a final note on this issue, take a look at Winston Churchill's famous reply to someone who suggested that he should not end a sentence with a preposition: "This is the sort of arrant pedantry up with which I will not put." *Arrant* means *complete* and *pedantry* means *excessive display of learning* or *slavish devotion to rules.* The joke, of course, is that the common expression "put up with" sounds ridiculous when the words are put in a strange order to avoid ending the sentence with a preposition.

Prepositions Wrap-Up

✓ Prepositions are often short little words, but they still play an important role in sentences. In general, the GMAT uses prepositions to do two things:

1. To make a sentence longer and separate major parts of the sentence (such as the subject and the verb) in order to obscure errors.
2. To test modifier errors (more on this in Chapter 6).

✓ The following prepositions are most commonly used in the English language (and on the GMAT!):

of	in	on
at	to	for

You are almost done with the parts of speech. It's time to move on to *conjunctions.*

Conjunctions

Conjunctions link words, phrases, and clauses, making lists or contrasts. All of the following are conjunctions:

and	but
yet	either . . . or
not only . . . but also	if
when	because

There are only a limited number of conjunctions in existence, but they're critically important to communication.

4

The following are the three types of conjunctions.

Coordinating Conjunctions

The coordinating conjunctions are **for, and, nor, but, or, yet,** and **so**. They can be remembered with the acronym FANBOYS. Without question, the most important coordinating conjunction is *and.* As was the case with pronouns, the biggest danger on Sentence Correction is that you will skip right past the conjunctions. Start training yourself to notice the FANBOYS.

The coordinating conjunctions can join anything from single words to entire sentences or complete ideas:

> *Peanut butter* **and** *jelly* go well together on a sandwich.

In the sentence above, the coordinating conjunction *and* joins two nouns.

> *You will come with me to my mother's house for Mother's Day,* **or** *I will break up with you right now.*

In the sentence above, the coordinating conjunction *or* joins two sentences to make a more complex sentence.

On the GMAT, you are tested on whether the *right* conjunction is being used. This is as much a question of meaning and logic as it is of grammar. For example:

> Many whale species are endangered, **but** they are overhunted.

Here, *but* does not fit the meaning of the rest of the sentence. Species are endangered, *but* they are overhunted? Logically, species become endangered *because* they are overhunted. *But* should be *because, since,* or *as.* Any of these three conjunctions would show the proper causal relationship between the two ideas. *Because, since,* and *as* fall into a different category of conjunction—*subordinating conjunctions*—which will be discussed soon.

Correlative Conjunctions

The primary correlative conjunctions are **either/or, neither/nor, both/and, whether/or**, and **not only/ but also**. (The last one can also be written **not only/but.**)

Each correlative conjunction has two parts; after each part could be a noun, a phrase, or an entire simple sentence.

The GMAT does like to test errors related to correlative conjunctions. You'll need to start training yourself to spot these correlative conjunctions and to make sure that the items after each of the two parts are the same part of speech or type of phrase.

Try to figure out why these two sentences are labeled "correct" and "incorrect":

> CORRECT: I like to eat **not only** steak **but also** ribs, pork chops, and chicken cutlets.
>
> INCORRECT: I like **not only** to eat steak **but also** ribs, pork chops, and chicken cutlets.

In the correct version, *not only* is followed by a noun (*steak*). The second part of the conjunction, *but also,* is followed by several nouns. Both parts answer the same question: "What do I like to eat?" This sentence is **parallel**: the words after each part of the conjunction are in the same form.

In the incorrect version, however, *not only* is followed by an infinitive (*to eat*), but *but also* is still followed by several nouns. The first part answers the question, "What do I like?" whereas the second part answers a different question, "What do I like *to eat?*" This sentence is NOT parallel and is incorrect.

Pop Quiz!

True or False: The sentence, "Profits were outstanding, and the company went bankrupt because of outrageously poor management," would be considered incorrect on the GMAT.

Answer is on page 81.

Here's another example:

> You can **either** wash these dishes **or** I will leave you forever.

Do the parts after *either* and *or* match? After *either* is a verb (*wash*). After *or* is a pronoun (*I*). Also, *I will leave you forever* is a complete sentence, while the first part, *wash these dishes,* is not. These portions are definitely not parallel. Here's a corrected version:

> **Either** you can wash these dishes, **or** I will leave you forever.

Now, *either* and *or* are both followed directly by pronouns. Even more importantly, *you can wash these dishes* and *I will leave you forever* are each complete sentences. The structure is now *Either [first sentence], or [second sentence].* The new compound sentence is now parallel.

You'll revisit this idea when you get to the section on parallelism in a couple of chapters.

Drill 4.5 — Find the Conjunction Errors

Circle the two parts of each correlative conjunction. Determine whether the sentence has an error and circle "Correct" or "Incorrect."

1. Critics allege that the company failed because of both market conditions and improper management. CORRECT/INCORRECT

2. Not only was the study flawed but also frivolous. CORRECT/INCORRECT

3. The king wishes to express that he is neither a despot nor oblivious to the concerns of the people. CORRECT/INCORRECT

4. The nation not only ranks very poorly in elementary education, but also trails every other nation in measures of child health. CORRECT/INCORRECT

5. The speaker is both entertaining and an inspiration. CORRECT/INCORRECT

Answers are on page 84.

Subordinating Conjunctions

Subordinating conjunctions introduce **dependent clauses**. A *dependent clause* and a *subordinate clause* are the same thing. The word *subordinate* means *lower in position* or *submissive.*

A **clause** is a group of words that could stand alone as a complete sentence. For example, *Nearly 10% of children in the United States are without health insurance* is a complete sentence. So is *This health care bill* *will help millions of families.* The word *because* is a subordinating conjunction. You can use it to make the first sentence *subordinate* to the second:

> Because nearly 10% of children in the United States are without health insurance, this health care bill will help millions of families.

That is, a subordinating conjunction attaches two smaller sentences into a single sentence in a way that makes one the main part of the sentence and the other dependent on it. The subordinating conjunction also gives information about the relationship between the main part (known as the **main clause** or **independent clause**) and the dependent part.

Some of the most common subordinating conjunctions are:

after	although	as
as if	as long as	because
before	even though	how
if	if only	in order
once	since	so that
than	that	though
unless	until	when
where	whether	while

You may recognize some of these words from earlier in the book—a number of the subordinating conjunctions can also serve as prepositions. Here's a simple way to tell: if a word such as *until* is followed by just a noun, pronoun, or gerund, it's a preposition, but if it introduces a clause, it's a subordinating conjunction.

> I studied until midnight.

In the example above, *until midnight* is a prepositional phrase.

> I intend to sleep until you wake me up.

In this second example, *until* is a subordinating conjunction and *you wake me up* is the subordinate clause.

Subordinating conjunctions are an important issue in understanding the structure of complex sentences. Students sometimes become confused when asked for the subject of a sentence, because it seems as though there are two or more subjects. If you identify a *subordinate clause* and a *main clause,* it is much easier to figure out the *main* subject of the sentence. Also, if *until* introduces a prepositional phrase, you can temporarily ignore it while looking at subject/verb issues, but if *until* introduces a subordinate clause with its own subject and verb, you will need to check that subject and verb for agreement, too.

Drill 4.6 — Find the Dependent Clause

For each sentence, circle the subordinating conjunction and underline the dependent clause.

1. The company's leadership began to falter after the board disagreed sharply over executive bonuses.

2. While freshly minted law school graduates greatly exceed the number of top law jobs available, prospective students continue to apply to law school in droves.

3. She ate as if she had been starved for weeks.

4. Unless you get your MBA, you cannot rise to the next level in this company.

5. I'll go if you do.

Answers are on page 84.

Conjunctions Wrap-Up

✓ The FANBOYS are coordinating conjunctions; they connect two parts of a sentence in a parallel way:

For And Not But Or Yet So

These conjunctions are special because they can connect two complete clauses, or sentences, in an equal manner.

✓ Other conjunctions also connect parts of sentences together:

- Correlative conjunctions, such as *either/or, neither/nor, both/and, whether/or,* and *not only/but also,* connect two parts of a sentence in a parallel, or equal, manner.
- Subordinate conjunctions, such as *although, because, after,* and *since,* make one of the clauses subordinate to, or dependent on, the other.

You now know more about English grammar than 75% of Americans and a great many GMAT test-takers. Nice! Now, it's time to move on to some drills to help solidify your new skills.

Mixed Drills

Mixed Drill 4.7 — Match the Word with the Part of Speech

Label each word a noun, pronoun, adjective, verb, adverb, preposition, or conjunction. Some words can play more than one role.

1. each	____________	11. at	____________
2. Scandinavian	____________	12. equivalent	____________
3. by	____________	13. no one	____________
4. really	____________	14. into	____________
5. under	____________	15. or	____________
6. yet	____________	16. hard	____________
7. only	____________	17. wrung	____________
8. fly-by-night	____________	18. so	____________
9. diverged	____________	19. without	____________
10. primarily	____________	20. finally	____________

Answers are on page 84–85.

Mixed Drill 4.8 — Identify Parts of Speech in Sentences

Label each underlined word a noun, pronoun, adjective, verb, adverb, preposition, or conjunction.

Example: Many men feel that miniature poodles are not real dogs.
adj noun verb adj noun verb adj noun

1. It may be true that Notre Dame alumni really care about football, but it is also true that they care about academics.

2. Thirty members of the marching band have voted to play Lady Gaga's "Poker Face" in the parade.

3. Russian players often beat the Americans in chess tournaments.

4. Class attendance and participation are important, but you cannot truly learn the material without reading primary sources, either in books or on the Internet.

5. The small boy was delighted, for he had received a jack-in-the-box for Hanukkah.

Answers are on page 85.

Mixed Drill 4.9 — Identify Certain Kinds of Errors

Each sentence below contains one of these errors:

A. A pronoun does not match its antecedent in number (that is, a singular pronoun refers to a plural noun or vice-versa).
B. A reflexive pronoun (such as *ourselves*) is used inappropriately.

Circle the error in the sentence and write A or B in the blank.

1. It seems that everyone has brought loved ones to watch them graduate. _____

2. The area is rife with pickpockets, so a tourist should keep their handbag close. _____

3. The administration has amended their requirement that students who want to graduate on time must submit their theses one month before graduation. _____

4. Each of the children is going to sing a little song for your grandmother and myself. _____

5. All students must consider the options and decide for himself or herself. _____

Answers are on page 86.

Mixed Drill 4.10 — Identify Certain Kinds of Errors

A. A pronoun is ambiguous.
B. The pronoun *one* is used incorrectly.
C. A subject and verb do not agree.
D. A verb is in the wrong tense.

Circle the error in the sentence and write A, B, C, or D in the blank.

1. From 1971 to 1975, he earns his undergraduate degree at Villanova. _____

2. The three employees who live in the townhouses by the river wants to move closer to work. _____

3. One cannot help but wonder if you could float to the sky by holding on to a very large number of helium balloons. _____

4. Graduates of Dartmouth and Yale are the most likely to report in surveys years later that they loved it. _____

5. The committee that controls the allocation of new funds and the dean often differs over policy. _____

Answers are on page 86.

Answers to Pop Quizzes

Prepositions, page **70**

In the sentence, "He wants to go," the word *to* is not a preposition, but in the sentence, "He went to the store," the word *to* is a preposition.

TRUE! *To* just before a verb is part of an infinitive (*to go*), but *to* followed by a noun (*to the store*) is a preposition used in a prepositional phrase.

Prepositions, page **71**

Sometimes the main subject of a sentence is located inside a prepositional phrase.

FALSE! Learn to identify prepositional phrases so that you can temporarily ignore them for the purpose of matching up subjects and verbs. The subject of the sentence will never be located inside a prepositional phrase. (There are a couple of rare exceptions that the *Manhattan Prep Sentence Correction GMAT Strategy Guide* discusses.)

Conjunctions, page **75**

The sentence, "Profits were outstanding, and the company went bankrupt because of outrageously poor management," would be considered incorrect on the GMAT.

TRUE! The meaning is illogical. For this sentence to make sense, *and* should be *but* (or *yet*, or some other word that conveys a contrast).

Answers to Drill Sets

Answers to Drill 4.1 — Find the Prepositions

The following words are (or can be) prepositions:

or	(in)	(out)
(before)	and	new
some	(with)	(into)
slow	(beside)	(outside)
(upon)	never	(underneath)
now	is	(about)
go	(off)	

The uncircled words in the drill are *not* prepositions:

Or and **and** are conjunctions.
Slow and **new** are adjectives.
Never is an adverb.
Some can be an adjective, pronoun, or adverb.
Now can be an adverb, noun, or conjunction.
Go and **is** are verbs.

Answers to Drill 4.2 — Find the Prepositional Phrases

1. [After a spell] [in the sun], a spot [in the shade] sounded delightful.
Complete sentence: *A spot sounded delightful.*

2. Seventy-five people [with asthma] marched [in the parade].
Complete sentence: *Seventy-five people marched.*

3. [In our club], to play [by the rules] is crucial.
Complete sentence: *To play is crucial.*

4. The committee, which meets monthly [for the purpose] [of discussing the fiscal management] [of the charitable fund], recommends passing the annual budget [on Monday].
Complete sentence: *The committee, which meets monthly, recommends passing the annual budget.*

5. To run [with the wolves] [on thirty consecutive cold winter mornings] [in Minsk, Belarus,] is to truly strengthen your spirit [in just one month]; to drink nothing [but cold mountain water] and eat nothing [but goat meat] [for thirty days] [in any of the former Soviet republics] is to truly strengthen your character [in a similarly spartan manner].

Complete sentence: *To run is to truly strengthen your spirit; to drink nothing and eat nothing is to truly strengthen your character.*

Answers to Drill 4.3 — Strip Out the Prepositional Phrases

1. The trolls [under the bridge] really just want to be understood. **CORRECT.**

2. The statistics [from the study] reveals that the populace [of the United States] is plagued [by poor health]. **INCORRECT.** *Reveals* should be *reveal.*

3. Each [of the spouses] [of the company's executives] have expressed their wish that the executives would work less and spend more time [with family]. **INCORRECT.** *Have* should be *has* to match the singular subject *each.* Also, *their* should be *his or her.*

4. Each [of the runners] who chose to run this marathon [in polyester] is experiencing serious chafing. **CORRECT.**

5. I ran [over the bridge], [through the woods], and [into your arms]. **CORRECT.** The *and* isn't technically canceled out, but that's okay. It was only there to link the three prepositional phrases together.

Answers to Drill 4.4 — Strip Out More Prepositional Phrases

1. The editor [of the newspaper] would later make his reputation [as a union firebrand]. **CORRECT.**

2. Construction [of the Parthenon], a temple [in the Athenian Acropolis], began [in 447 BC]. **CORRECT.**

3. Because provisions [of the new international trade agreement] specifies that imports must be inspected [for drugs], international disputes have already begun [over delayed shipments]. **INCORRECT.** *Specifies* should be *specify* in order to match the plural subject *provisions.*

4. A company that specializes [in the analysis] [of body language] purports, [from a one-minute video] [of a person's speech], to be able to ascertain numerous truths [about the person]. **CORRECT.**

5. Because the payment [of interest] is prohibited [under Sharia law], some practicing Muslims [in the U.K. and U.S.] are able to obtain what is known [in modern parlance] as an "Islamic mortgage," often an arrangement in which a bank purchases a home outright and rents it [to a tenant] who pays down principal as he or she accumulates ownership. **CORRECT.**

4

Answers to Drill 4.5 — Find the Conjunction Errors

1. Critics allege that the company failed because of both market conditions and improper management. **CORRECT.**

The parts following *both/and* are *market conditions* and *improper management.*

2. Not only was the study flawed but also frivolous. **INCORRECT.**

Not only is followed by the verb *was,* whereas *but also* is followed by the adjective *frivolous.* A correct version could read *The study was not only flawed but also frivolous.*

3. The king wishes to express that he is neither a despot nor oblivious to the concerns of the people. **INCORRECT.**

Neither is followed by *a despot* (*despot* is a noun) and *nor* is followed by *oblivious* (an adjective). A correct version could read *neither despotic nor oblivious.* (Despotic is an adjective.)

4. The nation not only ranks very poorly in elementary education, but also trails every other nation in measures of child health. **CORRECT.**

Ranks and *trails* are both verbs; the two parts of the sentence match nicely.

5. The speaker is both entertaining and an inspiration. **INCORRECT.**

Entertaining is an adjective and *inspiration* is a noun. A correct version could read *The speaker is both entertaining and inspiring.*

Answers to Drill 4.6 — Find the Dependent Clause

1. The company's leadership began to falter after the board disagreed sharply over executive bonuses.
dependent clause

2. While freshly minted law school graduates greatly exceed the number of top law jobs available,
dependent clause
prospective students continue to apply to law school in droves.

3. She ate as if she had been starved for weeks.
dependent clause

4. Unless you get your MBA, you cannot rise to the next level in this company.
dependent clause

5. I'll go if you do.
dependent clause

Answers to Mixed Drill 4.7 — Match the Word with the Part of Speech

1. pronoun (Can also be used as an adjective, as in *Each cell phone should be turned off.*)
2. adjective (Can also be used as a noun, as in *A Scandinavian came into the store.*)
3. preposition (Can also be used as an adverb, as in *He drove by.*)
4. adverb

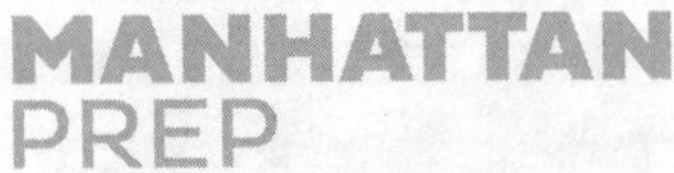

5. preposition (Can also be used as an adverb, as in *He went under.*)
6. conjunction
7. adverb or adjective
8. adjective
9. verb
10. adverb
11. preposition
12. adjective (Can be used as a noun, as in *This is an equivalent to an iPod.*)
13. pronoun
14. preposition
15. conjunction
16. adjective or adverb
17. verb (*Wrung* is the past tense of *wring,* as in *He wrung out the wet towel.*)
18. conjunction (Can also be used as an adverb, as in *She is so tall that she can touch the ceiling.*)
19. preposition
20. adverb

Answers to Mixed Drill 4.8 — Identify Parts of Speech in Sentences

1. It may be true that Notre Dame alumni really care about football, but it is
pronoun verb adj adj noun adv verb prep noun conj pronoun verb

also true that they care about academics.
adv adj pronoun verb prep noun

2. Thirty members of the marching band have voted to play Lady Gaga's
adj noun prep adj noun verb

"Poker Face" in the parade.
prep noun

3. Russian players often beat the Americans in chess tournaments.
adj noun adv verb noun prep adj noun

4. Class attendance and participation are important, but you cannot truly learn the
adj noun conj noun verb adj conj pronoun verb adv verb

material without reading primary sources, either in books or on the Internet.
noun prep adj noun conj prep noun conj prep noun

5. The small boy was delighted, for he had received a jack-in-the-box for Hanukkah.
adj noun verb adj conj pronoun verb noun prep noun

Answers to Mixed Drill 4.9 — Identify Certain Kinds of Errors

1. **A.** It seems that everyone has brought loved ones to watch them graduate.

Them is plural and does not match with *everyone,* which is singular. Fix this sentence by saying, "It seems that everyone has brought loved ones to watch *him or her* graduate," or the less awkward, "It seems that *all of the seniors have* brought loved ones to watch them graduate."

2. **A.** The area is rife with pickpockets, so a tourist should keep their handbag close.

A tourist is singular, so the sentence should refer to *his or her handbag.*

3. **A.** The administration has amended their requirement that students who want to graduate on time must submit their theses one month before graduation.

Administration is singular and does not match *their.* The sentence should say, "has amended *its* requirement." (The second *their* is correct—it refers to *students.*)

4. **B.** Each of the children is going to sing a little song for your grandmother and myself.

Myself should be replaced with the object pronoun *me.* There is no reason here to use the reflexive.

5. **A.** All students must consider the options and decide for himself or herself.

The students must decide for *themselves.*

Answers to Mixed Drill 4.10 — Identify Certain Kinds of Errors

1. **D.** From 1971 to 1975, he earns his undergraduate degree at Villanova.

Since the action occurred between 1971 and 1975, it took place in the past. The verb should be *earned.*

2. **C.** The three employees who live in the townhouses by the river wants to move closer to work.

The subject, *employees,* is plural and requires the plural verb *want.*

3. **B.** One cannot help but wonder if you could float to the sky by holding on to a very large number of helium balloons.

One and *you* cannot be mixed and matched. Either both pronouns should be *one* or both pronouns should be *you.*

4. **A.** Graduates of Dartmouth and Yale are the most likely to report in surveys years later that they loved it.

The pronoun *it* is singular. Though each school is singular, the sentence clearly lumps them into a (plural) group, so the sentence could substitute something like *they loved them.* Notice that it is awkward to use two such similar pronouns so closely together to refer to different antecedents. Additionally, this suggests that graduates of each school loved both of the schools. A better fix might be something like *they loved their schools* or *they loved their time in school.*

5. **C.** The committee that controls the allocation of new funds and the dean often differs over policy.

The subject is *The committee that controls the allocation of new funds and the dean*. You can shorten this in your head as *The committee and the dean*. (You could read the sentence to mean that the committee controls the dean, but that's an unlikely meaning.) The subject is plural; it requires the plural verb *differ*.

Note: Microsoft Word's grammar check caught only 1 out of the 10 errors in the previous two drills! You cannot depend on computers to fix your writing.

Chapter 5
of

GMAT Foundations of Verbal

Part 1: **Sentence Correction**

Subject/Predicate, Fragments & Run-ons, & Punctuation

In This Chapter. . .

Chapter 5

Subject/Predicate, Fragments & Run-ons, & Punctuation

Subjects and Predicates

Every complete sentence contains a **subject** and a **predicate**. It is possible for a complete sentence to be only two words long:

We went. Love hurts.

In both cases, the first word is the subject, and the second word is the predicate. Of course, most sentences are more complicated, but at minimum, a predicate always includes a working verb.

Sometimes, it is difficult to understand the meaning of a sentence without some background information, but that doesn't mean that the sentence isn't grammatically complete. For instance:

They gave it to us.

Who are *they*? What did they give to us? You have no idea. But the sentence is still complete—it has a subject (the pronoun *they*) and a predicate (*gave it to us).* The predicate contains a working verb (*gave*), plus some additional information. On the GMAT, this sentence would be incorrect, because *they* and *it* lack antecedents, but again, the sentence is complete.

In a command, the subject *you* is implied:

Go!

A "command" sentence that is more likely to appear in business or academic writing might look something like this:

> Consider the case of Watson and Crick.

Here, the sentence is understood to mean, "*You* consider the case of Watson and Crick." The subject is the pronoun *you*.

Subjects are generally nouns and pronouns (such as *we* and *love* in the examples above). As was discussed in the section on verbs, sometimes a gerund or infinitive can be a subject:

> *Dancing* is a great joy.
>
> *To die* for one's country is to pay the ultimate price.

Here, *dancing* is a gerund, and *to die* is an infinitive.

A group of words can be the subject of a sentence. Even a clause beginning with *that* can be the subject:

> *That forty people dropped out* is less a reason to condemn the program than to praise its rigor.

The subject is *That forty people dropped out.* That sounds like a very weird subject! You'd rarely hear such a construction in speech, but it's perfectly grammatical. You could also write the subject as *The fact that forty people dropped out.*

Now consider a much longer sentence:

> Each of us has saved for weeks to be able to attend the Madonna concert, where we will undoubtedly dance all night to Madonna's hits from the last twenty years, including "Papa Don't Preach," "Open Your Heart," "True Blue," "Express Yourself," "Ray of Light," "Beautiful Stranger," and "4 Minutes."

This rather silly example demonstrates how a *subject* is different from a *topic.* What is the *topic* of this sentence? Perhaps "Madonna" or "some people who really love Madonna." But what is the grammatical *subject*? It is the word *each.* It seems a bit weird that the subject would be one of the least interesting, least descriptive words in the sentence.

To be clear—the *subject* of a sentence is not the same as the *topic* of a sentence. In some languages, the idea of a *subject* and a *topic* are interchangeable. In English, a *topic* is what you're really talking about. Two people could disagree about the topic of a sentence. A topic is a matter of opinion. A subject is not. A *subject* is a grammatical concept; it is not about the meaning or main idea of the sentence.

A simple subject is just one word—in this case, *each.* A complete subject is the simple subject plus the other words that help to identify the simple subject—in this case, *each of us.* Most of the time, you want the *simple subject* of the sentence so you can ask questions, such as "Does the subject match the verb?"

Here are some guidelines for locating the subject of a sentence:

- The subject is usually a noun or pronoun, but sometimes it's a gerund, infinitive, phrase, or clause.
- One good way to find the main subject is to find the main verb and ask what or who is *doing* the action described by the verb.
- A subject can consist of two or more things joined by *and.* For instance, *Joe and Maria* could be a subject, as could *Dancing, drinking, and eating.*
- The subject is NOT located in a prepositional phrase. This is why you spent so much time learning to identify prepositions and prepositional phrases—so you can rule them out when looking for the subject.
- If you have a subordinate clause joined to a sentence with a subordinating conjunction, you want the subject that is *not* in the subordinate clause—the main subject will be in the main clause of the sentence.

Pop Quiz!

True or False: The subject of a sentence can be a phrase beginning with *that* or *to.*

Answer is on page 104.

Here are some more examples. Find the subject and the verb:

A big, fat, delicious chicken parmesan sandwich would be amazing right now.

The subject is *sandwich.* The adjectives *big, fat, delicious,* and *chicken parmesan* tell you more about the sandwich. The sandwich is performing the verb *would be.*

Earth and the other planets in our solar system orbit around the Sun.

The subject is *Earth and the other planets. In our solar system* is a prepositional phrase. The subject *Earth and the other planets* is performing the verb *orbit.*

None of the guests have arrived.

The subject is *none. Of the guests* is a prepositional phrase. The subject *none* is performing the verb *have arrived.*

Although rapper Tupac Shakur died in 1996, his music has been released on no fewer than eight posthumous albums.

The subject is *music.* Note that most people would say that the *topic* of the sentence is Tupac Shakur. However, *Tupac Shakur* is located within a subordinate clause (*although* is a subordinating conjunction). The main clause of the sentence is *his music has been released on no fewer than eight posthumous albums.* The subject *music* is performing the verb *has been released.*

Because his jokes were so offensive, we left before the show ended.

The subject is *we.* The first part of the sentence is the subordinate clause (*because* is a subordinating conjunction), and the second part, *we left before the show ended*, is the main clause. The subject *we* is performing the verb *left.*

There are 10 people waiting in the conference room.

In a sentence that begins with *there* and a form of *to be* (is, are, were . . .), the word *there* is NOT the subject—rather, the word *there* is a clue that the real subject will occur soon. Here, the subject is *people.* The subject *people* is performing the verb *are waiting.*

Notice that the compound verb is split up (*are* and *waiting* do not touch each other in the sentence). In this kind of sentence, it can be helpful to eliminate the word *there* and to put the sentence in a more normal order: *Ten people are waiting in the conference room.* This makes it more clear that *people* is the subject and *are waiting* is the verb.

Sentences also can run backwards. For instance: *Here comes the sun.* It's *the sun* that comes, not *here* that comes.

Beside the highway was the wreckage from the crash.

The sentence in the example above begins with a prepositional phrase, *Beside the highway.* Then there is a verb, *was.* Finally, the subject, *wreckage. From the crash* is another prepositional phrase. Put the sentence back in a more normal order to see the structure: *The wreckage from the crash was beside the highway.*

Drill 5.1 — Find the Subject

Circle the main subject of each sentence.

1. Each of the women in the study said that her arthritis had gotten worse since beginning the therapy.

2. Only a thin sliver of the specimen is needed to perform the test.

3. All of us agree.

4. There are a bank, a nail salon, and a day care center in this shopping plaza.

5. Amid the weeds and trash was my lost kitten.

Answers are on page 105.

Some sentences have more than one subject–verb pair:

> I like game shows, but I hate those reality dating shows in which people hurt each others' feelings for money and prizes.

This sentence consists of two independent clauses joined by a coordinating conjunction, *but*:

> I like game shows,
> but
> I hate those reality dating shows in which people hurt each others' feelings for money and prizes.

In the first clause, the subject *I* is performing the verb *like.* In the second clause, the subject *I* is performing the verb *hate.*

> Although *Ailurus fulgens* is commonly called the "red panda," the species is only distantly related to the giant panda and is actually more closely related to weasels and raccoons.

Ailurus fulgens is the subject of the first part of the sentence. Its verb is *is* or *is called.*

The species is the subject of the second part of the sentence. Its verbs are *is* and *is,* or *is related* and *is related.*

If you wanted to mark up the subjects and verbs visually (a process you want to be able to do mentally on the real GMAT), you could do so as follows:

> Although (*Ailurus fulgens*) <u>is</u> commonly called the "red panda," the (species) <u>is</u> only distantly related to the giant panda and <u>is</u> actually more closely related to weasels and raccoons.

Here subjects are circled and verbs are underlined. It doesn't exactly matter how you do the mark-ups. If you are making flash cards, though, try to be consistent. Don't mark every part of speech; focus on whatever's important in the sentence you're dealing with.

Pop Quiz!

True or False: In the sentence, "Although Italy is famous for pasta, noodles were invented by the Chinese," the dependent clause has the subject *Italy* and the independent clause has the subject *the Chinese.*

Answer is on page 104.

Subject/Predicate Wrap-Up

✓ A complete sentence must contain at least a verb, such as *Go*! On the GMAT, all sentence correction sentences will contain at least one main subject and one main verb (or predicate).

✓ Your first task is to find the subject so that you can see whether it matches with the verb. Subjects can be:

- nouns
- gerunds (*-ing* words, more rare)
- pronouns
- infinitives (more rare)

✓ Prepositional phrases always include nouns but these nouns are never the subject of a sentence.

Sentence Fragments & Run-on Sentences

A sentence fragment is a group of words that cannot stand alone as a sentence. A fragment either does not contain a subject–verb pair or it does but it also contains a subordinating word that doesn't allow the sentence to be a complete thought. Sentence fragments trying to stand alone are always wrong.

All of the following are sentence fragments:

Under the bridge at the edge of town.	No subject–verb pair
While it's lovely that you came to visit.	Subordinator: *while*
If it's true that Chandler was responsible for the project's failure.	Subordinator: *if*
The Japanese medal given for bravery.	No verb
Rushing the field during the football game.	No verb

These fragments are not complete sentences and cannot stand alone, but they would all be fine as part of larger sentences that include independent clauses:

The drug dealer was arrested under the bridge at the edge of town.

While it's lovely that you came to visit, I do think it's time you headed back home.

If it's true that Chandler was responsible for the project's failure, he will probably be fired.

The *bukosho*, the Japanese medal given for bravery, was instituted in 1944 by Imperial edict.

Rushing the field during the football game is strictly forbidden.

Note that in every example but the last one, the non-underlined part of the sentence can stand alone without the underlined portion. In the last example, *Rushing the field during the football game* is actually the subject of the sentence (specifically, *rushing* is the simple subject).

If a group of words lacks a verb, it is a sentence fragment. As you learned in the last section, all good sentences contain, at minimum, a subject and a verb. Note that *rushing* could be a noun (gerund) or a verb, but it can't be both at the same time.

REMINDER

To determine whether a word ending in *-ing* is a verb, look for helper verbs. If the *-ing* stands alone, it is not a verb.

Just one word can make the difference between being a complete sentence and being a fragment. In fact, you can turn a perfectly good sentence into a fragment by *adding* a word, such as *who* or *since* (a subordinating conjunction):

COMPLETE: My brother broke his foot.

INCOMPLETE: My brother **who** broke his foot.

INCOMPLETE: **Since** my brother broke his foot.

Notice that the words on the right do not feel like complete thoughts. If someone said either one aloud, you would wait impatiently for the person to continue speaking and finish his or her thought. The GMAT will try to make you accept a fragment as a sentence by using lots of long words. Don't be fooled. Demand complete thoughts!

A run-on sentence consists of two (or more) independent clauses joined without appropriate punctuation or a conjunction. For instance:

I pronounce "tomato" one way, you pronounce it a completely different way.

This so-called "sentence" consists of two independent clauses joined by only a comma. This specific kind of run-on sentence is called a comma splice. Run-on sentences, including comma splices, are always wrong.

To make this a real sentence, you need a conjunction or a semicolon (semicolons are discussed later in this chapter):

CORRECT: I pronounce "tomato" one way, **while** you pronounce it a completely different way.

CORRECT: I pronounce "tomato" one way**;** you pronounce it a completely different way.

Drill 5.2 — Find Fragments and Run-ons

For each sentence, circle "Complete Sentence," "Fragment," or "Run-on."

1. Scott Fitzgerald, planning, writing, and revising *The Great Gatsby* from 1922 to 1925 in Great Neck, Long Island. COMPLETE SENTENCE/FRAGMENT/RUN-ON

2. That the charge was true was the worst part. COMPLETE SENTENCE/FRAGMENT/RUN-ON

3. There are only seven of us because the twins couldn't make it. COMPLETE SENTENCE/FRAGMENT/RUN-ON

4. The decorated war general, who stormed the beach in Normandy in 1944. COMPLETE SENTENCE/FRAGMENT/RUN-ON

5. The company sold its machine parts and chemicals divisions, they hadn't made a profit in the last five years. COMPLETE SENTENCE/FRAGMENT/RUN-ON

Answers are on page 105.

Fragments & Run-ons Wrap-Up

✓ The GMAT will try to get you to fall for sentence fragments or run-ons.

✓ All correct GMAT sentences will contain an independent clause (at a minimum, at least one main subject and one main verb). If the sentence is lacking a main subject or verb, then the sentence is a fragment.

✓ Run-on sentences have too much of a necessary thing: they jam two independent clauses together without using a proper conjunction or punctuation mark to connect the clauses.

✓ It is possible for a correct sentence to contain more than one independent clause, as long as those clauses are connected appropriately.

Punctuation

The English language contains many punctuation marks: commas, periods, question marks, quotation marks, exclamation points, parentheses, hyphens, a couple different kinds of dashes, and more.

Fortunately, there are very few punctuation marks you need to care about for the GMAT. Perhaps most importantly, no one is going to test you on precise comma placement.

On the GMAT, commas can sometimes serve as a clue, helping you to understand sentence structure. So don't ignore commas entirely. But you will never mark an answer choice wrong because of a misplaced comma; if you're tempted to do so, ignore that impulse and look for some other issue to attack. In real life, the rules of comma placement involve quite a few judgment calls; while sometimes comma are mandatory, such as the ones in this sentence, in many cases the decision to use a comma or not is more a matter of style.

Do you have a strong opinion about whether another comma belongs in this sentence?

Please buy eggs, bread and milk.

The comma that many people (including most Americans, as well as the GMAT writers) would put after *bread* is called the *serial comma* or the *Oxford comma*. Even experts disagree about it. So, don't worry about it; the GMAT writers will use the Oxford comma themselves when giving a list, but they will not test you on whether it should or should not be used.

Two punctuation marks are discussed in this guide: semicolons and colons.

The Semicolon (;)

A semicolon connects two independent clauses. That is, the two parts on either side of the semicolon must be complete sentences, each one able to stand alone. They must also be closely related in meaning.

CORRECT: I have to admit that I hate spending Christmas with your parents; they always give me a ridiculous sweater and expect me to wear it.

What does it mean to be "closely related in meaning"? Everyone agrees that *I like milk; my brother prefers cola* is correct. But what about *I like milk; my brother likes bicycling*? That sentence looks very strange, but the question of whether the two parts are "closely related" is related to context. If someone had just asked the couple, "What are your very favorite things in the world?", then *I like milk; my brother likes bicycling* could indeed be a sensible answer.

MEMORIZE IT

The two parts on either side of a semicolon must be able to stand alone and must be closely related in meaning.

When you worry about clauses being closely related in meaning on the GMAT, what you are really trying to avoid is this:

INCORRECT: The volcano devastated the town; there was still hope.

This sentence violates the "closely related in meaning" rule because it needs a contrast word such as *however.* The contrasting meaning of the two clauses demands a contrasting conjunction. This rule is not specific to sentences containing semicolons. In *any* sentence, if *but, however,* or an equivalent word is needed, it is incorrect to leave it out.

CORRECT: The volcano devastated the town; however, there was still hope.

MEMORIZE IT

Do NOT use a semicolon before *and* or *but.* Use a semicolon before *however* and a comma after. In every case, the parts before and after the semicolon must be able to stand alone.

Here is another important rule: do not use a semicolon before *and* or *but.* A simple comma will do. For example:

INCORRECT: He applied to Harvard Business School; but he forgot to send his GMAT score.

INCORRECT: I like beer; and my grandmother likes bourbon.

In both cases, a comma should be used instead. Some people would use nothing at all in the second case, since the sentence is so short—this is a matter of style.

Pop Quiz!

True or False: The sentence, "The dog asked for a treat; he gave it one," correctly uses a semicolon to join two independent clauses.

Answer is on page 104.

Drill 5.3 — Correct the Punctuation Errors

Determine whether the sentence has an error and circle "Correct" or "Incorrect."

1. The cobblestone streets lent a certain historic charm; but they cost the city a mint to maintain. CORRECT/INCORRECT

2. I was offended; we left. CORRECT/INCORRECT

3. The 1950s in America were a period of prosperity and consumerism; programs such as *The Donna Reed Show, Leave it to Beaver,* and *Father Knows Best* portrayed comfortable suburban lifestyles made easier by modern appliances. CORRECT/INCORRECT

4. Although he won the election by a landslide; international bodies suspect serious irregularities in the voting process. CORRECT/INCORRECT

5. He needs a kidney transplant; without it, he'll die. CORRECT/INCORRECT

Answers are on pages 105–106.

The Colon (:)

The colon goes before a list or explanation:

> CORRECT: This recipe requires only three ingredients: sardines, tomato sauce, and olive oil.

The part of the sentence before the colon must be able to stand alone (that is, it must be an independent clause). Unlike semi colons, colons do *not* require the part after the colon to be a complete sentence:

> INCORRECT: I am going to the store to get: sardines, tomato sauce, and olive oil.

I am going to the store to get is not able to stand alone as a complete sentence. It can be fixed by removing the colon. A good rule is that if you don't need *any* punctuation there at all, a colon is wrong.

> **MEMORIZE IT**
> The part of a sentence before a colon must be an independent clause.

Sometimes, a list contains only one item. This is completely fine:

> CORRECT: I like only one kind of music: hip-hop.

Colons can also go before explanations, rules, or examples:

> CORRECT: I was fired today: my boss caught me trying to steal a laser printer.

This sentence is completely correct. The first part is able to stand alone. The second part (stealing) *explains* the first part (getting fired).

In some sentences, either a colon or a semicolon would work:

> CORRECT: Bill was tormented; the Packers lost again.

> CORRECT: Bill was tormented: the Packers lost again.

Grammar experts would say that using a colon would actually give more information, because the colon would make it clear that the Packers' loss was the *cause* of Bill's torment, whereas the semicolon just joins two related ideas, without being as clear about how the ideas are related.

On the GMAT, you will never have to decide between using a semicolon and using a colon, with everything else exactly the same. Just don't assume that either one is inherently wrong; check how each is used, following the rules discussed here.

Drill 5.4 — Examine the Colon

Determine whether the sentence has an error and circle "Correct" or "Incorrect."

1. I have really enjoyed hearing you lecture about: grammar, punctuation, and sentence structure. CORRECT/INCORRECT

2. We will do a soft launch of our new product in two markets: Los Angeles and New York. CORRECT/INCORRECT

3. It can hardly be said that the nation's government was negligent in planning for such a disaster: there had never been a volcanic eruption in the region in the whole of recorded history. CORRECT/INCORRECT

4. The protest was effective, but not without cost: sixteen people died. CORRECT/INCORRECT

5. He said something absolutely outrageous: "Shut up, Mr. President." CORRECT/INCORRECT

Answers are on page 106.

Drill 5.5 — Put It All Together

Each sentence below has a blank within the text. Circle your answer based on which would be correct in that spot: a colon, a semicolon, either a colon or a semicolon, or nothing at all.

1. I have always loved hockey ___ my dad is from Canada. COLON/SEMICOLON/EITHER/NOTHING

2. The investors are demanding that the board be replaced ___ however, we think we can convince the major players otherwise. COLON/SEMICOLON/EITHER/NOTHING

3. The administration has introduced such cost-saving measures as ___ cutting less popular classes, reducing opening hours in libraries and other buildings, and using work-study labor wherever possible. COLON/SEMICOLON/EITHER/NOTHING

4. I only need one thing from you ___ silence. COLON/SEMICOLON/EITHER/NOTHING

5. Many law school graduates are having serious trouble finding suitable employment ___ law schools are being criticized for a lack of transparency in releasing information about the employment rates of previous years' graduates. COLON/SEMICOLON/ EITHER/NOTHING

Answers are on page 106.

Punctuation Wrap-Up

✓ The two punctuation marks that are most commonly tested on the GMAT are the semicolon and the colon.

Punctuation Mark	Usage
;	Connect two complete sentences that are closely related
:	Connect a complete sentence (before the colon) to a list, example, or explanation

Answers to Pop Quizzes

Subjects and Predicates, page **93**

The subject of a sentence can be a phrase beginning with *that* or *to.*

TRUE! Here are examples: *That the architecture is so lovely is why I chose Yale. To love is the purpose of life.*

Subjects and Predicates, page **96**

In the sentence, "Although Italy is famous for pasta, noodles were invented by the Chinese," the dependent clause has the subject *Italy* and the independent clause has the subject *the Chinese.*

FALSE! The dependent clause is *Italy is famous for pasta* and its subject is indeed *Italy.* The independent clause is *noodles were invented by the Chinese.* Its subject is *noodles.* The verb is *were invented. By the Chinese* is a prepositional phrase.

Punctuation, page **100**

The sentence, "The dog asked for a treat; he gave it one," correctly uses a semicolon to join two independent clauses.

TRUE! Some students are thrown off by *he gave it one* as a complete clause, but it has a subject and a verb and can stand alone. Pronouns can be subjects of sentences, just as nouns can. (Of course, on the GMAT, you would need an antecedent for the pronoun *he*, but this sentence still correctly uses a semicolon to join two complete sentences.)

Answers to Drill Sets

Answers to Drill 5.1 — Find the Subject

1. Each of the women in the study said that her arthritis had gotten worse since beginning the therapy.

Of the women and *in the study* are prepositional phrases. The subject *each* is performing the verb *said.*

2. Only a thin sliver of the specimen is needed to perform the test.

Of the specimen is a prepositional phrase. The subject *sliver* is performing the verb *is needed.*

3. All of us agree.

Of us is a prepositional phrase. The subject *all* is performing the verb *agree.*

4. There are a bank, a nail salon, and a day care center in this shopping plaza.

In this shopping plaza is a prepositional phrase. Omit *there* and put the sentence in a more normal order to make the structure clear: *A bank, a nail salon, and a day care center are in this shopping plaza.*

5. Amid the weeds and trash was my lost kitten.

This sentence is backwards: it begins with a prepositional phrase and puts the subject after the verb. *Amid the weeds and trash* is a prepositional phrase. The verb is *was. Kitten* is performing the verb *was.* Put the sentence back in a more normal order to make the structure clear: *My lost kitten was amid the weeds and trash.*

Answers to Drill 5.2 — Find Fragments and Run-ons

1. FRAGMENT. Remember, words ending in *-ing* aren't verbs unless accompanied by helper verbs (for instance, *was planning* is a verb, but *planning, writing,* and *revising* alone are not verbs). This fragment lacks a true verb.

2. COMPLETE SENTENCE. The subject is *That the charge was true.* Rearranging the sentence may make it easier to understand the meaning: *The worst part was that the charge was true.*

3. COMPLETE SENTENCE. *There are only seven of us* is the main or independent clause. *Because the twins couldn't make it* is a subordinate clause.

4. FRAGMENT. This sentence lacks a main verb. *1944* should be followed by a comma and then a verb to pair with the subject *The decorated war general.*

5. RUN-ON. The two parts of the sentence should be joined with a conjunction (*since, because, as*) or a semicolon.

Answers to Drill 5.3 — Correct the Punctuation Errors

1. INCORRECT. Do not use a semicolon before "but." The sentence can be corrected by replacing the semicolon with a comma.

2. CORRECT. Although *we left* is very short, it has a subject and verb; both sides are independent clauses.

3. CORRECT. Both sides of the sentence are independent clauses.

4. INCORRECT. The first part of the sentence is a *dependent* clause. *Although he won the election by a landslide* cannot stand alone. The sentence could be fixed by removing the word *although* or by replacing the semicolon with a comma (but not both).

5. CORRECT. Both sides of the sentence are independent clauses.

Answers to Drill 5.4 — Examine the Colon

1. INCORRECT. The first part of the sentence cannot stand alone. The colon should be removed.

2. CORRECT. The first part is an independent clause, and the second part is a list of two items.

3. CORRECT. The first part is an independent clause, and the second part is an explanation for the first.

4. CORRECT. The first part is an independent clause, and the second part is an explanation for the first.

5. CORRECT. The first part is an independent clause, and the second part is a "list" of one item. Generally, a comma sets off a quote, but it is perfectly common and correct to use a colon when the quote is being used as a list item and the other rules of colons are followed.

Note: Four out of five of the examples above have been deliberately made correct. Students tend to think sentences are wrong when they see colons that are not before lists of three or more items. Colons are much more versatile than most people think!

Answers to Drill 5.5 — Put It All Together

1. EITHER. Both parts of the sentence are independent clauses, so a semicolon is fine. The second part is a plausible explanation for the first, thus making a colon fine as well.

2. SEMICOLON. Both parts of the sentence are independent clauses, but the second part is not an explanation, rule, or example; in fact, it is in opposition to the first part.

3. NOTHING. The part before the blank is not a complete sentence, so neither a semicolon nor a colon is appropriate.

4. COLON. The first part can stand alone, but not the second. The second part is a "list" of one item.

5. SEMICOLON. Both parts of the sentence are independent clauses, but the second part is not an explanation, rule, or example. In fact, it seems as though the *first* part is an explanation for the *second* part.

Chapter 6
of

GMAT Foundations of Verbal

Part 1: **Sentence Correction**

Modifiers, Parallelism, & Comparisons

In This Chapter...

Chapter 6

Modifiers, Parallelism, & Comparisons

Modifiers

A modifier describes something else in the sentence. It is not part of the core sentence. All prepositional phrases are modifiers, and there are also many other kinds of modifiers.

All of the underlined portions in the correct sentences below are modifiers:

> Ptolemy, <u>an accomplished mathematician</u>, used a symbol for zero as early as 130 AD.
>
> The students <u>who go to my school</u> are hardworking.
>
> Please complete this task <u>in a timely manner</u>.

Modifiers are one of the most difficult topics in GMAT Sentence Correction; for more advanced study, refer to the Manhattan Prep *Sentence Correction GMAT Strategy Guide*. However, there are a few common modifier errors that you can learn to spot right now.

Pop Quiz!

True or False: It can be helpful to ignore modifiers temporarily in order to help match up subjects and verbs.

Answer is on page 118.

Opening Modifiers or "Warmups"

When a sentence begins with what is often called a "warmup" followed by a comma, the thing being described should come directly after the comma. For instance:

Full of one million tons of trash, . . . (WHAT is full of trash?)

Hiking through the woods, . . . (WHO is hiking?)

The phrase at the beginning of the sentence does not have a subject. Whatever is *full of trash* or *hiking* should come directly after the comma. Consider the following:

INCORRECT: Full of one million tons of trash, the mayor suggested that a new landfill be built.

INCORRECT: Hiking through the woods, my backpack was stolen by bears.

Now, what's full of trash? The mayor! What's hiking? My backpack!

This type of grammar error is often unintentionally hilarious. There are several ways you could rewrite these sentences in order to fix them, but say you are only allowed to change the second part:

6

CORRECT: Full of one million tons of trash, the landfill was cited by the mayor as sorely in need of expansion.

CORRECT: Hiking through the woods, I had my backpack stolen by bears.

Sometimes, even opening modifiers ("warmups") used correctly sound a bit weird, because people almost never use this sentence pattern when speaking aloud. For instance:

CORRECT: Accomplished mathematicians and astronomers, the ancient Babylonians used a base-60 number system and were able to measure the length of the solar year with a high degree of accuracy.

The warmup creates a question—who are the *accomplished mathematicians and astronomers*? The question is answered right after the comma—*the ancient Babylonians.*

This sentence may sound odd, but it's fine.

That, Who, When, and Where

There are some rules to follow when using *that, who, when,* and *where*:

- Don't use *that* or *which* for people—instead, use *who*.
- Use *when* only for times.
- Use *where* only for places.

Here are some examples:

> INCORRECT: Young professionals *that* go to business school hope to increase their salary prospects.

Do not use *that* for people. Some experts disagree with the GMAT on this issue, but from our perspective, GMAT wins. The sentence should read *Young professionals who. . . .*

> INCORRECT: First-degree murder is *when* the killing was premeditated.

First-degree murder is not a time. You don't have to figure out on your own how to fix this sentence; you just need to know that it's wrong. Here is one correction: *One criterion for first-degree murder is that the killing was premeditated.*

> INCORRECT: Algebra II was *where* I learned to factor.

Algebra II is not a place. Algebra II probably took place in a classroom, and you could say *Room 201 is where I learned to factor*, but a physical location is not given in the sentence above. One correction: *Algebra II was the class in which I learned to factor.*

ADVANCED TIP

While *who* is only for people, *whose* can actually be used with objects. For instance, it is fine to say *I am going to fix all the tables whose legs are broken.*

Drill 6.1 — Find the Modifier Errors

Determine whether the sentence has an error and circle "Correct" or "Incorrect."

1. The two companies made an illegal agreement where they agreed to raise prices significantly on the first of the year. CORRECT/INCORRECT

2. Running the final mile of the marathon, Jeff doubted that he would be able to keep going. CORRECT/INCORRECT

3. Although Balaji managed to eat 75 hot dogs with incredible speed, the hot-dog-eating contest trophy ultimately went to another competitor. CORRECT/INCORRECT

4. A good haircut is when you leave the salon feeling great. CORRECT/INCORRECT

5. Once rivaling the Great Pyramids, an earthquake snapped the Colossus of Rhodes, a statue of the Greek god Helios, at the knees. CORRECT/INCORRECT

Answers are on page 119.

Modifiers Wrap-Up

Modifiers provide extra information about some word, action, or concept in a sentence. They could be removed from a sentence and you would still have a "core" or complete sentence.

✓ *Prepositional phrases* are always modifiers. They can modify nouns, verbs, or other words in a sentence.

✓ *Opening modifiers* start off sentences by providing information about something without telling you what that something is; the relevant noun should be placed just after the comma following an opening modifier.

✓ *Who* is always used to refer to people.

✓ *That* and *whose* can refer to people or other types of nouns.

✓ *When* refers to a time. *Where* refers to a place.

As mentioned earlier, you can learn more about the complex topic of modifiers in the *Sentence Correction GMAT Strategy Guide.*

6

Parallelism & Comparisons

When you list or compare two or more things, make sure your lists and comparisons are both logically and grammatically parallel.

Parallelism

First, consider a list:

> INCORRECT: The charges against him include financial crimes, human rights abuses, and that he murdered international aid workers.

What are the items in the list?

1. financial crimes
2. human rights abuses
3. that he murdered international aid workers

In #1 and #2, the main words are *nouns*: *crimes* and *abuses*; however, #3 in the list is an entire clause beginning with *that*. These items are not in the same format. You can correct this by putting the third item in the form of a noun:

> CORRECT: The charges against him include financial crimes, human rights abuses, and *the murders* of international aid workers.

Another example:

> INCORRECT: The college cut expenses by *laying off* staff and it stopped work on a new library.

This list has only two items:

1. laying off staff
2. it stopped work on a new library

Laying off and *it stopped work* are not in the same format: the first is part of a prepositional phrase and the second is a full clause. Here's one way to fix the sentence:

> CORRECT: The college cut expenses by laying off staff and *stopping* work on a new library.

Laying and *stopping* match both logically and grammatically.

Here is one more example:

> TRY IT: You can purchase tickets by phone or on the Web.

What are the two things in the list?

1. by phone
2. on the Web

Remember how *laying off* and *stopping* were considered parallel in the sentence above? Here, *by* and *on* are also parallel—the items in the list just have to be the same part of speech, not the exact same word. *By phone* and *on the Web* are both prepositional phrases, indicating *how* to purchase tickets.

Different expressions are used for telephones and the Internet, so each item in the list needs a different preposition. The sentence is correct. Prepositional phrases that are in parallel don't have to use the same preposition.

Comparisons

Now, consider a comparison:

INCORRECT: Montreal's mayor has been in office longer than Toronto.

Both *Montreal's mayor* and *Toronto* are nouns, but the comparison is illogical—the city of Toronto has not been in office. Logically, the sentence is trying to say that Montreal's mayor has been in office longer than *Toronto's mayor*. There are several ways to fix the problem:

CORRECT: Montreal's **mayor** has been in office longer than Toronto's **mayor**.

CORRECT: Montreal's **mayor** has been in office longer than Toronto**'s**.

CORRECT: The **mayor** of Montreal has been in office longer than **that** of Toronto.

In the last example, the word *that* stands in for *mayor* and creates a logical comparison. Here is a similar example that matches a format used frequently on the GMAT:

INCORRECT: The theories of astronomer Johannes Kepler superseded his teacher and colleague, Tycho Brahe.

6

What was just compared?

1. The theories of astronomer Johannes Kepler
2. his teacher and colleague, Tycho Brahe

The sentence compares a person's *theories* with *another person*. You need to compare *theories* to *theories* and *people* to *people*:

CORRECT: The **theories** of astronomer Johannes Kepler superseded **those** of his teacher and colleague, Tycho Brahe.

Pop Quiz!

True or False: It is not parallel to put singular nouns and plural nouns in the same list, or to compare them with one another.

Answer is on page 118.

Now consider an example with a different problem:

INCORRECT: I hate having to work late even more than to have to do what my horrible boss demands.

Here, working late and having to follow orders are logically the same kind of thing, but the way they are phrased in the sentence (*having to* and *to have to*) makes them a *grammatical* mismatch. This is really just a problem with parallelism, which you just practiced in the previous section.

> CORRECT: I hate having to work late even more than having to do what my horrible boss demands.

Phrases Beginning with "That" and "When"

Here's a special case that the GMAT likes to test:

> INCORRECT: I liked the birthday cake you made me better than when you called me names.

Okay, that sentence is pretty silly, but that's not the problem. Look at the two things being compared:

1. the birthday **cake** you made me
2. **when** you called me names

It is wrong to compare a thing (*cake*) with a period of time (*when* something happened). To correct the error, you can eliminate *when* or use *when* for both parts:

> CORRECT: I liked the birthday cake you made me better than the name-calling.

> CORRECT: I liked when you made me a birthday cake better than when you called me names.

Note that in the first correction, *when you called me names* was changed to *the name-calling* in order to create a noun, since *cake* is a noun and the two things being compared need to be grammatically parallel. A little bit of meaning was lost when that was done (*who* is doing the name-calling?). The second correction might be a bit better because it preserves the original meaning more closely.

Now try to spot a similar problem in a more GMAT-like example:

> INCORRECT: Cell-phone customers are much more likely to become incensed over additional charges they view as punitive than when obscure service fees are added to their monthly bills.

Did you find the error? Ask yourself, "What are the two things being compared?"

1. additional **charges** they view as punitive
2. **when** obscure service fees are added to their monthly bills

Once again, the sentence is comparing a thing (*charges*) with a time (*when* fees are added). The correct GMAT answer could use *when* for both parts of the sentence, but will probably just eliminate *when*, since the idea of a time isn't really important to the sentence:

POSSIBLE CORRECT ANSWER: Cell-phone customers are much more likely to become incensed **when** additional charges they view as punitive are applied to their accounts than **when** obscure service fees are added to their monthly bills.

MORE LIKELY CORRECT ANSWER: Cell-phone customers are much more likely to become incensed over **additional charges** they view as punitive than over **obscure service fees** that are added to their monthly bills.

Both of the sentences above are correct; the test won't make you choose between them.

MEMORIZE IT

Do not compare a phrase that starts with *that* to one that starts with *when, where, which,* or *who.*

One more related example—do not compare a phrase that starts with *that* to one that starts with *when, where, which,* or *who*:

INCORRECT: Liechtenstein is the only European nation that still has a monarchy with real—rather than largely ceremonial or diplomatic—power, and where the power given to the sovereign has actually increased in the current millennium.

6

What are the two things being compared?

Liechtenstein is the only European nation . . .

1. **that** still has a monarchy . . .

and

2. **where** the power given to the sovereign . . .

Here, *that* has the correct meaning and should be used in both spots:

CORRECT: Liechtenstein is the only European nation that still has a monarchy with real—rather than largely ceremonial or diplomatic—power, and that has actually increased the sovereign's power in the current millennium.

In the cases above in which you're given more than one possible correction, the GMAT would only ever give you *one* of those correct answers—you will not have to choose between two correct answers that differ only in matters of style.

Drill 6.2 — Find the Parallelism/Comparison Errors

Determine whether the sentence has an error and circle "Correct" or "Incorrect."

1. New York City's population is greater than Montana, Wyoming, Vermont, North Dakota, South Dakota, Delaware, and Rhode Island all added together. CORRECT/INCORRECT

2. While we think of our state parks as pristine stretches of nature, some parklands actually cost more than maintaining busy city streets. CORRECT/INCORRECT

3. Although the people revolted when their leader was found fixing election results, they scarcely made a sound when the same ruler was discovered siphoning campaign funds for personal use. CORRECT/INCORRECT

4. While the age at which Americans become parents has been steadily rising over past decades, most young people still say that parenthood is an important milestone in life, much as it was for their own progenitors. CORRECT/INCORRECT

5. Despite the contributions of many great American novelists and playwrights, Shakespeare's plays are still taught in schools more frequently and deeply than any American writer. CORRECT/INCORRECT

Answers are on page 119.

Parallelism & Comparisons Wrap-Up

✓ Certain sentence structures require two or more parts of a sentence to be parallel both logically and grammatically; some common structures include:

- Lists of two or more items
- Comparisons

✓ In parallel structures, do not mix *that* with *when*, *where*, *which*, or *who.*

You can learn more about parallelism and comparisons in Manhattan Prep's *Sentence Correction* guide.

Answers to Pop Quizzes

Modifiers, page **109**

It can be helpful to ignore modifiers temporarily in order to help match up subjects and verbs.

TRUE! Remember, prepositional phrases are modifiers, and one of the reasons you spent so much time on prepositional phrases was so you could learn to temporarily ignore them in order to get down to a "core sentence" that you can check for subject–verb agreement.

Parallelism & Comparisons, page **114**

It is not parallel to put singular nouns and plural nouns in the same list, or to compare them with one another.

FALSE! As long as the items in a list or comparison are all nouns, some can be singular and some plural. It's fine to say *I'm going to the store to buy rice, vegetables, and a carton of milk.*

Answers to Drill Sets

Answers to Drill 6.1 — Find the Modifier Errors

1. INCORRECT. An *agreement* is not a place, so *where* cannot be used.

2. CORRECT. Who is *running the final mile of the marathon*? The answer, *Jeff,* is correctly placed directly after the comma.

3. CORRECT. While this sentence might sound a bit strange, it is fine. The first part is NOT a warmup because it actually answers its own question: *Who* managed to eat 75 hot dogs? Balaji. Therefore, there is no requirement that any special word go directly after the comma.

4. INCORRECT. A haircut is not a time, so *when* cannot be used. *X is when Y* is generally a poor way to write any definition.

5. INCORRECT. *Once rivaling the Great Pyramids* is a warmup that raises a question: *What* was once rivaling the Great Pyramids? The answer to that question is *the Colossus of Rhodes*, which needs to come directly after the comma. Right now, the sentence is illogically saying that *an earthquake* once rivaled *the Great Pyramids.*

Answers to Drill 6.2 — Find the Parallelism/Comparison Errors

1. INCORRECT. New York City's *population* is being compared to *Montana, Wyoming, Vermont, North Dakota, South Dakota, Delaware, and Rhode Island all added together* (if you add all those states together, the answer is seven—seven states, that is, which is clearly not the point of this sentence). Corrected version: *New York City's population is greater than THE POPULATIONS OF Montana, Wyoming, Vermont, North Dakota, South Dakota, Delaware, and Rhode Island all added together.*

2. INCORRECT. *Parklands* is being compared to *maintaining* busy city streets. Corrected version: *. . . some parklands actually cost more to maintain than do busy city streets.* OR, *. . . the maintenance of some parklands actually costs more than that of busy city streets.*

3. CORRECT. The people *revolted*, and later they scarcely *made* a sound (*revolted* and *made* are both past tense verbs). The leader *was found fixing election results* and later *was discovered siphoning campaign funds.* These two actions match both grammatically and logically.

4. CORRECT. *Parenthood* is an important milestone in life for young people, much as *it* was for their own progenitors. The *it* stands for *parenthood* and the comparison is both grammatical and logical.

5. INCORRECT. *Shakespeare's plays* are being compared to *any American writer.* Do not compare plays to people! Corrected version: . . . *Shakespeare's plays are still taught in schools more frequently and deeply than are the works of any American writer.*

Chapter 7

of

GMAT Foundations of Verbal

Part 1: **Sentence Correction**

Idioms & Sentence Correction Wrap-Up

In This Chapter...

Chapter 7

Idioms & Sentence Correction Wrap-Up

Idioms

Idioms are expressions or figures of speech, such as *pushing up the daisies* (a cute reference to being dead—the person is pushing up flowers from under the ground).

On the GMAT, it rarely *rains cats and dogs,* and no one is described as *under the weather.* Idioms on the GMAT are a bit more subtle. For instance:

> INCORRECT: The meeting devolved into a fight between the marketing team with the sales team.

Many GMAT idiom errors are related to using the wrong preposition. In this case, the error concerns the preposition that goes with the word *between:*

> Incorrect pattern: between X with Y
>
> Correct pattern: between X and Y

The sentence should read *The meeting devolved into a fight between the marketing team AND the sales team.* Some of these patterns are not logical—that's why they're idioms. For instance, compare these two examples:

> I prohibit you <u>from leaving</u> school grounds. I forbid you <u>to leave</u> school grounds.

Both sentences are correct and mean the same thing. *Prohibit* and *forbid* mean the same thing. Why does *prohibit* go with the preposition *from* plus a gerund (*leaving*), while *forbid* goes with the infinitive form (*to leave*)? No reason. Idioms simply must be memorized.

Idioms in Sentence Correction versus Idioms in Reading Comprehension: There is a section on *Idioms* in the Reading Comprehension portion of this book, but that section is more about understanding the *meaning* of idioms when you read. This section is about identifying idioms that have been used incorrectly in Sentence Correction problems. There is certainly some overlap between the two sections, and understanding the meaning of idioms can be helpful in recognizing logical errors in Sentence Correction problems.

Some of the most common Sentence Correction idioms are covered here. Many more can be found in the chapter on idioms and in the appendix in the *Sentence Correction GMAT Strategy Guide.*

Label	**Definition**
RIGHT:	Expressions that the GMAT considers correct.
SUSPECT:	*Expressions that the GMAT seems to avoid if possible. These expressions are sometimes grammatically correct, but they may be wordy, controversial, or simply less preferred than other forms.*
WRONG:	*Expressions that the GMAT considers incorrect.*

ABILITY

RIGHT: I value my ABILITY TO SING.

WRONG: *I value my ABILITY OF SINGING.*
I value my ABILITY FOR SINGING.
I value the ABILITY FOR me TO SING.

7

ALLOW

RIGHT: The holiday ALLOWS Maria TO WATCH the movie today. (= permits)
Maria WAS ALLOWED TO WATCH the movie.
The demolition of the old building ALLOWS FOR new construction.
(= permits the existence of)

WRONG: *The holiday ALLOWED FOR Maria TO WATCH the movie.*
The holiday ALLOWED Maria the WATCHING OF the movie.
The holiday ALLOWS THAT homework BE done (or CAN BE done).
Homework is ALLOWED FOR DOING BY Maria.
The ALLOWING OF shopping TO DO (or TO BE DONE).

AND

RIGHT: We are concerned about the forests AND the oceans.
We are concerned about the forests, the oceans, AND the mountains.
We work all night, AND we sleep all day. (Note the comma before AND.)

SUSPECT: *We are concerned about the forests AND ALSO the oceans.*

WRONG: *We are concerned about the forests, ALSO the oceans.*

AS

RIGHT: AS I walked, I became more nervous. (= during)
AS I had already paid, I was unconcerned. (= because, since)
AS we did last year, we will win this year. (= in the same way)
JUST AS we did last year, we will win this year. (= in the same way)
AS the president of the company, she works hard. (= in the role of)
AS a child, I delivered newspapers. (= in the stage of being)
My first job was an apprenticeship AS a sketch artist.
AS PART OF the arrangement, he received severance.

SUSPECT: *AS A PART OF the arrangement, he received severance.*

WRONG: *My first job was an apprenticeship OF a sketch artist.*
They worked AS a sketch artist. (Needs to agree in number.)
WHILE BEING a child, I delivered newspapers.
AS BEING a child, I delivered newspapers.
WHILE IN childhood, I delivered newspapers.

AS . . . AS

RIGHT: Cheese is AS great AS people say.
Cheese is NOT AS great AS people say.
We have AS MANY apples AS need to be cooked.
We have THREE TIMES AS MANY pears AS you.
We have AT LEAST AS MANY apples AS you.
We have 10 apples, ABOUT AS MANY AS we picked yesterday.
His knowledge springs AS MUCH from experience AS from schooling.

SUSPECT: *Cheese is NOT SO great AS people say.*
We have AS MANY apples AS OR MORE apples THAN you.
We have AS MANY apples AS THERE need to be cooked.

WRONG: *Cheese is SO great AS people say.*
Cheese is SO great THAT people say.
Cheese is AS great THAT people say.
We have AS MANY apples THAN you.
We have SO MANY apples AS you.
We have AS MANY OR MORE apples THAN you.
We have THREE TIMES AS MANY MORE pears AS you.
We have 10 apples, ABOUT EQUIVALENT TO what we picked yesterday.
His knowledge springs NOT from experience AS from schooling.

BECAUSE

RIGHT: BECAUSE the sun SHINES, plants grow.
Plants grow BECAUSE the sun SHINES.
BECAUSE OF the sun, plants grow.

	BY SHINING, the sun makes plants grow. Plants grow, FOR the sun shines. (Grammatically correct but very formal.)
SUSPECT:	*Plants grow BECAUSE OF the sun, WHICH SHINES.* *Plants are amazing IN THAT they grow in the sun.* (Correct but wordy.) *The growth of plants IS EXPLAINED BY THE FACT THAT the sun shines.* (Correct but wordy.)
WRONG:	*Plants grow BECAUSE OF the sun SHINING.* *Plants grow AS A RESULT OF the sun SHINING.* *BECAUSE OF SHINING, the sun makes plants grow.* *BECAUSE the sun SHINES IS the REASON that plants grow.* *The ABILITY OF plants TO grow IS BECAUSE the sun shines.* *The growth of plants IS EXPLAINED BECAUSE OF the shining of the sun.* *The growth of plants IS EXPLAINED BECAUSE the sun shines.*

BOTH . . . AND

RIGHT:	She was interested BOTH in plants AND in animals. She was interested in BOTH plants AND animals.
WRONG:	*She was interested BOTH in plants AND animals.* *She was interested BOTH in plants AS WELL AS in animals.* *She was interested BOTH in plants BUT ALSO in animals.*

7

BUT

RIGHT:	I STUDY hard BUT TAKE breaks. I STUDY hard, BUT I TAKE breaks. ALTHOUGH I TAKE frequent naps, I STUDY effectively. DESPITE TAKING frequent naps, I STUDY effectively. I TAKE frequent naps, YET I STUDY effectively.
SUSPECT:	*DESPITE THE FACT THAT I TAKE frequent naps, I STUDY effectively.* *ALTHOUGH a frequent napper, I STUDY effectively.* (Note: ALTHOUGH should generally be followed by a clause.)
WRONG:	*I STUDY effectively ALTHOUGH TAKING frequent naps.* *ALTHOUGH I TAKE frequent naps, YET I STUDY effectively.* *ALTHOUGH I TAKE frequent naps, AND I STUDY effectively.* *DESPITE TAKING frequent naps, YET I STUDY effectively.*

CAN

RIGHT:	The manager CAN RUN the plant. The plant CAN CAUSE damage.
SUSPECT:	*It is POSSIBLE FOR the plant TO CAUSE damage.* *The plant POSSIBLY CAUSES damage.*

WRONG: *The manager HAS THE CAPABILITY OF RUNNING the plant.*
The plant HAS THE POSSIBILITY OF CAUSING damage.

CONSIDER

RIGHT: I CONSIDER her a friend.
(Note: I CONSIDER her intelligent. You can switch the order of the two objects, if one is long.)
I CONSIDER illegal the law passed last week by the new regime.
The law IS CONSIDERED illegal.

SUSPECT: *The judge CONSIDERS the law TO BE illegal.*

WRONG: *The judge CONSIDERS the law AS illegal* (or AS BEING illegal).
The judge CONSIDERS the law SHOULD BE illegal.
The judge CONSIDERS the law AS IF IT WERE illegal.

EITHER . . . OR

RIGHT: I will take EITHER the subway OR the bus.

WRONG: *I will take EITHER the subway AND the bus.*

EXPECT

RIGHT: We EXPECT the price TO FALL.
The price IS EXPECTED TO FALL. We EXPECT THAT the price WILL FALL.
IT IS EXPECTED THAT the price WILL FALL.
Inflation rose more than we EXPECTED.
There IS an EXPECTATION THAT the price will fall.

SUSPECT: *There IS an EXPECTATION the price WILL FALL.*
There IS an EXPECTATION OF the price FALLING.

WRONG: *The price IS EXPECTED FOR IT TO FALL.*
IT IS EXPECTED THAT the price SHOULD FALL.

FROM . . . TO

RIGHT: The price fell FROM 10 euros TO 3 euros.
The price fell TO 3 euros FROM 10 euros.

WRONG: *The price fell FROM 10 euros DOWN TO 3 euros.*
The price rose FROM 3 euros UP TO 10 euros.

IN ORDER TO

RIGHT: She drank coffee IN ORDER TO STAY awake.
She drank coffee TO STAY awake. (Infinitive TO STAY indicates purpose.)

SUSPECT: *She drank coffee IN ORDER THAT (or SO THAT) she MIGHT stay awake.*
She drank coffee SO AS TO STAY awake.

WRONG: *She drank coffee FOR STAYING awake.*
Coffee was drunk by her IN ORDER TO STAY awake (or TO STAY awake).
(Note: The subject COFFEE is not trying TO STAY awake.)

LIKE

RIGHT: LIKE his sister, Matt drives fast cars. (= both drive fast cars)
Matt drives fast cars LIKE his sister's.
(= both drive *similar* cars OR, less optimally, one of the cars he drives is his sister's)

WRONG: *Matt drives fast cars LIKE his sister does.*
LIKE his sister, SO Matt drives fast cars.

NOT . . . BUT

RIGHT: She DID NOT EAT mangoes BUT ATE other kinds of fruit.
She DID NOT EAT mangoes BUT LIKED other kinds of fruit AND later BEGAN to like kiwis, too.
A tomato is NOT a vegetable BUT a fruit.
A tomato is NOT a vegetable BUT RATHER a fruit.

WRONG: *She DID NOT EAT mangoes BUT other kinds of fruit.*

NOT ONLY . . . BUT ALSO

RIGHT: We wore NOT ONLY boots BUT ALSO sandals.
We wore NOT ONLY boots, BUT ALSO sandals. (Comma is optional.)
We wore NOT ONLY boots BUT sandals.
We wore NOT JUST boots BUT ALSO sandals.

SUSPECT: *We wore NOT ONLY boots BUT sandals AS WELL.*
We wore boots AND ALSO sandals.

WRONG: *We wore NOT ONLY boots AND ALSO sandals.*
We wore NOT ONLY boots BUT, AS WELL, sandals.

RATHER THAN

RIGHT: He wrote with pencils RATHER THAN with pens.

SUSPECT: *He wrote with pencils, BUT NOT pens.*

WRONG: *He wrote with pencils INSTEAD OF with pens.* (*Of with* is incorrect.)

REQUIRE

RIGHT: She REQUIRES time TO WRITE (*or* IN ORDER TO WRITE).
She REQUIRES her friend TO DO work.
Her friend IS REQUIRED TO DO work.

SUSPECT: *In this hostel, there is a REQUIREMENT OF work.*
There is a REQUIREMENT THAT work BE done.

WRONG: *She REQUIRES her friend DO work (*or MUST DO*) work.*
She REQUIRES her friend TO HAVE TO DO work.
She REQUIRES OF her friend TO DO work.
She REQUIRES THAT her friend DOES work (or SHOULD DO) *work.*
She REQUIRES THAT her friend IS TO DO work.
She REQUIRES DOING work (or THE DOING OF work).
She REQUIRES her friend DOING work.
In this hostel, there is a REQUIREMENT OF work BY guests.

SEEM

RIGHT: This result SEEMS TO DEMONSTRATE the new theory.
IT SEEMS THAT this result DEMONSTRATES the new theory.
IT SEEMS AS IF this result DEMONSTRATES the new theory.

SUSPECT: *This result SEEMS TO BE A DEMONSTRATION OF the new theory.*
This result SEEMS DEMONSTRATIVE OF the new theory.
This result SEEMS LIKE A DEMONSTRATION OF the new theory.

WRONG: *This result SEEMS AS IF IT DEMONSTRATES the new theory.*
This result SEEMS LIKE IT DEMONSTRATES the new theory.

SO . . . THAT

RIGHT: The book was SO SHORT THAT I could read it in one night.
The book was SHORT ENOUGH FOR me TO READ in one night.

SUSPECT: *The book was SO SHORT I could read it.* (THAT is preferred.)
The book was OF SUCH SHORTNESS THAT I could read it.
SUCH was the SHORTNESS of the book THAT I could read it.

WRONG: *The book had SO MUCH SHORTNESS THAT I could read it.*
The book was OF SUCH SHORTNESS, I could read it.
The book was SHORT TO SUCH A DEGREE AS TO ALLOW me to read it.

SO THAT

RIGHT: She gave money SO THAT the school could offer scholarships. (= purpose)

SUSPECT: *She gave money, SO the school was grateful.* (= result)

WRONG: *She gave money SO the school could offer scholarships.*

SUCH AS

RIGHT: Matt drives fast cars, SUCH AS Ferraris. (= example)
Matt enjoys driving SUCH cars AS Ferraris.
Matt enjoys intense activities, SUCH AS DRIVING fast cars.

SUSPECT: *Matt drives fast cars LIKE Ferraris.* (= similar to, but "example" is implied)
(Note: The GMAT has backed off from claiming that *like* cannot introduce examples, but it is probable that the use of *like* with examples will continue to be avoided.)

WRONG: *Matt drives Ferraris AND THE LIKE.*
Matt drives Ferraris AND OTHER cars SUCH AS THESE.
Matt trains in many ways SUCH AS BY DRIVING on racetracks.
Matt enjoys intense activities, SUCH AS TO DRIVE fast cars.

THAN

RIGHT: His books are MORE impressive THAN those of other writers.
This paper is LESS impressive THAN that one.
This paper is NO LESS impressive THAN that one.
This newspaper cost 50 cents MORE THAN that one.
MORE THAN 250 newspapers are published here.
Sales are HIGHER this year THAN last year.

WRONG: *His books are MORE impressive AS those of other writers.*
This paper is MORE impressive RATHER THAN that one.
This paper is MORE impressive INSTEAD OF that one.
This paper is NO LESS impressive AS that one.
This paper is NONE THE LESS impressive THAN that one.
This newspaper cost 50 cents AS MUCH AS that one.
AS MANY AS OR MORE THAN 250 newspapers are published here.
Sales are HIGHER this year OVER last year.

7

UNLIKE

RIGHT: UNLIKE the spiny anteater, the aardvark is docile.

WRONG: *UNLIKE WITH the spiny anteater, the aardvark is docile.*

WHETHER

RIGHT: I do not know WHETHER I will go.

SUSPECT: *I do not know WHETHER OR NOT I will go.*

WRONG: *I do not know IF I will go.* (IF requires a consequence.)

Drill 7.1 — Find the Idiom Errors

Correct the errors in each of the following sentences. Every sentence has at least one error.

1. Although I have the ability of doing gymnastics well, this time I fell off the balance beam.
2. The ostensible reason for Anne Boleyn's execution was because of adultery, although the charges were almost certainly fabricated wholesale.
3. She not only has deep relationships with all of the union leaders and also worked for the company for many years herself, so she is expected to be appointed as chairperson.
4. The study indicates more men are working in education, traditionally considered as a "female" profession.
5. The company's new product is so successful it will likely gain market share.

Answers are on page 140.

Idioms Wrap-Up

Great, you've learned some of the most commonly tested idioms on the GMAT!

If you are concerned about this topic, then start to make flash cards or use whatever memory devices you prefer to help you memorize the idioms in this chapter and in Chapter 9 of our *Sentence Correction GMAT Strategy Guide.* (The guide also contains an appendix of less commonly seen idioms that could still appear on the GMAT.)

Pop Quiz!

True or False: The sentence, "I prohibit you from breaking up the fight between Jared and Bill," is correct.

Answer is on page 139.

Parts of Speech and Sentence Structure Wrap-Up

You've covered a lot of ground. Now you've got to apply all this knowledge to Sentence Correction problems.

The table below gives a recap of what you already know about the parts of speech. It's not important that you draw these shapes, or any particular shapes at all, when you write out and analyze your own sentences. However, you do want to indicate the key issues somehow, such as the connection between a pronoun and its antecedent.

You will not write everything out during the test; rather, use the techniques below to help learn and remember the rules.

Parts of Speech

Symbol	Part of Speech	Example	Definition	Notes
N	Noun	*dog, happiness, production*	Represents a thing, person, or idea.	Countable noun: *one dog, two dogs* Uncountable noun: *happiness, bread*
Pro	Pronoun	*they, it, its*	Stands for a noun.	I found the dog after *it* ran away.
Adj	Adjective	*green, expensive*	Modifies a noun.	The *green* hat was *expensive*.
V	Verb	*chased, bark, belonged*	Shows what a noun does or is.	The dog chased *the scared* cat. Dogs bark. That hat belonged to Maxim.
Adv	Adverb	*quickly, very*	Modifies a verb, adjective, or adverb.	Dogs bark loudly.
Prep	Preposition	*of, for, on, during*	Expresses a relationship to a noun.	on the table for my mother
			Can modify verbs.	The book fell on the table.
			Can modify nouns.	This is a gift for my mother.
Conj	Conjunction	*and, or, because, although*	Creates a list, contrast, or other special relationship.	He and she are great. [We won] because [we rocked].

7

Sentence Structure

Likewise, you now know a ton about sentence structure.

The table below captures the basic forms of a sentence and some variations. Take a few minutes and look over these templates. If it helps you to learn, practice drawing out sentences yourself, but not everyone will need to do so.

Basic Templates

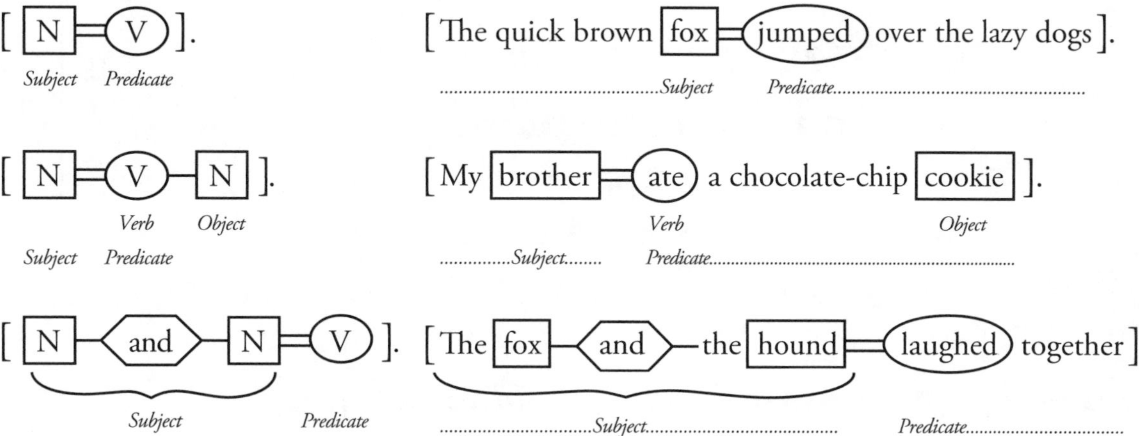

Combinations

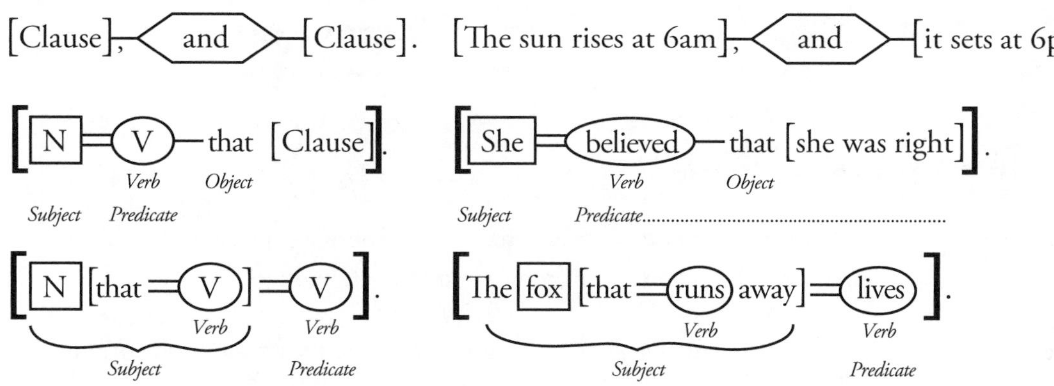

The SC Process

When answering SC questions on the GMAT, you'll need to work efficiently without hurting your accuracy. An introduction to the standard SC process is below; test it out on the questions in the drill found just afterwards. The explanations for the drill set not only provide the solution to the problem but also show how to use the SC process to answer that problem. You can also learn more about this process in Manhattan Prep's *Sentence Correction GMAT Strategy Guide.*

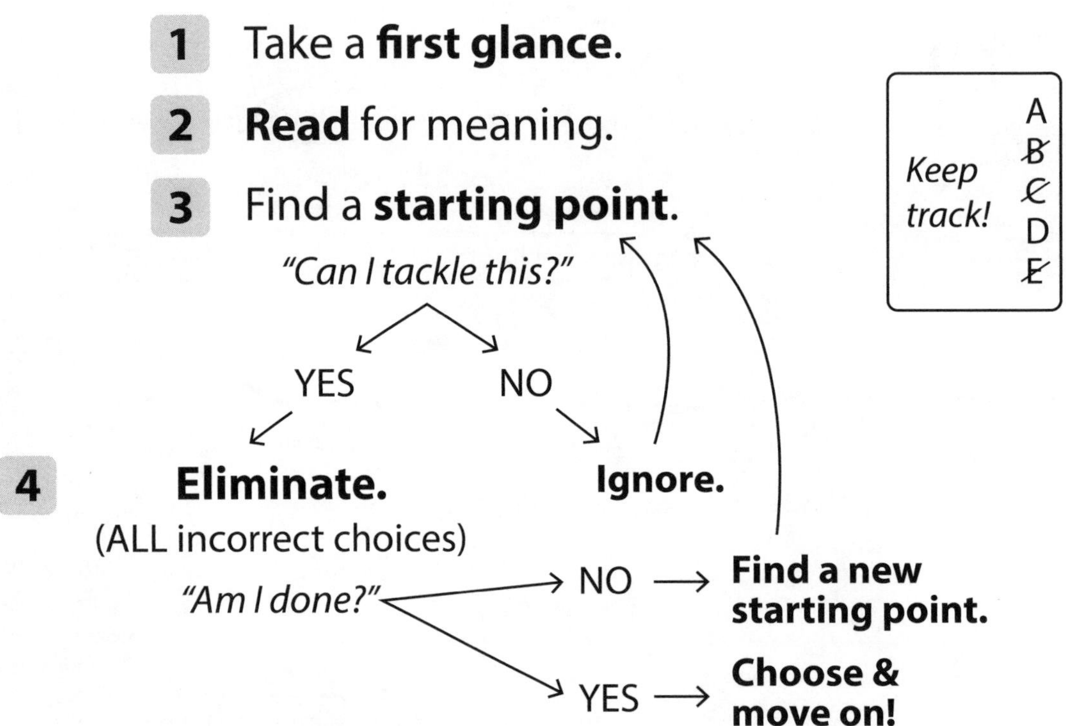

Step 1: Take a First Glance.

Your first glance will tell you that you have a Sentence Correction question (as opposed to Critical Reasoning or Reading Comprehension). It can tell you more than that, though!

Don't read the sentence yet. First, take a quick look at the beginning of the underline in the original sentence and at the first word or two of each answer choice. Depending on the differences that you see, you may immediately know one issue that the sentence is testing. For example, if the first two answers start with *is* and the last three start with *are*, you know the problem is testing subject–verb agreement. You also know that you will need to find the subject that goes with this verb so that you can decide whether the verb should be singular or plural.

Step 2: Read the sentence for meaning.

You're going to read for both meaning and grammar, actually, but this step emphasizes meaning because most people forget to pay attention to what the sentence is trying to say. This makes your job harder. Pay attention to the meaning.

Step 3: Find a starting point.

Either of the first two steps may have already given you your starting point. If you spotted a meaningful difference on the first glance, or if you found an error during your read-through of the original sentence, then you know where to start.

If not, then start comparing the answer choices to find other differences, until you find a particular difference that you know how to handle. If you find a difference that you don't know how to handle, ignore it and keep looking.

Step 4: Eliminate all incorrect choices.

First, track the answers on your scrap paper. Second, a particular error will often be repeated in more than one answer choice. Once you've found an error, make sure that you cross off all answer choices that contain that same error.

Repeat!

On most sentence correction problems, you will have to complete steps 3 and 4 at least twice in order to narrow down to one answer.

On harder questions, you may not be able to narrow down to one answer. You may have to decide to move on even though multiple answers remain. Don't be stubborn! Tackle what you know how to handle, ignore the rest, pick an answer, and move on.

Drill 7.2

The following are complete GMAT-style Sentence Correction problems testing issues discussed in this book. Note that answer choice (A) is always identical to the original sentence. For each question, write A B C D E on your paper and practice process of elimination. Cross off all of the answers that have mistakes. The remaining choice is the correct answer.

1. Avgolemono, or "egg lemon," is a soup or sauce made by mixing egg, lemon juice, and broth and <u>heat the mixture until it will thicken</u>.

   (A) heat the mixture until it will thicken
   (B) heat the mixture until it thickens
   (C) heating the mixture until it will thicken
   (D) heating the mixture until it thickens
   (E) heating the mixture until it had thickened

2. Soldier ants are sterile, wingless females that serve many roles within a colony, from <u>serving as sentinels and sound</u> a warning when danger is near.

   (A) serving as sentinels and sound
   (B) serving as sentinels and sounding
   (C) to serve as sentinels and to sound
   (D) serving as sentinels to sound
   (E) serving as sentinels to sounding

3. <u>That the consumer products division lacks credible leadership cannot be blamed for</u> the company's troubles.

   (A) That the consumer products division lacks credible leadership cannot be blamed for
   (B) That the consumer products division has a lack in credible leadership cannot blame
   (C) The consumer products division lacks credible leadership cannot be blamed for
   (D) The lack of credible leadership of the consumer products division is not blaming
   (E) It is not blameworthy that the consumer products division lacks credible leadership for

4. Many small businesses <u>are finding that it can avoid the fees associated with credit card merchant accounts,</u> using Internet-based credit card processing services, which typically take a percentage of sales but charge no setup fee or monthly service fee.

   (A) are finding that it can avoid the fees associated with credit card merchant accounts
   (B) are finding that they can avoid the fees associating with credit card merchant accounts
   (C) are finding that they can avoid the fees associated with credit card merchant accounts by
   (D) had found that they can avoid the fees associated to credit card merchant accounts by
   (E) have found that they can avoid the fees associated to credit card merchant accounts,

5. Confounded by the seemingly contradictory data, the experiment was suggested by the scientist to be re-run by his graduate students.

   (A) experiment was suggested by the scientist to be re-run by his graduate students
   (B) experiment was re-run by the graduate students at the suggestion of the scientist.
   (C) graduate students were suggested to re-run the experiment by the scientist.
   (D) scientist had suggested his graduate students re-run the experiment
   (E) scientist suggested that his graduate students re-run the experiment

6. The agency's top creative team, each member of which was asked to submit at least three ideas, remain stymied in its development of the new campaign.

   (A) which was asked to submit at least three ideas, remain
   (B) which was asked to submit at least three ideas, remains
   (C) which were asked to submit at least three ideas, remain
   (D) whom asked to submit at least three ideas, remains
   (E) whom was asked to submit at least three ideas, remains

7. The peanut, or groundnut, a legume probably first cultivated as long as 7,600 years ago in the valleys of Peru.

   (A) a legume probably
   (B) a legume was probably
   (C) is a legume probably
   (D) probably is a legume
   (E) the legume probably

8. The Paris Commune, hailed by many as an assumption of power by the working class, a government in 1871 that ruled France for less than two months.

   (A) a government in 1871 that ruled France for less than two months
   (B) a government that ruled France for less than two months in 1871
   (C) was a government who ruled France for less than two months in 1871
   (D) was a government that ruled France for less than two months in 1871
   (E) was a French government in 1871 that ruled for less than two months

9. Communards, or leaders of the Paris Commune, once mistook the painter Renoir, painting on the banks of the Seine River, for a spy.

    (A) mistook the painter Renoir, painting on the banks of the Seine River, for
    (B) mistook the painter Renoir, painting on the banks of the Seine River, as
    (C) mistook the painter Renoir, painting on the banks of the Seine River, to be
    (D) were mistaken of the painter Renoir, painting on the banks of the Seine River, for
    (E) were mistaken by the painting Renoir, painting on the banks of the Seine River, to be

10. The guests of the king had had plenty of time to glut themselves at the feast, and thus they were too stupefied, drunk, and startled to react effectively when rebels broke into the castle.

    (A) guests of the king had had plenty of time to glut themselves at the feast, and thus they were too stupefied, drunk, and
    (B) guests of the king had plenty of time to glut themselves at the feast, and thus they were too stupefied, drunk, and were too
    (C) king's guests had plenty of time to glut themselves at the feast, and thus they were too stupefied, too drunk, and were too
    (D) king's guests had had plenty of time to glut themselves at the feast, and thus they were too stupefied, too drunk, and were too
    (E) king's guests had plenty of time to glut themselves at the feast, but they were too stupefied, drunk, and

7

Answers are on page 140–145.

Now Go and Do Likewise

If you purchased this book or received it as part of a package of materials from Manhattan Prep, you have free access to an online bank of GMAT-style Verbal problems written expressly to supplement this book. Extensive explanations for each problem will help ensure that you understand why the right answer is right and the wrong answers are wrong.

When you have mastered the material in this book, you will be ready to work with our *Sentence Correction GMAT Strategy Guide*. Work through the chapters in that guide in the order presented, while referring back to this book whenever you need to clarify a particular rule or concept. As you work, test your skills by trying problems from one of *The Official Guide* books published by the makers of the official GMAT.

Now, turn to the next part on Critical Reasoning.

Answer to Pop Quiz

Idioms, page **131**

The sentence, "I prohibit you from breaking up the fight between Jared and Bill," is correct.

TRUE! Both of these idioms were covered at the beginning of the chapter. *Prohibit* goes with *from* and *between* goes with *and.*

Answers to Drill Sets

Answers to Drill 7.1 — Find the Idioms Errors

1. **Ability of doing** is wrong. Corrected sentence: *Although I can do* (or *am able to do,* or *have the ability to do*) *gymnastics well, this time I fell off the balance beam.*

2. **Reason . . . because** is wrong. Corrected sentence: *The ostensible reason for Anne Boleyn's execution was adultery, although the charges were almost certainly fabricated wholesale.*

3. **Not only . . . and also** and **appointed as** are wrong. Corrected sentence: *She not only has deep relationships with all of the union leaders but also worked for the company for many years herself, so she is expected to be appointed chairperson.*

4. **Indicates** ought to be followed by **that**, and **considered as** is wrong. Corrected sentence: *The study indicates that more men are working in education, traditionally considered a "female" profession.*

5. The correct idiom is **so . . . that**. Corrected sentence: *The company's new product is so successful that it will likely gain market share.*

Answers to Drill 7.2

7

1. **(D).** Issues tested: Parallelism, Verb Tense

Glance at the beginning of the underline and the beginning of each answer. The first word switches between *heat* and *heating*; this change, coupled with the word *and* just before, indicates that the sentence is likely testing parallelism. Keep this in mind as you read the sentence.

Next, read for meaning and find a starting point. The sentence describes a two-step process: *mixing* some ingredients and then *heat/heating* them. The words used to introduce the two steps should be parallel, so *heating* is correct. Eliminate answers (A) and (B).

Next, the soup is heated until the moment when it changes state, at which point you would stop heating it: the soup is heated *until it thickens.* Eliminate answers (C) and (E).

The correct answer is (D).

2. **(E).** Issues tested: Parallelism, Idioms

Glance at the beginning of the underline and the beginning of each answer. The first word switches between *serving* and *to serve*; this sentence may be testing sentence structure, modifiers, or idioms.

Next, read for meaning and find a starting point. The sentence describes the roles played by soldier ants but uses the incorrect idiom *From X and Y*; the correct idiom is *From X to Y.* Eliminate answers (A), (B), and (C).

Next, the idiom *From X to Y* requires the *X* and *Y* elements to be parallel. *Serving* is parallel to *sounding*, not *to sound*; eliminate answer (D).

The correct answer is (E).

3. **(A).** Issues tested: Sentence Structure, Meaning

Glance at the beginning of the underline and the beginning of each answer. The subject of the sentence changes from *That* to *The ... division* to *It*. The problem may be testing sentence structure or meaning.

Next, read for meaning and find a starting point. It likely sounds funny to have *that* be the subject but the structure is correct. It is the equivalent of saying *The fact that the division lacks credible leadership cannot be blamed for its troubles*, or *This fact cannot be blamed for the company's troubles.*

There are no other errors in the original sentence, but if you were not sure, you would examine the other choices. Because the original sentence did not provide a starting point, read answer (B) completely. Choice (B) is the equivalent of saying *The fact that the division has a lack ... cannot blame the company's troubles.* The lack of *credible leadership* can't blame something else; it can only be blamed for something. Answer (D) repeats this same error, so both (B) and (D) can be eliminated.

Answer (C) changes the subject: *The division lacks leadership cannot be blamed.* The sentence jams two verbs together without any kind of connecting word in between, the equivalent of saying *The pot contains soup cannot be heated.* Eliminate (C).

The reordering of the sentence in choice (E) creates an illogical meaning: *It is not blameworthy that the division lacks leadership for the company's troubles.* First, the sentence is saying that nobody is to blame for the lack of solid leadership. Next, it is saying that nobody is leading the company's troubles. Presumably, you want someone to lead the division out of trouble, not simply to preside over the troubles and let them continue.

The correct answer is (A).

4. **(C).** Issues tested: Verb tense, Pronouns, Modifiers/Meaning, Idioms

Glance at the beginning of the underline and the beginning of each answer. The verb tense changes from *are finding* to *had found* to *have found.* It will be important to figure out when the actions in the sentence are taking place.

Next, read for meaning and find a starting point. When talking about something that is ongoing in the present, you can correctly use the present tense *are finding* or the present perfect *have found.* The past perfect *had found* would only be used if there were another past event taking place later in the past; in this case, no such second past event exists in the sentence, so eliminate answer (D).

While the verb tense was fine in the original sentence, there are two errors. First, the singular pronoun *it* does not match the plural noun *businesses*; answer (A) is the only one that makes this mistake. Second, the modifier *using . . . services* does not explain the logical sequence of events: *businesses can avoid fees* ***by*** *using Internet-based services.* Eliminate answers (A), (B), and (E) for making this mistake.

Finally, three answers contain an idiom error. The correct idiom is *X associated with Y.* Answer (B) incorrectly says *fees associating with services*; answers (D) and (E) incorrectly say *fees associated to services.*

The correct answer is (C).

5. **(E).** Issues tested: Modifiers/Meaning, Verb Tense

Glance at the beginning of the underline and the beginning of each answer. The starting noun switches from *experiment* to *graduate students* to *scientist.* The sentence might be testing subject–verb agreement, pronouns, or modifiers.

Next, read for meaning and find a starting point. The sentence contains an opening modifier. Who was *confounded by the data?* Not the experiment! Eliminate answers (A) and (B).

The verb portion of the original sentence is also awkward. Passive voice always sounds a bit funny, but it can be correct. Check the remaining answers to see how they handle this part of the sentence. There are three options: *were suggested, had suggested,* or *suggested.*

In choice (C), *were suggested,* although many verbs can be written in passive voice, the verb *suggest* has limitations. A conclusion or something abstract can *be suggested,* but if someone suggests something to someone else, then don't write that one *person was suggested to do* something by another. Write that one *person suggested that* another *do* something, as in choice (E).

7

In choice (D), *had suggested,* past perfect requires a second past event that took place later in the past, but no such event exists in this sentence, so eliminate answer (D).

The correct answer is (E).

6. **(B).** Issues tested: Subject–Verb Agreement, Modifiers

Glance at the beginning of the underline and the beginning of each answer. The starting word switches from *which* to *whom*; as you read the sentence, ask yourself which option is the appropriate one to introduce the modifier.

Next, read for meaning and find a starting point. In the construction *each member of which/whom,* what does the *of which/whom* portion refer to?

This is at trap, actually. Normally, *which* or *whom* would immediately follow what it is modifying. In this case, though, the preposition *of* signals that it is referring to something further back in the sentence. *Each member of* what? Of the team. *Whom* is used to refer to a person; *which* is used to refer to a non-person, such as a team. The correct option is *which*; eliminate answers (D) and (E).

Next, decide about the last word in the choices: *remain* or *remains*. This is a verb, so it needs to match the subject in number. The portion of the sentence between the commas is a modifier, so it does not contain the main subject. The subject is *team* and the word is used in the singular, as evidenced by the later singular pronoun *its*. The verb, then, should also be singular: *remains*. Eliminate answers (A) and (C).

The correct answer is (B).

7. **(C).** Issues tested: Sentence Structure, Meaning

Glance at the beginning of the underline and the beginning of each answer. Three answers begin with a noun, *legume*, and two begin with a verb, *is*. Something appears to be going on with sentence structure.

Next, read the original sentence for meaning and find a starting point. The subject appears to be *peanut*, and everything that follows modifies *peanut*. The sentence has no verb; it is a sentence fragment. Answer (E) also lacks a verb. Eliminate both (A) and (E).

The other three choices all include a verb. Here are the core sentences of each:

> (B) The peanut a legume was probably cultivated.
>
> (C) The peanut is a legume probably cultivated.
>
> (D) The peanut probably is a legume.

Answer (B) smashes two subjects together without anything in between; it is the equivalent of saying *Sally a girl likes cheese*. Eliminate answer (B).

Answer (D) changes the meaning of the sentence. *Legume* is a standard classification of a food: either the peanut does or does not qualify as a legume, in the same way that an apple does or does not qualify as a fruit (as it turns out, both do qualify, respectively). The legume was *probably first cultivated* at a certain time. Answer (D), though, says that the peanut is probably a legume, not that it was probably first cultivated at a certain time. Eliminate (D).

The correct answer is (C).

8. **(D).** Issues tested: Sentence Structure, Modifiers/Meaning

Glance at the beginning of the underline and the beginning of each answer. Two start with a noun and three with a verb, so something appears to be going on with sentence structure.

Next, read for meaning and find a starting point. The subject could be *Paris Commune* or *government*, but no main verb exists in the sentence to go with either one. Eliminate choices (A) and (B) because they are sentence fragments.

Answers (C), (D), and (E) all correctly add the verb *was* to match the subject *Paris Commune.* Answer (C), though, refers to the government with the modifier *who.* This modifier is reserved for actual people, not words that refer to people; eliminate answer (C).

Answer (E) mixes up the modifiers enough to make the meaning ambiguous. What or whom did the French government rule? (It is possible for the government of a country to rule something other than that country.) In addition, when did they do this? *For two months in 1871.* The prepositional phrase *in 1871* should be next to *two months.* Eliminate choice (E).

The correct answer is (D).

9. **(A).** Issue tested: Idioms

We set a bit of a trap for you! This idiom tested in this problem was not presented in the idioms chapter. It is nearly impossible to memorize every idiom in a language, but the *Sentence Correction GMAT Strategy Guide* does present lists of idioms that have been tested on official GMAT questions in the past. If you run across an idiom you don't know, look it up in either the main idioms chapter or in the idioms appendix of that guide.

Glance at the beginning of the underline and the beginning of each answer. Is it *mistook* or *were mistaken*?

Read the sentence for meaning to figure that out. The sentence is using a particular idiom: *mistake X for Y.* The original sentence uses the idiom correctly.

Answers (B) and (C) use an incorrect idiom (*mistake X as Y* and *mistake X to be Y,* respectively). Eliminate both.

Answers (D) and (E) change up the idiom a bit. It is possible to say something like *The cat was mistaken for a dog.* In this case, though, the Communards were not *mistaken as Renoir,* nor were they *mistaken for a spy.* Rather, they *mistook Renoir for* someone else. Eliminate (D). They were also not *mistaken by Renoir to be a spy* (you still need to say *mistaken for a spy*). Eliminate (E).

The correct answer is (A).

10. **(D).** Issues tested: Verb Tense, Parallelism, Meaning

Glance at the beginning of the underline and the beginning of each answer. Should it be *guests of the king* or *king's guests*?

Read the sentence for meaning to figure that out. It turns out that this difference is a red herring: either form is just fine. What next? Should the verb be *had had* or *had*? The sentence discusses multiple events that took place at different times in the past, so it is appropriate to use the past perfect *had had* to refer to the longest-ago event. First, the guests *had had* too much to eat and drink; then rebels *broke in* and the guests were unable to react effectively. Eliminate answers (B), (C), and (E).

Next, check the list for parallelism:

(A) too stupefied, drunk, and startled

(D) too stupefied, too drunk, and were too startled

Answer (D) tosses in a verb where none is needed. Only the list in choice (A) is parallel.

Did the pronoun *they* sound ambiguous to you? When you spot a pronoun that might be ambiguous, check the answers: in this case, all five use the pronoun *they*, so it must be correct. This red herring, along with the *guests of the king*, was designed to get you to eliminate, or at least to doubt, the correct answer.

The correct answer is (D).

Chapter 8
of
GMAT Foundations of Verbal
Part 2: **Critical Reasoning**

Argument Structure

In This Chapter...

Chapter 8

Argument Structure

Have you ever witnessed or even taken part in the following kind of discussion?

Person A	**Person B**
Makes a statement of some kind.	
	Says something that doesn't address what Person A just said.
Responds with a random thought that popped into his head.	
	Confidently states an opinion as if it were a fact.
Talks in circles, leaving his true position unspoken.	
	Makes a mistaken assumption about what Person A wants.
Can't articulate what he really thinks.	
Winds up frustrated.	Winds up frustrated.

This sort of exchange is typical. In real life, people are generally bad at arguing.

Even folks who try to be fair-minded can be fuzzy in their thinking. For instance, people will hear both sides of an issue and then say, "Well, I need more information to decide." But they can't tell you what information they need. They can't identify specific flaws in the chains of logic they've heard, so they have no idea how to fix those flaws.

It doesn't have to be this way! GMAT Critical Reasoning (CR) questions force you to really understand arguments. In the context of the GMAT, the word *argument* doesn't usually mean "a verbal scuffle or debate" (*I had an argument with my significant other last night*). Rather, it means "a set of logically connected statements that put forth an assertion of some kind" (*She made the argument that we should replace the refrigerator*).

You "have" the first kind of argument, which is the verbal scuffle. In contrast, you "make" the second kind of argument, which is a case for some position.

As you study GMAT arguments—as you delve into their structure, their purpose, their flaws, and possible cures for those flaws—you will start to come across similar arguments all around you.

Most arguments on the GMAT are flawed in some fashion. So are most arguments in the real world.

Be warned: Once your eyes are opened, there's no going back to blind acceptance of the self-serving arguments of some salesperson or politician. But that's not a bad thing, right?

In short, improving on Critical Reasoning will make you better at reasoning critically in general. That's a pretty useful side effect of your preparation for the GMAT.

Arguments and Conclusions

A Critical Reasoning argument looks something like this:

> To be considered a form of cardiovascular exercise, an activity must raise the heart rate and keep it elevated for at least 20 minutes. Skydiving cannot properly be considered a form of cardiovascular exercise. While skydiving certainly does elevate a person's heart rate, the skydiver only experiences freefall for 60–70 seconds, followed by 5–6 minutes under a parachute—and, of course, it is not possible to string multiple dives immediately back-to-back.

Every argument contains certain building blocks, types of information that form the complete argument.

All arguments contain **premises**. A premise is a fact or an opinion that is intended to support some claim made by the author.

Most arguments also contain **conclusions**. The conclusion is the main claim made by the author.

Together, premises and conclusions make up the **core argument**. What is the core argument about skydiving?

Premise 1: cardio = raise heart rate AND keep high for 20+ m

Premise 2: skydiving raises heart rate BUT fall lasts only 6–8m

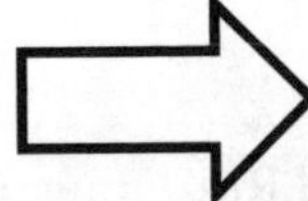

Conclusion: skydiving isn't cardio

The conclusion of an argument is the speaker's main point or claim. If you order the information chronologically, as in the diagram, the conclusion is the last piece of information in the sequence of events.

When an argument does contain a conclusion (as most arguments will), it's very important for you to correctly identify it.

Drill 8.1 — Find the Conclusion

Articulate the conclusion in each of the arguments. In some, you may be able to simply underline the conclusion. In others, you may have to rephrase the conclusion a bit, or combine two pieces of information.

1. Quoting sources in your papers without attributing the quotes to those sources is forbidden on this campus. Plagiarism is strictly forbidden by our code of conduct, and quoting without attribution is a form of plagiarism.

2. The difference between a weed and a garden plant depends entirely on the opinion of the person who owns the land. Thus, it is impossible to develop a flawless garden "weed killer" that kills all types of weeds and leaves all types of garden plants unharmed. The Vytex Company's attempt to develop a perfect garden weed killer will fail.

3. An anti-smoking policy would cause a loss of revenue to the bars in Melton. Since Melton is a small town, smokers would likely just drive an extra couple of miles to bars in any of the neighboring towns, none of which have anti-smoking policies.

4. The city parks are overcrowded, leading to long wait times for athletic fields and courts and lessening citizens' enjoyment of the parks. A new park should be built at the southern tip of the city, which does not have its own park. Because the heavily populated south of the city lacks a park, residents regularly travel to other parts of the city to use those parks, thus leading to overcrowding.

5. Some say that Saddlebrook College provides the best value in the state. Yet, this belief is simply not true: students at the state's Tunbridge College pay less, enjoy newer buildings and smaller class sizes, and earn higher incomes after graduation.

Answers are on page 162.

Building Blocks

You've learned the first two types of Critical Reasoning building blocks:

Premise: supports the author's conclusion

Conclusion: the main claim made by the author

There are two more building blocks to learn:

Counterpremise: A counterpremise, or counterpoint, goes against the author's conclusion in some way. Some arguments will contain this kind of information, but many do not.

Background: The argument also might introduce background information to provide context for the overall story.

The following exercise will help you practice finding these building blocks.

Drill 8.2 — Identify the Building Blocks

Label each piece of information according to the role that it plays in the argument.

1. Company spokesperson: An investor has accused the CEO of financial impropriety, citing as evidence a $50,000 payment made to the CEO's son although no work was performed. In fact, the payment was perfectly legitimate. The son's firm provides consulting services to the company and this was an advance payment of 10% of project fees for a new endeavor slated to start in the next month.

2. The female arkbird will lay eggs only when a suitable quantity of nesting material is available, and the climate is suitably moderate. This year, unseasonable temperatures have actually increased the amount of nesting material as trees and plants die, shedding twigs and leaves. For this reason, the arkbirds in this region can be expected to lay eggs soon.

3. John Doe pleaded not guilty to the charge of embezzlement, but was convicted after irrefutable evidence was found on his personal computer. It is illegal, however, to search a personal computer without the consent of the owner, so Doe's conviction will be overturned on appeal.

Answers are on page 163.

Plans

Some arguments will look like most of the ones that you've already seen (some type of logical argument is made), but others will be in the form of plans. Recall this argument (with a couple of small changes):

> The city parks are overcrowded, leading to long wait times for athletic fields and courts and lessening citizens' enjoyment of the parks. The mayor contends that a new park should be built at the southern tip of the city, which does not have its own park. Because the heavily populated south of the city lacks a park, residents regularly travel to other parts of the city to use those parks, thus leading to overcrowding.
>
> Which of the following, if true, most seriously undermines the mayor's plan to alleviate overcrowding at city parks?

Now, the argument is being put forth by the mayor, and the question stem explicitly lays out the goal of the plan: to alleviate overcrowding. The full plan is as follows:

Build a new park at the southern tip.

Residents in that area will stop going to other parks.

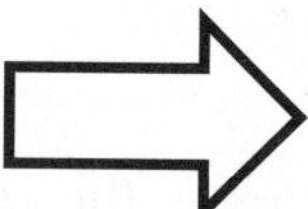

Overcrowding in other parks will be alleviated.

For any plan, the key point of attack is typically whether the plan will work the way that the author says it will. It's crucial to note precisely how the author states that the plan will work.

Trap answers will often try to go outside of the plan. For instance, a trap on this problem might revolve around building an indoor recreation center instead, so that it could be used in winter. Maybe the center would attract more people and thus alleviate park overcrowding, but the question will ask you to analyze the *given* plan, not how to achieve the same goal via a different plan.

In other words, don't think the way you would in the real world when someone presents you with a plan. Evaluate the exact plan as it stands.

You'll learn more about these types of arguments later; for now, just note that you will want to notice when the argument is presenting a plan.

Flaws in Arguments

Nearly all of the arguments that you see on the GMAT will be flawed. That is, the argument will contain weak points, and the question is going to ask you to analyze one of those weak points in some way.

You'll learn about some of these weaknesses here. In the next chapter, you'll learn about one more special kind of building block and the weaknesses associated with that building block.

1. Language Weaknesses

Some arguments use unjustified language. For example:

> People who jog more than 10 miles per week have a lower incidence of heart disease than people who exercise the same amount on stationary bicycles. Therefore, jogging is the best method of exercise for reducing heart disease.

The conclusion is in the final sentence: *jogging is the best method of exercise for reducing heart disease.* The word *best* is quite extreme. Jogging is the best method ever? Better than swimming, tennis, and a million other things? Even if you prove that jogging is better in some respect than stationary bicycling, all you can say is that jogging is better than one other activity, not that it's the best.

Watch out for these extreme words: *only, never, always, cannot, certainly, obviously, inevitably, most, least, best,* and *worst.* Look for dramatic predictions and assertions: *X costs far more than Y, an immediate increase in Z, or a sharp decline in W.* When you see extreme language, check whether this language is justified by other information in the argument. If not, you've just found a flaw in the argument.

Study Tip

Check whether extreme language is justified by the argument.

If you see something like this . . .

> Whenever there is political unrest in the world, the price of oil goes up. Thus, political unrest must be the most important influence on the price of oil.

. . . then think something like this:

> *Is it really the MOST important influence?*

8

In addition to unjustified language, arguments will sometimes use false synonyms or false equivalents. For example:

> Consumers used their cell phones more this month than last month, but they talked for fewer minutes. So they must have sent more text messages this month than last month.

Used their cell phones more is not necessarily equivalent to *sent more text messages.* There are plenty of other things to do on a cell phone; they could have been playing games, surfing the web, listening to music, and so on.

Vague language can also be problematic. Recall the *People who jog* argument:

> People who jog more than 10 miles per week have a lower incidence of heart disease than people who exercise the same amount on stationary bicycles. Therefore, jogging is the best method of exercise for reducing heart disease.

What on earth does it mean to *exercise the same amount* as someone who is jogging 10 miles? Does it mean biking for the same amount of *time* or the same *distance*? The same number of calories burned? It's much faster to ride 10 miles on a stationary bike than to jog 10 miles, so if the arguer means that the distances are the same, then there is potentially another reason (besides the author's conclusion) that the joggers have less heart disease: they are exercising more hours per week. *Exercise the same amount* is overly vague. Question any term that's **insufficiently precise**.

2. Selection Bias

Whenever you compare two groups, make sure that the two groups are legitimately comparable. This is particularly tricky when the two groups *seem* comparable—for instance, when they are both drawn from the same population.

There are several types of selection bias.

Unrepresentative Sample

Marketers, pollsters, and social scientists of all stripes use samples. It's impossible to ask everyone in the entire population for their opinions on single- versus double-ply toilet paper, so instead you ask 100 people. You have to ensure that the sample is representative, though. In particular, you have to be wary of volunteers. For example:

> Some customers who filled out a long survey for free said that they love our company. So our customers love our company.

Isn't there a possibility that this sample of customers is disproportionately comprised of people who like you? After all, they filled out a long survey for free. The potential for self-selection bias is strong here.

Survivor Bias

It is not logical to judge an entire group by concentrating only on who or what survived a process or time period while ignoring the nonsurvivors. It's easy to fall into this trap, though; after all, it's often hard to find out much about the people or things that didn't make it.

When you say *survive*, you might mean it literally—for instance, the population of living people over 100 years old (those who survived that long) is not representative of all people born 100 or more years ago. Those alive today are very likely different in important ways—better access to nutrition, fewer genetic maladies, etc. For example:

> A survey of living people over 100 showed lower rates of cigarette smoking than were shown in every other age group age 15 and up. Therefore, the rate of smoking is increasing.

Here, it is likely that those who lived to be 100 did so in part by not smoking, and that plenty of people born 100 or more years ago did smoke and did not live to be 100.

Survivor bias can also involve nonliving things:

> Most ancient Greek coins made of gold and silver have been found buried in the ground. So the ancient Greeks must have buried most of their gold and silver coins.

What about the ancient Greek coins that *weren't* buried? They were probably dispersed, melted down, or otherwise destroyed. The sample of surviving coins is not representative.

Ever-Changing Pool

Many groups of people have a rotating cast of members. If a civic club voted in favor of something yesterday and against it 20 years ago, you wouldn't automatically conclude that people in the club changed their minds over time; it's pretty likely that the club includes different people than it did back then. For example:

> A petition is circulating in Capital City opposing the building of a new sports center at State University, on land now occupied by abandoned strip malls. Five years ago, many city residents opposed the building of the new State University dormitory complex, yet in a poll this year, 80% of respondents said that building the dormitory complex had been a good idea. If the people who currently oppose the new Sports Center are patient, they will change their minds.

Five years ago, people opposed the new dorm, and now 80% of respondents to a poll like the dorm. Are the poll respondents the same population as the voters? Maybe the poll was conducted on or near campus; a high percentage of students in the poll would certainly skew results.

Even if the poll were representative of the city's current residents, it's not clear that they are the same residents as five years ago. Maybe some residents disliked the college's expansion plans enough to move out of town. Maybe the new dorm allowed the college to admit significantly more students, thus *diluting* the pool of people who disliked and still dislike the dorm.

If you see something like this . . .

> Students who joined social clubs at Hambone University last year and were elected officers of their clubs had lower grades on average than all students at Hambone over the last decade. Therefore, participation in social clubs at Hambone negatively impacts students' grades.

. . . then think something like this:

> *That may be true, but so what? Self-selection bias: these kids wanted to prioritize socializing by joining social clubs. Survivor bias: these students were elected officers, meaning that they made it even further into socializing. Ever-changing pool: students from last year are being compared with students over the last decade. The composition of the school may have changed over that time.*

3. Math Errors

You might not want to hear this, but even on the Verbal section of the GMAT, you can't completely get away from the Quant. A few Critical Reasoning arguments do trade on math issues. Fortunately, these issues almost never require any computation, and even in the worst case, you'll just be comparing one ratio to another.

When working with numbers on the GMAT, you'll generally be trying to find mathematically provable conclusions. Here's an example: *Alice worked fewer days last month than Bob worked, but she earned more dollars last month than Bob earned.* What can you definitely conclude? Alice had to have a higher *daily* wage (dollars per day) than Bob did.

You can't conclude that her hourly wage is higher; she may have worked a greater *total* number of hours than Bob did even though she worked fewer days. Also, notice that this conclusion is based only on inequalities and ratios. This is the way that the GMAT can avoid putting real numbers into arguments and yet still have a rigorous, airtight conclusion.

The GMAT also likes to mix up percents and real numbers. If David gets a 10% pay raise and Marie gets an 8% pay raise, who now has a higher salary? Without knowing how much the two people made before, it's impossible to tell. Don't confuse percents with actual numbers of dollars, people, etc.

Consider this argument:

> Cetadone, a new therapy for the treatment of addiction to the illegal drug tarocaine, has been proven effective in a study centered around Regis Hospital in the western part of the state of New Portsmouth. The study involved local tarocaine addicts who responded to a newspaper ad offering free treatment. Participants who received cetadone and counseling were 40% more likely to recover than were patients assigned to a control group and who received only counseling. Conventional therapies have only a 20% recovery rate. Therefore, the best way to reduce deaths from tarocaine overdose throughout all of New Portsmouth would be to fund cetadone therapy for all tarocaine addicts.

8

In this argument, 40% certainly looks like a higher number than 20%. And there are no real numbers of people here anywhere, so the argument is not confusing a percent with a real number.

However, the 20% is an actual *recovery rate for* conventional therapies.

The 40% is a *percent increase on an unknown figure*—the recovery rate of the control group. You have no way to compare this to an actual 20% recovery rate. For instance, what if the control group had a 50% recovery rate? Then the cetadone group would have a 70% recovery rate (1.4 × 50). But what if the control group had a 1% recovery rate? Then the cetadone group would have a 1.4% recovery rate, making it much less successful than conventional therapies. Be ready to test some extreme cases (high and low) to see whether the conclusion actually holds.

In short, if any numbers or numeric relationships are presented in an argument, determine whether they are being cited in a logical way. This is the exact same reasoning about percents and percent change that you will need for the Quantitative part of the exam (and, of course, the math on the actual math section is much harder than anything that would ever occur in Critical Reasoning), so it pays in numerous ways to have a solid knowledge of percents.

A few other standard mathematical relationships show up in Critical Reasoning as well:

Rate × Time = Distance
Profit = Revenue − Costs
Revenue = Price × Quantity
(Dollars per Hour) × Hours = Dollars

You have to know these for the Quant section of the test, of course. Ratios in general (such as *dollars per hour, miles per gallon*, etc.) are fair game. Again, you won't have to compute anything; you need to be able to follow a couple of steps to a mathematical conclusion.

4. Big Leaps in Logic

Sometimes, a conclusion makes too big of a leap in logic. For example:

> For over 100 years, the nation of Relmeer has had a mutual defense pact with the neighboring country of Gherfu. Yet, last month, the government of Relmeer fell to an invasion from the United Provinces of Antocia. Thus, Gherfu is at fault for not abiding by the mutual defense pact.

8

Gherfu was supposed to help Relmeer, but Antocia completely defeated Relmeer anyway. Therefore, Gherfu didn't help? There is no way to tell that. Maybe Relmeer and Gherfu are small nations, and the United Provinces of Antocia is a very large and powerful nation. Maybe Gherfu did absolutely everything it could. Maybe soldiers from Gherfu died valiantly in battle, trying to protect Relmeer. Here is another example:

> Amateur boxers wear headgear to protect against brain injuries from boxing. Yet, last year, three amateur boxers suffered serious brain injuries in the ring while wearing the headgear. Therefore, the headgear does not protect against brain injuries.

Well, it certainly seems true that the headgear is not 100% effective (although it would be helpful to confirm that the injured boxers were wearing the headgear correctly). However, there is a huge gap between saying that the headgear is not 100% effective (not much in life is), and saying that it *does not protect*. There are lots of things—automobile airbags, sunscreen, bulletproof vests—that do not provide 100% protection, but certainly still have a protective effect.

Here's another example, this time with a choice of two multiple-choice answers:

> Pancreatic cancer patients as a group have only a 5% survival rate after five years. With a surgical procedure called the Whipple, followed by chemotherapy and radiation, this survival rate can be increased. Therefore, this course of treatment is the best option for all pancreatic cancer patients strong enough to undergo the surgery.
>
> What does this argument assume?
>
> (A) People who receive the Whipple operation followed by chemotherapy and radiation are likely to live longer than five years.
>
> (B) No other treatment has a better or equivalent rate of effectiveness.

Note that this argument has another kind of error as well: it uses unjustified language. This course of treatment is the "best"? In making that conclusion, the argument assumes that other treatments must be worse. You are to take as fact that this course of treatment increases the survival rate, but what if some other course of treatment increases the rate *even more*? The author has neglected to rule out this possibility. The answer is (B).

What about incorrect choice (A)? An argument that asserts that a particular plan is the "best" one does not have to assert that that plan is likely to work—only that nothing else is *more* likely to work. In the case of a very deadly disease, sadly, even the very best treatment may not be that effective. As it turns out, the course of treatment described above leads to a five-year survival rate around 20%—thus, even with the "best" treatment, patients are not likely to survive five years.

One subset of a big leap in logic has to do with causation. Many conclusions assert that something is the cause of something else. If you claim that *sunscreen protects against skin cancer*, you are asserting that the presence of sunscreen at least contributes to the absence of skin cancer. Causation can also be assumed by this sort of conclusion: *To reduce the elk population, wolves should be reintroduced to the park.* This conclusion assumes that the presence of wolves will cause a reduction in the elk population. **Look closely at the verb**: *cause, make, force, lead to, prevent, protect, increase/decrease, reduce.* Also look at infinitives (*to reduce*), which often indicate goals. The achievement of goals requires causation.

The situation is often scientific or medical. For example:

> Research has shown that very tall people are more likely to have thyroid problems. So being very tall leads a person to have thyroid problems.

When an argument **jumps to a causal relationship**, question that relationship. Couldn't it be the other way around? Maybe thyroid problems cause people to be very tall. Or maybe they're both caused by something else (e.g., genetic factors).

Consider this argument:

> According to a recent study, cats that eat Premium Cat Food have healthier coats and shed less hair than those that do not. The higher cost of Premium Cat Food will be offset by a reduction in the need for cat grooming and house-cleaning services.

Two things are happening at the same time: cats are eating Premium Cat Food, and they are shedding less. The conclusion is that owners will save money on certain services by feeding their cats Premium Cat Food. This conclusion clearly assumes that Premium Cat Food causes the healthier coats and reduced shedding. But is it necessarily the case that the cat food has these beneficial effects?

Perhaps people who can afford to purchase Premium Cat Food (and choose to do so) also provide their cats with grooming, top-notch health care, or other amenities that reduce shedding and make coats healthier. Perhaps people who spend more on cat food tend to have special breeds of cats that naturally shed less.

When changes or events occur at the same time or in sequence, don't assume that X necessarily caused Y. It could be that Y caused X. It could also be that something else entirely caused both X and Y.

Here's a summary of the argument flaws you've learned so far:

1. Language Weaknesses	Unjustified language (e.g., an extreme word) False synonyms or false equivalents
2. Selection Bias	Unrepresentative sample Survivor bias Ever-changing pool
3. Math Errors	Conclusion not mathematically justifiable Percentages vs. real numbers
4. Big Leaps in Logic	Conclusion makes huge leap. For example: • something good is the absolute best! • A and B both happen, so A causes B

Drill 8.3 — Match Similar Arguments

Six arguments are presented below. Not all arguments are complete—some lack conclusions.

Match each argument with a partner—that is, an argument that uses the same pattern or shares the same problem. You should wind up with three pairs of arguments. Articulate the pattern for each pair.

1. **Running Study:** A study concluded that running is the optimal form of exercise to effect significant changes in overall health. Study participants ran five miles per day, six days a week, for three months. At the end of the study, the participants were shown to have lost weight, reduced their cholesterol levels, and increased their cardiovascular fitness. Further, running is inexpensive and easy to do year-round in most locations.

2. **Freight Trains:** In a survey of working freight trains, a recent study found that engines built before 1960 had better tolerances and higher-grade steel than engines built since 1960. Therefore, freight train engines were constructed according to higher quality standards before 1960 than afterward.

3. **New Product:** To make a profit this quarter, Company X must increase sales of its old product while also introducing a new product that is as profitable as the old one. Whenever Company X introduces a new product, sales of the old product drop sharply.

4. **Heart Murmurs:** A veterinarian noticed more potentially fatal heart murmurs in puppies than in dogs over 15 years old. Thus, the veterinarian concluded that the diet and care given to dogs must have declined over the last 15 years.

5. **Peacekeeping Force:** For the violence in Kirkenberg to be stopped, the majority of surrounding nations must vote to send in a peacekeeping force, and the wealthy nation of Nandia must provide funding. If Nandia becomes involved in any way regarding Kirkenberg, at least half of the nations surrounding Kirkenberg will vote against intervening in Kirkenberg.

6. **Cost Cutting:** Company G determined that there were two available methods to cut production costs for its main product line: change suppliers for certain raw materials or automate certain steps in the assembly of the product. Automation will save more money than changing suppliers, so Company G will maximize its savings by automating certain steps of the assembly.

Answers are on pages 164–165.

Answers to Drill Sets

Answers to Drill 8.1 — Find the Conclusion

1. **Quoting sources in your papers without attributing the quotes to those sources is forbidden on this campus.** In order, the chain of logic could be summarized: quoting without attribution is plagiarism; plagiarism is forbidden; therefore, quoting without attribution is forbidden.

2. **The Vytex Company's attempt to develop a perfect garden weed killer will fail.** The chain of logic is as follows: the difference between weed and plant is based on personal opinion; therefore, it's impossible to develop a "weed killer" that kills all weeds but no plants; therefore, Vytex's attempt to develop such a product will fail. Note that there seem to be two conclusions here! The first one is sometimes called an intermediate conclusion; only the final one is considered the main conclusion.

3. **An anti-smoking policy would cause a loss of revenue to Melton's bars.** The chain of logic is as follows: if smokers can't smoke in bars in Melton, they'll go to other bars in nearby towns; therefore, Melton's bars will lose revenue.

4. **A new park should be built at the southern tip of the city.** The chain of logic is as follows: the southern tip of the city doesn't have a park; residents in that area go to parks in other areas; those other parks are overcrowded; therefore, a new park should be built at the southern tip of the city.

5. **It is not true that Saddlebrook College provides the best value in the state.** Careful! The conclusion isn't that *Tunbridge College provides the best value in the state*—the speaker has simply pointed out that Saddlebrook can't be the best value, since another college is a better value. It could be that Saddlebrook and Tunbridge are actually the 10th and 7th best values in the state, for instance.

The speaker's statement of the conclusion is that "this belief is simply not true." You have to go back to the previous sentence and substitute in what the speaker means by *this belief.* Don't go beyond what is explicitly stated in the passage.

Be literal. Think about when you say things such as *Uncle Jay thinks he's the smartest person in our family? Even my eight-year-old is better at math than he is!* You're not arguing that your eight-year-old is the smartest person in the family—you're just pointing out that Uncle Jay can't be the best, since at least one other person is above him.

Answers to Drill 8.2 — Identify the Building Blocks

1. Company spokesperson:

An investor has accused the CEO of financial impropriety, citing as evidence a $50,000 payment made to the CEO's son although no work was performed.	*Counterpremise*
In fact, the payment was perfectly legitimate.	*Conclusion*
The son's firm provides consulting services to the company and this was an advance payment of 10% of project fees for a new endeavor slated to start in the next month.	*Background Premise*

2. The female arkbird will lay eggs only when a suitable quantity of nesting material is available, and the climate is suitably moderate.	*Premise*
This year, unseasonable temperatures have actually increased the amount of nesting material as trees and plants die, shedding twigs and leaves.	*Premise*
For this reason, the arkbirds in this region can be expected to lay eggs soon.	*Conclusion*

The most common building blocks are premises and conclusions. Many arguments, like the second one, will not contain counterpremises or background information.

3. John Doe pleaded not guilty to the charge of embezzlement but was convicted after irrefutable evidence was found on his personal computer.	*Background Counterpremise*
It is illegal, however, to search a personal computer without the consent of the owner,	*Premise*
so Doe's conviction will be overturned on appeal.	*Conclusion*

At first, the fact that *irrefutable evidence* of his guilt was found may seem like a premise. The conclusion, however, is that his *conviction will be overturned*, so irrefutable evidence of his guilt doesn't support that claim. Rather, the idea that this evidence is not permissible supports the claim that his conviction will be overturned.

8

Answers to Drill 8.3 — Match Similar Arguments

#1 "Running Study" and #6 "Cost Cutting"

Pattern: *One particular plan has a good result. Therefore, it is the best way to accomplish a certain goal.*

Both cases use **unjustified language** in the conclusion. According to the running study, it does sound like running will help people to improve their health. There is no information to suggest, however, that this is the optimal, or best, way to do so. Running might work for some people but not others. Or tennis might be even better than running. Running is good, but there is no evidence to say that it is the best.

The cost cutting argument is a bit trickier. If automation saves more money than changing suppliers, then doesn't that mean that automation is the better choice? Sure! But the conclusion states that, by automating certain steps, the company will *maximize* its savings. What if it *also* changes suppliers? Nothing in the argument prevents the company from taking both steps.

#2 "Freight Trains" and #4 "Heart Murmurs"

Pattern: *Right now, some things towards the end of their life cycle are better than some things towards the beginning of their life cycle. So the older things must have been better to start with.*

The problem in both cases is **survivor bias**. In the case of the freight train engines, it is very likely that the poorly built engines from before 1960 have long since fallen apart—only the best ones are left running. So the argument is illogically comparing the *best* old engines with *all* newer engines. New engines that were badly built haven't yet had much of a chance to fall apart. In the case of the dogs, the 15-year-old dogs are probably mostly the ones who never had heart murmurs in the first place, since their littermates who did have potentially fatal heart murmurs did not live to be 15 years old, sadly.

Just as it would be unfair to compare one university's *best* graduates with *all* of another university's graduates, it is illogical to compare a group that has been weeded out (in this case, by long periods of time) with another group that hasn't.

#3 "New Product" and #5 "Peacekeeping Force"

Pattern: *In order to solve a problem, two things must happen. If one thing happens, the other one can't. (Therefore, the solution cannot take place.)*

The first argument presents as fact that *to make a profit this quarter, Company X must increase sales of its old product while also introducing a new product that is as profitable as the old one.* If this is true—that this is the only way to make a profit this quarter—then the next premise makes it impossible to make a profit, since *whenever Company X introduces a new product, sales of the old product drop sharply.* This is not a paradox, nor is the argument flawed. It's just that the plan won't work. This situation might be called the **self-defeating plan**.

The peacekeeping plan is similarly doomed. For the violence to stop, two things must happen: surrounding nations must vote to send in forces, and Nandia must give money. But if Nandia gives money, the other nations won't vote to send in forces. In other words, the plan will fail.

Chapter 9
of
GMAT Foundations of Verbal
Part 2: **Critical Reasoning**

Assumptions & Diagramming

In This Chapter...

Chapter 9

Assumptions & Diagramming

What Is an Assumption?

At the end of the last chapter, you learned about a particular category of flawed argument: big leaps in logic. Big leaps can be obvious, but arguments can also make smaller and more subtle—but no less problematic—leaps.

These leaps are the result of an **assumption**. The author assumes something to be true without actually supplying evidence or even just asserting that this thing is true.

Consider this argument:

> Surprisingly, the impoverished nation of Beltraja has several hospitals that practice good sanitation and employ well-trained doctors. However, these doctors report that thousands of patients per year die because of a shortage of antibiotics. Therefore, a relief plan to provide regular shipments of antibiotics to Beltraja's hospitals should save lives.

This seems like a pretty decent argument. Note that the conclusion is not too extreme—the argument does not say that *all* of the people will be saved. There are some gaps, however:

People are dying because of a lack of antibiotics.

↓

Give the hospitals antibiotics.

↓

Some of the people won't die.

In either arrowed location, what is the author assuming? For one, the author assumes that the dying people are close enough to the hospitals to be treated. Perhaps it is the case that the few hospitals mentioned in the argument are all in Beltraja's main city, and the dying patients are mostly in rural areas, far from the city.

The author also assumes that the shipments make it to the hospitals and the patients; the antibiotics are not, for instance, intercepted by a corrupt government or hospital official and sold on the black market.

Assumptions are the fifth, unspoken building block of arguments. The author assumes something is true without actually stating that thing or providing evidence that it is true.

About half of the question types on the GMAT revolve around the weak points of an argument, assumptions that the author is making. If you can identify the author's assumptions, then you are halfway toward answering the question correctly.

Try this one:

> Consumption of fast food contributes to obesity. If a fast food restaurant is permitted to open right next door to the local high school and to sell to students during lunchtime, the students will become obese and the school's scores on a national fitness test will decline.

List the steps leading to the conclusion (it's okay if you use a different number of "steps" than the lines given):

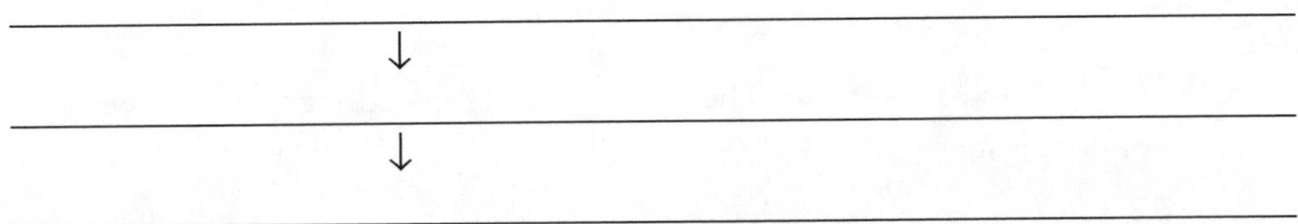

Here's one possible response:

Fast food place sells to students.
↓
Students become obese.
↓
Students do worse on fitness test.

There are some significant assumptions in this argument.

The author assumes students will eat at this restaurant in the first place (and regularly enough to become obese). The author also assumes either that this fast food is unhealthy and will contribute to obesity or that students will generally avoid healthy items and purchase the unhealthy ones.

The author further assumes that obese people generally score lower on a national fitness test. The argument doesn't actually detail what is required on the national fitness test, let alone how a subject's weight is a factor in performance on such a test. What if doing well on the test isn't any less likely for obese people?

Changing an argument to make a "larger" claim can introduce even more assumptions. Here's the Beltraja argument again, with a few changes (in bold):

> Surprisingly, the impoverished nation of Beltraja has several hospitals that practice good sanitation and employ well-trained doctors. However, these doctors report that **approximately 3,000** patients per year die because of a shortage of antibiotics. Therefore, a relief plan to provide regular shipments of antibiotics to Beltraja's hospitals **will save thousands of patients per year**.

The original conclusion seemed pretty reasonable—if people are dying because of a lack of antibiotics, sending some antibiotics ought to save some indeterminate number of people (technically, if you save just two people, you've "saved lives").

But, in this new version of the argument, the original problem has been quantified—about 3,000 people are dying. The new conclusion is that you'll save *thousands*, which implies at least 2,000. Can the plan save approximately two-thirds of the people who are dying? That is a much more ambitious goal, and more evidence would help support such a big conclusion. For instance, the author is assuming that antibiotics *alone* will save at least two-thirds of these people. Perhaps there are other medical complications that would still threaten lives, even if antibiotics are made available.

Some common types of assumptions are listed below. Anything the author assumes to be true in drawing his or her conclusion, though, is considered an assumption, even if it does not fall into the following categories.

Assumes Shared Beliefs

Here, the arguer assumes that the listener will share certain basic beliefs—some of which are mere impressions, prejudices, and so on. Here is an example:

> Smalltown Cinema currently prohibits movie attendance by unaccompanied teenagers under age 16. If this restriction is lifted, the theater's operating expenses will increase because of an increased need for cleaning services and repairs to the facility.

Some people read this argument and do not immediately see the flaw. Restate the argument in a simpler way to clarify the argument's structure:

> *IF unaccompanied teenagers under age 16 are allowed in the theater...*
>
> *THEN the theater will have to pay for cleaning and repairs.*

What's missing in the middle of that argument? What does the arguer need to prove in order to make the argument valid?

Consider a slightly different example:

> Smalltown Cinema currently prohibits movie attendance by elderly women. If this restriction is lifted, the theater's operating expenses will increase because of an increased need for cleaning services and repairs to the facility.

Isn't the argument now kind of strange? The speaker seems to think that elderly women make a mess in theaters and break things.

The speaker has made the assumption that elderly women disproportionately mess up and damage theaters. The reason that the assumption was so easy to spot in this case was that it was *not* something most of us intuitively believe.

However, many people take it for granted that teenagers make messes and are more likely to break things. The speaker in the original argument played on a general prejudice against teenagers. Although the speaker's argument depends on the idea that "teenagers under age 16 are more likely to make theaters dirty and to damage the facilities," the speaker didn't even bother to *write* that—and he or she certainly didn't *prove* it. Don't take anything for granted, and don't bring in outside ideas.

Here's another example:

> The Urban Apartment Towers complex has seen a number of police visits to the property recently, resulting in the police breaking up loud parties held by young residents and attended by other young people. These police visits and the reputation for loud parties are hurting the complex's reputation and ability to attract new residents. To reduce the number of police visits and improve profitability, management plans to advertise its vacant apartments in a local publication for people aged 50 and up.

What is this argument assuming but not proving? That *people aged 50 and up are less likely to have loud parties or attract police visits.* This doesn't sound like a totally unreasonable assumption, but it's an assumption nonetheless. It's the arguer's job to prove such an assumption. It's your job to notice that the arguer hasn't done so.

If you see something like this . . .

> Spider silk cannot be made in a lab; it can only be harvested directly from live spiders. So it is impractical to produce spider silk on an industrial scale.

. . . then think something like this:

> *That assumes that you can't "farm" spiders to produce the silk. Maybe you can!*

Assumes Skill and/or Will

For people to do something, they have to be able to do it, certainly, but they also have to want to. Both skill and will are necessary.

Some arguments give you one piece but not the other. A recommendation that *everyone should exercise two hours every day* might give reasons why people should want to do so, but ignore the fact that not everyone *can* exercise that much (e.g., people who are seriously ill). Consider the following example:

> The school should offer fresh vegetables at every lunch. Children who eat fresh vegetables are healthier, and fresh vegetables are cheaper than processed food, so the budget can accommodate the change.

What's the problem here? Maybe the school can afford to offer vegetables (the skill side). The argument makes a nod toward the will side: maybe the *parents* would want their kids to eat fresh vegetables. But what about the will of the children themselves? How many kids eat fresh vegetables voluntarily?

The *Urban Apartment Towers* argument on the previous page also has a skill/will problem. Maybe over-50 people in the local area cannot afford to live in the Towers. And how badly do people over 50 want to live in an apartment complex that has a reputation for loud parties? It's the responsibility of the arguer to answer.

Assumes the Future Equals the Past

To comply with consumer protection laws in the United States, investment firms have to tell you that "past performance is no guarantee of future results." So why do they trumpet the fact that their precious metals mutual fund exceeded its benchmark for the past three quarters?

Because they know that people fall into this logical trap. Of course, in many ways the future *will* be like the past. If you didn't assume so, you would go crazy. But this assumption goes too far. In the late 1990s, people kept plowing money into Internet stocks, believing that the ride wouldn't end (or wouldn't end yet!).

Remember that the future does not have to mimic the past. In a sense, every plan and proposal is guilty of this error, since every plan and proposal is forward-looking but uses the past as evidence. But some plans are more guilty than others.

If you see something like this . . .

> The price of the stock went up eight months in a row, when the market was flat. Therefore, I should buy this stock.

. . . then think something like this:

> *How do you know that it will keep going up? Maybe the stock has already risen too far. Maybe the increase is random: after all, if enough people flip coins, someone will flip heads eight times in a row.*

An Introduction to Argument Diagramming

Remember this argument from Chapter 8?

> To be considered a form of cardiovascular exercise, an activity must raise the heart rate and keep it elevated for at least 20 minutes. Skydiving cannot properly be considered a form of cardiovascular exercise. While skydiving certainly does elevate a person's heart rate, the skydiver only experiences freefall for 60–70 seconds, followed by 5–6 minutes under a parachute—and, of course, it is not possible to string multiple dives back-to-back.

The argument gets pretty complex. You can use a diagram to help you map out the parts and remember the major pieces of information.

Here's an example of a diagram one student might write:.

CE: ↑ heart rate 20+ min

Ⓒ SD ≠ CE

SD too short

This student used some abbreviations and symbols, but you probably have figured out what most of them mean. CE stands for *cardiovascular exercise* and SD stands for *skydiving.* The up arrow means *increase* and 20+ means *at least 20 minutes.* The ≠ symbol is shorthand for a common piece of information in arguments: one thing does not represent or go along with another. Finally, the Ⓒ is this student's way of denoting the conclusion of the argument.

Is that the only way to diagram this argument? Definitely not! Someone else might draw something like this:

cardio = > HR ≥ 20m

BUT S only 6-7m ⟶ S <u>not</u> cardio

This student used different abbreviations of course, but she also just laid things out differently in general. Instead of writing things out line by line as she read, she read the whole argument first, then laid it out according to the logical flow of information. She writes the conclusion off to the right after the arrow to set it apart from the rest of the argument.

There are many ways to diagram Critical Reasoniing arguments. On some, you might even want to make a table or draw a picture. Your task will be to find the right style for you. Whether you use variables or abbreviations to refer to entire premises (*B = the company will go bankrupt*) or merely words (*FF = fireflies*) will depend on the complexity of the argument and your own preferences.

Keep one important principle in mind as you develop your diagramming style: abbreviate aggressively! You'll only need to use the diagram for about 60–90 seconds after you're done creating it. You can abbreviate down to single variables and still remember what they stand for 90 seconds later!

Here are some additional examples of symbols that you could use:

≈ similar to; almost the same as happening simultaneously

∴ therefore

[ ] [assumptions]

Next, arrange the pieces of the argument in a logical order, one that makes sense for you. If you prefer to write each piece of information as you read, then use symbols or arrows to indicate what leads to what (and make sure to mark the conclusion). If you prefer to read first and then diagram, you can reorder the information to put the conclusion last or to the right (or first, if you prefer, as long as you are consistent).

Try this argument:

> A study of 120 elderly, hospital-bound patients in the United Kingdom showed that daily consumption of Nutree, a nutritional supplement containing vitamins, fiber, and sugar, increased by an average of four months the typical life expectancy for patients of the same age and physical condition. Thus, anyone who wants to live longer should drink Nutree every day.

Here is one possible diagram; can you decipher the abbreviations and symbols used?

S: old, hosp take N daily → +4 mo avg LE

∴ N daily → ↑ LE for all

[old vs. all?]

The diagram starts by attributing the information to a *study* (S:) and then conveys the study results. N is *Nutree* and LE is *life expectancy*. It's generally a good idea to rearrange the content slightly to clarify relationships or to fit a pattern you're used to. For instance, always putting causes on the left and effects on the right is a fine habit to adopt.

The last line is not stated in the argument. The student is noticing an assumption (a bad one!): the study only followed elderly people in the hospital. Would the same results hold true for everyone? The conclusion assumes so, but this may not be valid.

Drill 9.1 — Diagramming Arguments

Try diagramming these arguments in the space provided below each one. Try to brainstorm any assumptions or pinpoint any weaknesses in the argument. (Note: You saw the first two arguments earlier in this book.)

1. The difference between a weed and a garden plant depends entirely on the opinion of the person who owns the land. Thus, it is impossible to develop a flawless garden "weed killer" that kills all types of weeds and leaves all types of garden plants unharmed. The Vytex Company's attempt to develop a perfect garden weed killer will fail.

2. The city parks are overcrowded, leading to long wait times for athletic fields and courts and lessening citizens' enjoyment of the parks. A new park should be built at the southern tip of the city, which does not have its own park. Because the heavily populated south of the city lacks a park, residents regularly travel to other parts of the city to use those parks, thus leading to overcrowding.

3. Van Hoyt College has produced at least one Rasmussen Scholar per year for the past decade. Therefore, Van Hoyt College is a very good school.

4. Researcher: The female arkbird will lay eggs only when a suitable quantity of nesting material is available and the climate is suitably moderate. This season, the arkbirds in our local habitat will be laying eggs because unusual temperature patterns have increased the amount of nesting material preferred by the arkbird.

5. The SML-1 is a test of computer programming abilities used by Human Resources departments to make hiring decisions and assess employees. The Cyvox Corporation reported an average score of 65 out of 100 for its job applicants. At Vectorcom Company, employees achieved an average score of 83—nearly 20 points higher than Cyvox. Therefore, Vectorcom's employees are better computer programmers than Cyvox's.

Answers are on pages 178–180.

Answers to Drill Set

Answers to Drill 9.1 — Diagramming Arguments

Below are sample diagrams; of course, yours may look really different. If you find that the sample diagrams make it easier to see the argument's flaws, then consider ways to modify your own diagramming.

1. Vytex's Weed Killer

Weed or plant? depends owner

∴ no perfect W-K b/c OD

© ∴ V's W-K will fail

This student used the abbreviation OD, which stands for *opinions differ*. It's not uncommon for an argument to have some kind of debate, so you might use *deb* or *OD* (or anything else you like, as long as you're consistent!) as your standard shorthand for "there is not a consensus on this issue."

Note that there are also two sets of therefore symbols. The student used the triangle dots to show a series of conclusions, then labeled the final conclusion with the © symbol.

If it is impossible to define what a weed is, then the argument is correct that it is impossible to develop a weed killer that will kill every type of weed. The argument assumes, though, that people don't actually agree on what is a weed and what is a plant. The argument also assumes that a *perfect weed killer* must kill every last type of weed. Perhaps customers would consider a product *perfect* if it kills the most common types of weeds for a particular climate or geographic area.

2. Overcrowded Parks

9

P crowd long waits

b/c S no park, ppl travel ⟶ Build P in S

[impl: reduce crowd]

The student uses S to mean *southern tip of the city*. Notice that this diagram shows a horizontal orientation, with the conclusion to the right, while the diagram for the first problem shows a more vertical orientation. You can use whichever orientation you like, but it's a good idea to be consistent in how you draw your diagrams.

The author assumes that if a new park is built at the southern tip, then the residents there won't travel to other parts of the city. What if, for example, these residents are visiting relatives who live in other areas of the city? Or what if their children play on sports teams that meet in the other parks?

Further, the argument never specifies the volume of southern residents traveling to other areas of the city; it says only that (some) residents do regularly travel to those existing parks. What if they make up only 1% of the people who use the existing parks? Reducing usage by 1% is unlikely to relieve overcrowding.

3. Van Hoyt College

VH: ≥ 1 RS/y for 10y

∴ VH = v. good

[valid metric?]

This student included a note in brackets; use brackets to denote weaknesses or assumptions that you brainstorm when reading the argument. In this case, the student is questioning whether the number of Rasmussen Scholars is actually an appropriate metric to determine that a school is a very good school. What if it is relatively easy to become a Rasmussen Scholar but most of Van Hoyt's students still can't qualify? Or, what if the school always chooses at least one Rasmussen Scholar every year, regardless of the quality of the students?

4. Arkbirds

R: A needs

1) nesting

AND } lay eggs

2) mod climate

Now: unusual temp → nesting → will lay eggs

[what about #2?]

The argument specifies that the arkbird requires two things in order to lay eggs. The first one, nesting materials, is present this season, but what about the second one? What are *unusual temperature patterns*?

The required *suitably moderate* climate is one that is relatively mild, neither too hot nor too cold. Unusual temperature patterns could be anything—they could be mild or too hot or too cold or varying wildly from day to day. It's not clear that *this season* actually fulfills the second requirement.

5. Vectorcom vs. Cyvox

SML: test of CP skill

C appl: 65/100
V empl: 83/100 → V empl > C empl

[empl? or appl??]

Be careful with the language on this one! Know which groups you need to compare. The argument provides data for Cyvox *applicants* and Vectorcom *employees*, then draws a conclusion about the employees of both companies. Perhaps Cyvox only hires the people who score the best on the SML-1 test. If so, it's possible that Cyvox employees actually have higher test scores, on average, than Vectorcom employees.

Chapter 10

of

GMAT Foundations of Verbal

Part 2: **Critical Reasoning**

Question Types & Trap Answers

In This Chapter…

Decoding the Question Stem

Trap Wrong Answers

Answers to Drill Sets

Chapter 10

Question Types & Trap Answers

You have spent all of the Critical Reasoning (CR) portion of this book so far discussing *arguments*. Of course, it is also crucially important to understand the question being asked about that argument.

People make a lot of mistakes when they don't pay enough attention to the question. Many times, a careless student will read an argument and pick an answer that seems to "go along" with the argument, but the answer does not do what the question specifically asks!

GMAT questions fall into a few broad categories:

Questions about assumptions: These include questions that ask directly about assumptions, as well as questions that ask you to strengthen and weaken arguments.

Questions about evidence: These questions might ask you to draw an inference or conclusion. Or they might ask you to resolve a discrepancy or a paradox (an apparent contradiction that may not really be contradictory).

Questions about structure: These questions will sometimes have two bold statements within the argument and ask you to pick the answer that tells the role of those two statements. Alternatively, a question might ask you how one person responds to another person's argument.

Decoding the Question Stem

The **question stem** will tell you what kind of question you have been asked. It's crucial, therefore, to learn how to decode the various question stems. The most common GMAT CR question types are discussed below; you can find a deeper discussion of these and other, less common question types in the Manhattan Prep *Critical Reasoning GMAT Strategy Guide.*

Here are some sample question stems for Assumption family questions.

1. The argument depends upon which of the following assumptions?

2. Which of the following, if true, most strongly supports the argument above?

3. Which of the following, if true, would most weaken the claim that Vectorcom's employees are better computer programmers than Cyvox's?

What is each question asking you to do?

1. The argument depends on which of the following assumptions?

This question asks directly about assumptions. It is important to deconstruct the argument, finding the premises and the conclusion and, if possible, brainstorming assumptions, before reading the answer choices. If you are able to brainstorm assumptions, the task of evaluating the answer choices will be easier.

For the Cyvox vs. Vectorcom argument from Drill 9.1, a correct assumption answer might read: "The average score for Cyvox's employees is not appreciably higher than the average score for all Cyvox applicants."

2. Which of the following, if true, most strongly supports the argument above?

This question asks you to strengthen the argument. To do so, you must know what the argument's assumptions are. The correct answer will be a new piece of information that does not have to be true, but if it is true, then the argument is strengthened.

For the Cyvox vs. Vectorcom argument from Drill 9.1, a correct strengthen answer might read: "The average score for applicants at a particular company is typically about the same as the average score for those who are eventually hired by that company."

Notice that this choice doesn't make the argument definitely true. Strengthen answers will rarely make the argument airtight. Rather, they will introduce a new piece of information that, if true, increases the likelihood that the conclusion is valid. If average applicant scores tend to be about the same as average employee scores, then it is more likely that the argument is valid.

3. Which of the following, if true, would most weaken the claim that Vectorcom's employees are better computer programmers than Cyvox's?

This question asks you to weaken the argument. To do so, you must know what the argument's assumptions are. The correct answer will be a new piece of information that does not have to be true, but if it is true, then the argument is weakened.

For the Cyvox vs. Vectorcom argument from Drill 9.1, a correct weaken answer might read: "The average score for applicants at a particular company is typically lower than the average score for those who are eventually hired by that company."

Notice that this choice doesn't make the argument definitely false. Weaken answers will rarely destroy the argument. Rather, they will introduce a new piece of information that, if true, increases the likelihood that the conclusion is bad. If average applicant scores tend to be lower than average employee scores, then this explains why Vectorcom would have higher employee scores than Cyvox's applicant scores, and this diminishes the advantage that the original argument seemed to assign to Vectorcom's employees. Here are sample question stems for the two Evidence family questions, along with descriptions of what each type is asking you to do.

4. Which of the following conclusions can most properly be drawn from the information above?

This question asks you to make an inference from the facts given in the argument. The argument itself will not contain a conclusion.

The test writers are not asking you to come up with one of the flawed conclusions that the assumption-type arguments contain. Rather, they are asking you to deduce, or to conclude something that must be true from the given information. For instance, if last month Meme Corporation both increased its price on its flagship product and sold more units of the product than it had in the prior month, then Meme corporation's revenues from this product must be higher last month than the month before.

5. Which of the following, if true, most helps to explain the surprising finding?

These questions ask you to explain some kind of contradiction or discrepancy in the information provided. For instance, Meme Corporation sold more units of a particular product this year than last year, but revenues for this product declined. They sold more but revenues went down? What could explain this strangeness? A correct answer might read: "Meme Corporation had to reduce the retail price of this product by 15% due to increased competition." Ah! Well, if they aren't making as much money on a per-product basis, then it's entirely possible for revenues to decline even if they sell more units.

In a paradox question (or a question that mentions a *contradiction* or *discrepancy*), there is always a perfectly reasonable explanation for something that looks like a contradiction or impossibility. Pay attention to the exact wording; the subtle differences are often what crack the problem open.

These five question types are among the most commonly tested on the GMAT. There are others, but you can wait to learn those when you feel you're ready to move to the *Critical Reasoning GMAT Strategy Guide*.

Drill 10.1 — Decoding the Question Stem

For each example, determine the question type. Which words most help you to make this determination?

1. Which of the following, if true, casts the most serious doubt on the politician's argument?

2. The consultant's statements, if true, best support which of the following conclusions?

3. Which of the following, if true, most helps to explain the apparent discrepancy between increasing incidence of fatal illness and the increased life expectancy among the same population?

4. The conclusion drawn above is based on the assumption that

5. Each of the following, if true, provides some support for hiring based in part on results of the personality test described EXCEPT:

Answers are on page 197.

Trap Wrong Answers

The GMAT is also going to try to make things tricky when you get to the answer choices. Sometimes, an incorrect answer is actually going to look *better* to you than the correct answer will look. How can you spot and avoid such traps?

First, understand how the GMAT set up the trap in the first place. If you understand how the trap works, you are much more likely to be able to avoid it.

A. Faulty Comparisons

You were first introduced to this idea during the Language Weaknesses discussion (under Flaws in Arguments) in chapter 8. Answer choices can make faulty comparisons, too! Consider some sample answers for this argument that you've seen before:

> A study of 120 elderly, hospital-bound patients in the United Kingdom showed that daily consumption of Nutree, a nutritional supplement containing vitamins, fiber, and sugar, increased by an average of four months the typical life expectancy for patients of the same age and physical condition. Thus, anyone who wants to live longer should drink Nutree every day.
>
> The argument depends upon which of the following assumptions regarding daily consumption of Nutree?
>
> (A) It is the top method for increasing life expectancy.
>
> (B) Among the people in the study, younger patients achieved a greater increase in life expectancy than older patients.
>
> (C) The demonstrated benefits are not limited to older, institutionalized patients.

One of the answers is correct, but the other two make some type of faulty comparison.

The study tested only elderly, hospital-bound patients, but the conclusion attempts to apply to everyone. The author is assuming, then, that the study results do actually apply to other groups of people than elderly, hospital-bound patients—a match for correct answer (C).

Relative vs. absolute: Answer (A) mistakes a relative statement for an absolute. Yes, Nutree has been shown to increase life expectancy for a certain group of people; in that sense, Nutree is a benefit or a good thing. Is it the *best* way to increase life expectancy? The argument provides no information to support this extreme statement.

When the argument provides evidence that something is good or better than another thing, that doesn't necessarily make it the best or only way, nor does it mean that you definitely want to do that good thing. Likewise, evidence that something is bad or worse than another thing doesn't make it the worst, nor does it mean that you definitely don't want to do that thing. Be careful not to draw an absolute conclusion when you have been given only relative information.

Note: On Critical Reasoning, don't automatically cross off an answer just because it contains an extreme word. Think through the logic. It's entirely possible that an argument would provide support for some kind of absolute outcome; if so, then an extreme word in the answer may be just fine. Check for proof in the text!

Irrelevant comparison or distinction: Answer (B) draws a distinction that is irrelevant for the given argument. The argument never distinguishes between the older and the younger patients in the study group. In particular, the GMAT might do this when the distinction would seem to make logical sense. After all, older patients are less likely to live as long just because they are *older*. If the argument doesn't make the distinction, though, then an answer choice that makes such a distinction is a trap.

B. Misinterpret the Argument

If you misread something in the argument, then you are, of course, going to have trouble answering that question correctly. One common mistake is to bring in outside or real-world knowledge and incorrectly interpret the conclusion.

For example:

> Tuition at Low-Ranked College is $500 per semester. Tuition at University of High Rank is $6,000 per semester. Therefore, if I go to Low-Ranked College, I will spend less money to earn my degree.
>
> Which of the following, if true, most seriously undermines the argument?
>
> (A) I'll get a worse education at Low-Ranked College.
>
> (B) University of High Rank students make an average of $35,000 a year, while students at Low-Ranked College make an average of $12,000 a year.
>
> (C) Fees and books cost $5,800 per semester at Low-Ranked College and $200 per semester at University of High Rank.

What's the trap? Many people interpret the conclusion as something like "I should go to Low-Ranked College" or "Low-Ranked College is the better choice." The argument does not say this, however. The argument says only that *if* you go, *then* you'll spend less money to earn your degree.

The trap here is to **articulate the wrong conclusion** to yourself. Don't bring in any real-world knowledge or baggage. Stick closely to the conclusion as written in the argument.

If you articulate the wrong conclusion here, then you might fall for trap answers (A) and (B). Both undermine the (wrong) conclusion that you should go to Low-Ranked College. Only answer (C) undermines the conclusion as given. According to this answer, you'll pay $6,300 per semester at Low-Ranked College and only $6,200 per semester at University of High Rank.

Try another:

> It is true that students who meditate at least once a week do better on the GMAT than those who never meditate. This finding does not show that meditation causes people to do better, since students who meditate are more likely than other students to have adequate time to study.

Which of the following, if true, most strongly supports the argument above?

(A) A person who meditates but has little time to study is more likely to give up other activities to allow more study time than a person who does not meditate and also has little time to study.

(B) Among people who meditate, the more frequent the meditation, the better that person does on the test, on average.

(C) Among the students who have adequate time to study, those who do not meditate do just as well on the test as those who do meditate.

In this case, the author has set up the argument to try to get you to misidentify the conclusion. What's the trap?

The author acknowledges a fact: *students who meditate ate least once a week do better on the GMAT than those who never meditate.* The tricky part is the beginning of the next sentence: *This finding does **not** show that meditation causes people to do better.*

Yes, that word is bolded, underlined, and italicized. This is the trap! Many people have already assumed that the *it is true* language means that there is a causal relationship, but the author says that there is *not* a causal relationship. Rather, according to the author, there is some other reason why these two things happen together.

If you get this conclusion wrong, then you're going to be supporting, or strengthening, the wrong argument. Indeed, trap answers (A) and (B) both support the mistaken conclusion that regular meditation causes someone to do better on the test. These are the opposite of the correct answer.

Answer (C) indicates that the key is having enough time to study in the first place. If you do, then it doesn't matter as much whether you do or do not meditate. In this scenario, perhaps people who meditate have more time on average to study because they just have more free time in general. After all, they have the time to meditate at least once a week. Therefore, answer choice (C) is correct.

Finally, did you note that incorrect answer (B) also tossed in an irrelevant comparison? The argument compares never meditating to meditating at least once a week. It doesn't distinguish between those who meditate a little and those who meditate a lot.

The wording of a question stem might also cause you to articulate the wrong conclusion. For instance, what if the Low-Ranked College question had asked:

Which of the following, if true, most seriously supports a claim that a degree from Low-Ranked College will not cost less than a degree from University of High Rank?

Say what? That sentence is seriously confusing! The question stem gives a different conclusion than the one in the argument: in this case, the question stem claims that a degree from Low-Ranked College will not cost less, and you're asked to support this claim. This is the same thing as undermining the original conclusion given in the argument. If you support, or undermine, the wrong conclusion, you're going to get the question wrong.

Another common mistake is to misinterpret the question stem, or simply to get turned around, and **answer the wrong question**. It can be easy during the stress of the test to get turned around; make sure that you write down S for Strengthen or W for Weaken (or some similar abbreviations) so that you don't mistakenly pick a Weaken answer when the question asked you to Strengthen.

C. Superficial Word Matches

Have you ever had this happen? You narrow down to two answer choices but you don't know how to choose between them. One of them feels better, though, because many of the words in the answer choice match directly with language from the argument, while the other one doesn't match so exactly. So you pick the one that "matches" better . . . and later you discover that you fell into a trap.

If the GMAT made every correct answer feel like a perfect fit, then way too many people would be answering hard questions correctly. How do they get you to cross off the right answer or at least contemplate doing so?

Try this problem out; when you're done, see if you can articulate why the correct answer is designed to sound less good than at least one of the wrong answers:

> Researcher: People who study for 30 minutes a day aren't as likely to reach their goal score on the GMAT as those whose study sessions last 90 minutes a day. But those who study for more than 5 hours a day are less likely to reach their goal score on the GMAT than those who study for less than 5 hours a day. So everyone should study for more than 90 minutes a day but less than 5 hours a day.
>
> Which of the following, if true, most seriously weakens the conclusion above?
>
> (A) In some cases, daily study periods of an hour are sufficient to allow the student to achieve his or her preferred result.
>
> (B) The length or quantity of a student's study is less important than the quality of that study.
>
> (C) When studying is split among multiple sessions in a day, taking a break of 90 minutes or more between sessions can result in a failure to reach one's goal score.

Did you spot the trap or fall into it?

Let's start with trap answer (B). It might be true that quality of study is more important than quantity of study, but the argument addresses only length of study. This choice makes an irrelevant distinction between two types of study, one of which is never addressed in the argument.

The next trap answer is (C). Look at all the exact language matches: *sessions* [in] *a day, 90 minutes, reach* [one's] *goal score.* So what's the problem?

The 90 minutes referred to here is not the same 90 minutes referred to in the argument. In the answer, the 90 minutes represents a break, not study time. It's possible for someone to study for 15 minutes, take a 2-hour break, and then study for another 15 minutes. It's also possible for someone to study for 90 minutes, take a 90-minute break, and then study for another 90 minutes. According to the argument data, the first person studied a non-optimal length of time and the second person studied an optimal length, yet both match the language in trap answer (C): they split their studies into multiple sessions and took breaks of 90 minutes.

Why is it tempting to eliminate correct answer (A)? First, it uses some synonyms instead of direct language matches: *daily* instead of *a day*; study *periods* instead of study *sessions*; *preferred result* instead of *goal score.* All of these are valid synonyms, though: they mean the same thing! Further, this choice talks about a one-hour time frame, which is not mentioned in the argument.

Logically, though, the information about this one-hour time frame does weaken the argument! If some people can reach their goal scores by studying only one hour a day, then the claim that *everyone* should study at least 90 minutes a day is weakened. By contrast, trap answer (C) doesn't fit logically, since anyone studying any length of time could take 90-minute breaks.

Dealing with the superficial word match trap is tricky, since sometimes the correct answer really does match the language of the argument. Your first line of defense is to think about the actual logic of the information and how it fits with the argument. When this doesn't work, though, and you find yourself with two answers that both seem okay, one with exact language matches and one with synonyms, take two steps:

1. Check the synonyms to make sure that they're valid based on the information given in the argument. If not, eliminate this choice.
2. If the synonyms are all valid, guess this choice, on the theory that the trap is to get someone to fall for the other answer: superficial word matches with faulty logic.

Drill 10.2 — Spotting the Trap Answers

Test out what you've just learned. Give yourself approximately two minutes per question to try each of the full Critical Reasoning problems in this set. Note: You have seen some of the arguments before.

1. For the violence in Kirkenberg to be stopped, the majority of surrounding nations must vote to send in a peacekeeping force, and the wealthy nation of Nandia must provide funding. If Nandia becomes involved in any way regarding Kirkenberg, at least half of the nations surrounding Kirkenberg will vote against intervening in Kirkenberg.

   The claims above most strongly support which of the following conclusions?

   (A) Nandia is the wealthiest nation in the region surrounding Kirkenberg.

   (B) Violence in Kirkenberg is likely to result in unrest in other countries in the region.

   (C) It is unlikely that the violence in Kirkenberg will be stopped.

   (D) Most nations surrounding Kirkenberg oppose the current leadership in Nandia.

   (E) The peacekeeping forces would not have sufficient equipment without financial support from Nandia.

2. The Urban Apartment Towers complex has seen a number of police visits to the property recently, resulting in the police breaking up loud parties held by young residents and attended by other young people. These circumstances are hurting the complex's reputation and ability to attract new residents. To reduce the number of police visits and improve profitability, management plans to advertise its vacant apartments in a local publication for people aged 50 and up.

   Which of the following, if true, would cast the most doubt regarding the effectiveness of the management's plan?

   (A) No recent police visits to Urban Apartment Towers have been to the apartments of residents over the age of 50.

   (B) A substantially cheaper apartment complex may be built in a neighboring town.

   (C) Residents over the age of 50 are more likely to call police in circumstances in which young people would not call.

   (D) A nearby condominium complex of similar size had far fewer police visits last year than Urban Apartment Towers.

   (E) Relative to young people, people over 50 are much more likely to host parties with fewer than 10 guests

3. Lexton University began offering Biology 101 courses online as well as in a traditional classroom setting. Students in all sections of the course were given the same final exam. On average, the students in the online sections received higher scores on the final exam than students in the traditional classroom-based sections. Therefore, the students in the online sections learned more about biology than did students in the classroom-based sections.

   The argument above is based on which of the following assumptions?

   (A) Final exam scores accurately represent how much students learned about biology.

   (B) Most current Lexton students report that they would be interested in taking some but not all of their courses online.

   (C) Students from Burbain College who took only online accounting courses scored better on the accounting licensing exam than students who took only traditional classroom-based accounting courses.

   (D) Lexton University should begin offering other introductory courses online.

   (E) In post-course surveys, the students enrolled in the online sections reported studying an average of two more hours per week than students in the classroom-based sections.

4. A plastics factory next to Hullson River dumps its waste, which contains toxin A, directly into the river. The amount of waste the factory dumps into the river is directly proportional to the amount of plastic the factory produces. This year the factory produced 50% more plastic than last year. Yet, measurements taken 50 yards downstream of the toxic dump site show that concentrations of toxin A were significantly lower than they were at the same site last year.

Which of the following, if true, does the most to explain the surprising finding?

(A) The factory is considering adopting a production technique that would drastically reduce the amount of toxin A produced.

(B) Unseasonably heavy rains have increased the volume of water in Hullson River by 75%.

(C) In studies, high concentrations of toxin A in water have been shown to inhibit certain species of fish from laying eggs.

(D) When the plastic factory produces more plastic, the concentration of toxin A within the waste dumped into the river increases.

(E) Another factory, located upstream from the plastics factory, produces waste containing toxin B and dumps that waste into the river.

5. In Mountain Village, the frequency of bears entering residential neighborhoods has recently increased due to a shortage of food in the forest in which the bears live. In order to track the location of these bear visits, Mountain Village has set up a special phone number that residents are asked to call if they see a bear in a residential neighborhood.

   Which of the following, if true, most strongly supports the claim that the plan will have its intended effect?

   (A) A neighboring town decreased bear entries into residential neighborhoods by installing trash cans with specially designed lids that bears cannot open.

   (B) The new phone number that residents are asked to call has not been widely publicized.

   (C) Bears generally pose no threat to humans although they may behave aggressively toward small domestic animals.

   (D) Residents have been educated as to how to scare the bears away without making them more aggressive.

   (E) Bears generally enter residential neighborhoods during the daytime hours when many residents are outside.

Answers are on pages 197–201

Answers to Drill Sets

Answers to Drill 10.1 — Decoding the Question Stem

1. *Weaken* (*cast doubt* is a synonym for weaken).

2. *Inference.* Careful! The word *support* makes this seem like a strengthen question. Note what you're supporting though: one of *the following conclusions.* Where are those conclusions located? In the answer choices! You'll need to infer, or deduce, what must be true from the information given in the argument.

3. *Explain a discrepancy.* Pick the answer that resolves the discrepancy by providing a reasonable explanation for what looked, at first, like a contradiction.

4. *Assumption.* The question asks you to find something that the author assumes in drawing his conclusion in the argument above.

5. *Strengthen (EXCEPT).* This is a tricky one. In this case, the word *support* does signal a Strengthen question because the question itself tells you the conclusion to support (you should base part of your hiring decision on this personality test!). If a question asks you to support a conclusion given in the argument or question stem, then it is a Strengthen question. If a questions asks you to support a conclusion given in the answer choices, then it is an Inference question.

In addition, this is an EXCEPT question. Four of the answers will strengthen the conclusion; these four answers are all wrong. One answer will *not* strengthen the conclusion. This answer will not necessarily weaken the conclusion; it might do nothing at all to the conclusion. This answer is the correct one.

Answers to Drill 10.2 — Spotting the Trap Answers

1. **(C).** You first saw this argument in Chapter 8.

The question asks you to support a conclusion found in the answer choices, so this is an Inference problem.

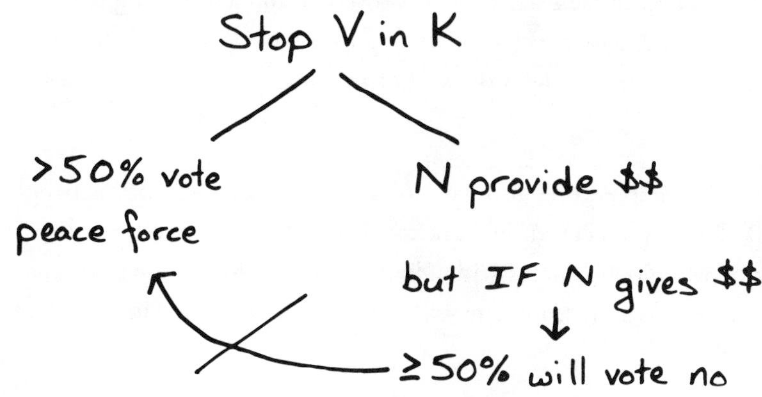

In order for the violence to stop, two things must happen: (1) at least 50% of surrounding nations have to vote to send in a peacekeeping force, *and* (2) Nandia has to provide funding. But, if Nandia does actually provide that funding, then *at least half* of the other nations will vote against sending in the peacekeeping force.

What must be true, given this information? On the one hand, Kirkenberg needs funding from Nandia. On the other, if it gets that funding, then it won't have 50% or greater support from the surrounding nations for the peacekeeping force. Things don't look good for Kirkenberg. Answer (C) is correct: it looks pretty unlikely that the violence in Kirkenberg can be stopped.

Answer (A) goes too far with the word *wealthiest*. Nandia is described only as *wealthy*, not the *wealthiest*. Answer (B) goes beyond the scope of the argument; no information is provided as to what may be going on in other countries.

Answers (D) and (E) both introduce information that goes beyond what the argument discusses. On Inference questions, stick tightly to the information presented. Don't bring in outside information. Answer (D) talks about the *current leadership* and answer (E) talks about *equipment*, neither of which is addressed in the argument.

2. **(C).** You first saw this argument in Chapter 9.

The question asks you to *cast doubt* on the plan, or weaken the argument.

Young: loud parties, police

hurting UAT

Plan: target 50+ yrs ⟶ ↓ police, ↑ profit

What is the plan? There have been a bunch of loud parties held and attended by young people and the police have been called. The complex is getting a bad reputation and having trouble attracting new residents. The plan is to *advertise to people aged 50 and up* in order to *reduce the number of police visits and improve profitability*. What assumptions is the author making and how might these assumptions weaken the argument?

The author assumes older people won't also have loud parties; however, maybe people over 50 have the loudest parties of all. That would certainly weaken the argument. The author also assumes older people are going to want to move into a complex with a bad reputation for loud parties and police visits. The part about profitability is also a big leap: why will having older residents improve profitability?

If older people do move in, and they are also more likely to call the police over various issues, as answer (C) states, then bringing in older residents makes it less likely that management's plan to reduce the number of police visits is going to work.

If answer (A) is true, it might actually *strengthen* the assumption that older people don't have loud parties. Answer (B) doesn't address the management's plan for Urban Apartment Towers specifically.

Answer (D) is a faulty comparison: the size might be similar, but the residents' ages might be far different, the layout of the complex might be different enough to minimize noise, and so on.

Answer (E) matches a lot of the language from the argument, but the meaning of those words is off. Plus, if anything, this might actually strengthen the argument by showing that older people typically have smaller parties (though you'd also have to assume that smaller parties are quieter parties, which isn't a given).

3. **(A).** This is a brand-new argument.

The question asks you to identify an assumption made by the author.

Bio 101: online or trad

online exam > trad exam ⟶ Ⓒ online learned more

[maybe already knew more?]

LU offers the same class both online and in a traditional classroom. On the final exam, the online students did better than the others. The argument concludes that the online students learned more during the course. What is the author assuming?

She assumes that a higher final exam score actually means they learned more during the course. Maybe, for some reason, those students knew more about biology before the class started. Maybe they're better at taking tests in general. Maybe they cheated!

Answer (A) matches the assumption.

Answers (B) and (D) don't address the actual events that occurred. Note that (D) follows from the conclusion: if it really is the case that people learn better online, then maybe it would be a good idea for Lexton to offer more online classes. The question didn't ask this, though; the question asked you to find an assumption used to draw the conclusion.

Answer (C) is an irrelevant comparison. While it might be the case that data from another college showing that students learned more from an online course would help the argument, note that this choice does not actually say the online Burbain students learned more in their accounting course. The choice shows the same data that Lexton presented: certain students did better on an exam, but who knows why they did better?

Answer (E) sounds good. If the online students studied two more hours per week, then it makes sense that they did better. But this is a trap; the choice is too specific. Remember, the question asked: What is the author assuming to be true? The author does not have to assume that the students studied an average of two hours more, specifically. They could have studied one hour more on average or three hours more on average, or any other number. The online students could even have studied less if they studied more efficiently!

4. **(B).** This is another new argument.

The question asks you to explain a *surprising finding*. This is an Explain a Discrepancy question.

waste (with A) ⟶ river

> plastic = > waste; +50% plastic this yr

BUT conc of A much lower?? How?

The plastics factory dumps waste, including toxin A, straight into the river. It produced more plastic this year so, according to the argument, it should also be dumping more waste. But measurements show that there's a lot less toxin A in the river this year than last year. How come?

The argument doesn't say that the amount of toxin A produced is directly proportional to the waste produced. Maybe the factory did have more waste but it changed something in its manufacturing process (or something else) and that reduced how much toxin A was produced? Or maybe the equipment used to measure the toxin levels changed or is faulty somehow?

It turns out to be another explanation entirely. Answer (B) indicates that it's been raining a lot, which significantly increased the amount of water in the river. The argument says that the concentration levels were measured, or the percentage of toxin A in the water. But if the water volume is much higher, then the *concentration* levels could go down even if there's just as much (or more!) toxin A in the water this year as last year. If you add a teaspoon of salt to a cup of water, that water is going to taste a lot saltier than if you added a teaspoon of salt to a gallon of water.

Answer (A) might explain a *future* reduction in toxin A, but the argument is discussing what has already happened. Answers (C) and (E) are irrelevant; you need to explain the surprising info about toxin A, not something about fish laying eggs or anything about toxin B.

Answer (D) might look good because it matches a lot of the language from the passage, but be careful! It is actually the opposite of what you need. If it's the case that more production of plastic leads to more toxin A, then the finding that the concentrations have decreased is even more surprising. Your task is not to show why something is surprising. Your task is to explain, or to resolve, that discrepancy.

5. **(E).** This is another new argument.

The question asks you to strengthen the plan. What is that plan?

↓ food → ↑ bears in nbrhd

Plan: call phone # → track location

Because of a food shortage, a lot more bears are coming into the neighborhoods (abbreviation: *nbrhd*). The village is asking people to call in when they see a bear so that the village can track the location of the bears.

What is the author assuming? First, the author assumes that people will actually see the bears. What if they hide among the trees and bushes or only come out at night? Second, the author assumes that people will pick up the phone and call. Perhaps the residents just don't care.

Answer (E) fits one of the assumptions: if the bears come during the daytime hours and residents are often outside at that time, then it's more likely that they'll actually see the bears.

Answer (A) goes after the wrong conclusion. The village isn't trying to stop the bears from coming (at least not yet). The stated goal is just to track the location of the bears. Answer (D) is similarly tempting: if you run into a bear, it would definitely be helpful to know how to scare it off! This still isn't the goal of the plan, though.

Answer (B) weakens the argument; if people don't know the number, how can they call, even if they see a bear?

Answer (C) might explain why the village wants to track the bears' locations, but it does not address whether the plan will work.

Chapter 11

of

GMAT Foundations of Verbal

Part 2: **Critical Reasoning**

Putting It All Together

In This Chapter...

Critical Reasoning "Hints" Drill
Critical Reasoning Wrap-Up
Answers to Drill Set

Chapter 11

Putting It All Together

You've learned a lot about how to handle Critical Reasoning (CR). It's time to put it all together in a full drill set of questions.

This set is designed both to test you on what you've learned and to stretch your brain some. Some of the question types are ones that you learned in the preceding chapters. Others are types you haven't learned about yet! Do your best and consider this your introduction to the next level of CR study: the Manhattan Prep *Critical Reasoning GMAT Strategy Guide*, where you will learn about the full set of CR question types, including strategies for deconstructing complicated arguments, eliminating trap answers, and identifying tricky correct answers.

Critical Reasoning "Hints" Drill

The following drill contains 10 Critical Reasoning questions, representing a variety of question types.

Every problem is followed by one or more hints; cover up these hints with a piece of paper. If you don't feel you need a hint, then go ahead and answer the question.

If you do want a hint, read them one at a time. If you don't need them all, don't use them all! Read only as much as you need to have an idea of what to do next.

Answers begin on page 214.

Question #1

President of Teachers' Union: **Many people are convinced that declining test scores in our district are the fault of teachers.** Yet, our school district has recently seen a large influx of enrolling students who do not speak any English at all. Nearby districts that have seen a similar influx of students who do not speak English have all experienced much larger drops in test scores. It is a testament to the skill and dedication of our teachers that test scores in our district have dropped so little.

The bold statement in the argument plays which of the following roles?

(A) It is the main conclusion of the argument.
(B) It is a finding that the argument seeks to explain.
(C) It introduces an explanation that the argument seeks to refute.
(D) It provides support for the main conclusion of the argument.
(E) It is a judgment that the argument corroborates.

HINT #1: Try to answer this question in your own words before you read the answer choices. In order to do so, it will help to diagram.

HINT #2: Try to label each piece of information using the CR building block categories.

HINT #3: What is the conclusion? How does the boldface information relate to the conclusion?

Question #2

The drug Nephoprene has been proven to help certain harmful medical conditions, but it also has serious side effects. Doctors are responsible for weighing the benefits of a drug against the possible harm to the patient from side effects, and most doctors have chosen not to prescribe Nephoprene even to patients who would experience benefits.

The considerations given best serve as part of an argument that

(A) Nephoprene will not cure patients
(B) most doctors have determined that the side effects of Nephoprene outweigh the benefits
(C) patients who want to take Nephoprene are not able to obtain prescriptions for it
(D) not all patients with medical conditions that can be helped by Nephoprene will actually experience benefits when taking it
(E) most drugs have some side effects, whether mild or more serious

HINT #1: *The considerations given best serve as part of an argument that* indicates that the answer choices contain an argument. The word argument is a synonym for conclusion.

HINT #2: If the answers contain conclusions, then the question is an Inference question.

HINT #3: On Inference questions, your task is to find an answer that must be true based on the information from the argument.

Question #3

A candidate for governor has suggested repealing the state law requiring cigarette advertisers to print a warning label about the dangers of smoking on every cigarette pack, and instead requiring cigarette manufacturers to publish recent data and studies about the dangers of smoking on websites that the manufacturers will create for this purpose. The candidate argues that the plan will provide consumers with more detailed information so that they may make better decisions about smoking.

The argument assumes which of the following?

(A) It is harder to break an addiction to alcohol than to cigarettes.
(B) Consumers are willing and able to visit the websites and evaluate the data and studies presented.
(C) Competing candidates for governor have not introduced the same or a superior plan relating to cigarette warnings.
(D) Most people are not able to break their addictions to cigarettes.
(E) Smoking will become more popular if this plan is not enacted.

HINT #1: This is an assumption question.

HINT #2: Your task on assumption questions is to find something that fills the gap between the author's premises and the author's conclusion. What is the author assuming to be true in drawing his conclusion?

HINT #3: This argument is a plan. In general, the author assumes the plan will work as stated. What are the weak points in the plan?

Question #4

Researchers have noted that panda bears that have given birth to live young live longer in the wild. Therefore, these researchers have concluded that giving birth to live young increases a panda's lifespan.

The argument makes which of the following assumptions?

(A) Pandas that have given birth to live young will not be killed by predators.
(B) Since male pandas cannot give birth, female pandas live longer than male pandas.
(C) Pandas that are already likely to live longer are not more likely to give birth to live young.
(D) Female pandas are not likely to die while giving birth.
(E) Pandas that have given birth to multiple live young are likely to live even longer than pandas that have given birth to only a single live offspring.

HINT #1: This is an Assumption question.

HINT #2: Your task on Assumption questions is to find something that fills the gap between the author's premises and the author's conclusion. What is the author assuming to be true in drawing his or her conclusion?

HINT #3: In the sequence of events, what causes what?

Question #5

Newspaper editorial: It is important that penalties for drug dealing on school grounds remain extremely severe. If the penalties became less severe, more students would become addicted to drugs.

Which of the following is an assumption that supports drawing the conclusion above from the reason given for that conclusion?

(A) Drug dealers are already being deterred from drug dealing on school grounds due to the penalties currently in place.
(B) Drug use is harmful to the academic careers of students.
(C) Drug dealing on school grounds is punished more harshly than drug dealing off school grounds.
(D) Those who deal drugs on school grounds are not students at those schools.
(E) There is a significant chance that some of those addicted to drugs will ultimately die from drug-related causes.

HINT #1: This is an Assumption question.

HINT #2: Your task on assumption questions is to find something that fills the gap between the author's premises and the author's conclusion. Can you brainstorm anything that the author is assuming to be true?

Question #6

In the last 10 years, usage of pay phones in Bridgeport has dropped by 90%. Since cell phone usage is much higher among middle- and upper-income residents of Bridgeport than among lower-income residents, the Bridgeport City Council has decided to remove pay phones from middle- and upper-income neighborhoods, while retaining those in lower-income neighborhoods, reasoning that this plan will respond appropriately to demand for pay phones and thereby inconvenience very few people.

Which of the following, if true, would most strongly support the claim the plan to retain pay phones in lower-income neighborhoods only will have the intended effect?

(A) In certain areas, pay phone usage has dropped only 50% to 60% over the past 10 years.
(B) Middle-income residents are more likely to use pay phones than high-income residents.
(C) Some lower-income residents do use cell phones.
(D) People who need a pay phone are most likely to use one within two miles of their home.
(E) Eliminating pay phones would save the city money.

HINT #1: This is a Strengthen question.

HINT #2: Your goal on Strengthen questions is to find a new piece of information that, if true, would make the conclusion at least a little more likely to be valid.

HINT #3: Can you brainstorm any assumptions before looking at the answer choices?

Question #7

The Orange Corporation is conducting market research in preparation for the launch of its new device, the 3-D eSlate. Thus far, in Orange's market research, two groups have emerged as likely buyers of the eSlate: medical professionals and people making more than $250,000 a year. Since the number of medical professionals in the target market plus the number of people making more than $250,000 a year in the target market is over 20 million people, and since Orange typically achieves a sales rate of 25% or more in its target markets, Orange will sell over 5 million units of the eSlate.

Which of the following, if true, would most weaken the author's conclusion?

(A) Nearly 45% of medical professionals in the target market have already purchased a similar product from a competitor.
(B) The eSlate has many more uses for education professionals than for medical professionals.
(C) Many people with astigmatism and other vision problems will have trouble using the 3-D features of the eSlate.
(D) Many medical professionals make more than $250,000 a year.
(E) People who make more than $250,000 a year buy more electronic devices than people who make less than $250,000 a year.

HINT #1: This is a Weaken question.

HINT #2: Your task is to find a new piece of information that, if true, will make the argument a little less likely to be valid. You do not need to destroy the argument.

HINT #3: What is the argument assuming? What do the numbers tell you and what *don't* they tell you?

Question #8

A study of full-time employees in Langlia revealed that female workers take more days off from work due to illness than do male workers. The same study also revealed that female workers are more likely than male workers to go into work when they are sick.

Which of the following conclusions can most properly be drawn from the information above?

(A) Langlian employers prefer that sick employees stay home so as to avoid infecting others.
(B) Childbearing and related medical conditions are responsible for the increase in sick days among Langlian female workers.
(C) In Langlia, both male and female workers sometimes call in sick when they are actually healthy.
(D) In Langlia, female workers are sick on more work days than male workers.
(E) Female workers in Langlia are more conscientious about their jobs than are male workers.

HINT #1: This is an Inference question.

HINT #2: The correct answer to an Inference question will be something that must be true given the information in the argument.

Question #9

This year, the Rocktown school district offered a free summer enrichment program called "History Rocks" to its rising fourth-grade students. Therefore, fourth graders in the Rocktown school district will score better this year on American history tests.

Each of the following, if true, would strengthen the author's conclusion EXCEPT:

(A) "History Rocks" focuses entirely on American history.
(B) The majority of the district's rising fourth graders attended the program.
(C) For the past five years, Rocktown students have scored lower, on average, on American history tests than have students in neighboring towns.
(D) The material on fourth-grade history tests in Rocktown is substantially similar to the material being covered in the enrichment program.
(E) It has been proven that students retain knowledge better when learning one subject at a time, as is the case in the "History Rocks" program.

HINT #1: This is a bit of a weird question type: it's asking you what does *not* strengthen the conclusion. What kind of answer would fit the bill?

HINT #2: The four wrong answers should strengthen the conclusion. The correct answer should either weaken it or do nothing to it.

Question #10

Over the past three decades, the number of hospital beds available for inpatient psychiatric treatment in the United States has declined from 4 per 1,000 population to 1.3 per 1,000 population. Over the same period in Japan, beds increased from 1 per 1,000 population to 2.9 per 1,000 population. Also during this period, annual mortality rates for persons with mental disorders have risen substantially in the United States, while declining in Japan.

Which of the following, if true, would cast the most serious doubt on the conclusion that the reduction in hospital beds is principally responsible for the increase in mortality in the United States?

(A) The number of hospital beds available for inpatient psychiatric treatment in Canada has declined over the past three decades, with no increase in mortality.

(B) Due to advances in medical care and training over the past three decades, outpatient treatment is more effective than inpatient treatment for many mental disorders.

(C) The incidence of mental disorders in Japan has been decreasing, even as the country has increased the number of beds available for inpatient psychiatric treatment.

(D) Over the past three decades, Japan has offered state-sponsored health insurance to all citizens, while the United States has not.

(E) Over the past three decades, the incidence of mental disorders that are more likely to end in death has risen in the United States and declined in Japan.

HINT #1: This is a Weaken question.

HINT #2: Your task on Weaken questions is to find an answer that makes the argument less likely to be valid.

HINT #3: When the question stem contains specific information about the argument, that information typically either is the conclusion or is referring to the conclusion.

Critical Reasoning Wrap-Up

Congratulations! You have made it all the way through the Critical Reasoning portion of this book.

When you're ready, access the online Question Banks associated with this book. You'll gain additional practice with GMAT-style Critical Reasoning problems that were designed to help you improve your performance.

Our *Critical Reasoning GMAT Strategy Guide* is highly recommended for continued study. This guide has much, much more to say about particular question types in Critical Reasoning, and includes more specific methods of argument diagramming and ways to eliminate tricky wrong answers. In conjunction with the strategy guide, you'll also want to practice problems from the *Official Guide* books, which contain real past GMAT questions.

Now, you can proceed to the third and final topic area of this book: Reading Comprehension.

Answers to Drill Set

Answers to Drill 11.1 — Putting It All Together

Note: Sample diagrams are shown for each problem. The abbreviations used may vary in order to illustrate multiple styles in which different people might diagram arguments.

1. **(C).**

↓ scores → T fault

P: BUT >> S can't speak E

sim schools: ↓↓ scores

Ⓒ our T: drop is less!

This question type was not presented earlier in the guide, but it asks about the building blocks that you learned about in Chapter 8.

When the question asks you to "describe the role" of a particular boldface statement, first find the conclusion of the argument. Then, see how the boldface statement relates to that conclusion.

The president of the union claims that, in fact, the test results are good. Other districts with similar student bodies had even bigger drops in test scores. How does the boldface statement relate to this claim?

The boldface statement claims that the declining test scores are a problem and the fault of the teachers; this goes against the president's claim. The correct answer, then, is not (A), (D), or (E), which all support the conclusion.

Between (B) and (C), the key is whether the argument is trying to *explain* or *refute* the boldface information. Since the argument actively goes against what the boldface statement claims, the correct answer is (C).

2. **(B).**

N = helpful but bad SE

most D: no N, even when helps

The wording of the question stem indicates that the answer choices contain an *argument,* or conclusion. If the answer choices contain a conclusion, then this is an Inference question. On Inference questions, your task is to find something that must be true according to the information given in the argument.

If doctors are responsible for weighing the benefits against the side effects and most decide not to prescribe Nephoprene, these doctors must have decided that the benefits were not worth the side effects. Answer (B) is a match.

Choice (A) is a good trap: if Nephoprene did cure patients, then wouldn't the doctors prescribe it even if it had bad side effects? Not necessarily. What if the side effect is to cause a heart attack that may kill the patient?

Answer (C) may or may not be true; the argument says only that most doctors don't prescribe Nephoprene.

Answers (D) and (E) are probably true about drugs in general, but this particular argument does not provide evidence to support either answer.

3. **(B).**

C: stop warning on pack

move to web

© > dtl ⟶ better decision

[too much dtl ?]

On Assumption questions, your task is to find the answer that plugs the gap between one of the premises and the conclusion. What is this author assuming to be true, but not stating outright?

In this case, the argument makes many assumptions:

> That people make smoking decisions rationally (not based on addiction or other personal preferences)
> That people will visit the website
> That people will be able to understand the information presented on the website

Answer (B) matches with the second and third assumptions listed above. Answers (A) and (C) both make irrelevant distinctions; alcohol addiction is not at issue, nor are competing plans from other candidates.

Answer (D) is a potential reason why the plan might not help people to break the addiction, but this is not what the question asked! Make sure you're answering the right question. Answer (E) is out of scope; the general popularity of smoking is not addressed.

4. **(C).**

wild P live baby, live longer

∴ live baby → live longer

[causation?]

On Assumption questions, your task is to find the answer that reflects something the author assumes to be true in order to draw his or her conclusion.

The author assumes that one thing causes another: that giving birth to live young causes the panda to live longer. Perhaps it's the case that the pandas who are healthier in the first place are more likely both to give birth to live young and to live longer.

Answer (C) correctly articulates the author's assumption, though the negative language is tricky. The author assumes that pandas that are likely to live longer in general are *not* also more likely to give birth to live young. This has to be assumed in order to conclude that giving birth to live young causes a panda to live longer.

Answers (A) and (D) explain why these female pandas live as long as or longer than other female pandas, but since it is a fact that pandas that have given birth to live young live longer, these answers don't really have an impact on the argument.

Answer (B) refers to male pandas, but the argument is only about female pandas; this distinction is irrelevant.

Answer (E) might be a good answer if you were asked to strengthen the conclusion, but this information about multiple vs. single births is an irrelevant comparison. The conclusion doesn't hinge upon the number of live births, just whether the panda has given live birth at all.

5. **(A).**

↓ pen → ↑ addict S

∴ keep severe pen

[when not at school?]

On assumption questions, your task is to find the answer that reflects something the author assumes to be true in order to draw his or her conclusion. Here are some assumptions in the argument:

- The students will take the drugs.
- The students have money to buy the drugs.
- At least some students who take the drugs will become addicted.
- Drug dealers are aware of and deterred by different levels of penalties in different situations.

Answer (A) is a very close match with the last idea. The argument certainly does assume that drug dealers care about what the penalties are—it assumes that the current high penalties are keeping drug dealers away, and that lower penalties would increase their activities.

Answers (B) and (E) are reasonable to believe, but the argument says nothing about academic work or death.

Answer (C) has a similar problem. The argument addresses only drug dealing on school grounds; comparing this situation to drug dealing off of school grounds is irrelevant.

The argument does not make any assumptions about who is dealing the drugs, so answer (D) is out of scope.

6. **(D).**

B: PP use ↓ 90% → remove PP M+U

M+U cell >> L cell keep PP L (meet demand)

On Strengthen questions, your job is to find something that would make the argument more likely to be valid. The correct answer does not have to make the argument definitely true.

What does the author assume in drawing the conclusion that dropping pay phones from middle- and upper-income neighborhoods while leaving them in lower-income neighborhoods will be the best way to meet *demand* and *inconvenience very few people*?

First, the author assumes that there is some correlation between cell phone usage and pay phone usage. Those who don't use cell phones as much, the reasoning goes, are more likely to use pay phones. (Note the vagueness of the phrase *cell phone usage*. Are lower-income residents less likely to have phones at all? Or do they just use their phones less?)

The author also assumes that people are most likely to want to use pay phones in their own neighborhoods (as opposed to, say, traveling to an area with lousy cell phone reception, where a pay phone might be someone's only option!).

Answer (D) matches the assumption that the lower-income residents are using pay phones close to home.

Answer (A) is tempting but it's a trap. The choice doesn't indicate *where* these statistics apply! If usage has dropped 90% overall but only 50%–60% in upper-income neighborhoods, then the conclusion is actually weakened.

Answer (B) makes an irrelevant distinction—in order to evaluate this argument, you don't need any data splitting the upper- and middle-income groups from each other.

The argument doesn't assume that no lower-income residents use cell phones; it only requires that their usage is lower. Answer (C) is incorrect.

Answer (E) addresses the wrong conclusion! The question is not whether the plan is a good idea in general or whether the city should implement the plan. Rather, the conclusion states that following the plan will meet demand and avoid inconveniencing people; these considerations have nothing to do with whether the city will save money.

7. **(D).**

1) MP
2) > $250k/y   1+2 > 20m ppl

© if 1/4 buy ⟶ > 5m units sold
[math right?]

On Weaken questions, your job is to find an answer that will make the argument at least somewhat less likely to be valid. The correct answer will not usually completely invalidate the argument.

Did you discover any assumptions in the argument, particularly with respect to those numbers?

The company is targeting two markets: medical professionals and people who make more than $250,000 a year. Do those two groups have any overlap? For example, what if 1 million medical professionals also make more than $250,000 a year? How were they counted?

Since the argument simply adds up to the two numbers, it counts these people twice. In the worst case scenario, imagine that there are 10 million medical professionals who make more than $250,000 a year. Total, then, there are only 10 million people, not 20 million.

The concluding calculation is based on the assumption that there are 20 million people in the target markets. If there are fewer than 20 million people, then a *25% or greater* sales rate may not result in 5 million units sold.

Answer (D) addresses this weakness in the argument. If it is true that there is overlap between the two groups, then Orange is less likely to hit 5 million units in sales.

Answers (A) and (E) introduce some numbers; evaluate how they would impact the argument. If nearly 45% have already purchased a similar product, then perhaps not as many people are left to buy Orange's new product. But the company is only depending on a *25% or greater* sales rate, so there are still plenty of customers left (and the fact that so many medical professionals have bought a similar product seems to indicate a certain amount of demand).

Answer (E) makes an irrelevant distinction. The argument is concerned only with those who make more than $250,000 a year.

Answer (B) also makes an irrelevant comparison; the argument does not address the market for education professionals.

Without knowing what percentage of the population is affected by *astigmatism and other vision problems*, it's impossible to assess the impact of choice (C) on the argument. The company is only targeting a *25% or greater* sales rate. Further, the choice says only that people would have trouble using certain features; this does not mean that they would not buy the product at all.

8. **(D).**

W sick days > M

W work sick > M

This is an Inference question; it is asking you to deduce something that must be true from the information given in the argument.

If women in Langlia take more sick days *and* are more likely to go to work when they are sick, then they must be sick on more work days in general than men are. Answer (D) is a match.

Answer (A) is reasonable to believe in the real world but the argument contains no information about the preferences of employees. Likewise, the argument provides no information about the conscientiousness of employees, so answer (E) is also wrong.

Answer (B) goes too far. While childbearing and related medical conditions might be one cause of the difference between women and men in Langlia, the argument provides no information as to why women are sick more than men.

Answer (C) also goes too far. The argument restricts itself to days taken off *due to illness*, not days taken off when the sun is shining or someone would rather go to the movies.

9. **(C).**

free HR class to 4th graders ⟶ 4th will ↑ score on AH tests

This EXCEPT question is a variation on a regular Strengthen question. The four wrong answers will strengthen the argument. The correct answer will either weaken the argument or do nothing at all to it—but the correct answer will *not* strengthen the argument.

There are a great many assumptions in this argument. The argument assumes that students will actually sign up for and attend the free class. It assumes that the material in "History Rocks" is the same kind of material tested on American history tests (maybe "History Rocks" teaches the history of Ancient Greece, for instance), and that the students will remember what they learned long enough to score well on tests during the upcoming school year.

Choices (A) and (D) strengthen by filling the gap related to whether "History Rocks" teaches the same kind of material tested on American history tests.

Choice (B) strengthens by filling the gap related to whether students will actually sign up for and attend the free class.

Choice (E) strengthens by filling the gap related to whether students will remember what they learned long enough to score well on tests during the upcoming school year.

Choice (C) provides information that might explain why Rocktown wants to offer the free summer program, but this information does not address whether the plan will work as intended. As such, it neither strengthens nor weakens the plan; it doesn't address the plan at all.

10. **(E).**

US	Japan
bed ↓ from 4 to 1.3	bed ↑ from 1 to 2.9
↑↑ die	↓ die

Ⓒ ↓ bed → ↑ die

The question asks you to cast doubt on, or weaken, the conclusion that the reduction in hospital beds for inpatient psychiatric treatment in the United States is the primary cause for the increase in mortality among this population.

In order to weaken the idea that the reduction in beds is the cause, you could find another plausible cause for the increase in mortality rate. There are many possible alternatives: an increase in poverty or illegal drug use, a change in treatment plans or health insurance policies, and so on.

Note that, though the body of the argument addresses both the United States and Japan, the conclusion is limited specifically to the United States. Expect a trap or two in the answer choices revolving around Japan.

Answer (A) goes outside the scope of the argument by discussing Canada. While it might be true that Canada and the United States are similar in various ways, data about Canada does not weaken the conclusion about the United States.

Likewise, answer (B) brings up the idea of outpatient treatment, but the argument specifically refers to inpatient treatment. Further, this choice might explain why the number of inpatient hospital beds has declined, but it does not address the mortality issue.

Answer (C) is the Japan trap. The conclusion relates specifically to the situation in the United States. The knowledge that the incidence of mental disorders in Japan has been decreasing does not apply to the claim about the United States.

Answer (D) is tempting. Perhaps mortality is higher in the United States because not as many people have access to health insurance? Here's the catch: this lack of access has existed over the entire three-decade period. So why did the United States have an increase in mortality during this period?

Choice (E) is the correct answer. If certain types of mental disorders that are more likely to result in death are on the rise in the United States, but not in Japan, then that provides an alternative reason why the United States had an increase in mortality rates. The number of beds might have had nothing to do with it.

Chapter 12
of
GMAT Foundations of Verbal
Part 3: Reading Comprehension

How to Read on the GMAT

In This Chapter...

Chapter 12

How to Read on the GMAT

Reading Comprehension

Reading Comprehension passages on the GMAT are typically 1–5 paragraphs in length and appear on the left-hand side of the screen, while one question at a time appears on the right-hand side.

If the passage is long, you will be able to scroll up and down the left-hand side of the screen while the right-hand side remains static. A typical passage is accompanied by three or four questions. Since you can see only one question at a time, you won't know until you answer the third question whether a fourth one will appear. This is how the screen will be laid out:

The passages are excerpts from longer works, generally in the fields of business, history, science, and social science. Since the passages have been greatly shortened and adapted, they sometimes seem to begin abruptly; the passages lack the background information or interesting introduction you are accustomed to in much of your reading.

Some of the questions ask about specific details in the passage, while others ask about the main idea, the structure of the passage, or the author's purpose in including certain information. Still other questions ask you to make inferences—this is an area where, as you will see, the hard work you've already done on Critical Reasoning will pay off in RC as well.

Some people think that you can't improve on RC—after all, you've known how to read for 20 or more years at this point, right?

These people are completely wrong! It is absolutely possible to improve a great deal on RC, if you are willing to do the work.

Time to get started!

Why GMAT Reading Comprehension Is Hard *(Don't Skip This Intro!)*

Why is it hard to read a passage and answer questions about it? After all, you're reading this book right now, right? Obviously, you can read just fine. And, on the GMAT, you're allowed to look back at the passage anytime you want. So why does anyone get *anything* wrong?

There are several answers to that question. One is that GMAT reading passages are a lot harder to read than this book and your time is quite limited. Some people respond to these circumstances by rushing through the reading so much that they gain little more than a superficial understanding of the passage. Some of the trap answer choices you will encounter are set up for just this circumstance.

Others will read as they were taught to do in school: slowly and thoroughly, while taking extensive notes along the way. This is great for comprehension but won't work on the GMAT because you are not given much time. You'll have to rush on the questions, or rush later in the Verbal section, either of which will lead to careless mistakes.

So what do you need to do? You need to learn how to read in a balanced way: carefully enough to learn the main ideas and the main contrasts, or changes of direction, in a passage, while mentally setting aside much of the nitty-gritty detail for now—until you are asked a question about it.

You may be thinking: well, if I have to learn it later, I'd rather just read it all carefully right now. Here's the beauty of the GMAT: you *don't* have to learn it all later. You will be asked just three or four questions for each passage. You will literally be able to ignore certain details and examples forever, because you won't be asked about every detail in the passage.

Things can (and will!) go wrong at the level of the question, too. For instance, consider this question:

What is the function of the second paragraph in relation to the rest of the passage?

That's a pretty specific question, but someone who is rushing or not reading carefully might interpret the question too loosely.

For example, if you interpret the question as, "What's going on with paragraph two?", you are likely to pick a wrong answer, because some of the wrong answers may, in fact, be *true*. To be clear: *some of the wrong answers in GMAT RC are 100% true facts.* But they are facts that, for instance, do not explain the role of the second paragraph in relation to the rest of the passage. An answer choice can be true and yet not answer the particular question asked.

In the next several chapters, you'll learn how to read on the GMAT and how to answer the different kinds of questions you'll be asked.

Find the Simple Story

Quick! Your boss is about to go into a conference call with her boss. The subject: what your department has accomplished in the past 12 months. You have five minutes to prepare your boss for this call; what do you do?

You don't have much time, obviously, so you're going to have to summarize pretty heavily. Plus, your boss doesn't have a lot of time to learn a bunch of detailed facts. You're going to have to put together the *simple story* for your boss (and hers!).

You work at a biotech firm; here's an excerpt from the introduction of a paper your division recently published, reflecting what you've done for the past 12 months:

> *The previously made observation that the most rare variants in the human genome are also the most responsible for disease is supported by this new study that demonstrates that more common genome variants are less likely to be found in functional regions of the genome, and the functional regions are those that are actually expressed, such as in the form of disease.*

Wow. That's a mouthful. Strip out the technical detail: what's the basic story?

prev idea: rare variants → ↑ disease

new study: supports

The basic story is two-fold:

1. Originally, "rare variants of the genome" (whatever that is) were thought to be most responsible for causing disease, and
2. the new study supports that original idea. Hooray!

How? Why? You don't care. Not at this stage of the GMAT game, anyway. You've got the main idea; if you get a question about how, exactly, the new study supports the original theory, you can come back to that part of the sentence and try to understand it better. (And if you don't get such a question, you can ignore that detail forever.)

In order to find the simple story, you're going to need to figure out several things:

- What is the main point of each paragraph?
- What major contrasts, or changes of direction, exist?
- What is the overall main idea of the entire passage?

Following is information on how to develop these ideas during your first read-through of the passage.

A Balanced Read

Here's how to conduct a balanced read of a passage, gathering the main ideas while not getting too tangled up in the details:

1. Get oriented. Read the first couple of sentences carefully and write down the main idea of that first paragraph.

2. Find the main ideas of the remaining paragraphs. Pay particular attention to any language that signals foreshadowing, contrast, or a change of direction.

3. Know *why* the details are there but not *what* they say at anything more than a high level.

4. Articulate the simple story. When you're done with the first read-through, you want to know the main point of the entire passage, as well as the major twists and turns of the story.

You'll have to do all of the above in about two to three minutes! In other words, you'll need to learn this process well so that you can read efficiently and not get bogged down in details.

Here is how to effectively execute each of the four steps.

Step 1: Get oriented.

Read the first two or three sentences of the first paragraph carefully. They are going to set the context for the entire story. If the first paragraph is on the shorter side, read the entire thing carefully.

Jot down a few notes to summarize what the first paragraph conveys. You can write as you read, or you can wait until you've finished the paragraph to write—different people prefer different approaches. Either way, do take the time to articulate explicitly to yourself the point of the first paragraph, even if you only jot down a couple of words as a reminder.

Focus on the main ideas. Don't try to learn the details!

Now, you might begin to understand how you can do all of this in just two to three minutes: you aren't actually going to pay a ton of attention to the annoying details.

> **How do I find the main point of the whole passage?**
>
> Ultimately, you want to be able to articulate the simple story. The heart of that story is the main point of the entire passage.
>
> This main point could be located anywhere, but it is most often located in the first paragraph or the beginning of the second paragraph.

Step 2: Find the main idea of the remaining paragraphs.

Whoever wrote the passage had some reason for including each paragraph. Your task is to figure out what that reason is.

> What is the main idea of each paragraph?
>
> Why is it included in the passage?

For the most part, the first sentence or two of the paragraph will help you to answer these questions. After that, you're going to start to get into detail, which you're mostly going to ignore. (See Step 3 for more on how to handle detail.)

Do, though, look for language that signals summaries or conclusions (Therefore, . . .) or changes of direction (However, . . .). You can turn your brain back on and pay attention when you see that kind of big-picture language.

As before, jot down a few words to help you remember the main idea of the paragraph, as well as any major conclusions or contrasts that you think may be important.

Step 3: Minimize the details.

Don't spend time trying to memorize, or even understand, examples, technical discussions, or other detailed information. Instead, focus on why the detailed information is there.

> Why is this detail here?
>
> Is it an example to illustrate the main idea of the paragraph?
>
> Is it evidence to support a contention the author is making?
>
> Does the detail explain how some theory works?

Other than that, don't try to understand what all of the detail means. Seriously! Each passage contains more detail than you will be asked about in the questions, so why bother trying to learn things that you're never going to need?

Instead, you'll come back to the particular details you need once you're offered a question that depends on that detail. You'll learn how to do that in a later chapter.

Step 4: Articulate the simple story.

By the end of your read-through, you will hopefully be able to articulate the simple story of the passage. In order to do this, you will have to accomplish two tasks:

1. Articulate the main point of the passage.

    Why did the author bother to sit down and write this passage in the first place? She had some thesis that she was trying to establish.

    Perhaps there was an old way of explaining some phenomenon but new research has uncovered a better explanation. Perhaps there are two competing business principles or processes, each of which has its positive points, but neither of them is perfect. Perhaps the author wants to contend that a series of historical events occurred for a particular reason.

    In general, the main point is not a simple recitation of facts. The author is interested in discussing not just *what* happened but *why* it may have happened (or, possibly, what the future implications might be).

2. Find the main contrasts, or changes of direction, in the story.

    Every passage has at least one contrast or change of direction; this kind of information makes for good questions! Contrasting information also underpins the story the passage is trying to tell.

    Common change of direction signals include such words and phrases as however, but, yet, unexpectedly, it was once thought, now, and more recent research shows.

Remember your biotech company's discovery from earlier in the chapter? Perhaps the full simple story is something like this:

> The original theory was that the more rare variants of the genome were more likely to lead to disease. Our recent research shows that more common variants are less likely to lead to disease, which indirectly supports the original theory. Direct support, however, is better than indirect support, so more research should be done in the coming year to try to more directly support the original hypothesis.

The passage would have far more technical detail of course, but you're not going to get all caught up in it. You're going to pick out the simple story that your boss can tell her boss to make the case that your department should be given more research funds for the coming year.

Practicing a Balanced Read

That's a lot to remember. Time to put it into practice!

First, create a "cheat sheet" for yourself, including your major goals and the steps that you want to follow. Then test out the process by reading the following passage and taking some notes.

Try to stick to the roughly two-minute time frame you want to use on the real test. If your reading speed is just not fast enough right now, that's okay; give yourself an extra minute or so. Do *not*, though, use extra time to try to understand thoroughly, memorize, or take notes on every last detail in the passage! Stick to your goal: find the simple story.

During salary negotiations, some career advisors recommend that the job seeker allow the company to make the initial salary offer. Proponents of this approach assert that making an initial offer that is too high or too low can hurt a party's position. For example, if a job seeker initially requests a lower salary than the employer was prepared to provide, then the end result is likely to be a lower final salary offer than might have been attained had the candidate allowed the company to start the negotiations. Thus, the party that initially does not name a salary is in a better position to protect its interests even while allowing the opposing side to feel more in control of the negotiations.

Critics of this approach emphasize the importance of anchors, cognitive focal points that direct any given negotiation. Under the anchoring principle, the initial offer becomes the number to which all other numbers are compared. The party who makes the initial offer is able to define the range of the negotiation and thereby has more significant influence over the final deal. In order to avoid undermining their own interests, job seekers would purposely start negotiations at a higher-than-expected anchor point, but not a point so high that the company in question balks at negotiating entirely.

Harvard Law School's Program on Negotiation suggests one further step: establish an anchor without making an explicit offer. A candidate might mention, for instance, that a colleague recently accepted a similar position at a specified salary, or that the average salary for people with similar qualifications falls within a particular range. Such anchoring tactics may diminish the sometimes adversarial effect of a direct offer.

How did it go? Below you'll find an example of what a strong GMAT test-taker might think and write while reading this passage.

Lines 1–7:

Hmm. Some *advisors say the person should let the company make the initial offer—but not all? And* proponents *are recommending this? I wonder whether the passage is also going to talk about what opponents think. This may be some foreshadowing. I think I'll read a little further before I write anything down.*

Lines 7–17:

Okay, there's at least one good reason for the individual to let the company make the offer: if you unknowingly start too low, then the company's likely to offer you less than it otherwise might have. In that case, you're better off waiting to see what the company offers first.

I still think they're going to talk about a different point of view . . . [glancing at the beginning of paragraph 2] . . . yep, critics! Okay, so I'm going to make a little table to map out the main points here.

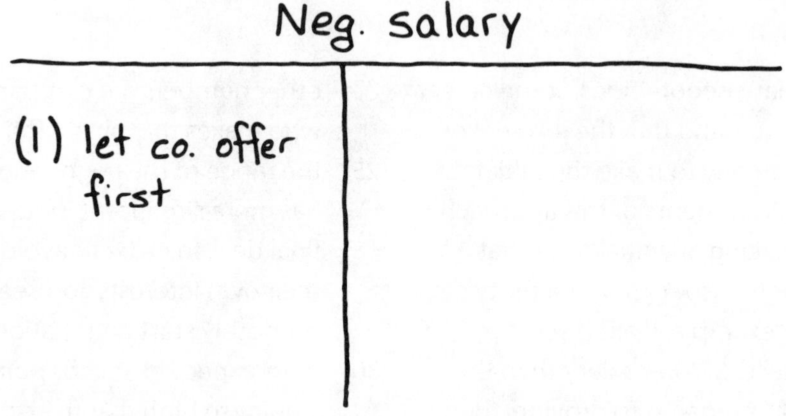

(Note: the number shows the paragraph in which that info is found.)

Lines 18–23:

Anchors are . . . cognitive focal points? [Reads it again.] Nope, I have no idea what that means. Okay, don't get hung up on that. Keep going. The second sentence makes more sense. The initial number is an "anchor" because all of the future numbers get compared to the initial number. And apparently that means you get more influence over the final deal.

Lines 23–32:

Oh, interesting. So the final deal will probably be within some range of the initial starting point. If so, and if you can set that initial starting point, then I can see how you'd have more influence over the final deal. But what if you start too low, like the first paragraph said?

Ah, I see. You purposely start out at the higher end, maybe more than you know they'll pay. But at least you're getting them to start from a higher point. Yeah, if I were negotiating a salary, I'd definitely rather start higher and negotiate down a bit than start too low and leave money on the table.

Neg. salary

(1) let co. offer first	(2) indiv offer first and high end up ↑↑ overall?

Okay, one more paragraph to go. Is there a third theory?

Lines 33–43:

No, they're still talking about the second theory. Apparently, making a direct offer might come across as "adversarial," but you might be able to get around that by citing statistics about the salary for similar positions (vs. just making a direct offer yourself). Harvard Law School says so!

Neg. salary

(1) let co. offer first	(2) indiv offer first and high end up ↑↑ overall? (3) cite similar stats

So what's the overall story here?

There are two different theories for negotiating a salary. First, the job seeker should let the company make the first offer, so that the job seeker doesn't inadvertently go too low. Second, the job seeker should make the first offer and make it on the high side, "anchoring" the subsequent negotiations around this higher number. The job seeker might start by citing statistics for similar positions to solidify the anchor.

It sounds like the second theory offers more upside and a stronger negotiating position, as long as you don't mistakenly offer too low a salary to start.

During the test, you can't write that all out—there's not enough time! If you generally struggle to articulate the simple story in your head, though, then you may want to write it out now. With enough practice, you'll become proficient at articulating the story to yourself, without having to write it down.

There was a major difference in the way that the test-taker handled paragraph 1 versus paragraph 2. She understood paragraph 1 immediately, so well that she was able to free up some brain cells to speculate about what might be coming next.

By contrast, she got hung up on the first sentence of the second paragraph. She wasn't sure what that whole *cognitive focal point* thing was, but she kept going to the second sentence and that helped her understand what this new theory was about. Then, notice that she was again able to start thinking about the bigger picture when she got to the detail: her thoughts and notes didn't even mention the idea of making an offer that is high *but not so high* as to stop negotiations.

Rather, she connected the overall idea of making an initial high offer to the contrasting recommendation in the previous paragraph: don't make the initial offer at all! She even thought about how this would apply if she were negotiating an offer herself; putting yourself into the RC passage or CR argument is a great way to wrap your brain around the complexities under discussion.

Finally, she tried to anticipate what might be coming in the third paragraph but she wasn't right. That's okay. It's still a good exercise to try to anticipate. If you're right, you'll feel vindicated and will remember the information better; if you're wrong, you'll be curious to see what the next paragraph really is talking about . . . and you'll remember the information better. Either way, you win!

Ready for another one? Try this passage; it's longer, so on the real test, you'd want to take about three minutes. (Again, you can give yourself some extra time now, earlier in the learning process, but do *not* use that extra time to get into detail that you should be skimming for now.)

In 1901, divers exploring the remains of a ship wreck off the coast of Greece discovered a contraption believed to have been used by Ancient Greeks to predict solar eclipses. The Antikythera Mechanism was composed of a fixed-ring dial representing the 12 months of the Egyptian calendar and an inner ring representing the 12 zodiac signs. Inside, a complex assembly of bronze gears mechanically replicated the irregular motions of the Moon caused by its elliptical orbit around the Earth through the use of two gear-wheels, one of which was slightly off-center, connected by a pin. Regarded as the world's first analog computer, the Antikythera Mechanism involved remarkably intricate physics considering that, only 300 years earlier, the Ancient Greeks still believed the world was flat. Accurately predicting lunar and solar eclipses, as well as solar, lunar, and planetary positions, it predated similar technology by 1,000 years. The timing and nature of its existence remains one of science's great puzzles to this day. How and by whom was it created?

Today, scientists understand much more about the complexities of the orbital revolutions that cause solar eclipses to occur; for instance, the Earth's orbit around the Sun is also elliptical such that, depending on the time of year, the Earth is gradually traveling nearer to or farther from the Sun. Further, since the plane of the Moon's revolution around the Earth is not the same as the plane of the Earth's revolution around the Sun, all calculations predicting a solar eclipse must be completed in three dimensions. While in modern times the use of satellites, telescopes, and other high-tech equipment has greatly enhanced our capacity for such calculations, when the Antikythera Mechanism was created, the sole source of information available to scientists was observation of the night sky. It is thus not surprising that, under certain circumstances, the device is inaccurate by up to 38 degrees; what is astonishing is that the device is remarkably accurate over a wide range of conditions.

Recent analysis dating the device to 205 BC, earlier than previously thought, suggests that the eclipse prediction mechanism was based not on Greek trigonometry but on Babylonian arithmetical methods borrowed by the Greeks. This conjecture makes plausible Cicero's claim that Archimedes created the mechanism, as Greek trigonometry was nonexistent in 205 BC.

What did you think? The second one is longer than the first one, of course. It also has more technical detail. Were you able to push through and ignore detail that was too hard to grasp right away? Or did you get hung up at certain points, enough that your understanding of the overall passage was negatively impacted? This is what you're going to learn to do better right now.

Let's go back to the strong-at-RC test-taker and see how she would think her way through this passage.

Lines 1–5:

Ship wreck—cool. A hundred years ago. "A contraption believed to have been used to predict solar eclipses." Something technical and they're not 100% sure what it was for, but they think it was for predicting an eclipse (Moon covering Sun).

Lines 5–24:

Calling that thing AM. Showed the 12 months and the zodiac signs. Complex inside showed the Moon's orbit around the Earth. "Remarkably intricate"—okay, so it was impressive, maybe ahead of its time? Yes: AM was accurate and it "predated similar technology by 1,000 years."

Lines 24–27:

Puzzle: who made it and how? But it's still a puzzle "to this day" so what's the rest of the passage about? A new theory about who and how? Speculation?

(1) AM found, spec: anc Grk, predict solar eclipse?
AM= sophis, not sure how made or who

Note: *Spec* is short for speculation: the passage says the AM was *believed* to have been used by ancient Greeks. *Sophis* is short for sophisticated.

Lines 28–31:

Now, scientists know a lot more about calculating eclipses; this is highlighting how amazing it was that the Ancient Greeks were able to figure this stuff out.

Lines 31–41:

Ugh, lots of detail about how solar eclipses work. Skimming, skimming . . .

(1) AM found, spec: anc Grk, predict solar eclipse?
AM= sophis, not sure how made or who

(2) Now: DTL eclipse

Note: *DTL* is this test-taker's shorthand for "the passage has lots of detail about this topic, if I need to come back to it later."

Lines 41–52:

Oh, here we go. Today, there are lots of tools to help calculate this stuff, but when AM was made, all they had was what they observed in the sky. It's pretty amazing that it's as accurate as it is.

(1) AM found, spec: anc Grk, predict solar eclipse?
AM= sophis, not sure how made or who

(2) Now: DTL eclipse
AM= surpris acc.

Lines 53–62:

Hmm, now they think AM was made even earlier than they previously thought. Maybe it was created by Arch? Evidence based on math. Speculating, but still no answers about who made it and how.

(1) AM found, spec: anc Grk, predict solar eclipse?
AM= sophis, not sure how made or who

(2) Now: DTL eclipse
AM= surpris acc.

(3) C: made by Arch(?)
evid given (math)

Note: *Evid given* is this test-taker's shorthand for "the passage provides specific evidence to support this claim or contention."

Simple story:

AM created by Ancient Greeks to predict solar eclipses. Mystery: who made it and how could they do this relatively accurately when all they had was observation of the night sky? Remarkably sophisticated given what they had to work with. Para 2 gets into how lots of detail about how to predict an eclipse. But Para 3 only speculates about when it was created and by whom, and we still don't know how they made it, so the mystery hasn't actually been resolved.

Did you notice how much of the technical detail the test-taker skimmed right over, particularly in paragraphs 2 and 3?

This is where you don't want to let yourself get hung up and distracted from your goal: find the simple story.

It's going to take a lot of training to get yourself to the point that you are comfortable just leaving that detail for later. At first, you're going to feel that something is wrong, that you can't possibly understand everything because you're not learning that detail right now. And you're right—you aren't going to understand everything thoroughly. That's not your goal.

Remember, the passage will give you more detail than you actually need in order to answer the questions. You only want to bother learning the details that you need, so don't waste precious time and mental energy learning something when you aren't even sure yet whether you'll get a question about it.

Speaking of questions, it's time to move to the next chapter, where you'll tackle General questions, including Main Idea questions.

Chapter 13

of

GMAT Foundations of Verbal

Part 3: **Reading Comprehension**

Main Ideas & General Questions

In This Chapter…

What Is a Main Idea?

General Questions

Answers to Drill Sets

Chapter 13

Main Ideas & General Questions

What Is a Main Idea?

In order to be able to articulate the Simple Story, you have to understand the main idea that a passage is trying to convey. But what does a main idea look like on the GMAT, and how can you be sure you've found it?

GMAT main ideas are not quite the same as "real world" main ideas.

Non-GMAT reading passages—including news articles, editorials, and academic papers—often have pretty straightforward main ideas, such as:

- Here's how bees pollinate certain plants.
- There are several different methods for seeding a cotton field (and here are the options).
- The death penalty should not be applied to mentally disabled criminals (and here are some reasons why).

A GMAT main idea is not likely to take the form "Here are some facts." A GMAT passage always has a Point: the author is trying to make the case for a specific thesis. In the last chapter, the second passage asserted that the Antikythera Mechanism is still a mystery to this day and the author spent the rest of the passage supporting this thesis.

Nor is a GMAT passage likely to say "I believe this conclusion and here are my reasons." GMAT main ideas are more nuanced. Even when a writer is arguing "for" something, she or he will typically present multiple points of view. It might not be that obvious that the author prefers one of the views. In the negotiation passage from the last chapter, the author never stated a preference for one theory, but did provide a lot of supporting evidence as to why the anchoring theory may be better.

Find the Point

Most of the time, the point will fall into one of a few categories:

1. A change (Here's a situation—but now there's a new set of circumstances/theory/explanation.)
2. A twist (Here's something that seems straightforward—but it's not what you think!)
3. A judgment call (Here are two options—and now I'm going to tell you which one is better!)

From now on, the **point** will refer to the overarching main idea of an entire passage. Individual paragraphs may also have their own main ideas.

Many passages take the form, "The [noun] was doing something, but now it's doing something else," or "A group of people thought something for a particular reason, but now the reason is wrong, so maybe the thing they were thinking isn't really true (but we need more information to find out)." Some GMAT points do give opinions, but the opinion will usually be contrasted against a view presented in the first paragraph ("A certain group of people have traditionally thought *X*—but actually, *Y*!").

Where to Look

The point is often articulated in a single, discrete sentence in the passage, though sometimes it may be spread over a couple of sentences. It is most often found in the first paragraph or the beginning of the second paragraph (though it could technically be anywhere in the passage). Of course, you need to read the first paragraph to understand that the second paragraph is presenting a *change, twist,* or *judgment call.* Often, the first paragraph sets up an idea or situation, and then the second paragraph provides a contrast that gives you the point.

Often, the first sentence or two will provide background information or set context, but sometimes the opening sentence will give you the point. For instance, if the first line begins, "A stunning new theory has changed everything we thought we knew about the rotation of the Earth around the Sun," then that's almost certainly the main idea right there. It's pretty likely that the passage will tell you a little bit about what people have traditionally thought, before returning to explaining that stunning new theory.

While you are reading through a GMAT passage for the first time, imagine a small voice in the back of your mind saying something like, "Facts facts facts facts facts! BUT WHAT?!" (Imagine that in a silly voice. *Facts facts facts facts facts!* The facts are not the main idea—keep looking!)

Try that out in the exercise below.

Drill 13.1 — Find the point.

As you read, jot down notes to help you find the point of each passage and the main idea of each individual paragraph. If appropriate, identify whether the passage has a change, a twist, or a judgment call.

1. Freelancing

As the proportion of Australian workers who are self-employed has boomed in the past decade, the topic of wealth creation for freelancers has become much more prevalent in business magazines. A standard maxim among such publications is that a sole proprietor is best off treating her business as a much larger enterprise with a set of core departments, including but not limited to executive, production, human resources, marketing, and finance functions. In effect, the freelancer would devote time and attention to each "department" in order to optimize her chances of success, and would, unaided, create content, advertising campaigns, contracts, and quarterly budgets.

Most freelancers, however, presently operate in the creative realm, encompassing not only traditional arts such as photography and writing but also more technical services such as computer programming and software engineering. Such creative forms of labor demand highly specialized skills. For the creative freelancer, then, whose most valued asset is labor, conceptualizing one's business in such a fashion risks the dilution of the company's most important resource: the freelancer's skills. Distributing one's labor across platforms is a zero-sum game that may yield positive results in some scenarios but not necessarily all. A photographer who spends his time developing a marketing plan may consequently jeopardize his public image by failing to devote sufficient effort to expanding his portfolio via new and high-value artwork. Moreover, because "word of mouth" is typically considered the most powerful means of marketing in a creative industry, the potential benefits of such a trade-off are far from certain.

The point of the passage:

____

____

____

____

The main idea of paragraph 1:

____

____

____

The main idea of paragraph 2:

____

____

____

2. Polymers

Synthetic polymers are man-made polymers colloquially referred to as "plastics." These polymers can be classified in many ways, perhaps the most useful regarding how they respond to heat. For example, thermosets are permanently set plastics; they do not melt, even when subjected to high temperatures. Thermoplastics, however, become malleable when heated and can be remolded as they are cooled. As a result, thermoplastics can be recycled more easily than thermosets and are used in the manufacture of toys, water bottles, and other goods that are typically used for limited time periods and subsequently discarded. Thermosets are more difficult to recycle and are often used as adhesives or sealants in high-wear settings, circumstances in which the less malleable nature of the material is a distinct advantage, despite the inability to recycle at a later date.

Thermoplastics can be further differentiated as amorphous or semi-crystalline. While both amorphous and semi-crystalline thermoplastics melt when heated, amorphous thermoplastics soften gradually in response to heat while semi-crystalline thermoplastics remain solid until a precise melting point. Semi-crystalline thermoplastics tend to be tougher, suitable for weight-bearing goods such as folding chairs, whereas amorphous thermoplastics are more common for products that break apart easily, such as packing peanuts.

The contrasting molecular structures of the various plastics underpin the way in which each responds to heat. Thermoset polymers are chemically "cured," involving the formation of chemical bonds and resulting in rigid, three-dimensional molecular structures. Unlike thermosets, thermoplastics are two-dimensional chains connected by intermolecular forces. In amorphous thermoplastics, the molecules are randomly ordered, resembling a jumble of yarn, while semi-crystalline thermoplastics feature ordered molecular "crystals."

The point of the passage:

____
____
____
____

The main idea of paragraph 1:

____
____
____

The main idea of paragraph 2:

____
____
____

The main idea of paragraph 3:

____
____
____

Answers are on pages 251–253.

General Questions

General questions test your understanding of the overall point and the simple story. General questions fall into one of two main categories:

1. Primary purpose: What is the point of the passage?

2. Paragraph: What is the purpose of a specific paragraph?

Try this main idea question for the Freelancing passage.

As the proportion of Australian workers who are self-employed has boomed in the past decade, the topic of wealth creation for freelancers has become much more prevalent in business magazines. A standard maxim among such publications is that a sole proprietor is best off treating her business as a much larger enterprise with a set of core departments, including but not limited to executive, production, human resources, marketing, and finance functions. In effect, the freelancer would devote time and attention to each "department" in order to optimize her chances of success, and would, unaided, create content, advertising campaigns, contracts, and quarterly budgets.

Most freelancers, however, presently operate in the creative realm, encompassing not only traditional arts such as photography and writing but also more technical services such as computer programming and software engineering. Such creative forms of labor demand highly specialized skills. For the creative freelancer, then, whose most valued asset is labor, conceptualizing one's business in such a fashion risks the dilution of the company's most important resource: the freelancer's skills. Distributing one's labor across platforms is a zero-sum game that may yield positive results in some scenarios but not necessarily all. A photographer who spends his time developing a marketing plan may consequently jeopardize his public image by failing to devote sufficient effort to expanding his portfolio via new and high-value artwork. Moreover, because "word of mouth" is typically considered the most powerful means of marketing in a creative industry, the potential benefits of such a trade-off are far from certain.

The primary purpose of the passage is to

(A) describe a current debate taking place among authors of a certain type of literature
(B) attack a particular theory as fundamentally untenable
(C) explain the prevalent theory of a particular business area
(D) discuss how one principle of business may not be optimal in all cases
(E) contrast two views with respect to a particular business area

How did that go? Before you keep reading, look over your work for a moment. What was hard about the problem? Did your understanding of the point go along with the correct answer? What was tempting about some of the wrong answers?

When a new question pops up on the screen, your first task is to figure out what kind of question it is. In this case, the language *primary purpose* indicates that this is a Primary Purpose, or main idea, question.

Next, you want to reread or remember whatever information you have about the main idea and articulate in your own words what you think the answer should say.

If you've gotten a good grasp of the simple story from your read-through, then you likely won't have to go back to the passage to reread anything for main idea questions. For the Freelancing passage, the point is something like *Some people think freelancers should run themselves like a business, but this could be detrimental for those working in creative fields.*

Finally, you're ready to go find a match in the answer choices. Look for something that goes along with the idea you've articulated to yourself. Here's how a strong RC test-taker might think through the five answers on this problem.

Answer	**Thoughts**
(A) describe a current debate taking place among authors of a certain type of literature	*The first paragraph does say that business magazines recommend that people run themselves like a business . . . but the contrasting paragraph doesn't say anything about the magazines. It sounds like the author's opinion, not a debate among magazine writers. Eliminate.*
(B) attack a particular theory as fundamentally untenable	*Too strong. The author says only that the theory might not apply to a certain type of freelancer. Eliminate.*
(C) explain the prevalent theory of a particular business area	Prevalent *means dominant or the most widespread. Maybe the "act like a business" theory is dominant but this choice entirely misses the contrasting point of view. Eliminate.*
(D) discuss how one principle of business may not be optimal in all cases	*Yes, this is it. There is this theory, or principle, but it could turn out to be bad for certain people. I think this is it, but I'm going to check the last one to make sure.*
(E) contrast two views with respect to a particular business area	*Oh, this one's tricky. My first thought was that this one is right, too, but now that I'm rereading it . . . it doesn't say quite the right thing. It's not about a particular business area. That would mean, hey, we're only talking about photographers. Rather, the first group has a theory it thinks applies to everyone, and the author is pointing out that it might not apply to people working in creative fields (emphasis on the plural—many fields!). Eliminate.*

The correct answer is **(D)**.

Congratulations! You just used the 4-step RC Process to answer your first question. Here's a summary of the process:

Step 1: Identify the question.

Step 2: Find the support.

Step 3: Predict an answer.

Step 4: Eliminate and find a match.

In the coming chapters, you'll learn more about how to use the process for the different question types found on RC. Now, test out your newfound skills on some more problems.

Drill 13.2 — Answer the General Questions

For each passage, answer the General question provided. Practice using the 4-step process to answer the question.

Passage 1: Anchoring

During salary negotiations, some career advisors recommend that the job seeker allow the company to make the initial salary offer. Proponents of this approach assert that making an initial offer that is too high or too low can hurt a party's position. For example, if a job seeker initially requests a lower salary than the employer was prepared to provide, then the end result is likely to be a lower final salary offer than might have been attained had the candidate allowed the company to start the negotiations. Thus, the party that initially does not name a salary is in a better position to protect its interests even while allowing the opposing side to feel more in control of the negotiations.

Critics of this approach emphasize the importance of anchors, cognitive focal points that direct any given negotiation. Under the anchoring principle, the initial offer becomes the number to which all other numbers are compared. The party who makes the initial offer is able to define the range of the negotiation and thereby has more significant influence over the final deal. In order to avoid undermining their own interests, job seekers would purposely start negotiations at a higher-than-expected anchor point, but not a point so high that the company in question balks at negotiating entirely.

Harvard Law School's Program on Negotiation suggests one further step: establish an anchor without making an explicit offer. A candidate might mention, for instance, that a colleague recently accepted a similar position at a specified salary, or that the average salary for people with similar qualifications falls within a particular range. Such anchoring tactics may diminish the sometimes adversarial effect of a direct offer.

1. Which of the following best describes the purpose of the third paragraph of the passage?

    (A) To argue that Harvard Law School's principle is the best of the principles discussed
    (B) To conclude that following the anchoring principle is more likely to result in a higher starting salary
    (C) To suggest that diminishing any potential adversarial effects should be the primary concern of the candidate
    (D) To offer a counter example to the principle discussed in the prior paragraph
    (E) To provide additional guidance regarding the operation of the anchoring principle

2. Polymers

Synthetic polymers are man-made polymers colloquially referred to as "plastics." These polymers can be classified in many ways, perhaps the most useful regarding how they respond to heat. For example, thermosets are permanently set plastics; they do not melt, even when subjected to high temperatures. Thermoplastics, however, become malleable when heated and can be remolded as they are cooled. As a result, thermoplastics can be recycled more easily than thermosets and are used in the manufacture of toys, water bottles, and other goods that are typically used for limited time periods and subsequently discarded. Thermosets are more difficult to recycle and are often used as adhesives or sealants in high-wear settings, circumstances in which the less malleable nature of the material is a distinct advantage, despite the inability to recycle at a later date.

Thermoplastics can be further differentiated as amorphous or semi-crystalline. While both amorphous and semi-crystalline thermoplastics melt when heated, amorphous thermoplastics soften gradually in response to heat while semi-crystalline thermoplastics remain solid until a precise melting point. Semi-crystalline thermoplastics tend to be tougher, suitable for weight-bearing goods such as folding chairs, whereas amorphous thermoplastics are more common for products that break apart easily, such as packing peanuts.

The contrasting molecular structures of the various plastics underpin the way in which each responds to heat. Thermoset polymers are chemically "cured," involving the formation of chemical bonds and resulting in rigid, three-dimensional molecular structures. Unlike thermosets, thermoplastics are two-dimensional chains connected by intermolecular forces. In amorphous thermoplastics, the molecules are randomly ordered, resembling a jumble of yarn, while semi-crystalline thermoplastics feature ordered molecular "crystals."

2. The passage is primarily concerned with

(A) providing examples of real-world uses for various related substances
(B) contrasting the chemical compositions of various substances
(C) presenting a useful basis for classifying a set of related substances
(D) assessing the pros and cons of recycling various types of substances
(E) outlining the primary categories of a set of related substances and proposing uses for each category

3. Greek Wreck

In 1901, divers exploring the remains of a ship wreck off the coast of Greece discovered a contraption believed to have been used by Ancient Greeks to predict solar eclipses. The Antikythera Mechanism was composed of a fixed-ring dial representing the 12 months of the Egyptian calendar and an inner ring representing the 12 zodiac signs. Inside, a complex assembly of bronze gears mechanically replicated the irregular motions of the Moon caused by its elliptical orbit around the Earth through the use of two gear-wheels, one of which was slightly off-center, connected by a pin. Regarded as the world's first analog computer, the Antikythera Mechanism involved remarkably intricate physics considering that, only 300 years earlier, the Ancient Greeks still believed the world was flat. Accurately predicting lunar and solar eclipses, as well as solar, lunar, and planetary positions, it predated similar technology by 1,000 years. The timing and nature of its existence remains one of science's great puzzles to this day. How and by whom was it created?

Today, scientists understand much more about the complexities of the orbital revolutions that cause solar eclipses to occur; for instance, the Earth's orbit around the Sun is also elliptical such that, depending on the time of year, the Earth is gradually traveling nearer to or farther from the Sun. Further, since the plane of the Moon's revolution around the Earth is not the same as the plane of the Earth's revolution around the Sun, all calculations predicting a solar eclipse must be completed in three dimensions. While in modern times the use of satellites, telescopes, and other high-tech equipment has greatly enhanced our capacity for such calculations, when the Antikythera Mechanism was created, the sole source of information available to scientists was observation of the night sky. It is thus not surprising that, under certain circumstances, the device is inaccurate by up to 38 degrees; what is astonishing is that the device is remarkably accurate over a wide range of conditions.

Recent analysis dating the device to 205 BC, earlier than previously thought, suggests that the eclipse prediction mechanism was based not on Greek trigonometry but on Babylonian arithmetical methods borrowed by the Greeks. This conjecture makes plausible Cicero's claim that Archimedes created the mechanism, as Greek trigonometry was nonexistent in 205 BC.

3. Which of the following best describes the relationship of the second paragraph to the passage as a whole?

(A) It provides evidence to support the main idea introduced earlier in the passage.
(B) It presents a hypothesis that is rejected in the final paragraph of the passage.
(C) It offers an example of a theory proposed in the first paragraph of the passage.
(D) It suggests a solution to a problem described earlier in the passage.
(E) It draws a parallel between two phenomena discussed in the passage.

Answers are on pages 253–257.

Answers to Drill Sets

Answers to Drill 13.1 — The Point

The answers below show one possible way to take notes and articulate the point and main ideas; your wording won't match exactly, of course. Ask yourself: Were you able to paraphrase in order to state the point concisely? Did you understand the purpose of each paragraph? Do you know the type of detail found in each paragraph?

1. Freelancing (pg. 242)

(1) Bus Pub: FL should run as business w/ dep'ts, etc.

(2) auth: BUT creative FL might be hurt by this

The point: While some freelancers might benefit from treating themselves as a complete business, freelancers working in creative fields may find that this approach hurts them (because they're better off spending more time creating whatever they make).

Main idea of paragraph 1: A *standard maxim* says that freelancers should treat themselves like a business, with multiple departments that they "run" as a larger company would.

Main idea of paragraph 2: BUT (twist!) freelancers working in creative fields might find this harmful rather than helpful; they may need to keep creating stuff in order to sustain their businesses.

When a passage tells you that something is a *standard maxim* or attributes something to conventional wisdom, there's a pretty good chance that the passage is about to give you a twist: "Here's what most people think (or what people used to think), but (twist!) here's how you should really be thinking about it now."

2. Polymers (pg. 244)

(1) man-made Poly = plastic

★ most useful: classify by heat

(1)

TS	TP
set	
can't melt	can melt
	easier to recycle

(2)

A	SC
gradual melt	melt fast @temp
	tougher

(3) structure

DTL	DTL

Notice that, for the third paragraph, the test-taker either started to get bored or decided that the paragraph was too technical. She just wrote *DTL* to signal that more detail about the chemical structure can be found by going back into the third paragraph. This is a great strategy to use when the passage gets too technical.

The point: The most useful way to classify man-made plastics is based on how they respond to heat.

Main idea of paragraph 1: Same as the point. (Support: two types of plastics respond differently to heat.)

Main idea of paragraph 2: One of the two types from the previous paragraph can be split into two subgroups based on . . . you guessed it . . . how they respond to heat.

Main idea of paragraph 3: The heat thing is based on the fact that these different kinds of plastic have different molecular structures. (Ignore the word *molecular* as much as possible! They have different structures.)

The point of this passage is tough to spot, even though it's right in the second sentence. When the point is given to you early, you often can't be sure that it is the point until you get through more of the passage. In this case, the technical detail is distracting, too, so how are you going to pick up that the second sentence is, in fact, the point?

The key words are these: *perhaps the most useful.* The polymers can be classified in many ways? That's just a fact. *Perhaps the most useful* way is based on how they respond to heat? That's an opinion or a claim, and claims make for a good point.

Answers to Drill 13.2 — Answer the General Questions

1. Anchoring: (E) To provide additional guidance regarding the operation of the anchoring principle

Step 1: Identify the question.

The language *purpose of the third paragraph* in the question stem indicates that this is a Paragraph question.

Step 2: Find the support.

Review your notes on the third paragraph or glance back at the first sentence or two of the paragraph.

Step 3: Predict an answer.

The paragraph *suggests one further step* to what was discussed in the prior paragraph. In other words, the paragraph is elaborating on the anchoring principle. The correct answer should convey this idea.

Step 4: Eliminate and find a match.

Answer choice	Explanation
(A) To argue that Harvard Law School's principle is the best of the principles discussed	Paragraph 3 discusses a particular tactic for the anchoring principle; it does not discuss a separate principle. Further, the passage does not say that this tactic is the best of any tactic.
(B) To conclude that following the anchoring principle is more likely to result in a higher starting salary	The second paragraph might be interpreted as arguing this for the anchoring principle, but the third paragraph does not do this (nor does the passage as a whole *conclude* this).
(C) To suggest that diminishing any potential adversarial effects should be the primary concern of the candidate	The paragraph suggests that this is or should be one concern of a job candidate, but provides no information that it should be the *primary* concern.
(D) To offer a counterexample to the principle discussed in the prior paragraph	This choice directly contradicts the passage. The third paragraph *supports* the second paragraph. The third paragraph provides a refinement, or "further step," that can be taken with the anchoring principle introduced in the second paragraph.
(E) To provide additional guidance regarding the operation of the anchoring principle	CORRECT. The third paragraph describes an additional way in which the anchoring principle can be used effectively.

Notice that one of the trap answers (arguably) describes a paragraph of the passage, but not the paragraph that the question asks about. This is a common trap on Paragraph questions.

Also keep an eye out for answer choices that directly contradict what the passage says. Someone reading too quickly could easily reverse the information mentally. This is one reason it is so important to predict the answer in your own words before going to the choices!

2. Polymers: (C) presenting a useful basis for classifying a set of related substances

Step 1: Identify the question.

The language *primarily concerned with* in the question stem indicates that this is a Primary Purpose, or main idea, question.

Step 2: Find the support.

Ideally, you will have determined the main idea during your read-through of the passage; if you need to refresh your memory, return to your map.

Step 3: Predict an answer.

On main idea questions, Steps 2 and 3 are often compressed into one. The point of the passage is something like *probably the best way to classify man-made plastics is based on how they respond to heat.*

Step 4: Eliminate and find a match.

Answer choice	Explanation
(A) providing examples of real-world uses for various related substances	They do give some real-world uses, but that's not the main point. The examples are there to support the contention about classifying based on reaction to heat.
(B) contrasting the chemical compositions of various substances	The third paragraph does talk about this a bit, but it's not the overall point, which should connect to the whole passage.
(C) presenting a useful basis for classifying a set of related substances	CORRECT. This matches the point. The *related substances* are the various kinds of plastics, and the *useful basis for classifying* these plastics is the way they respond to heat.
(D) assessing the pros and cons of recycling various types of substances	This information is mentioned only as part of the passage detail; it is not the main point.
(E) outlining the primary categories of a set of related substances and proposing uses for each category	So close! This one looks good right up until the word *proposing*. The author doesn't propose anything related to usage of the plastic; rather, the author mentions what they are already used to build.

Notice that several of the incorrect answers mention details that are present in the passage; in other words, they represent true information from the passage. They just don't represent the *main idea*, which should relate to and encompass the passage as a whole. In the future, watch out for traps that do reflect something the passage said but don't answer the specific question asked.

The other trap answer is very close to correct but takes things one step too far with the word *proposing*. Watch out for trap answers that are 90% right but mess things up via just one or two wrong words.

3. Greek Wreck: (A) It provides evidence to support the main idea introduced earlier in the passage.

Step 1: Identify the question.

The language *the relationship of paragraph two to the passage as a whole* in the question stem indicates that this is a Paragraph question. Your task is to determine what role this paragraph plays in the overall simple story.

Step 2: Find the support.

Review your notes on the second paragraph, paying attention to how it relates to the other paragraphs. Or glance back at the second paragraph, as well as several lines immediately before and after it.

Step 3: Predict an answer.

One test-taker's map of this passage might look like this:

(1) AM found, spec: anc Grk, predict solar eclipse?
AM= sophis, not sure how made or who
(2) Now: DTL eclipse
AM= surpris acc.
(3) C: made by Arch (?)
evid given (math)

The point is something like *We still don't know who made AM or how it was made, but it was surprisingly accurate at predicting solar eclipses.* The first paragraph introduces the point. The second paragraph talks about how very complex eclipses are, underscoring the surprising fact that the AM is pretty accurate given that whoever made it didn't have any of the sophisticated equipment that is available today.

The second paragraph, then, is providing additional information to support the claim made in the first paragraph (that AM is surprisingly accurate given how old it is).

Step 4: Eliminate and find a match.

Answer choice	**Explanation**
(A) It provides evidence to support the main idea introduced earlier in the passage.	CORRECT. This matches what the second paragraph does.
(B) It presents a hypothesis that is rejected in the final paragraph of the passage.	Whoops! Time to look at the third paragraph, too. That paragraph talks more about who might have invented AM. The third paragraph isn't rejecting anything from the second paragraph, so this choice can't be right.
(C) It offers an example of a theory proposed in the first paragraph of the passage.	This one's closer. The first paragraph, though, didn't propose a theory as to who made this thing or how it was made; it just says that we still don't know.
(D) It suggests a solution to a problem described earlier in the passage.	The first paragraph could be described as a discussion of a problem, or conundrum. But the second paragraph does not propose a solution to that conundrum. (The third paragraph could be described this way.)
(E) It draws a parallel between two phenomena discussed in the passage.	Drawing a parallel would be making a connection between two separate phenomena, or events. The passage does not discuss two such events. Further, the second paragraph elaborates on the point discussed in the first paragraph, so answer (A) is a better match.

When there are several paragraphs, you may begin Steps 2 and 3 by reviewing only the paragraph with the point and the paragraph about which the question asks. When you get to the answers, though, you might realized that you also need to look at another paragraph, as the wording of answer (B) required. If you like, you can look at all paragraphs first. Alternatively, you can delay reviewing all paragraphs until you know for sure that an answer choice requires you to do so.

Answer (D) exemplifies a common trap on Paragraph questions: the answer choice describes a different paragraph in the passage. This information is true; it just doesn't answer the question asked.

Chapter 14

of

GMAT Foundations of Verbal

Part 3: **Reading Comprehension**

Specific Questions

In This Chapter...

Specific Detail Questions
Inference Questions
Specific Purpose Questions
Answers to Drill Sets

Chapter 14

Specific Questions

Specific questions require you to get into the detail of the passage. The questions can ask you to perform different kinds of analyses. In this chapter, you'll learn about the three most common Specific question types and you'll have a chance to practice your new skills.

Specific Detail Questions

Specific Detail questions ask you to find and "regurgitate" specific facts from the passage. That sounds kind of gross! It's not as bad as it sounds: your task is to find a specific piece of information in the passage and then find the answer choice that most accurately matches that piece of information. Many people like this particular type of RC question best because it really can be just like repeating back what someone has already told you.

Try out this short passage and question.

In the early 1940s, women's participation in the U.S. labor market changed dramatically as a result of the labor shortages resulting from the drafting of men to fight in World War II. Although persistent and institutionalized discrimination had discouraged women from paid work during the 1930s, the wartime government used patriotic propaganda to encourage women to work in defense industries. While women's employment was still viewed as an extraordinary measure for extraordinary times—and the female worker as merely filling in for a soldier to whom the job "properly" belonged—gender barriers were lowered somewhat during this period, and pay began to equalize. Despite these moves toward women's participation in the workforce, however, shifting forces in the post-war labor market meant that fewer American women worked outside the home in 1952 than in 1942.

According to the passage, which of the following was true of working women in the United States during World War II?

(A) As soon as soldiers returned home from the war, women were happy to give up their paid jobs and return to the home.

(B) Women exhibited extraordinary levels of skills relative to what was expected of them.

(C) Wages for women were closer to the typical wages paid to males than had been the case in earlier decades.

(D) Gender barriers began to equalize, allowing women greater access to jobs outside the home.

(E) Women were better suited than men to certain tasks needed in the defense industries.

1930s: W ≠ hold jobs

WWII 1940s: M → war, W → jobs

(P) good for W: discrim ↓, pay more =

BUT 1952 W work < 1942

The point: Discrimination went down and pay became more equal when more women joined the work force during World War II, but 10 years later, fewer women were working outside the home.

Step 1: Identify the question.

The language *according to the passage* indicates that this is a Specific Detail question. The question stem further indicates that you are looking for information about working women in the United States during World War II. (Note: You may already know that World War II took place from 1939 to 1945. If not, the first sentence of the passage indicates that the war was going on in the early 1940s.)

Step 2: Find the support.

The 1940s time frame was mostly detailed in the middle of the passage. The information about the 1930s (that women were discouraged from working) was pre-war and the information about 1952 was post-war.

Find the relevant text and, in order to get full context, start reading two to three lines before the "meat" of the text. Here's the relevant text (*lines 6–18*) for the wartime period:

> *Although persistent and institutionalized discrimination had discouraged women from paid work during the 1930s, the wartime government used patriotic propaganda to encourage women to work in defense industries. While women's employment was still viewed as an extraordinary measure for extraordinary times—and the female worker as merely filling in for a soldier to whom the job "properly" belonged—gender barriers were lowered somewhat during this period, and pay began to equalize.*

Step 3: Predict an answer.

So what was true? The government encouraged women to work. They were still viewed as filling in, not the real workers. But gender barriers were lowered a bit and pay got a little bit more equal.

Step 4: Eliminate and find a match.

(A) Based on the last sentence of the paragraph, it sounds like the women did eventually give up their jobs, but nothing indicates that they did so happily, nor does the passage indicate that this occurred *as soon as* the men returned home. Eliminate.

(B) The passage does use the word *extraordinary*, but in a different context. The fact that women were doing what was usually "man's work" was viewed as *extraordinary*, or very unusual. The passage does not indicate how competent the women were at their jobs. Eliminate.

(C) Yes! This matches the language *pay began to equalize*. It was not as equal before (*in earlier decades*) and it began to become more equal during the wartime 1940s.

(D) This answer choice mashes together two different parts of the same sentence, confusing the meaning. The passage says that *gender barriers were lowered* and that *pay began to equalize. Barriers* can't be *equalized*; they either prevent someone from doing something, or they are lowered or removed, allowing someone to do something more easily. Eliminate.

(E) The passage does not indicate anything about the competence or skills of women in the workforce in the 1940s.

The correct answer is **(C)**.

For Specific Detail questions, your four steps are as follows:

Step 1: Identify the question.

According to the passage . . .

The passage mentions which of the following . . .

Step 2: Find the support.

Don't rely on your memory, and don't even rely on your handwritten passage map exclusively. Use your passage map to figure out where you need to go in the original source passage.

Step 3: Predict an answer.

Read the text that you identified as important and try to answer the question in your own words.

Step 4: Eliminate and find a match.

Cross off any answer choices that are far from what you predicted or that contradict what the passage actually said. If you have more than one answer left, check the remaining choices against the relevant text from the passage.

Inference Questions

Inference questions are quite different from Specific Detail questions. When the GMAT asks you to infer something, it is not asking you to repeat back something that the passage already told you. Rather, the GMAT is asking you to draw a conclusion that must be true based on the information given in the passage. For example, what can you infer from this sentence?

> As opposed to typical artifacts from the period, the newly named Rozzi Urn depicts a battle scene.

A valid GMAT inference might be:

> Typical artifacts from the period in question do not depict battle scenes.

You might be thinking, "Duh. That's what the first sentence just said." But it isn't, not quite. The inference "flips" the given information into something new that absolutely must be true based on the original information. That's what you're looking to do on the GMAT: take a little baby step away from the given information to get to something that must be true.

On the GMAT, you will get into trouble if you infer the way that most people infer in the real world. In the real world, if someone tells you that *cats make the best pets*, you'd probably think that this person has a cat, or used to have a cat, or maybe wants to get a cat. None of these things has to be true however. On the GMAT, a valid inference *must be able to be proved true* based on some information from the passage. (For instance, it must be true that this person doesn't think that dogs make equally good pets.)

When answering an Inference question, the following are indicators of a WRONG answer:

- Answers that are *probably* true (but not definitely)
- Answers that require additional assumptions (such as about what people might have been thinking when they did something, or about what will happen in the future)

By the way, not every Inference question uses the word *infer*. Many questions use words such as *suggest* or *imply*. All these questions will be treated the same way: find the relevant information in the passage and pick something that MUST be true based on that information.

Drill 14.1 — What Can You Infer?

Determine what else must be true for each statement given. If you get stuck, try "flipping" the information.

1. Toads, unlike frogs, lack teeth and spend most of their time on land.

2. Irish-American groups pressed for a more accurate treatment of the Irish Potato Famine in textbooks used in American schools.

3. The company's household products division was responsible for 40% of its profits in 2010. The balance of its profits came from its beauty products, baby care, and health products divisions, with 25% of the balance coming from the baby care division.

4. Unlike most skinks, the crocodile skink of Papua New Guinea is nocturnal or crepuscular (active in the early mornings and at dusk).

5. In 1980, Canadian expenditures on these measures were only slightly lower than U.S. expenditures on these same measures. Throughout the 1980s and early 1990s, the Canadian expenditures increased by a constant rate of 2% per year and the U.S. expenditures by a constant rate of 3% per year.

6. In 2008, Ecuador became the first nation in the world to pass a constitution codifying the rights of nature.

7. Because of monumental shifts in the social behavior studied by the researcher in the 1970s, the researcher's methodology has proved to be of more lasting value than her results.

Answers are on pages 280–281.

Now that you've had some practice drawing GMAT inferences, try this full question.

In the early 1940s, women's participation in the U.S. labor market changed dramatically as a result of the labor shortages resulting from the drafting of men to fight in World War II. Although persistent and institutionalized discrimination had discouraged women from paid work during the 1930s, the wartime government used patriotic propaganda to encourage women to work in defense industries. While women's employment was still viewed as an extraordinary measure for extraordinary times—and the female worker as merely filling in for a soldier to whom the job "properly" belonged—gender barriers were lowered somewhat during this period, and pay began to equalize. Despite these moves toward women's participation in the workforce, however, shifting forces in the post-war labor market meant that fewer American women worked outside the home in 1952 than in 1942.

Which of the following can be inferred regarding women's employment during the period discussed in the passage?

(A) Discrimination against women in the workplace increased between 1942 and 1952.
(B) Women's job qualifications decreased during the period 1942–1952.
(C) The end of World War II caused many men to come home and take back jobs they had once held.
(D) Increased economic prosperity in the 1950s meant women didn't have to work.
(E) More women worked outside the home in 1942 than 10 years later.

1930s: W ≠ hold jobs

WWII 1940s: M → war, W → jobs

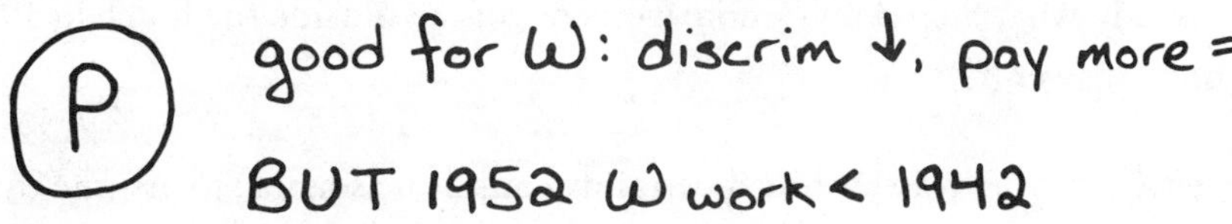

P
good for W: discrim ↓, pay more =
BUT 1952 W work < 1942

The point: Some good came of more women joining the workforce during World War II, but this good regressed after the war ended. (Note: This is worded a bit differently than it was earlier; different people will word the point in somewhat different ways!)

MEMORIZE IT

If a passage tells you that something happened, and an Inference answer choice gives a *possible reason* why that thing happened, that choice is wrong! Do not assign causes for things you are told have happened.

Step 1: Identify the question.

The word *inferred* indicates that this is an Inference question. The question stem further indicates that you need to infer something about *women's employment.*

Step 2: Find the support.

Most of the passage is about the topic of women's employment, so remind yourself of the major time frames:

> *. . . discrimination discouraged women from paid work during the 1930s*
>
> *. . . wartime government . . . encourage[d] women to work*
>
> *. . . fewer women worked outside the home in 1952 than in 1942*

MEMORIZE IT

Do not pick an answer that is merely "consistent with" something you were told in the passage. The correct answer must be able to be proven true from the passage.

Note: The passage contains additional detail about wartime employment; if none of the answers matches on your first pass, you can narrow down and review the more specific details about the 1940s.

Step 3: Predict an answer.

The correct answer should "flip" what the passage says. If women were discouraged from working in the 1930s but encouraged in the 1940s, then there was a change in behavior or attitudes toward women working. If fewer women worked outside the home in 1952, then more worked outside the home in 1942.

Step 4: Eliminate and find a match

(A) *Discrimination* was mentioned for the 1930s, not 1942 or 1952. Eliminate.
(B) The passage indicates that fewer women worked outside the home in 1952 than in 1942, but it does not say *why*. One possibility might have to do with job qualifications, but this does not have to be true.
(C) This sounds pretty good—that's probably what happened when the war ended. Leave this choice in.
(D) The passage doesn't mention anything about economic prosperity. Eliminate.
(E) This is exactly what Step 3 says: more women worked outside the home in 1942! But what about answer (C)?

It turns out that answer (C) is a big trap. While it certainly sounds reasonable to assume that a lot of men came back from World War II and took their old jobs back, the passage doesn't provide the information needed to make this inference. What if most of the soldiers died or were too injured to resume their old jobs? What if they came back and wanted to take new jobs, not resume their old ones? The passage does state that fewer women worked outside the home by 1952, but it does not provide information to infer that soldiers specifically took back their old jobs.

The correct answer is **(E)**.

For Inference questions, your four steps are as follows:

Step 1: Identify the question.

It can be inferred . . .

The author implies . . .

The passage suggests . . .

Step 2: Find the support.

As with all Specific questions, don't rely on your memory. Use your little handwritten map of the passage to figure out where you need to go in the passage.

Step 3: Predict an answer.

Read the text that you identified as important and try to answer the question in your own words. If you're not sure how to flip the language, just identify the relevant text on which the inference should be based.

Step 4: Eliminate and find a match.

Cross off any answer choices that could be true but do not have to be true (as well as any that can't be true, of course!). The correct answer must be able to be proven from the text of the passage.

Specific Purpose Questions

Specific Purpose questions ask you *why* the author mentions a specific piece of information. (For this reason, these questions are also sometimes called Why questions.)

It's important to recognize when the author is asking you *why* vs. *what*. The answers to the questions *What are you studying?* and *Why are you studying it?* are quite different! To see an illustration of how a *Why* question works, try out the problem below.

In the early 1940s, women's participation in the U.S. labor market changed dramatically as a result of the labor shortages resulting from the drafting of men to fight in World War II. Although persistent and institutionalized discrimination had discouraged women from paid work during the 1930s, the wartime government used patriotic propaganda to encourage women to work in defense industries. While women's employment was still viewed as an extraordinary measure for extraordinary times—and the female worker as merely filling in for a soldier to whom the job "properly" belonged—gender barriers were lowered somewhat during this period, and pay began to equalize. Despite these moves toward women's participation in the workforce, however, shifting forces in the post-war labor market meant that fewer American women worked outside the home in 1952 than in 1942.

The author mentions *the female worker as merely filling in for a soldier to whom the job "properly" belonged* primarily in order to

(A) argue that women should not have taken jobs away from soldiers
(B) assert that women were generally less competent than men to do the jobs in question
(C) establish that persistent and institutionalized discrimination still predominated in the workplace
(D) acknowledge that the changes brought about for female workers during this time period were not universally positive
(E) explain why gender barriers were lowered somewhat during the period In question

1930s: W $\neq$ hold jobs

WWII 1940s: M $\rightarrow$ war, W $\rightarrow$ jobs

(P) good for W: discrim $\downarrow$, pay more =

BUT 1952 W work $<$ 1942

The point: Some good came of more women joining the work force during World War II, but this good regressed after the war ended.

You know the drill now! Use the four-step process to answer the question.

Step 1: Identify the question.

The words *in order to* indicate that this is a Specific Purpose, or Why, question. Why did the author include the specific line quoted in the question stem?

Step 2: Find the support.

On Why questions, you'll need to make sure you have the full context. The sentence or two preceding the quoted text will typically tell you why the author introduced that text, so start a bit before the quoted text, in this case lines 6–18:

> *Although persistent and institutionalized discrimination had discouraged women from paid work during the 1930s, the wartime government used patriotic propaganda to encourage women to work in defense industries. While women's employment was still viewed as an extraordinary measure for extraordinary times—and the female worker as merely filling in for a soldier to whom the job "properly" belonged—gender barriers were lowered somewhat during this period, and pay began to equalize.*

Step 3: Predict an answer.

Before the war, women experienced a lot of discrimination. Then the government started encouraging women to work. The *While* start to the next sentence indicates a twist: although the fact that women were working was still viewed as something they wouldn't (or even shouldn't) be doing if the men hadn't gone off to war, some things did get better for women.

The author is showing the two sides of the coin. The country needed women to work, and the fact that so many did helped to lower gender barriers, but many people still felt that the situation was, or should be, only temporary.

Step 4: Eliminate and find a match.

(A) The men were off at war; they were literally unavailable to take the jobs. The government encouraged the women to fill in. Eliminate.
(B) The passage mentions nothing about the competency of either men or women. Eliminate.
(C) While it is likely true that discrimination still existed, the passage doesn't provide enough information to say that it predominated. All the passage indicates is that conditions did get at least somewhat better for women during this period. Eliminate.
(D) Yes! The sentence does list two positives (gender barriers lowered, pay more equalized), but the specific line quoted is a negative for women. The author is showing both sides of the coin.
(E) Just the opposite, in fact! The lowering of gender barriers was a positive for women. The fact that they were still viewed as filling in for men to whom the jobs "properly" belonged is a negative.

The correct answer is **(D)**.

For Specific Purpose (or Why) questions, your four steps are as follows:

Step 1: Identify the question.

in order to . . .

serves primarily to . . .

Step 2: Find the support.

Don't rely on your memory. Use your little handwritten map of the passage to figure out where you need to go in the passage. Make sure to start a sentence or two before the specific text cited, as the set-up for a Why answer often occurs just before the cited information is given in the passage.

Step 3: Predict an answer.

Read the text that you identified as important and try to answer the question in your own words.

Step 4: Eliminate and find a match.

Cross off any answer choices that are far from what you predicted or that contradict what the passage actually said. If you have more than one answer left, check the remaining choices against the relevant text from the passage.

Congratulations! You've made it through the three most common specific question types tested on RC passages. Make your own summary sheet that indicates the four-step process for each question type (you can just copy what's here, but you'll remember better if you write it in your own words). Test out your newly acquired skills in the following drill set.

Drill 14.2 — Try Full Passages

First, grab your smart phone or another timer: you're going to time yourself while working on these drills! Each passage has a suggested time limit given; you may work a little more quickly or a little more slowly than this suggested time limit.

Before answering the questions, articulate the point to yourself, as well as the purpose of each paragraph. Use the 4-step process to answer the questions.

Ready? Go!

Passage 1: Supernovae (6.5 minutes)

A supernova is a brief stellar explosion so luminous that it can outshine an entire galaxy. While the explosion itself typically lasts less than fifteen seconds, the light emitted by the supernova can take weeks or months to fade from view. During that time, a supernova can emit an amount of energy equivalent to the amount of energy the Sun is expected to radiate over its entire lifespan; the heat thus generated can create heavy elements, such as mercury, gold, and silver. Although supernovae explode frequently, few of them are visible to the naked eye from the Earth.

For millennia, humans have recorded supernova sightings; speculation about the origin and meaning of the phenomenon helped to develop modern models of scientific thought. Tycho Brahe was the first to postulate that the source of the explosion must be very far away from the Earth. After the sighting of a new supernova in 1604, Galileo sought to explain the phenomenon and built upon Tycho's theory in a series of lectures widely attended by the public in Padua, Italy. The lectures not only sought to explain the origin of the "star" (some posited that perhaps it was merely "vapour near the Earth"), but also seriously undermined the views of most philosophers and scientists at the time that the heavens were unchangeable. This idea was foundational to the geocentric worldview underpinned by a central and all-important the Earth, around which other celestial bodies revolved. Galileo's observations of the 1604 supernova helped to promote a heliocentric worldview, in which the planets (including the Earth) revolved around the Sun.

1. The primary purpose of the passage is to

   (A) explain the origins and history of supernovae
   (B) describe a shift in thought as a result of a natural event
   (C) juxtapose two opposing views about supernovae
   (D) establish the validity of a theory jointly held by two prominent scientists
   (E) illustrate how the scientific process works

2. The passage suggests that which of the following is true of the heliocentric model of the galaxy?

   (A) Tycho and other scientists agreed with Galileo that it was superior to the geocentric view.
   (B) It held that the Earth was the all-important center of the galaxy.
   (C) It was proved true based on data gathered from the 1604 supernova event.
   (D) It was later superceded by the geocentric worldview.
   (E) Prior to 1604, it was not the predominant theory describing the relationship between the planets and the Sun.

3. The passage mentions which of the following as a result of the supernova of 1604?

   (A) The supernova created and dispersed the heavy elements out of which the Earth and everything on it is made.
   (B) Tycho and Galileo worked together to promote the heliocentric worldview.
   (C) The public was interested in hearing lectures about the phenomenon.
   (D) Galileo's lectures were opposed by most philosophers and scientists.
   (E) Those who thought the supernova was "vapour" were proved wrong.

Passage 2: Freelancing (6.5 minutes)

As the proportion of Australian workers who are self-employed has boomed in the past decade, the topic of wealth creation for freelancers has become much more prevalent in business magazines. A standard maxim among such publications is that a sole proprietor is best off treating her business as a much larger enterprise with a set of core departments, including but not limited to executive, production, human resources, marketing, and finance functions. In effect, the freelancer would devote time and attention to each "department" in order to optimize her chances of success, and would, unaided, create content, advertising campaigns, contracts, and quarterly budgets.

Most freelancers, however, presently operate in the creative realm, encompassing not only traditional arts such as photography and writing but also more technical services such as computer programming and software engineering. Such creative forms of labor demand highly specialized skills. For the creative freelancer, then, whose most valued asset is labor, conceptualizing one's business in such a fashion risks the dilution of the company's most important resource: the freelancer's skills. Distributing one's labor across platforms is a zero-sum game that may yield positive results in some scenarios but not necessarily all. A photographer who spends his time developing a marketing plan may consequently jeopardize his public image by failing to devote sufficient effort to expanding his portfolio via new and high-value artwork. Moreover, because "word of mouth" is typically considered the most powerful means of marketing in a creative industry, the potential benefits of such a trade-off are far from certain.

4. According to the passage, which of the following statements about the present-day freelancer population in Australia is true?

   (A) It is increasingly preoccupied with the question of how to create more wealth.
   (B) The majority of the freelancer population is composed of creative professionals.
   (C) Most freelancers are artists.
   (D) Many freelancers see themselves as structurally identical to larger corporations.
   (E) It has redefined the priorities of the publishing industry.

5. It can be inferred from the passage that the author believes "word-of-mouth" marketing

   (A) is more prevalent in photography than in other industries
   (B) is a form of marketing that requires no work on the freelancer's part
   (C) calls into question the utility of a particular business model
   (D) lends credence to a photographer's choice to develop a marketing plan
   (E) underscores the importance of rejecting a widely held view

6. The author of the passage mentions the photographer (in line 34) primarily in order to

   (A) provide an example of an instance in which the principle being discussed could be problematic
   (B) suggest that, for this category of worker, the principle being discussed is rarely useful
   (C) promote the idea that photography should be viewed as an exception to a general rule
   (D) illustrate that marketing decisions are unique in that they should be considered based upon context
   (E) remind readers that artistic integrity is more important than marketing for a true artist

Passage 3: Cargo Cults (8.5 minutes)

Cargo cults are religious movements that have appeared in isolated tribal societies following interaction with technologically advanced cultures. Such cults arose in earnest in the years following World War II, as members of tribal societies came into contact with radios, televisions, guns, airplanes, and other "cargo" brought to Melanesian islands as part of the Allied war effort. Members of native societies, having little knowledge of Western manufacturing, found soldiers' explanations of the cargo's provenance unconvincing. Some concluded that the "cargo" had come about through spiritual means, created by the deities and ancestors of the native people, and that the foreigners had attracted the cargo to themselves through trickery, or through an error made by the deities and ancestors. Cargo cults arose for the purpose of attracting material wealth back to its "rightful owners" via religious rituals that sought to mimic the actions of the foreigners in order to attract cargo. On the island of Tanna in Vanuatu, cult members constructed elaborate airstrips and control towers intended to attract airplanes; soldiers in re-created U.S. Army uniforms conducted parade ground drills with wooden rifles.

Members of cargo cults commit the fallacy of confusing a *necessary* condition with a *sufficient* one. It is true that an airstrip and a control tower are necessary for executing a safe landing of an airplane; they are not, however, sufficient to attract an airplane in the first place. Thus, the term "cargo cult" has arisen as an idiom to describe those who mimic the superficial appearance of a procedure without understanding the underlying purpose, meaning, or functioning of that procedure.

In the book *Surely You're Joking, Mr. Feynman!*, physicist Richard Feynman dedicates a chapter to "cargo cult science," the appearance of real science without an understanding of the underlying workings of real science. For example, through meticulous experimentation, a researcher named Young discovered that laboratory rats were using the sounds made by a maze's floorboards to memorize positions within the maze, thus invalidating experimental results. When the maze was put on a floor of sand, this cue was removed, and future experiments were more valid. However, some scientists—cargo cult scientists—went on running rats through a maze without the sand, publishing their results and going about the motions of science without, as Feynman argues, actually doing science.

7. The primary purpose of the passage is to

   (A) offer a suggestion for improving the results of scientific experiments
   (B) explain the origin and wider adaptation of a particular term
   (C) demonstrate that cargo cults mistakenly confuse preceding events with causal events
   (D) argue that it is important for scientists to take into account the research of other scientists in their fields
   (E) establish that the cargo cult members' mistakes in logic could be remedied through the scientific method

8. The passage suggests that some residents of Tanna concluded that they were the "rightful owners" (lines 23) of the "cargo" because

   (A) they didn't believe the reasons given for the goods' actual origins
   (B) they believed all possessions were created by deities
   (C) they believed they were owed a debt by their ancestors
   (D) military forces had given them the cargo
   (E) guns and airplanes were unknown to them prior to World War II

9. The author introduces the example of the researcher named Young (lines 49–55) in order to

   (A) demonstrate the difference between a necessary cause and a sufficient one
   (B) explore the contributions to science made by Feynman and his students
   (C) establish that members of cargo cults cannot also be members of the scientific research community
   (D) argue that the scientific method is not the only means by which to conduct a scientific experiment
   (E) illustrate how some scientists might not be conducting rigorous scientific research

10. According to the passage, the similarity between cargo cult members and practitioners of cargo cult science can most appropriately be described in which of the following ways?

   (A) Both use inappropriate equipment to try to force a phenomenon to occur.
   (B) Both refuse to accept the principles of the scientific method.
   (C) Both adhere to certain processes without fully understanding how those processes function.
   (D) Both believe that forces outside of their control may impact their lives or research.
   (E) Both would benefit from enhanced scientific education.

Passage 4: Anchoring (6.5 minutes)

During salary negotiations, some career advisors recommend that the job seeker allow the company to make the initial salary offer. Proponents of this approach assert that making an initial offer that is too high or too low can hurt a party's position. For example, if a job seeker initially requests a lower salary than the employer was prepared to provide, then the end result is likely to be a lower final salary offer than might have been attained had the candidate allowed the company to start the negotiations. Thus, the party that initially does not name a salary is in a better position to protect its interests even while allowing the opposing side to feel more in control of the negotiations.

Critics of this approach emphasize the importance of anchors, cognitive focal points that direct any given negotiation. Under the anchoring principle, the initial offer becomes the number to which all other numbers are compared. The party who makes the initial offer is able to define the range of the negotiation and thereby has more significant influence over the final deal. In order to avoid undermining their own interests, job seekers would purposely start negotiations at a higher-than-expected anchor point, but not a point so high that the company in question balks at negotiating entirely.

Harvard Law School's Program on Negotiation suggests one further step: establish an anchor without making an explicit offer. A candidate might mention, for instance, that a colleague recently accepted a similar position at a specified salary, or that the average salary for people with similar qualifications falls within a particular range. Such anchoring tactics may diminish the sometimes adversarial effect of a direct offer.

11. According to the passage, the proponents of the two theories differ in that

    (A) one group believes that remaining silent is the better way to negotiate, while the other group believes that active conversations are necessary
    (B) one group believes that its theory will lead to the best possible salary outcome for the job seeker, while the other group believes that its theory will lead to the best possible salary outcome for the company
    (C) one group believes that a high anchoring point should be set, while the other group believes that a low anchoring point should be set
    (D) one group believes that the party to make the starting offer has the stronger negotiating position, while the other group believes that the party to make the starting offer has the weaker negotiating position
    (E) one group believes that an adversarial negotiating approach is preferable, while the other group believes that a non-adversarial approach is preferable

12. The passage suggests that, when following the anchoring principle, a job candidate who begins negotiations by offering a modest salary level will likely end up with

    (A) a lower salary offer than he would have secured if he had made an initial offer that was extremely low
    (B) a salary similar to that of someone who allowed the company to set the initial anchor point
    (C) a lower salary than he would have secured if he had offered a higher starting level
    (D) a higher salary than he would have secured if he had offered a higher starting level
    (E) a higher salary than he would have secured if he had allowed the company to make the initial offer

13. The author cites the Program on Negotiation (lines 33–34) in order to

    (A) establish that a reputable institution supports one negotiation method over another
    (B) acknowledge a controversy associated with a particular negotiation method
    (C) demonstrate that a single negotiation method is not sufficient for all possible situations
    (D) assert that one negotiation method is markedly superior to another
    (E) introduce an additional tactic for use with a specific negotiation method

Answers are on pages 281–297.

Answers to Drill Sets

Answers to Drill 14.1 — Inference Drill

1. Since toads are presented as *unlike frogs* in a specific way, it must be true that frogs have teeth and do NOT spend most of their time on land. (If you said "frogs spend most of their time in the water," then you were using outside information—for all you know from the sentence, frogs spend most of their time in the air.)

2. If Irish-American groups *pressed for a more accurate treatment*, they must have thought that the treatment of the Irish Potato Famine in textbooks used in American schools was not accurate enough.

3. *The balance* means the rest or the remainder. So if household products accounted for 40% of its profits and baby products for 25% *of the balance*, then baby products accounted for 25% of the leftover 60%. One-fourth of 60% is 15%. Thus, household accounted for 40% and baby for 15%, for a total of 55%, so the other two divisions, beauty and health, combined for 45%.

4. The clue is *unlike most skinks*. Since the crocodile skink is active at night (*nocturnal*) or in the early morning or at dusk, pretty much the only time that leaves for the regular skinks is daytime. Thus, most skinks are active in the daytime. (If you've never heard of a skink, don't worry—almost no one has. No previous knowledge of skinks is required here.)

5. The Canadian expenditures were lower in 1980 and then grew at a slower rate than the already higher American expenditures. Throughout the given time period of the 1980s and early 1990s, then, U.S. expenditures were consistently higher (or Canadian expenditures were consistently lower).

Think a little more about #5. Since you know for sure that American expenditures throughout the period were always higher and also grew at a faster rate, you could also infer some fairly random-sounding (but not really random) facts, such as:

> Canadian expenditures in 1987 were lower than American expenditures in 1989.

That sounds out of scope, but actually, that statement must be true based on the original information—if American expenditures are higher throughout the entire period, and the gap between the American and Canadian expenditures widens every year, then you can safely conclude that American expenditures will always be greater than Canadian expenditures from the same year or an earlier year.

6. If Ecuador was the first nation to pass this particular type of constitution, then you can infer that, prior to 2008, no country had passed this type of constitution. You could even infer something that might sound too specific at first: As of 2001, Germany did not codify the rights of nature.

7. It might be helpful to paraphrase the original argument before making an inference. The argument is saying something like: *Since a lot has changed since the 1970s, the researcher's methodology is still valuable but the actual results are not as valuable.*

What can you infer from that? Her results are out of date.

Answers to Drill 14.2 — Try Full Passages

Passage 1: Supernovae

Main point: A particular type of phenomenon (supernova) helped some scientists to support a new model (the Earth revolves around the Sun).

Paragraph 1: Supernovae expend a huge amount of energy and some can be seen from the Earth.

Paragraph 2: Supernovae ended up being part of the support for a new, heliocentric worldview (the Earth revolves around the Sun, not the other way around).

Passage map:

(1) SN: explode, really bright
DTL

(2) SN spec → modern sci thought
TB 1st: SN really far away
1604 G: origin, undermine P
G: Earth revolves around sun

1. (B) describe a shift in thought as a result of a natural event

Step 1: Identify the question.

The words *primary purpose* indicate that this is a Primary Purpose question.

Step 2: Find the support.

Ideally, you will have determined the main idea during your read-through of the passage; if you need to refresh your memory, return to your map.

Step 3: Predict an answer.

The point of the passage: A particular type of phenomenon (supernova) helped some scientists to support a new model (the Earth revolves around the Sun).

Step 4: Eliminate and find a match.

Answer Choice	**Explanation**
(A) explain the origins and history of supernovae	The first paragraph does explain what supernovae are. The origins are not explored, however, nor does this choice account for the message in the second paragraph.
(B) describe a shift in thought as a result of a natural event	CORRECT. Some scientists used supernovae as one piece of evidence in support of a new scientific model.
(C) juxtapose two opposing views about supernovae	The passage does discuss two opposing views (geocentric vs. heliocentric), but these are not views *about supernovae.*
(D) establish the validity of a theory jointly held by two prominent scientists	The passage does not indicate that Galileo and Tycho's theory is now valid. (Be careful not to bring in your own outside knowledge!)
(E) illustrate how the scientific process works	This choice is too broad. One could argue that the scientific process was in use, but the purpose of the passage is much more specific.

2. (E) Prior to 1604, it was not the predominant theory describing the relationship between the planets and the Sun.

Step 1: Identify the question.

The word *suggests* indicates that this is an Inference question.

Step 2: Find the support.

The question asks about the heliocentric model; this is first referenced later in lines 27–41 of the second paragraph:

> *The lectures not only sought to explain the origin of the "star" (some posited that perhaps it was merely "vapour near the Earth"), but also seriously undermined the views of most philosophers and scientists at the time that the heavens were unchangeable.*

> *This idea was foundational to the geocentric worldview underpinned by a central and all-important the Earth, around which other celestial bodies revolved. Galileo's observations of the 1604 supernova helped to promote a heliocentric worldview, in which the planets (including the Earth) revolved around the Sun.*

Step 3: Predict an answer.

At the time, *most philosophers and scientists* believed in something called the *geocentric* view. But *Galileo's observations of the supernova helped to promote a heliocentric* view. The heliocentric view, then, was relatively new, and Galileo did not agree with most of the others.

Step 4: Eliminate and find a match

Answer Choice	**Explanation**
(A) Tycho and other scientists agreed with Galileo that it was superior to the geocentric view.	The argument indicates only that Galileo built upon Tycho's supernovae theory, not that Tycho agreed with the heliocentric worldview. Further, no other scientists are also cited as agreeing with Galileo.
(B) It held that the Earth was the all-important center of the galaxy.	The geocentric view holds this, not the heliocentric view.
(C) It was proved true based on data gathered from the 1604 supernova event.	The passage does not indicate that the heliocentric model was proved true at any point.
(D) It was later superseded by the geocentric worldview.	At the time, *most philosophers and scientists* believed the geocentric view; the heliocentric view is presented as new or gaining in importance, after the geocentric view.
(E) Prior to 1604, it was not the predominant theory describing the relationship between the planets and the Sun.	CORRECT. Since *most philosophers and scientists* believed in the geocentric worldview prior to Galileo's lectures, it must be the case that the heliocentric view was not the predominant theory prior to those lectures.

3. (C) The public was interested in hearing lectures about the phenomenon.

Step 1: Identify the question.

The language *mentions which of the following* indicates that this is a Specific Detail question.

Step 2: Find the support.

What happened as a result of the 1604 supernova? Lines 22–23 talk about this:

> *After the sighting of a new supernova in 1604, Galileo sought to explain the phenomenon and built upon Tycho's theory in a series of lectures widely attended by the public*

in Padua, Italy. The lectures not only sought to explain the origin of the "star" (some posited that perhaps it was merely "vapour near the Earth"), but also seriously undermined the views of most philosophers and scientists at the time that the heavens were unchangeable.

Step 3: Predict an answer.

Multiple things occurred as a result of the 1604 supernova. Start with the first one or two and check the answers for a match. If that doesn't work, read a little further and check the answers again.

Galileo gave some lectures to the public. He tried to explain where the supernova came from. He also ended up undermining what most scientists at the time thought.

Step 4: Eliminate and find a match.

Answer Choice	**Explanation**
(A) The supernova created and dispersed the heavy elements out of which the Earth and everything on it is made.	The first paragraph does mention that a supernova can create heavy elements, but the Earth must already have existed when the 1604 supernova, specifically, was observed (by people living on the Earth!).
(B) Tycho and Galileo worked together to promote the heliocentric worldview.	The passage indicates only that Galileo built on some of Tycho's earlier work, not that the two worked together.
(C) The public was interested in hearing lectures about the phenomenon.	CORRECT. The passage indicates that Galileo's lectures on the supernova were *widely attended by the public.*
(D) Galileo's lectures were opposed by most philosophers and scientists.	Galileo's theory did undermine the theory followed by most of his peers, but the passage does not indicate that his peers opposed what he had to say.
(E) Those who thought the supernova was "vapour" were proved wrong.	The vapour idea was one hypothesis; the passage does not indicate that the 1604 supernova or Galileo's lectures outright disproved this (or any other) hypothesis.

Note that the detail mentioned in the correct answer was so minor that you might not have called it out specifically when reviewing the passage. That's okay. As long as you have just re-read the two or three pertinent sentences, either you will be able to recall those kinds of seemingly more minor details or you will be able to re-check the text quickly since you have just identified the relevant couple of sentences.

Passage 2: Freelancing

Main point: The "freelancer as a company" idea might work for some businesses, but freelancers should be careful that they're not actually harming their businesses, especially those working in creative fields.

Paragraph 1: Business magazines say that a freelancer should still have all the "departments" that a larger company would have.

Paragraph 2: The author thinks this won't always work, especially for those in the creative realm. If creative freelancers take too much time away from actually creating stuff, then the overall business may be hurt.

Passage map:

(1) Bus Pub: FL should run as business w/ dep'ts, etc.

(2) auth: BUT creative FL might be hurt by this

4. **(B) The majority of the freelancer population is composed of creative professionals.**

Step 1: Identify the question.

The language *according to the passage* indicates that this is a Specific Detail question.

Step 2: Find the support.

The passage mentions Australian freelancers in the very first sentence *(lines 1–5)*:

> *As the proportion of Australian workers who are self-employed has boomed in the past decade, the topic of wealth creation for freelancers has become much more prevalent in business magazines.*

The passage adds additional information about this population at the beginning of the second paragraph *(lines 18–23)*:

> *Most freelancers, however, presently operate in the creative realm, encompassing not only traditional arts such as photography and writing but also more technical services such as computer programming and software engineering.*

Step 3: Predict an answer.

> In Australia, a higher proportion of self-employed workers are freelancers today than 10 years ago, and most of them work in creative fields.

Step 4: Eliminate and find a match.

Answer Choice	**Explanation**
(A) It is increasingly preoccupied with the question of how to create more wealth.	The passage says that business magazines are talking about this more, not that freelancers are becoming preoccupied with the topic.
(B) The majority of the freelancer population is composed of creative professionals.	CORRECT. The first sentence of the second paragraph indicates this.
(C) Most freelancers are artists.	This is a tricky answer! *Operating in the creative realm* does not necessarily mean that someone is an artist. The title of artist is more narrow than the idea of working in the creative realm in general.
(D) Many freelancers see themselves as structurally identical to larger corporations.	The passage does not indicate that this is the case.
(E) It has redefined the priorities of the publishing industry.	While the passage does say that business magazines are writing more about wealth creation for freelancers, no information is provided to say that the priorities of the publishing industry have been redefined.

5. (C) calls into question the utility of a particular business model

Step 1: Identify the question.

The word *inferred* indicates that this is an inference question.

Step 2: Find the support.

"Word-of-mouth" marketing is mentioned at the end of the passage in lines 34–43:

> *A photographer who spends his time developing a marketing plan may consequently jeopardize his public image by failing to devote sufficient effort to expanding his portfolio via new and high-value artwork. Moreover, because "word of mouth" is typically considered the most powerful means of marketing in a creative industry, the potential benefits of such a trade-off are far from certain.*

Step 3: Predict an answer.

> As a photographer contributes to his portfolio, he may gain much wider reach via word-of-mouth marketing. Taking time away from the portfolio to write up a marketing plan might actually hurt this photographer's business. So the author believes that word of mouth marketing could be valuable enough, in some cases, to negate the idea that a freelancer should run himself as a complete business.

Step 4: Eliminate and find a match.

Answer Choice	Explanation
(A) is more prevalent in photography than in other industries	The photographer is just one example; the author doesn't compare photography to other industries.
(B) is a form of marketing that requires no work on the freelancer's part	No, expanding the portfolio is work!
(C) calls into question the utility of a particular business model	CORRECT. The author uses this as an example of why the "run as a business" theory might not be useful for all freelancers.
(D) lends credence to a photographer's choice to develop a marketing plan	If anything, the opposite! If he's developing a marketing plan, he might have to take time away from building his portfolio, which would have potentially helped expand his word of mouth.
(E) underscores the importance of rejecting a widely held view	This choice goes too far. The author doesn't completely reject the theory; rather, the author points out that it would not necessarily be the right path for everyone.

6. (A) provide an example of an instance in which the principle being discussed could be problematic

Step 1: Identify the question.

The language *primarily in order to* indicates that this is a Specific Purpose, or Why, question.

Step 2: Find the support.

The photographer is first mentioned later in the second paragraph. Start a sentence or two before, as the answer to a Why question often hinges on the information just prior (lines 25–39):

> *For the creative freelancer, then, whose most valued asset is labor, conceptualizing one's business in such a fashion risks the dilution of the company's most important resource: the freelancer's skills. Distributing one's labor across platforms is a zero-sum game that may yield positive results in some scenarios but not necessarily all. A photographer who spends his time developing a marketing plan may consequently jeopardize his public image by failing to devote sufficient effort to expanding his portfolio via new and high-value artwork.*

Step 3: Predict an answer.

The photographer is an example to illustrate how someone could risk the dilution of [his] skills and to establish that the "run as a business" plan might not work in all scenarios.

Step 4: Eliminate and find a match.

Answer Choice	Explanation
(A) provide an example of an instance in which the principle being discussed could be problematic	CORRECT. This is exactly why the example of the photographer is introduced.
(B) suggest that, for this category of worker, the principle being discussed is rarely useful	The passage specifically states that the *principle may yield positive results in some scenarios but not necessarily all.* This language does not match the usage *rarely useful.*
(C) promote the idea that photography should be viewed as an exception to a general rule	The author does not use photography as an exception to the rule. Rather, the author uses this example to illustrate her main point.
(D) illustrate that marketing decisions are unique in that they should be considered based upon context	This choice is confusingly worded. Luckily, you can use just the first half to answer: *marketing decisions are unique.* The passage does not indicate this.
(E) remind readers that artistic integrity is more important than marketing for a true artist	Some people may believe this, but the passage does not indicate this.

Passage 3: Cargo Cults

Main point: A particular phenomenon (cargo cult) has evolved into a general term that can apply to other groups (including modern groups), not just isolated tribes.

Paragraph 1: WWII: Technologically advanced groups brought technology to isolated tribal societies who thought the technology was spiritual in nature. They developed cargo cults that tried to "attract" the technology back to them.

Paragraph 2: Cargo cult is now a term to describe anyone who superficially mimics something without really understanding what's going on.

Paragraph 3: Feynman wrote about a scientific example of cargo cult science, dealing with lab rats.

① tribe interact Western → CC
gods created equip
get it back via rituals

② CC = stepping thru motions
not really understanding

③ F: "CC science" same def as
ex: Young, rats

7. **(B) explain the origin and wider adaptation of a particular term**

Step 1: Identify the question.

This is a Primary Purpose question.

Step 2: Find the support.

Ideally, you will have determined the main idea during your read-through of the passage; if you need to refresh your memory, return to your map.

Step 3: Predict an answer.

The main point, as articulated earlier, is:

> A particular phenomenon (cargo cult) has evolved into a general term that can apply to other groups (including modern groups), not just isolated tribes.

Step 4: Eliminate and find a match

Answer Choice	Explanation
(A) offer a suggestion for improving the results of scientific experiments	While you might surmise that Feynman's suggestion is "don't be a cargo cult scientist," the point of the overall passage doesn't rest on scientific experiments.
(B) explain the origin and wider adaptation of a particular term	CORRECT. This matches the main point.
(C) demonstrate that cargo cults mistakenly confuse preceding events with causal events	This choice is confusing. The examples given in the first paragraph do go along with this idea. The broader point, however, is that the term cargo cult itself has expanded in usage and meaning.
(D) argue that it is important for scientists to take into account the research of other scientists in their fields	Most people would agree with this, but it is not the main point of this particular passage.
(E) establish that the cargo cult members' mistakes in logic could be remedied through the scientific method	This is a mash-up of some ideas in the passage. The cargo cult members are making logical mistakes, but the passage doesn't focus on employing the scientific method to fix these mistakes. (This could apply to the scientists in paragraph 3, but not to the tribal members in paragraph 1.)

8. (A) they didn't believe the reasons given for the goods' actual origins

Step 1: Identify the question.

The word *suggests* indicates that this is an Inference question.

Step 2: Find the support.

The question references specific lines. As always, start a sentence or two before the actual reference, in this case lines 10–25:

> *Members of native societies, having little knowledge of Western manufacturing, found soldiers' explanations of the cargo's provenance unconvincing. Some concluded that the "cargo" had come about through spiritual means, created by the deities and ancestors of the native people, and that the foreigners had attracted the cargo to themselves through trickery, or through an error made by the deities and ancestors. Cargo cults arose for the purpose of attracting material wealth back to its "rightful owners" via religious rituals that sought to mimic the actions of the foreigners in order to attract cargo.*

Step 3: Predict an answer.

> In the absence of what they considered a convincing explanation, some tribe members came up with their own explanation: their own deities (gods) and ancestors made this stuff but were *tricked* by the foreigners . . . so the foreigners are not the rightful owners. Therefore, the tribe members must be the rightful owners (according to their reasoning).

Step 4: Eliminate and find a match.

Answer Choice	**Explanation**
(A) they didn't believe the reasons given for the goods' actual origins	CORRECT. They found the soldiers' explanations *unconvincing.* In other words, they didn't believe the (true!) reasons given, so they eventually came up with their own explanation.
(B) they believed all possessions were created by deities	The word *all* is too extreme. The cargo in question was believed to be made by deities or ancestors, but no reference is made to *all possessions.*
(C) they believed they were owed a debt by their ancestors	The passage does say that they believed the cargo to be created by deities and ancestors, but it says nothing about the ancestors specifically owing them a debt.
(D) military forces had given them the cargo	If the military had given them the cargo, then they would not have needed to *attract [it]* back to themselves.
(E) guns and airplanes were unknown to them prior to World War II	The passage says that they had *little knowledge of manufacturing,* but does not provide evidence to infer that these objects were completely *unknown* to the islanders.

9. (E) illustrate how some scientists might not be conducting rigorous scientific research

Step 1: Identify the question.

The *in order* to language indicates that this is a Specific Purpose question. Why did the author introduce the example of Young?

Step 2: Find the support.

Support can be found in lines 45–62:

> *. . . physicist Richard Feynman dedicates a chapter to "cargo cult science," the appearance of real science without an understanding of the underlying workings of real science. For example, through meticulous experimentation, a researcher named Young discovered that laboratory rats were using the sounds made by a maze's floorboards to memorize positions within the maze, thus invalidating experimental results. When the maze was put on a floor of sand, this cue was removed, and future experiments were more valid. However, some scientists—cargo cult scientists—went on running rats through a maze without the sand, publishing their results and going about the motions of science without, as Feynman argues, actually doing science.*

Step 3: Predict an answer.

Young supports Feynman's contention that some (other) scientists are going through the motions of science without actually conducting good science.

Step 4: Eliminate and find a match.

Answer Choice	Explanation
(A) demonstrate the difference between a necessary cause and a sufficient one	Paragraph 2 mentions the concept of necessary and sufficient, not paragraph 3.
(B) explore the contributions to science made by Feynman and his students	The passage doesn't indicate that Young was Feynman's student or that Feynman had anything to do with Young's experiment.
(C) establish that members of cargo cults cannot also be members of the scientific research community	Though it's true that the islanders probably aren't also members of the scientific research community, the passage doesn't say that such a crossover is impossible. In fact, Feynman contends that certain scientists are basically members of a scientific cargo cult.
(D) argue that the scientific method is not the only means by which to conduct a scientific experiment	While this may be true in the real world, the passage doesn't introduce Young's experiment for this reason.
(E) illustrate how some scientists might not be conducting rigorous scientific research	CORRECT. The other scientists did not take Young's research findings into account; they just kept performing bad experiments.

10. (C) Both adhere to certain processes without fully understanding how those processes function.

Step 1: Identify the question.

The language *according to the passage* signals that this is a Specific Detail question.

Step 2: Find the support.

The question asks for a similarity between the islanders in paragraph 1 and the cargo cult scientists in paragraph 3. The answer should have something to do with the definition of cargo cults, which can be found in lines 38–43 of paragraph 2:

> *Thus, the term "cargo cult" has arisen as an idiom to describe those who mimic the superficial appearance of a procedure without understanding the underlying purpose, meaning, or functioning of that procedure.*

Step 3: Predict an answer.

People in both groups are operating with only a superficial understanding of the situation at hand.

Step 4: Eliminate and find a match.

Answer Choice	**Explanation**
(A) Both use inappropriate equipment to try to force a phenomenon to occur.	The islanders do this, but the scientists do not.
(B) Both refuse to accept the principles of the scientific method.	The scientific method is not mentioned with relation to the islanders. (It also isn't accurate to say that the scientists refuse to accept the principles of the scientific method; rather, they appear not to understand those principles.)
(C) Both adhere to certain processes without fully understanding how those processes function.	CORRECT. This matches the way in which the term *cargo cult* is used.
(D) Both believe that forces outside of their control may impact their lives or research.	If anything, the opposite is true. The islanders think things are within their control; otherwise, they would not take steps to try to attract the cargo to themselves.
(E) Both would benefit from enhanced scientific education.	This may be true for the scientists, but the topic of scientific education is irrelevant for the islanders.

Passage 4 — Anchoring

Main point: Two camps: (1) let the other side start so that you don't start too low by accident, and (2) you start with a higher offer to set the anchoring point for remaining negotiations. Second option addresses the concerns of the first.

Paragraph 1: Negotiation approach: let the other side go first, so that you don't underbid.

Paragraph 2: Alternative strategy: go first to set the "anchor" point for future negotiations. Start on the high side.

Paragraph 3: Harvard supports #2: start by giving a stat for someone else or an average.

Passage map:

Neg. salary

(1) let co. offer first	(2) indiv offer first and high end up ↑↑ overall? (3) cite similar stats

11. (D) one group believes that the party to make the starting offer has the stronger negotiating position, while the other group believes that the party to make the starting offer has the weaker negotiating position

Step 1: Identify the question.

According to the passage indicates that this is a Specific Detail question.

Step 2: Find the support.

Return to your notes summary for this question. The first paragraph summarizes the position of the first group and the second and third paragraphs summarize the position of the second group.

Step 3: Predict an answer.

One group thinks that the job seeker should let the company offer first. The other group thinks that the job seeker should offer first and should specifically offer a salary at the high end of an acceptable range.

Step 4: Eliminate and find a match

Answer Choice	**Explanation**
(A) one group believes that remaining silent is the better way to negotiate, while the other group believes that active conversations are necessary	The first paragraph does mention a party that declines to make the initial offer, but only at first. If one side never speaks, it's impossible to negotiate! The passage doesn't indicate that either side supports remaining silent throughout the negotiation.
(B) one group believes that its theory will lead to the best possible salary outcome for the job seeker, while the other group believes that its theory will lead to the best possible salary outcome for the company	Both groups think that their theory will help the *job seeker.*
(C) one group believes that a high anchoring point should be set, while the other group believes that a low anchoring point should be set	One group does believe in setting a high anchoring point, but the other does not believe in setting a low anchoring point.
(D) one group believes that the party to make the starting offer has the stronger negotiating position, while the other group believes that the party to make the starting offer has the weaker negotiating position	CORRECT. The anchoring group does believe that the party making the opening offer is in the stronger position. The other group does believe that making the opening offer puts that party in a weaker position.
(E) one group believes that an adversarial negotiating approach is preferable, while the other group believes that a non-adversarial approach is preferable	The passage does not say that either group believes in an adversarial approach to negotiations.

12. (C) a lower salary than he would have secured if he had offered a higher starting level

Step 1: Identify the question.

The word *suggests* indicates that this is an Inference question.

Step 2: Find the support.

Support can be found in lines 21–32:

> *Under the anchoring principle, the initial offer becomes the number to which all other numbers are compared. The party who makes the initial offer is able to define the range of the negotiation and thereby has more significant influence over the final deal. In order to avoid undermining their own interests, job seekers would purposely start negotiations at a higher-than-expected anchor point, but not a point so high that the company in question balks at negotiating entirely.*

Step 3: Predict an answer.

The anchoring strategy is to figure out a reasonable salary range and then start the negotiation by offering something at the high end (but still reasonable/within range). According to the theory, the job seeker will end up with a better salary in the end because he will have established a high anchor point around which future counteroffers will be based.

So what might happen if someone offers only a modest salary level to start? This scenario is basically what the proponents of the first theory fear: if you start too low, you are more likely to end up with a lower salary than you might otherwise have gotten (after all, the company is unlikely to make a counteroffer that is higher than what you initially propose!).

Step 4: Eliminate and find a match.

Answer Choice	Explanation
(A) a lower salary offer than he would have secured if he had made an initial offer that was extremely low	*Extremely* low is lower than *modest* (which is low but not extremely so). Thus, the modest initial offer would anchor at a higher point and would likely lead to a higher salary in the end than an extremely low initial offer would.
(B) a salary similar to that of someone who allowed the company to set the initial anchor point	According to the anchoring principle, making a modest offer initially will set a low anchor for the negotiations and will likely lead to a lower outcome. Allowing the company to make the initial offer runs the risk of establishing a low anchor as well, because the company wants to offer as little as it can to secure the candidate. However, the passage offers no way to compare these two effects.
(C) a lower salary than he would have secured if he had offered a higher starting level	CORRECT. The anchoring principle says that if you start with a higher offer, you'll be more likely to end up with a higher salary in the end. If you start with a more modest salary, then, you'll be likely to end up with a lower offer instead.
(D) a higher salary than he would have secured if he had offered a higher starting level	The anchoring principle says the opposite: if the initial offer is too modest, then he will likely end up with a *lower* offer.
(E) a higher salary than he would have secured if he had allowed the company to make the initial offer	The anchoring principle is theorized to work to the candidate's benefit when he starts with a high offer, not a modest offer.

13. (E) introduce an additional tactic for use with a specific negotiation method

Step 1: Identify the question.

The *in order to* language indicates that this is a Specific Purpose question.

Step 2: Find the support.

Because the citation is at the beginning of a paragraph and this is a Why question, remind yourself of the purpose of the prior paragraph. Paragraph 2 *(lines 33–43)* introduces the anchoring principle and explains how it works.

> *Harvard Law School's Program on Negotiation suggests one further step: establish an anchor without making an explicit offer. A candidate might mention, for instance, that a colleague recently accepted a similar position at a specified salary, or that the average salary for people with similar qualifications falls within a particular range. Such anchoring tactics diminish the sometimes adversarial effect of a direct offer.*

Step 3: Predict an answer.

The third paragraph introduces *one further step* to follow when using the anchoring principle. The information, then, elaborates on the principle introduced in the previous paragraph.

Step 4: Eliminate and find a match.

Answer Choice	**Explanation**
(A) establish that a reputable institution supports one negotiation method over another	The passage doesn't indicate that Harvard's Program on Negotiation prefers one method to the other.
(B) acknowledge a controversy associated with a particular negotiation method	Although the *sometimes adversarial effect* might be viewed as a potential *controversy*, a controversy associated with a negotiation method would be a debate about its efficacy or its side effects. The fact that a direct offer sometimes has an adversarial effect is not presented as a controversy itself.
(C) demonstrate that a single negotiation method is not sufficient for all possible situations	This choice may be true in the real world, but the passage itself does not say this. Moreover, in this context, the word *demonstrate* is a synonym of *prove*; you would need a level of mathematical certainty to demonstrate, or prove, this.
(D) assert that one negotiation method is markedly superior to another	The information from the Program on Negotiation does not in any way denigrate (or even mention!) the other method (i.e., letting the other party make the first offer).
(E) introduce an additional tactic for use with a specific negotiation method	CORRECT. The given information does represent an additional tactic that can be used with one of the methods presented in the passage: namely, being the first to set an anchor in salary negotiations.

Chapter 15

of

GMAT Foundations of Verbal

Part 3: **Reading Comprehension**

How to Get Better at RC

In This Chapter...

Chapter 15

How to Get Better at RC

Improving Your Reading in General

Learning to become a better reader takes time and practice; if you are not planning to take the GMAT for six months or longer, then you have the time to become a better (and faster!) reader in preparation for the GMAT, business school, and life in general.

The following article was first published on Manhattan Prep's GMAT blog; it has been updated exclusively for this edition of *GMAT Foundations of Verbal*.

How to Improve Your Reading Skills for Reading Comprehension

If you don't already read university-level material (in English) every day, then today is the day to start! But it's not enough just to read this material. You'll need to make sure that you are also learning how to comprehend and analyze the complex ideas found in this kind of writing.

How? You're about to learn!

Reading Passages on the GMAT

Reading on the GMAT is not exactly like reading in the real world (when was the last time someone gave you just three minutes to read something?), but it can mimic certain work situations. You typically have more to do than you have time to do carefully, so you have to prioritize, and GMAT reading is no different.

GMAT reading passages are also typically more dense than the kinds of things you're reading on a daily basis, so you're going to need to seek out more academically focused material with which to practice.

Non-GMAT Reading Sources

For those who are learning English, and aren't planning to take the GMAT for at least six months to a year, you may want to begin with business and science articles in newspapers such as *The Wall Street Journal* or magazines such as *The Economist.* These sources are a bit too "casual" and easy to read compared to most GMAT material, but they can provide you with a good way to build foundational skills.

Sources that are closer to "GMAT-speak" include:

- *Scientific American* for the harder science passages
- *The University of Chicago Magazine* (particularly feature articles)
- *Harvard Magazine* (particularly research articles)

Look for article titles or summaries that sound decently challenging to you.

How to Read from non-GMAT Sources

So how can you learn GMAT-specific lessons from these non-GMAT reading sources? (Note: The recommendations below are geared toward helping you prepare for the GMAT; we would recommend somewhat different strategies if you were looking for pure comprehension without artificial time limits.)

First, GMAT reading material rarely provides a long introductory section or much of a conclusion, but those features are quite common in news and magazine articles. Skip the first paragraph or two (possibly several) and dive in somewhere in the middle. Read approximately three to five paragraphs (depending upon the length: you want about 200–400 words), and give yourself a time limit: two minutes for a shorter length and three minutes for a longer one.

Don't expect to get 100% comprehension from what you read initially; after all, you aren't actually paying close attention to the full text. Don't give yourself extra time; stop when that buzzer buzzes. Part of your task is to become comfortable with reading quickly and actually *not* fully comprehending what you just read.

Then, try to articulate the following:

- The main point of each individual paragraph
- The main idea of the entire article (or at least of this section of the article) without having to go back to the introductory paragraph; don't expect to get it exactly right, since you aren't actually reading the entire article.
- "Judgment" language (opinions, hypotheses, comparisons)
- "Changes in direction" in the text that you read: "however" language, two differing points of view, etc.

Then, go read more and gauge your accuracy. Read a couple of additional paragraphs. Does that change your answers to the exercises above? How? Why? Read a bit more and do the same. Finally, read the entire article.

When you start to feel more comfortable with this type of reading, add another layer of complexity: what might they ask you about the details of the article? What can you infer for GMAT purposes? (That is, what is not stated but must be true based upon information given in the article?) Do you understand the detail well enough that you could summarize it for someone else, possibly using easier language?

Content

To start, you might read articles that cover all kinds of content. GMAT Reading Comp passages come in one of four main categories: Physical Sciences, Biological Sciences, Social Sciences, and Business. As you study, ask yourself: if your RC ability the same regardless of the type of content. Or, do you tend to struggle more with certain kinds of content? If the latter is true, then start doing some more non-GMAT reading in those areas.

What do you do when you hit a particular sentence that makes you think, "What in the world does that mean?" Examine the nearby text, looking for context that can help you to decipher the meaning.

For example, do you remember this text from the Cargo Cult passage?

> Members of cargo cults commit the fallacy of confusing a necessary condition with a sufficient one. It is true that an airstrip and a control tower are necessary for executing a safe landing of an airplane; they are not, however, sufficient to attract an airplane in the first place.

What in the world is that *necessary* vs. *sufficient* stuff all about? Hey, the sentence right after offers an example! Use the example to understand the original point.

The tribe members would build an airstrip, thinking that that would "make" planes arrive and land. If a plane does want to land there, then you do need to have some kind of airstrip. But just having the airstrip doesn't guarantee that a plane is going to show up. The airstrip is *necessary* for a plane to land, but the airstrip is not *sufficient* to guarantee that a plane will land. That's what that abstract first sentence means.

Most of the time, when an RC passage offers a complex sentence, one of two things will happen. If the sentence is trying to convey a bigger idea, then the passage will offer an example or some other information to help you comprehend that big idea. If the sentence is about some crazy detail, on the other hand, then you may not ever need to figure it out because you may not get a question about that detail. (And if you do, the passage will often offer additional explanation or an example to help you.)

Takeaways

1. If you want to be a better reader, practice reading from non-GMAT sources. If necessary, build up from "lighter" sources, such as *The Wall Street Journal* and *The Economist*, to more GMAT-like material, such as scientific and university magazines.

2. Answer certain questions about the material that you read: What's the overall point? What's the purpose of each paragraph? What are the main judgments made? What changes of direction exist?

3. If any specific content areas tend to give you trouble, practice those areas more. Learn to look for other clues in the text that will help you to comprehend the tough sentence or information.

How to Study from the Official Guides

You will definitely want to use the *Official Guide* books to study Reading Comprehension (as well as the other sections of the exam). These books contain real test questions from past official GMAT tests.

Working out of a book is, of course, different from taking an exam or practice test on a computer. On the RC section, the difference is even more pronounced. Here are some important differences:

The *Official Guide*	**The Real GMAT (a computer-adaptive exam)**
You can write in the book.	You can't write on the screen.
There are 3–9 questions per passage (usually 5–7).	There are 3–4 questions per passage.
Questions are at all levels of difficulty.	Questions adapt to your level of ability.
You can see all the questions at once.	You can only see one question at a time.
You can skip questions and go back to previous questions.	As on all of the GMAT, you must answer every question and you cannot go back.
You must time yourself.	A clock on the screen counts down.

Perhaps the most obvious difference between the *Official Guide* and the real exam is the number of questions per passage. The *Official Guide* gives as many as nine questions for a single passage, but on a computer-adaptive exam, you would see only the three or four questions that have been selected for your level of performance (based on how well you've been doing on the Verbal section in general).

You want to make your *Official Guide* practice as much like the real GMAT as possible. Therefore, next are some instructions for studying from the *Official Guide*.

First, **treat the book like a computer screen**. Prop it up vertically. It's pretty annoying to read that way, isn't it? You're going to have to look up to read and down to write on a separate piece of paper . . . just as you will on the real exam. Start practicing that way now.

Next, **plan to do only three or four questions**, not all of the questions given. The more you do, the more of an advantage you have because you already know so much more about the passage. If there are more than four questions, try doing just the even questions first. In a couple of months, you can try the passage again, this time doing the odd questions.

Answer each question before moving to another. Because you can see all of the questions at once, it's tempting to jump around. Don't. Also, if you suddenly realize that you made a mistake on an earlier question, don't go back and look at that problem again now. Make your practice experience mimic what will happen on the real test.

Finally, **time yourself**. Give yourself about 2 to 3 minutes to read (depending on length, complexity, and your reading speed). Plan to average about 1.5 minutes per question (though General questions should take closer to 1 minute). Add up that time and give yourself one block of time for the particular passage and three or four questions you're about to do.

On the real GMAT, you will first see a passage and just one question on the screen. If you wish, you can read that question (it is recommended to preview the question stem only, not read all the answer choices) before you read the passage. Note that, on the real exam, you will not see the other questions, so do not preview any others before reading the passage.

STUDY TIP

When reviewing the problem that you've done, imagine that, on every question, you have to argue with four other people, each of whom insists that one of the other answers is correct. Imagine convincing each of those people why he or she is wrong.

Once you finish a passage . . . you're not actually done! You're going to learn how to get better by analyzing the passage and questions. Read on to learn how!

How to Diagnose Problems in Your Reading Comprehension Process

Once you've completed a set of RC questions, compare your understanding of the passage now with what you understood before you answered any of the questions. Do you still think the point is the same? Or do you have a better understanding now of the point the passage was really trying to make? Did you change your mind about the purpose of any of the paragraphs, or any of the judgments or changes in direction going on in the passage?

If your later understanding of the main ideas is much stronger, then re-read the passage now to try to figure out what you missed on your first read-through that you want to pay attention to on future first readthroughs. Did you rush too much and skim or skip over important parts of the main messages? Did you get too sucked into certain details and lose sight of the big picture? Adjust your reading process accordingly.

Next, take a look at the questions. Analyze each one based on the 4-step process. Did you:

- correctly identify the question type? If not, what type of question is it and how will you know next time?
- find the proper support in the passage? If not, why not? Did you misread or misunderstand the question? Did you get confused about some of the details in the passage? Did you forget or decide to skip this step entirely? How will you fix these problems for next time?
- articulate an answer in your own words? If you did but your answer was inaccurate, see whether you can articulate a better answer now (including why it's a better answer!). If you couldn't do so, figure out why. It may be that this question was too hard to do so.
- know what kind of characteristics the correct answer should have, based on the question type? For instance, on an Inference question, did you think about making sure that the answer was something that must be true? If not, figure out how you should verify your thinking for the correct answer next time.
- spot and eliminate trap answers? What traps did you fall into (or almost fall into) and why? How will you avoid those types of traps in future?

When people study, they typically feel great when answering questions correctly and disappointed when they get something wrong. But if you're answering everything correctly, then you are not actually challenging yourself and learning how to get better! Your goal is to improve, right? So, when you get something wrong, change your mindset: get a little bit excited, because you are about to learn how to get a better score on the GMAT!

How to Plan Your Study Sessions

Don't do more than one passage in a row; review and analyze your work between passages so that you can apply the lessons and get even better next time.

A good study session for Reading Comp might consist of the following:

- Make 10–15 new flash cards from Part 4 of this book (Vocabulary and RC Idioms) and quiz yourself on your existing flash cards.
- Read 1–2 non-GMAT articles using the instructions from the previous section.
- Do one passage according to the instructions above, including analyzing all of your work afterwards. (For official passages and questions, try one of the *Official Guide* books.)
- Quiz yourself on your new flash cards, as well as your flash cards from previous sessions.

Practice RC several times a week, but make sure to mix in study sessions for other question types (Verbal, Quant, and IR). You'll learn better if you keep cycling back around to different topics and question types.

Next Steps

Congratulations! You are almost done with the Reading Comprehension section of this book! You just have one last task: a problem set that will test you on everything that you've just learned.

As you complete the problem set below, follow all of the steps of the RC process:

1. Find the main point and the purpose of each paragraph.
2. Create a passage map to keep track of the location of this information.
3. Use the 4-Step Process to answer each question

    Step 1: Identify the question.

    Step 2: Find the support.

    Step 3: Predict an answer.

    Step 4: Eliminate and find a match.

When you're done, analyze your work and articulate to yourself what you want to do differently next time in order to get better. Then try another passage and do it all over again.

But don't stop there! Part 4 of this book is chock full of GMAT vocabulary words and idioms; use the lists and exercises there to help improve your understanding of individual words and phrases on the GMAT.

When you feel ready, you can move up to Manhattan Prep's *Reading Comprehension GMAT Strategy Guide*, where you will reinforce what you have already learned and also learn strategies for tackling harder passages and questions.

Put It All Together: Four Full GMAT Passages and Questions

Complete each passage, together with its questions. Each passage has a suggested time limit, though you may work a little more quickly or slowly than average. Don't rush so much that you make careless mistakes, and don't take so much extra time that your performance on other questions in a test section would be negatively impacted.

Passage 1: Greek Wreck (9 minutes)

In 1901, divers exploring the remains of a ship wreck off the coast of Greece discovered a contraption believed to have been used by Ancient Greeks to predict solar eclipses. The Antikythera Mechanism was composed of a fixed-ring dial representing the 12 months of the Egyptian calendar and an inner ring representing the 12 zodiac signs. Inside, a complex assembly of bronze gears mechanically replicated the irregular motions of the Moon caused by its elliptical orbit around the Earth through the use of two gear-wheels, one of which was slightly off-center, connected by a pin. Regarded as the world's first analog computer, the Antikythera Mechanism involved remarkably intricate physics considering that, only 300 years earlier, the Ancient Greeks still believed the world was flat. Accurately predicting lunar and solar eclipses, as well as solar, lunar, and planetary positions, it predated similar technology by 1,000 years. The timing and nature of its existence remains one of science's great puzzles to this day. How and by whom was it created?

Today, scientists understand much more about the complexities of the orbital revolutions that cause solar eclipses to occur; for instance, the Earth's orbit around the Sun is also elliptical such that, depending on the time of year, the Earth is gradually traveling nearer to or farther from the Sun. Further, since the plane of the Moon's revolution around the Earth is not the same as the plane of the Earth's revolution around the Sun, all calculations predicting a solar eclipse must be completed in three dimensions. While in modern times the use of satellites, telescopes, and other high-tech equipment has greatly enhanced our capacity for such calculations, when the Antikythera Mechanism was created, the sole source of information available to scientists was observation of the night sky. It is thus not surprising that, under certain circumstances, the device is inaccurate by up to 38 degrees; what is astonishing is that the device is remarkably accurate over a wide range of conditions.

Recent analysis dating the device to 205 BC, earlier than previously thought, suggests that the eclipse prediction mechanism was based not on Greek trigonometry but on Babylonian arithmetical methods borrowed by the Greeks. This conjecture makes plausible Cicero's claim that Archimedes created the mechanism, as Greek trigonometry was nonexistent in 205 BC.

1. It can be inferred from the third paragraph that

    (A) the Ancient Greeks were more sophisticated than most people believe
    (B) Babylonian arithmetical methods predate Greek trigonometry
    (C) the greatest thinker in Ancient Greece was Archimedes
    (D) information obtainable by modern-day telescopes was also available in Ancient Greece
    (E) the Antikythera Mechanism was more likely to accurately predict a solar eclipse than modern-day technology

2. According to the passage, which of the following statements about the Antikythera Mechanism is true?

    (A) It was created by Archimedes.
    (B) It is 1,000 years old.
    (C) It was created in the 1900s.
    (D) It was the world's first digital computer.
    (E) It could be 38 degrees inaccurate.

3. According to the passage, which of the following is true about the orbit of the Earth around the Sun?

    (A) It renders predicting solar eclipses impossible without a telescope.
    (B) It is explainable using Greek trigonometry.
    (C) It is, unlike the Moon's orbit around the Earth, elliptical.
    (D) It is, like the Moon's orbit around the Earth, elliptical.
    (E) It is in the same plane as the Moon's orbit around the Earth.

4. The passage suggests which of the following about models that predict solar eclipses?

    (A) Until the last century, it was impossible to create models that would accurately predict solar eclipses.
    (B) When it was discovered in 1901, the Antikythera Mechanism was the only model available to predict solar eclipses.
    (C) The Antikythera Mechanism is not the only model that attempts to predict solar eclipses.
    (D) The calendar months and the zodiac signs are both important for tracking the irregular motions of the Moon.
    (E) The unpredictability of such models makes them suitable only as curiosities or antiques.

Answers are on pages 316–320.

Passage 2: Polymers (6.5 minutes)

Synthetic polymers are man-made polymers colloquially referred to as "plastics." These polymers can be classified in many ways, perhaps the most useful regarding how they respond to heat. For example, thermosets are permanently set plastics; they do not melt, even when subjected to high temperatures. Thermoplastics, however, become malleable when heated and can be remolded as they are cooled. As a result, thermoplastics can be recycled more easily than thermosets and are used in the manufacture of toys, water bottles, and other goods that are typically used for limited time periods and subsequently discarded. Thermosets are more difficult to recycle and are often used as adhesives or sealants in high-wear settings, circumstances in which the less malleable nature of the material is a distinct advantage, despite the inability to recycle at a later date.

Thermoplastics can be further differentiated as amorphous or semi-crystalline. While both amorphous and semi-crystalline thermoplastics melt when heated, amorphous thermoplastics soften gradually in response to heat, while semi-crystalline thermoplastics remain solid until a precise melting point. Semi-crystalline thermoplastics tend to be tougher, suitable for weight-bearing goods such as folding chairs, whereas amorphous thermoplastics are more common for products that break apart easily, such as packing peanuts.

The contrasting molecular structures of the various plastics underpin the way in which each responds to heat. Thermoset polymers are chemically "cured," involving the formation of chemical bonds and resulting in rigid, three-dimensional molecular structures. Unlike thermosets, thermoplastics are two-dimensional chains connected by intermolecular forces. In amorphous thermoplastics, the molecules are randomly ordered, resembling a jumble of yarn, while semi-crystalline thermoplastics feature ordered molecular "crystals."

5. According to the passage, semi-crystalline thermoplastic polymers differ from thermoset polymers in which of the following ways?

   (A) Semi-crystalline thermoplastic polymers melt at a specific temperature, whereas thermoset polymers soften gradually in response to heat.
   (B) Semi-crystalline thermoplastic polymers melt at a specific temperature, whereas thermoset polymers do not melt even when subjected to high temperatures.
   (C) Semi-crystalline thermoplastic polymers soften gradually in response to heat, whereas thermoset polymers melt at a specific temperature.
   (D) Semi-crystalline thermoplastic polymers soften gradually in response to heat, whereas thermoset polymers do not melt even when subjected to high temperatures.
   (E) Semi-crystalline thermoplastic polymers do not melt even when subjected to high temperatures, whereas thermoset polymers melt at a specific temperature.

6. The passage implies which of the following about the recycling of synthetic polymers?

   (A) The molecular structure of a synthetic polymer at least partially determines whether the polymer can be recycled.
   (B) Semi-crystalline thermoplastic polymers can be recycled more easily than amorphous thermoplastic polymers can be.
   (C) Thermosets would be easier to recycle if manufacturers would choose less malleable starting materials.
   (D) Polymers are more difficult to recycle in general than are other substances.
   (E) The "curing" process allows the final product to be more easily recycled in future.

7. Which of the following plastic products best exemplifies an amorphous thermoplastic polymer as it is presented in the passage (lines 28–29)?

   (A) The caulking that seals ceramic tiles on an outdoor swimming pool
   (B) A step-ladder that can bear a weight of up to 250 pounds
   (C) A toy water gun that remains solid until it is heated to a precise temperature
   (D) A sheet of insulation intended to withstand drastic temperatures
   (E) A yogurt container that gradually melts when exposed to increasing temperatures

Answers are on pages 320–324.

Passage 3: Language (8 minutes)

Jakobson argues that languages differ primarily in what they must convey rather than what they may convey. He asserts that, accordingly, if language shapes how we think, it does so by determining what speakers are *obligated* to think about rather than what they are *allowed* to think about. This view is both a departure from the behaviorist stance that all thought is inherently linguistic (and that there is therefore no distinction) and a rejection of the pure "mould theories" advanced by Whorf, which argue that all thought is shaped by language. Rather, Jakobson suggests, some thoughts are shaped by language and some are not.

The Aboriginal tongue Guugu Yimithirr, as an illustration, lacks coordinates related to the self such as "in front of," "behind," "left of," and "right of," and instead relies strictly on geographic coordinates—east, west, south, and north. Native Guugu Yimithirr speakers are able to identify which direction is north without a compass, while native English speakers do not typically develop this intuitive sense of cardinal direction. Whorf would argue that this difference is merely one of myriad ways in which linguistic patterns codify our thoughts, but Jakobson would more specifically point to the requisite aspects of Guugu Yimithirr that are lacking in English. In other words, Guugu Yimithirr speakers are forced to consider cardinal direction, while English speakers are free to consider it or not. Studying how languages constrain us, Jakobson believes, could lead to new discoveries in regard to how we think. For instance, a language in which common terms denote gender ("him") imposes information on listeners, whereas one in which gender is irrelevant ("they") leaves more open to interpretation.

8. The author of the passage is primarily concerned with

    (A) contrasting multiple theories in a discipline
    (B) discussing a particular theory and its implications
    (C) presenting a new theory that supplants the previously dominant theory
    (D) examining the origins of an academic position
    (E) reconciling two historically opposed views

9. According to the passage, which of the following statements best describes mould theories of language?

    (A) Some thoughts are shaped by language and some are not.
    (B) There is no difference between thought and language.
    (C) Languages differ primarily in their restrictiveness.
    (D) Language influences all thought.
    (E) Thought influences all language.

10. The passage suggests that which of the following is more restrictive for a speaker?

    (A) Directions that reflect personal orientation, as compared to those that rely only on cardinal keys
    (B) Pronouns in which gender is embedded, in contrast to pronouns that are gender-neutral
    (C) Pronouns that are gender-neutral, as opposed to pronouns for which gender is inherent
    (D) Mould theories compared to behaviorist theories
    (E) Jakobson's view in comparison to Whorf's view

11. With respect to the relationship of language to thought, the passage indicates that Jakobson believes that

    (A) language shapes some thoughts
    (B) most thoughts are shaped by language
    (C) if thoughts are shaped by language, language must be shaped by thoughts
    (D) the two are not interrelated
    (E) linguistic patterns codify all thought

Answers are on pages 325–329.

Passage 4: Switzerland (9.5 minutes)

Note: This passage has five related questions. On the real test, you will be given no more than four questions per passage. Your time limit here reflects the fact that the more questions you have, the faster it should be to answer the later questions (because you know more by then!).

Switzerland has three official national languages (French, Italian, and German) and two major religions (Catholicism and Protestantism). This level of diversity has often led to conflict and even violence in other countries, but Switzerland has maintained a peaceful coexistence since its establishment as a federal state in 1848. What could explain this unusual stability? A new study examines well-defined topographical and political boundaries separating groups and draws some surprising conclusions. In Switzerland, landscape elements tend to separate linguistic groups, while political cantons, which are similar to states or provinces, tend to separate religious groups. The study suggests that these physical or geographical barriers allow for partial autonomy among disparate groups within a single country and thus foster peace.

The study considered the effect of physical separations, such as those caused by lakes and mountain ranges, determining the scale of these boundaries via an edge detection algorithm that calculates topographical heights. Where a sharp contrast in height, such as a cliff, also continued for a significant distance, the researchers designated a physical boundary between groups. Throughout the regions separated by these types of boundaries, a quiet reign of peace has persisted for nearly two centuries. Where such boundaries do not exist, however, politically or linguistically mixed cantons are more prevalent and violence is more common. One such canton, Jura, has both a history of conflict and a porous mountain range that does not fully separate linguistic groups.

Some researchers hypothesized that political boundaries might encourage stability in places where physical boundaries are absent. However, existing evidence suggests that political boundaries might not be sufficient to discourage violence. For example, Jura was formed in 1979 in response to sustained attacks between a local German-speaking Protestant population and another French-speaking Catholic population. The new canton created an autonomous political region for the French-speaking Catholic population, though the French-speaking Protestant region chose to remain affiliated with the German-speaking Protestants in the existing canton of Bern, valuing similar religion over similar language. Because of remaining linguistic differences, conflict in the region continued. A proposal to combine the French-speaking Protestant areas with the French-speaking Catholic areas is currently being considered, despite little evidence that any boundaries except physical ones effectively temper violence.

12. In the passage, the author is primarily interested in

    (A) suggesting a modification to a flawed theory
    (B) initiating a debate about the true cause of a historical conflict
    (C) introducing a theory that seeks to answer a particular question
    (D) arguing that one method for addressing a question is preferable to another
    (E) explaining the development of an established theory

13. According to the passage, which the following is true about physical boundaries between populations within the same country?

    (A) They are the only proven method for fostering peace.
    (B) They allow distinct groups to live more autonomously and peacefully than might otherwise be the case.
    (C) They can be the result of natural or man-made landscape elements.
    (D) They are less effective than political boundaries in maintaining peace in a region.
    (E) They are more easily overcome with the advent of modern technology and transportation.

14. The author of the passage discusses the history of the canton Jura in order to

    (A) prove definitively that physical boundaries are the key to maintaining peace among disparate political and religious groups
    (B) remind readers that it is extremely difficult to sustain peace in all regions of a country
    (C) speculate about how Switzerland might finally resolve the ongoing conflicts in the region
    (D) provide an example of a canton in which the lack of physical boundaries appears to exacerbate differences of opinion among the populace
    (E) suggest that there are alternative methods to reduce conflict among warring groups when physical boundaries are not present

15. Which of the following is true of the study of topographical boundaries discussed in the passage?

    (A) It considered the length as well as the height of natural boundaries.
    (B) It was conducted by French and German researchers.
    (C) It did not take into account man-made physical boundaries.
    (D) It concluded that physical boundaries are necessary in order to ensure a certain level of peace among the population.
    (E) It rated mountains as more effective barriers than lakes.

16. It can be inferred from the passage that Switzerland's political boundaries

(A) are responsible for its remarkable history of peaceful coexistence among diverse groups
(B) are typically based upon natural geographic boundaries
(C) lead to more conflict in French- and German-speaking areas than in Italian-speaking areas
(D) are capable of being changed
(E) should be based upon language similarities, not religious similarities

Answers are on pages 330–335.

Put It All Together: Answers

Passage 1: Greek Wreck

Main point: The Antikythera Mechanism pretty accurately predicts solar eclipses. It's unclear who invented it and how.

Paragraph 1: The Antikythera Mechanism for predicting solar eclipses is a mystery: who made it and how did they make it?

Paragraph 2: Modern understanding of the factors involved makes it even more surprising that the ancient mechanism was as accurate as it was.

Paragraph 3: Archimedes might have created it in 205 BC.

Passage map:

(1) AM found, spec: anc Grk, predict solar eclipse?
AM= sophis, not sure how made or who

(2) Now: DTL eclipse
AM= surpris acc.

(3) C: made by Arch(?)
evid given (math)

Note: DTL stands for detail, signaling that a certain part of the passage contains more detail about a particular topic.

1. (B) Babylonian arithmetical methods predate Greek trigonometry

Step 1: Identify the question.

The word *inferred* in the question stem indicates that this is an Inference question.

Step 2: Find the support.

Support can be found in lines 53–62:

> *Recent analysis dating the device to 205 BC, earlier than previously thought, suggests that the eclipse prediction mechanism was based not on Greek trigonometry but on Babylonian arithmetical methods borrowed by the Greeks. This conjecture makes plausible Cicero's claim that Archimedes created the mechanism, as Greek trigonometry was nonexistent in 205 BC.*

Step 3: Predict an answer

What can be inferred? The device was once thought to have been created later than 205 BC. If they now think that it was based on Babylonian arithmetical methods, then those methods must have been in existence already in 205 BC.

Step 4: Eliminate and find a match.

Answer Choice	Explanation
(A) the Ancient Greeks were more sophisticated than most people believe	The paragraph doesn't address what most people believe about how sophisticated the Ancient Greeks were.
(B) Babylonian arithmetical methods predate Greek trigonometry	CORRECT. This matches the predicted answer: the Babylonian methods were already in existence by 205 BC. The passage states that Greek trigonometry was *nonexistent in 205 BC*, so the Babylonian math predated the Greek math.
(C) the greatest thinker in Ancient Greece was Archimedes	The paragraph indicates only that Cicero thinks Archimedes may have created the mechanism; it does not mention other *thinkers*.
(D) information obtainable by modern-day telescopes was also available in Ancient Greece	The third paragraph does not indicate this; in fact, the second paragraph appears to contradict it.
(E) the Antikythera Mechanism was more likely to accurately predict a solar eclipse than modern-day technology	The third paragraph does not indicate this; if anything, the second paragraph implies the opposite.

2. (E) It could be 38 degrees inaccurate.

Step 1: Identify the question.

According to the passage indicates that this is a Specific Detail question. What is true of the Antikythera Mechanism? The passage includes several facts.

Step 2: Find the support.

Details can be found throughout the passage:

> *. . . was composed of a fixed-ring dial representing the twelve months of the Egyptian calendar and an inner ring representing the 12 zodiac signs.* (lines 6–9)
>
> *Regarded as the world's first analog computer, the Antikythera Mechanism involved remarkably intricate physics . . .* (lines 16–18)
>
> *. . . under certain circumstances, the device is inaccurate by up to 38 degrees.* (lines 48–50)
>
> *Recent analysis dating the device to 205 BC . . .* (lines 53–54)

Step 3: Predict an answer.

The correct answer should match one of the descriptive facts given about the Antikythera Mechanism.

Step 4: Eliminate and find a match.

Answer Choice	Explanation
(A) It was created by Archimedes.	Cicero claims this; the passage indicates, however, that the creator is still not definitively known.
(B) It is 1,000 years old.	It *predated similar technology by 1,000 years*, but it is believed to have been created in 205 BC, more than 2,000 years ago.
(C) It was created in the 1900s.	It was discovered in 1901; it was created much earlier.
(D) It was the world's first digital computer.	The first paragraph indicates that it was considered the world's first *analog* computer.
(E) It could be 38 degrees inaccurate.	CORRECT. This information is found in the last sentence of the second paragraph, lines 49–50.

3. (D) It is, like the Moon's orbit around the Earth, elliptical.

Step 1: Identify the question.

According to the passage indicates that this is a Specific Detail question.

Step 2: Find the support.

Support can be found in the second paragraph:

> *. . . the Earth's orbit around the Sun is also elliptical such that, depending on the time of year, the Earth is gradually traveling nearer to or farther from the Sun*. (lines 31–35)

Step 3: Predict an answer.

The orbit is elliptical, which seems to mean that the Earth is sometimes closer to the Sun and sometimes farther away.

Step 4: Eliminate and find a match.

Answer Choice	**Explanation**
(A) It renders predicting solar eclipses impossible without a telescope.	The passage indicates that the Antikythera mechanism was relatively reliable even without telescopes.
(B) It is explainable using Greek trigonometry.	The third paragraph discusses trigonometry in relation to the Antikythera Mechanism (and, further, says that it was probably *not* used).
(C) It is, unlike the Moon's orbit around the Earth, elliptical.	The the Earth's orbit is elliptical . . . what about the Moon's? Check the passage. Paragraph 1: *the irregular motions of the Moon caused by its elliptical orbit around the Earth* (lines 11–13). The Moon's orbit is also elliptical.
(D) It is, like the Moon's orbit around the Earth, elliptical.	CORRECT. The orbits of the Earth and of the Moon are both elliptical.
(E) It is in the same plane as the Moon's orbit around the Earth.	The second paragraph indicates that the opposite is true: the two planes are not the same.

At times, while reviewing answer choices, you will have to return to the passage to confirm some detail or add some information. In this case, the question stem did not mention the Moon's orbit, but answers (C) and (D) did. When that happens, return to Step 2 and find the necessary proof in the passage.

4. (C) The Antikythera Mechanism is not the only model that attempts to predict solar eclipses.

Step 1: Identify the question.

The word *suggests* indicates that this is an Inference question. The question asks about models that predict solar eclipses in general, not just the Antikythera Mechanism in particular, so expect the correct answer to be based on broader information about such devices.

Step 2: Find the support.

Support can be found in the first and second paragraphs:

> *Accurately predicting lunar and solar eclipses, as well as solar, lunar, and planetary positions, it predated similar technology by 1,000 years.* (lines 21–24)

While in modern times the use of satellites, telescopes, and other high-tech equipment has greatly enhanced our capacity for such calculations, when the Antikythera Mechanism was created, the sole source of information available to scientists was observation of the night sky. (lines 41–47)

Step 3: Predict an answer.

The correct answer should convey something that must be true about solar eclipse prediction models in general.

Step 4: Eliminate and find a match.

Answer Choice	**Explanation**
(A) Until the last century, it was impossible to create models that would accurately predict solar eclipses.	The Antikythera Mechanism is described as fairly accurate, and it was created approximately 2,000 years ago.
(B) When it was discovered in 1901, the Antikythera Mechanism was the only model available to predict solar eclipses.	The passage indicates only that this was the earliest known model, not that it is or was the only one at the time of its discovery.
(C) The Antikythera Mechanism is not the only model that attempts to predict solar eclipses.	CORRECT. The first paragraph says that the Antikythera Mechanism *predated similar technology by 1,000 years* (lines 23–24). In other words, at least one additional type of solar eclipse model was made.
(D) The calendar months and the zodiac signs are both important for tracking the irregular motions of the Moon.	This is mentioned only in relation to the Antikythera Mechanism specifically.
(E) The unpredictability of such models makes them suitable only as curiosities or antiques.	The Antikythera Mechanism is described as relatively accurate, not unpredictable. Further, *such models* is too broad; ancient models might be considered antiques, but the question stem could refer to any models that predict solar eclipses, including modern ones.

Passage 2: Polymers

Main point: The most useful way (perhaps) to classify plastics is based on how they respond to heat.

Paragraph 1: The most useful way (perhaps) to classify plastics is based on how they respond to heat.

Paragraph 2: One type, thermoplastics, can be broken into two subgroups, with their own characteristics relative to heat.

Paragraph 3: The different molecular structures determine how each one responds to heat.

Passage map:

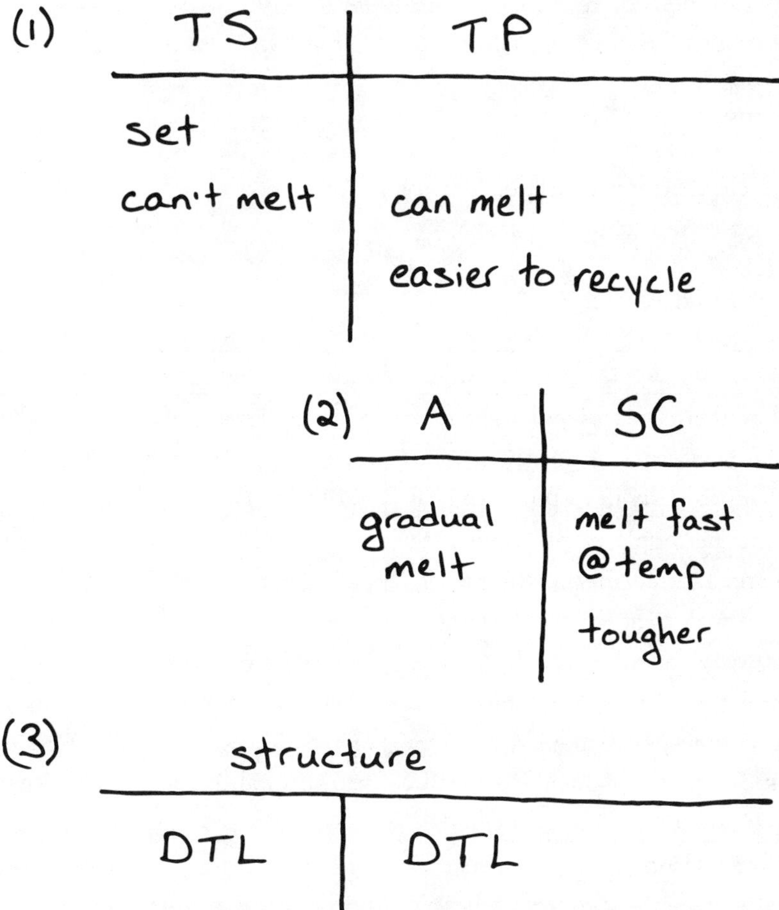

(1) man-made Poly = plastic
★ most useful: classify by heat
(1) TS
TP
set
can't melt
can melt
easier to recycle
(2) A
SC
gradual melt
melt fast @temp
tougher
(3) structure
DTL
DTL

Note: DTL stands for detail, signaling that a certain part of the passage contains more detail about a particular topic.

5. (B) Semi-crystalline thermoplastic polymers melt at a specific temperature, whereas thermoset polymers do not melt even when subjected to high temperatures.

Step 1: Identify the question.

According to the passage indicates that this is a Specific Detail question. The question asks specifically about the difference between thermoplastics and thermosets.

The passage further subcategorizes the thermoplastics; will you need to look at the subcategories in order to answer the question? Glance at the answer choices to see. Yes!

Step 2: Find the support.

Support can be found in the first and second paragraphs:

> *For example, thermosets are permanently set plastics; they do not melt, even when subjected to high temperatures. Thermoplastics, however, become malleable when heated and can be remolded as they are cooled.* (lines 5–11)

> *. . . amorphous thermoplastics soften gradually in response to heat while semi-crystalline thermoplastics remain solid until a precise melting point.* (lines 28–31)

Step 3: Predict an answer.

Thermosets don't melt; thermoplastics do. Amorphous ones soften gradually while semi-crystalline ones stay set until hitting a certain temperature.

Step 4: Eliminate and find a match.

Answer Choice	Explanation
(A) Semi-crystalline thermoplastic polymers melt at a specific temperature, whereas thermoset polymers soften gradually in response to heat.	The description of semi-crystalline is true, but the second half describes amorphous thermoplastics, not thermosets.
(B) Semi-crystalline thermoplastic polymers melt at a specific temperature, whereas thermoset polymers do not melt even when subjected to high temperatures.	CORRECT. Both descriptions match what the passage says.
(C) Semi-crystalline thermoplastic polymers soften gradually in response to heat, whereas thermoset polymers melt at a specific temperature.	The first portion describes amorphous plastics, not semi-crystalline. The second portion describes semi-crystalline plastics, not thermosets.
(D) Semi-crystalline thermoplastic polymers soften gradually in response to heat, whereas thermoset polymers do not melt even when subjected to high temperatures.	The first portion describes amorphous plastics, not semi-crystalline. The description of thermosets is true.
(E) Semi-crystalline thermoplastic polymers do not melt even when subjected to high temperatures, whereas thermoset polymers melt at a specific temperature.	The definitions are reversed; the first portion describes thermosets and the second portion describes semi-crystalline plastics.

6. (A) The molecular structure of a synthetic polymer at least partially determines whether the polymer can be recycled.

Step 1: Identify the question.

The word *implies* indicates that this is an Inference question. Recycling is mentioned in the first paragraph.

Step 2: Find the support.

Support can be found in the first paragraph:

> *As a result, thermoplastics can be recycled more easily than thermosets . . . Thermosets are more difficult to recycle . . .* (lines 11–23)

Step 3: Predict an answer.

The passage directly states that thermoplastics are easier to recycle than thermosets, so what is the inference? The information seems to imply that the rigidity of the material determines how easy or hard it is to recycle.

Step 4: Eliminate and find a match.

Answer Choice	**Explanation**
(A) The molecular structure of a synthetic polymer at least partially determines whether the polymer can be recycled.	CORRECT. The ability to recycle is based, at least in part, on each type's response to heat. The third paragraph indicates that the molecular structure determines (*underpins*) the way in which each responds to heat.
(B) Semi-crystalline thermoplastic polymers can be recycled more easily than amorphous thermoplastic polymers can be.	Read carefully! If anything, the passage implies that the reverse would be true. Semi-crystalline plastics are more rigid than amorphous plastics.
(C) Thermosets would be easier to recycle if manufacturers would choose less malleable starting materials.	Another trap! The passage does mention malleability in relation to thermosets: *the less malleable nature of the material is a distinct advantage, despite the inability to recycle at a later date* (lines 20–23). If anything, the passage implies that more malleable starting materials would make the materials easier to recycle.
(D) Polymers are more difficult to recycle in general than are other substances.	The passage does not discuss other materials.
(E) The "curing" process allows the final product to be more easily recycled in future.	The "curing" process is mentioned in relation to thermosets, which are more *difficult* to recycle.

This is a tough problem. Many people would have to go through the answers twice on this one, because the evidence on which to base the inference requires you to combine two pieces of information from different parts of the passage. These kinds of *synthesis* problems are among the hardest on the test.

7. (E) A yogurt container that gradually melts when exposed to increasing temperatures

Step 1: Identify the question.

Surprise! This is an uncommon type that was not introduced earlier in this guide. You'll recognize these in the future because they ask you to extrapolate beyond the passage. In this case, you need to come up with a real-life example of an amorphous thermoplastic—something that fits the description of this type of plastic.

Step 2: Find the support.

Support can be found in lines 26–37 of the second paragraph:

> *While both amorphous and semi-crystalline thermoplastics melt when heated, amorphous thermoplastics soften gradually in response to heat . . . amorphous thermoplastics are more common for products that break apart easily, such as packing peanuts.*

Step 3: Predict an answer.

The product should be something that melts gradually or relatively steadily when heated, and/or a product designed to break apart easily.

Step 4: Eliminate and find a match.

Answer Choice	Explanation
(A) The caulking that seals ceramic tiles on an outdoor swimming pool	The first paragraph indicates that thermosets, not amorphous thermoplastics, are used as *sealants in high-wear settings.* (line 19)
(B) A step-ladder that can bear a weight of up to 250 pounds	The second paragraph indicates that semi-crystalline thermoplastics, not amorphous thermoplastics, are *suitable for weight-bearing goods* (lines 33–34).
(C) A toy water gun that remains solid until it is heated to a precise temperature	The second paragraph indicates that semi-crystalline thermoplastics melt in this way, not amorphous thermoplastics.
(D) A sheet of insulation intended to withstand drastic temperatures	Thermosets would be able to withstand drastic temperatures; amorphous thermoplastics melt when exposed to heat.
(E) A yogurt container that gradually melts when exposed to increasing temperatures	CORRECT. Amorphous thermoplastics melt gradually when exposed to heat.

Passage 3: Language

Main point: In contrast to some other theorists, Jakobson thinks that language shapes some thoughts but not others.

Paragraph 1: Jakobson differs from some other theorists. He thinks that languages shape how we think based upon what we're obligated to think about: *some thoughts are shaped by language and some are not* (lines 15–16).

Paragraph 2: Guugu Yimithirr example: Jakobson has a certain interpretation, in contrast to Whorf's interpretation.

Passage map:

1. J: what language MUST convey vs. MAY convey

language → some thoughts (not all)

≠ behaviorist, W's mould (L → all T)

2. unlike E, G uses NSEW and G ppl just know

G forces direction, E doesn't

J: studying constraints → how we think?

Note: The "does not equal" symbol signals that Jakobson's views disagree with the views shown on this line of the map. The question mark at the end of the last line signals that Jakobson believes the one *could* lead to the other, not that it definitely does. You may choose to use longer abbreviations than the single letters used here, but don't take the time to write out the full names of people, languages, etc.

8. (B) discussing a particular theory and its implications

Step 1: Identify the question.

Primarily concerned with signals that this is a Primary Purpose question.

Step 2: Find the support.

Ideally, you will have determined the main idea during your read-through of the passage; if you need to refresh your memory, return to your map.

Step 3: Predict an answer.

On Primary Purpose questions, use your map and your understanding of the main point to articulate an answer. The passage is focused primarily on what Jakobson thinks, though it does mention that his views don't go along with those of two other positions (the behaviorist views and Whorf's mould theories). The other views are presented primarily as a contrast to Jakobson's views.

Step 4: Eliminate and find a match.

Answer Choice	**Explanation**
(A) contrasting multiple theories in a discipline	The passage does mention two alternative opinions in one sentence in the first paragraph, but the primary focus is on Jakobson's theory.
(B) discussing a particular theory and its implications	CORRECT. The passage primarily discusses Jakobson's point of view, describing it in the first paragraph and illustrating it via the Guugu Yimithirr example in the second paragraph. The passage concludes by mentioning broader implications at the end of the second paragraph.
(C) presenting a new theory that supplants the previously dominant theory	The passage doesn't indicate that either of the earlier theories was dominant, nor does it indicate that Jakobson's theory is the new dominant theory.
(D) examining the origins of an academic position	The passage doesn't address how Jakobson came to develop his theory in the first place.
(E) reconciling two historically opposed views	The passage does not reconcile the opposing points of view. No information indicates that the groups have come to agreement.

9. (D) Language influences all thought.

Step 1: Identify the question.

According to the passage indicates that this is a Specific Detail question. The mould theories were mentioned in the first paragraph.

Step 2: Find the support.

Support can be found in lines 4–14 of the first paragraph:

> *. . . if language shapes how we think, it does so by determining what speakers are* obligated *to think about rather than what they are* allowed *to think about. This view is both a departure from the behaviorist stance that all thought is inherently linguistic (and that there is therefore no distinction) and a rejection of the pure "mould theories" advanced by Whorf, which argue that all thought is shaped by language.*

Step 3: Predict an answer.

Jakobson's theory goes against the mould theories. The mould theories argue that all thought is shaped by language.

Step 4: Eliminate and find a match.

Answer Choice	Explanation
(A) Some thoughts are shaped by language and some are not.	Jakobson believe this; this is not part of Whorf's mould theories.
(B) There is no difference between thought and language.	The behaviorist position promotes this view, not the mould theories.
(C) Languages differ primarily in their restrictiveness.	Jakobson believe this; this is not part of Whorf's mould theories.
(D) Language influences all thought.	CORRECT. This is how the passage describes the mould theories: *all thought is shaped by language* (lines 13–14). In other words, language shapes (or influences) all thought.
(E) Thought influences all language.	This is the opposite of the description of the mould theories, which says that *all thought is shaped by language* (lines 13–14), not that all thought shapes or influences language.

10. (B) Pronouns in which gender is embedded, in contrast to pronouns that are gender-neutral

Step 1: Identify the question.

The word *suggests* indicates that this is an Inference question. The phrase *more restrictive* might lead you to consider the constraints imposed by a language.

Step 2: Find the support.

Support can be found in lines 33–44 at the end of the passage:

> *. . . Guugu Yimithirr speakers are forced to consider cardinal direction, while English speakers are free to consider it or not. Studying how languages constrain us, Jakobson believes, could lead to new discoveries in regard to how we think. For instance, a language in which common terms denote gender ("him") imposes information on listeners whereas one in which gender is irrelevant ("they") leaves more open to interpretation.*

Step 3: Predict an answer.

Since Guugu Yimithirr doesn't contain certain descriptive words, the speakers are forced to use north, south, east, and west. That's restrictive. Also, if more specific information is required or built in (such as gender), that's more restrictive.

Step 4: Eliminate and find a match.

Answer Choice	**Explanation**
(A) Directions that reflect personal orientation as compared to those that rely only on cardinal keys	This choice is the opposite of what the question asks. The cardinal directions are described as more restrictive, because the speakers cannot use personal orientation.
(B) Pronouns in which gender is embedded, in contrast to pronouns that are gender-neutral	CORRECT. This matches one of the restrictive examples given in the passage.
(C) Pronouns that are gender-neutral, as opposed to pronouns for which gender is inherent	The passage states the opposite: the gendered pronouns are more restrictive than the gender-neutral pronouns.
(D) Mould theories compared to behaviorist theories	The restrictiveness of language is not mentioned in relation to the competing theories.
(E) Jakobson's view in comparison to Whorf's view	The restrictiveness of language is not mentioned in relation to the competing theories.

11. (A) language shapes some thoughts.

Step 1: Identify the question.

The language *the passage indicates* signals that this is a Specific Detail question.

Step 2: Find the support.

Support can be found in the first paragraph:

> *. . . if language shapes how we think, it does so by determining what speakers are* obligated *to think about rather than what they are* allowed *to think about.* (lines 4–8)
>
> *. . . some thoughts are shaped by language and some are not.* (lines 15–16)

Step 3: Predict an answer.

According to Jakobson, it isn't the case that language always shapes how we think. Sometimes it does and sometimes it doesn't.

Step 4: Eliminate and find a match.

Answer Choice	Explanation
(A) language shapes some thoughts	CORRECT. This matches the last sentence of the first paragraph.
(B) most thoughts are shaped by language	The passage indicates only that Jakobson thinks that *some* thoughts are shaped by language, not *most*.
(C) if thoughts are shaped by language, language must be shaped by thoughts	This choice is trying to mix up confusing language from the passage. Jakobson asserts only that some thoughts are shaped by language and some thoughts are not.
(D) the two are not interrelated	Jakobson does believe that the two are interrelated at least some of the time.
(E) linguistic patterns codify all thought	This reflects Whorf's point of view, not Jakobson's.

Passage 3: Switzerland

Main point: Physical boundaries separating groups with significant differences (e.g., language, religion) can help to maintain peace.

Paragraph 1: A study suggests that Switzerland is unusually peaceful despite being very diverse (religion and language) because physical or geographical barriers keep groups separated.

Paragraph 2: In areas with significant physical barriers, things have been peaceful. In areas without these boundaries, there's been a lot of conflict.

Paragraph 3: Some hypothesized that political boundaries might reduce conflict, but the evidence shows otherwise.

Passage map:

1) S: 3 Ls, 2 Rs
usually conflict, but not in S. Why?
Study: phys barriers may explain

2) Study: DTL
signif. phys barrier: peaceful
no barrier: > conflict (eg. J)

3) political boundary work too?
not really
eg J

Note: DTL stands for detail; you can use this abbreviation to signal that a paragraph contains a lot of detail that you might want to return to later (if you're asked a question about that detail). Other abbreviations may not be exactly the way you would write them; just make sure that you aren't taking too much time to write out more detail than you need.

12. (C) introducing a theory that seeks to answer a particular question

Step 1: Identify the question.

The language *primarily interested in* signals that this is a Primary Purpose question.

Step 2: Find the support.

Ideally, you will have determined the main idea during your read-through of the passage; if you need to refresh your memory, return to your map.

Step 3: Predict an answer.

A study indicates that physical or geographic barriers may be what helps diverse areas to maintain peace.

Step 4: Eliminate and find a match

Answer Choice	Explanation
(A) suggesting a modification to a flawed theory	The passage discusses a new theory, not an existing one that was then altered.
(B) initiating a debate about the true cause of a historical conflict	The passage does talk about an area that has experienced conflict historically, but there is not a debate about the specific cause of a specific conflict.
(C) introducing a theory that seeks to answer a particular question	CORRECT. The first paragraph asks a question (*What could explain this unusual stability?* lines 9–10) and introduces a theory that seeks to answer that question.
(D) arguing that one method for addressing a question is preferable to another	The rejected political boundaries theory might be considered a second method, but it can't be said that one is *preferable* to the other. Rather, the political boundaries theory was introduced as a potential alternative when no physical boundaries exist.
(E) explaining the development of an established theory	The passage does not indicate that the geographic boundaries theory is established; in fact, it describes the study as *new*.

13. (B) They allow distinct groups to live more autonomously and peacefully than might otherwise be the case.

Step 1: Identify the question.

According to the passage indicates that this is a Specific Detail question.

Step 2: Find the support

Support can be found in the first and second paragraphs:

> *The study suggests that these physical or geographical barriers allow for partial autonomy among disparate groups within a single country and thus foster peace.* (lines 18–22)
>
> *Throughout the regions separated by these types of boundaries, a quiet reign of peace has persisted for nearly two centuries.* (lines 32–35)

Step 3: Predict an answer.

The passage indicates that physical barriers help keep the peace.

Step 4: Eliminate and find a match.

Answer Choice	**Explanation**
(A) They are the only proven method for fostering peace.	The passage discusses only one other possible method (political boundaries) for fostering peace. It does not indicate that physical boundaries are the only available method.
(B) They allow distinct groups to live more autonomously and peacefully than might otherwise be the case.	CORRECT. This matches the language from the passage.
(C) They can be the result of natural or man-made landscape elements.	Be careful not to bring in outside knowledge! The passage only mentions natural barriers as examples of *physical boundaries*. You do not know whether *man-made* landscape elements would work in the same way as natural elements (such as cliffs), or in fact whether the author would consider man-made features *physical boundaries* at all. (This is not to say that the author is excluding man-made features; you simply do not know how man-made features are treated.)
(D) They are less effective than political boundaries in maintaining peace in a region.	The passage says the opposite: they are more effective than political boundaries in maintaining peace.
(E) They are more easily overcome with the advent of modern technology and transportation.	This choice is a trap for someone who is rushing or getting tired and not reading carefully. *Barriers* sound like they may need to be *overcome*, but the passage does not discuss this; rather, the barriers are seen as a positive.

14. (D) provide an example of a canton in which the lack of physical boundaries appears to exacerbate differences of opinion among the populace

Step 1: Identify the question.

The language *in order to* indicates that this is a Specific Purpose, or Why, question. Remember to read a bit before you try to figure out why the author introduced the topic of Jura.

Step 2: Find the support.

Support can be found in lines 35–42 at the end of the second paragraph:

> *Where such boundaries do not exist, however, politically or linguistically mixed cantons are more prevalent and violence is more common. One such canton, Jura, has both a history of conflict and a porous mountain range that does not fully separate linguistic groups.*

Step 3: Predict an answer.

Jura doesn't have physical boundaries and it has experienced lots of conflict. This supports the theory that physical boundaries help keep the peace.

Note: The third paragraph has some more detail about Jura, but it is often enough to understand the main idea or first mention of the example. If the information in the second paragraph isn't enough to narrow down to one answer, then return to the third paragraph.

Step 4: Eliminate and find a match.

Answer Choice	**Explanation**
(A) prove definitively that physical boundaries are the key to maintaining peace among disparate political and religious groups	The example supports the theory but does not prove it true definitively.
(B) remind readers that it is extremely difficult to sustain peace in all regions of a country	Although it is likely true that peace is difficult to sustain everywhere, this is not why the author introduces the example. Rather, the author is further supporting the physical barrier theory.
(C) speculate about how Switzerland might finally resolve the ongoing conflicts in the region	The passage does not indicate any effective solutions; in fact, the final example given at the end of the third paragraph is dismissed as unlikely to be effective.
(D) provide an example of a canton in which the lack of physical boundaries appears to exacerbate differences of opinion among the populace	CORRECT. Jura is used specifically as an example to support the physical barrier theory.
(E) suggest that there are alternative methods to reduce conflict among warring groups when physical boundaries are not present	Jura has had lots of conflict, not reduced conflict. The political barrier theory is unlikely to be effective, according to the passage.

15. (A) It considered the length as well as the height of natural boundaries.

Step 1: Identify the question.

What *is true of* something discussed in the passage? This language signals a Specific Detail question. *Topographical* is mentioned in the first and second paragraphs.

Step 2: Find the support.

Support can be found in the first and second paragraphs:

> *A new study examines well-defined topographical and political boundaries separating groups and draws some surprising conclusions*. (lines 10–13)

> *The study considered the effect of physical separations, such as those caused by lakes and mountain ranges, determining the scale of these boundaries via an edge detection algorithm that calculates topographical heights. Where a sharp contrast in height, such as a cliff, also continued for a significant distance, the researchers designated a physical boundary between groups.* (lines 23–32)

Step 3: Predict an answer.

The study used an algorithm to calculate height differences. They also considered the length of the boundary. If the barrier had some defined combination of length and height differences, it was called a physical barrier.

Step 4: Eliminate and find a match.

Answer Choice	**Explanation**
(A) It considered the length as well as the height of natural boundaries.	CORRECT. This matches the language of the passage.
(B) It was conducted by French and German researchers.	The passage does not indicate who conducted the study.
(C) It did not take into account man-made physical boundaries.	The only examples mentioned are natural (e.g., *cliffs*), but that does not mean that man-made barriers were actually excluded from or ignored by the research. It's possible that they were included but just not mentioned in the passage.
(D) It concluded that physical boundaries are necessary in order to ensure a certain level of peace among the population.	The study claimed only that physical boundaries could help maintain peace, not that such boundaries are necessary to maintain peace.
(E) It rated mountains as more effective barriers than lakes.	Though the passage does mention using both height and length when designating something a barrier, it does not actually indicate which types of barriers the study considered most effective.

16. (D) are capable of being changed

Step 1: Identify the question.

The language *inferred* indicates that this is an Inference question. The first and third paragraphs discuss Switzerland's political boundaries.

Step 2: Find the support.

Support can be found in the first and third paragraphs:

> *In Switzerland, landscape elements tend to separate linguistic groups while political cantons, which are similar to states or provinces, tend to separate religious groups.* (lines 13–18)

> *Jura was formed in 1979 . . . The new canton created an autonomous political region for the French-speaking Catholic population . . . Because of remaining linguistic differences, conflict in the region continued. A proposal to combine the French-speaking Protestant areas with the French-speaking Catholic areas is currently being considered, despite little evidence that any boundaries except physical ones effectively temper violence.* (lines 49–68)

Step 3: Predict an answer.

Political cantons are typically separated by religion. The separation in Jura didn't actually fix things, though, and they're thinking about combining based on language instead, even though trying to set political boundaries hasn't been shown to be effective.

Step 4: Eliminate and find a match.

Answer Choice	Explanation
(A) are responsible for its remarkable history of peaceful coexistence among diverse groups	The passage suggests that *geographical boundaries* are responsible for maintaining the peace, not *political boundaries.*
(B) are typically based upon natural geographic boundaries	The passage discusses *political boundaries* as separate from *geographical boundaries.*
(C) lead to more conflict in French- and German-speaking areas than in Italian-speaking areas	The passage doesn't provide any specific information about Italian-speaking areas.
(D) are capable of being changed	CORRECT. As noted in the third paragraph, the boundaries were changed at least once, in 1979 with the creation of Jura, and the Swiss are considering another proposal to change them again.
(E) should be based upon language similarities, not religious similarities	The passage indicates that *political* boundaries don't seem to work, no matter what they're based on.

Chapter 16
of
GMAT Foundations of Verbal
Part 4: **Vocabulary & RC Idioms**

Vocabulary & RC Idioms

In This Chapter...

Chapter 16
Vocabulary & RC Idioms

Why Learn Vocabulary for the GMAT?

At the simplest level, it's pretty hard to do well on a test that requires reading if you can't comprehend what you're reading.

The vocab list in this section contains words that have appeared in the *Official Guide* or other official GMAT materials in the Reading Comprehension, Critical Reasoning, and Sentence Correction sections, as well as words from other sources at the same reading level. Following the vocab list is an RC idioms guide, that serves the same purpose as the vocab list, but focuses on expressions or phrases rather than single words.

This list includes only words and phrases that are general enough that they are likely to appear again. For instance, a GMAT reading passage about sea urchins might contain many biology terms that would be defined within the passage (or else would not be needed to answer the questions). Those words would not be included here.

Another type of word you will likely see on the GMAT but not on this list is "glued-together" words—words that hardly anyone has seen before, but that can be puzzled out by looking at the component parts. Don't let these kinds of words shake your confidence. Each one is just two medium-level words or word parts stuck together. For example:

Circumstellar – around a star
Deradicalized – something made not radical or extreme
Historicophilosophical – both historical and philosophical
Knowingness – quality of knowing something

Because these types of words can be deconstructed into two easier words, this chapter does not include such super-specialized words.

This portion of the book is geared mostly for non-native speakers. If you are a native speaker of English and don't feel that you have issues with vocabulary, still take a quick look over both lists—you will probably discover some new things. Or you could skip straight to the drills at the back of this section to make sure that you're on the right track.

While these lists are most tied to Reading Comprehension, learning these words will also help your Critical Reasoning and even your Sentence Correction. You might eliminate a correct Sentence Correction answer choice because you don't know how to use the word *seemingly,* or because you don't know that you could use the word *ranks* in the sense of *The university has many distinguished people among the ranks of its alumni.*

Many of these words are words that people just "read over" without even realizing that they don't know the word. If you saw a word like *omphaloskepsis* somewhere, you would definitely realize you didn't know it, and you might look it up (it means the contemplation of one's bellybutton as a meditation aid). But if you saw a much more boring, familiar-looking word used in a new way, as in *Her work is **informed** by a background in ancient Greece* or *The board won't **condone** noncompliance,* you would be much more likely to just pass over those words—at the expense of your comprehension. (Both *inform* and *condone* appear in the list.)

If you see an easy looking word in the list, don't skip over it! There's a good chance it's here because it has another meaning that not everyone is aware of. For instance:

- A *novel* is a book, but as an adjective, *novel* means *new and original.*
- *Conversant* looks like *converse,* but does it really mean the same thing? (Actually, it means *knowledgeable.*)
- Everyone knows the word *qualified,* right? Then how about the use of *qualified* in "Dr. Wong could give only *qualified* approval to the theory, as the available data was limited in scope." Why is Dr. Wong's approval "only" qualified? *Qualified* is good, right? *Qualified* here means *limited, conditional, holding back.*

Of course, if you have an impending GMAT deadline, you may not have time to learn vocabulary. It is more important that you spend time on things on which you are tested directly. If you have limited time, at least look over this list. You will probably see a few words you have always wondered about!

How to Learn Vocabulary for the GMAT

First, try to make connections to related concepts or ideas that will help you to learn the meaning of a word. For instance, if you know that a *blunt* knife is bad at cutting, then it makes sense that *blunt* as a verb means *weaken* or *take the edge off*—for example, you can *blunt* criticism by also offering praise. A good number of the words on the list may stick with you after just a single read, if you can make these kinds of connections to other words or contexts that you already know.

In order to keep the list a reasonable length, if a word has been included because of a less common meaning, the common one will *not* be included, too. So, for instance, when it says that *grade* means *blend into* or *slant,* don't worry that you're going crazy—of course, *grade* can also refer to what teachers do when they mark your papers.

While some of the words on the list might make sense and stick in your brain relatively easily, some of the words will take some memorization. To make a good vocabulary flash card, put the word on the front (and the part of speech, if it helps you). Put the definition on the back. It is also helpful to write an example sentence. It's fine if the example sentence illustrates the meaning of the word only to you—in fact, the more personal it is, the more likely you are to remember it. If you've written, "I can't *countenance* my spouse's tantrums" on a flash card, you're pretty likely to remember the meaning of *countenance.*

Here is a sample flash card:

Aberrant
(adj)

Also *abberration* (noun)

Abnormal, deviant

Losing rather than gaining weight over the holidays is certainly an aberration.

This student happened to include some extra information—the noun form of *aberrant.* You might also include some synonyms for the word, to help you learn a group of words with a related meaning. The richer your flash cards, the more likely you are to learn from them (even from the act of making them)!

Many students make the mistake of memorizing dictionary definitions of words without really understanding those definitions or being able to comfortably use those words in sentences.

You want to learn words such as *advent* and *dubious* the same way you know words such as *study* and *mistake*—that is, you use those words all the time, effortlessly, and in a variety of situations. Because you will not be taking a vocabulary test, but rather using vocabulary in understanding other types of Verbal problems, you need to be able to read and understand these new words quickly and normally.

Memorization is important. But while vocabulary lists, flash cards, and the like are excellent tools, some of the best vocabulary accrual occurs when you are reading difficult material and you go look up a word you just read in context. For sources of difficult material, try *The Economist, Scientific American,* or the articles posted on aldaily.com (that's *Arts and Letters Daily*).

If you read a definition and you don't really understand it, look the word up someplace else! One great place is www.learnersdictionary.com, which defines words in a simple way for English language learners.

It can also be helpful to ask someone, or to simply Google the word to see how other people are using it. Some students have had success typing the word into an online translation engine and reading a definition in their native language (only do this if you don't understand the English definition).

Finally, of course, you will learn words much better if you use them. Try pairing up with a study partner and sending each other emails using words off your list (you can probably think of plenty of other ways to use technology to practice vocab socially).

Once you have studied the definition, read the word in context, and worked the word into conversation three times (this can cause your friends to look at you funny, but it'll be worth it!), that word is probably yours for life.

TIP

You can look up words on dictionary.com, thefreedictionary.com, or m-w.com, but if you want simpler definitions, try learnersdictionary.com.

Vocabulary List for the GMAT

Abate – Reduce or diminish.

Her stress over spending so much money on a house **abated** when the real estate broker told her about the property's 15-year tax **abatement**.

Aberration, Anomaly – Something that stands out or is abnormal. *Outlier* is similar.

The election of a liberal candidate in the conservative county was an **aberration** (or **anomaly**), made possible only by the sudden death of the conservative candidate two days before the election.

Acclaim – Great praise or approval.

Accord, Discord – Accord is agreement, and discord is disagreement.

Our management is **in accord with** regulatory agencies about tightening standards.

Acquisitiveness – Desire to acquire more, especially an excessive desire.

The firm did well in buying up its competitors as a means of growth, but its **acquisitiveness** ultimately resulted in problems related to growing too quickly.

Acreage – Land measured in acres.

Our property is large, but much of the **acreage** is swampland not suitable for building.

Adhere to and **Adherent** – To adhere to is to stick to (literally, such as with glue, or metaphorically, such as to a plan or belief). An adherent is a person who sticks to a belief or cause.

The **adherents** of the plan won't admit that, in the long term, such a policy would bankrupt our state.

Employees who do not **adhere** to the policy will be subject to disciplinary action.

Ad-lib – 1) Make something up on the spot, give an unprepared speech; 2) Freely, as needed, according to desire.

We have ended our policy of rationing office supplies—pens may now be given to employees **ad-lib**.

Adopt – Take and make one's own; vote to accept. You can adopt a child, of course, or a new policy. To adopt a plan implies that you didn't come up with it yourself.

Advent – Arrival.

Before the **advent** of the Internet, people often called reference librarians to look up information for them in the library's reference section.

Adverse – Unfavorable, opposed.

A noisy environment is **adverse** to studying, and lack of sleep can have further **adverse** effects.

Agency – The ability to use power or influence.

Some climate change deniers acknowledge that the planet is heating up, but argue that human **agency** does not affect the climate.

Aggravate – Make worse.

Allowing your band to practice in our garage has greatly **aggravated** my headache.

Altogether – Completely, overall. **Altogether** is an adverb, and is one word. It is not the same as *all together,* as in *Let's sing all together.*

It was an **altogether** stunning new design.

Ambivalent – 1) Uncertain, unable to decide; 2) Wanting to do two contradictory things at once.

The health care plan has been met with **ambivalence** from lawmakers who would like to pass the bill but find supporting it to be politically impossible.

Amortize – Gradually pay off a debt, or gradually write off an asset.

A mortgage is a common form of **amortized** debt—spreading the payments out over as long as 30 years is not uncommon.

Analogous – Corresponding in a particular way, making a good **analogy**.

Our situation is **analogous** to one in a case study I read in business school. Maybe what worked for that company will work for us.

Annex – To add on, or something that has been added on. An annex to a building is a part built later and added on, or a new building that allows an organization to expand.

Annihilate – Completely destroy.

Annul – Make void or null, cancel, abolish (usually of laws or other established rules). Most people associate this word with marriage—a marriage is annulled when a judge rules that it was invalid in the first place (because of fraud, mental incompetence, etc.), so it is as if it never happened.

> Can we appreciate the art of a murderer? For many, the value of these paintings is **annulled** by the artist's crimes.

Anoint – The literal meaning is to rub or sprinkle oil on, especially as part of a ceremony that makes something sacred. The word is used metaphorically to refer to power or praise being given to someone who is thought very highly of. For instance:

> After Principal Smitters raised test scores over 60% at her school, it was only a matter of time before she was **anointed** superintendant by a fawning school board.

Antithetical to – Totally opposed to; opposite.

> The crimes of our chairman are totally **antithetical** to what the Society for Ethical Leadership stands for.

Application – Act or result of applying. Of course, you can have an **application** to business school, but you can also say something like:

> Company morale is at an all-time low, so the **application** of a severe cost-cutting policy may drive even more employees to look for new jobs.

Apprentice – A person who works for someone else in order to learn a trade (such as shoemaking, weaving, etc.) from that person.

Arbiter – Judge, umpire, person empowered to decide matters at hand. *Arbitration* is typically a formal process in which a professional *arbitrator* decides a matter outside of a court of law.

> Professional mediators **arbitrate** disputes.

> The principal said, "As the final **arbiter** of what is and is not appropriate in the classroom, I demand that you take down that poster of Miley Cyrus."

Archaic – Characteristic of an earlier period, ancient, primitive.

> The school's **archaic** computer system predated even floppy disks—it stored records on tape drives!

> Sometimes, when you look up a word in the dictionary, certain definitions are marked "**archaic**"—unless you are a Shakespeare scholar, you can safely ignore those **archaisms**.

Aristocracy – A hereditary ruling class, nobility (or a form of government ruled by these people).

Artifact – Any object made by humans, especially those from an earlier time, such as those excavated by archaelogists. Variant spelling: *artefact.*

> The archaeologists dug up countless **artifacts**, from simple pottery shards and coins to complex written tablets.

> The girl's room was full of the **artifacts** of modern teenage life: Justin Bieber posters, *Twilight* books, and a laptop open to Facebook.

Ascribe to/ascription – To *ascribe* is to give credit; *ascription* is the noun form.

> He **ascribed** his good grades **to** diligent studying.

> The boy's mother was amused by the **ascription to** his imaginary friend **of** all the powers he wished he had himself—being able to fly, having dozens of friends, and never having to eat his broccoli.

Assert – Affirm, claim, state, or express (that something is true).

Assimilation – The process by which a minority group adopts the customs and way of life of a larger group, or the process by which any new thing begins to "blend in." Words like *Westernization* or *Americanization* refer to the process of *assimilation* into Western culture, American culture, etc.

Attain – Achieve.

Attribute to – Give credit to.

Atypical – Not typical.

Backfire – To produce an unexpected and unwanted result. The literal meaning refers to an engine, gun, etc., exploding backwards or discharging gases, flame, debris, etc., backwards, thus possibly causing injury.

> The company's new efficiency measures **backfired** when workers protested and staged a walk-out, thus stopping production completely.

Balance – The remaining part or leftover amount. This is related to the idea of a **bank balance**—a **balance** is what you have left after deductions.

> The publishing division accounted for 25% of the profits, and the film division for **the balance**. This means that the film division provided 75% of the profits.

Baldly – Plainly, explicitly. (This is the same word as in losing one's hair.) To say something *baldly* is to be blunt. People are sometimes shocked or offended when things are said too bluntly or *baldly*.

An article in *Mother Jones* explained that Maine is not very diverse: "It is, to put it **baldly**, one of the whitest states in the union."

Balloon – 1) Swell or puff out; 2) Increase rapidly. Also, in finance, a *balloon payment* is a single payment at the end of a loan or mortgage term that is much larger than the other payments.

During the dot-com bubble, the university's investments **ballooned** to three times their former value.

When he won the award, his chest **ballooned** with pride.

Befall – Happen to (used with something bad). The past tense is **befell**.

Disaster **befell** the company once again when the CEO was thrown from a horse.

Belie – Contradict or misrepresent.

The actress's public persona as a perky "girl next door" **belied** her private penchant for abusing her assistants and demanding that her trailer be filled with ridiculous luxury goods.

The data **belie** the accepted theory—either we've made a mistake, or we have an amazing new discovery on our hands!

Benevolent – Expressing goodwill, helping others or charity.

Benign – 1) Harmless; 2) Kind or beneficial; 3) Not cancerous.

He was relieved when the biopsy results came back, informing him that the growth was **benign**.

He's a **benign** fellow. I'm sure having him assigned to your team at work will be perfectly pleasant, without changing the way you do things.

Blight – Disease that kills plants rapidly, or any cause of decay or destruction (noun); ruin or cause to wither (verb).

Many potato farmers have fallen into poverty as a result of **blight** killing their crops.

Gang violence is a **blight** on our school system, causing innocent students to fear even attending classes. In fact, violence has **blighted** our town.

Blunt – To dull, weaken, or make less effective.

The new therapy has severe side effects, but they can be **blunted** somewhat with anti-nausea medication and painkillers.

Blur – To make blurry, unclear, indistinct.

In Japan, company titles are taken very seriously and roles are sharply defined, whereas in the United States—especially in smaller firms—roles are often **blurred** as everyone is expected to pitch in on a variety of projects.

Bogus – Fake, fraudulent.

The back of this bodybuilding magazine is just full of ads for **bogus** products—this one promises 22-inch biceps just from wearing magnetic armbands!

Bolster – Strengthen or support.

The general requested reinforcements to **bolster** the defensive line set up at the border.

Many people use alcohol to **bolster** their confidence before approaching an attractive person in a bar.

Broad – Wide, large; in the open (*in broad daylight*); obvious, clear; liberal, tolerant; covering a wide scope of things. (*Broad* is also a mildly derogatory term for women, in case you're wondering—of course, no one would ever be called *a broad* on the GMAT.)

The panel was given **broad** discretionary powers. (That pretty much means that the panel can do whatever they want.)

Brook – Suffer or tolerate. Often used with the word *no.* You could say *The dictator will not* **brook** *dissent,* but a more common usage would be *The dictator will* **brook** *no dissent.*

Buffer – Something that separates two groups, people, etc., who potentially do not get along. When the United States was controlled by England, the state of Georgia was colonized as a *buffer* between the English colonies and Spanish Florida. A breakwater of rocks would act as a *buffer,* protecting the beach against crashing waves.

Bureaucracy – 1) Government characterized by many bureaus and petty administrators; 2) Excessive, seemingly meaningless requirements.

Some nations have a worse reputation for **bureaucracy** than others—in order to get a Visa, he had to file papers with four different agencies, wait for hours in three different waiting rooms, and, weeks later, follow up with some petty **bureaucrat** who complained that the original application should've been filed in triplicate.

Bygone – Past, former; that which is in the past (usually plural, as in the expression *let bygones be bygones*, which means let the past go, especially by forgiving someone).

At the nursing home, residents reminisced about **bygone** days all the time.

Bypass – Avoid, go around; ignore. The word can be a noun or a verb. Literally, a *bypass* is a stretch of highway that goes *around* an obstacle (such as a construction site). A synonym for *bypass* (verb) is *circumvent,* as in *to circumvent (or bypass) the normal approval process by going straight to the company president.*

Canon – Body of accepted rules, standards, or artistic works; *canonical* means authorized, recognized, or pertaining to a canon. Note that the spelling of *canon* is not the same as *cannon* (a large weapon). The *Western canon* is an expression referring to books traditionally considered necessary for a person to be educated in the culture of Europe and the Americas.

School boards often start controversies when replacing **canonical** books in the curriculum with modern literature; while many people think students should read works more relevant to their lives, others point out that *Moby Dick* is part of the **canon** for a reason.

Chancy – Risky, not having a certain outcome. This word comes from the idea of taking a lot of chances or depending on chance.

Channel – To direct or guide along a particular course. Of course, *channel* can also be a noun (television channel, the channel of a river, channels of communication). As a verb, you might *channel* your energy toward productive purposes.

Checked – Restrained, held back. A *check* or *checks* can also be used to mean *safeguards, limitations.* This is the same *checks* as in *checks and balances,* which refers to an aspect of the U.S. system of government in which the Executive, Judicial, and Legislative branches all have power over each other, so no one branch can gain too much power. The expression *held in check* means *restrained, held back.*

Once the economy took a turn for the worse, the investors began to **hold** spending **in check.**

The situation isn't so simple—while the warlords are surely criminals of the worst degree, they are the only force **checking** the power of the dictator.

Chronological – Arranged in or relating to time order.

Joey, I'm afraid you've done the assignment wrong—the point of making a timeline is to put the information in **chronological** order. You've made an alphabetical-order line instead!

Clamor – Noisy uproar or protest, as from a crowd; a loud, continuous noise. (*Not* the same word as *clamber,* to scramble or climb awkwardly.)

> As soon as a scent of scandal emerged, the press **clamored** for details.

> The mayor couldn't even make herself heard over the **clamor** of the protestors.

Clan – Traditional social unit or division of a tribe consisting of a number of families derived from a common ancestor. Metaphorically, a *clan* could be any group of people united by common aims, interests, etc.

Cloak – To cover or conceal. Often used as *cloaked in.* (Literally, a *cloak* is a large, loose cape, much like a winter coat without arms.)

> Apple's new products are often **cloaked in** mystery before they are released; before the launch of the iPad, even tech reviewers had little idea what the new device would be.

Coalesce – Come together, unite; fuse together.

> While at first, everyone on the team was jockeying for power and recognition, eventually, the group **coalesced** and everyone was happy to share credit for a job well-done.

> East and West Germany **coalesced** into a single country in 1990.

Coercion – Force; use of pressure, threats, etc., to force someone to do something.

Coexistence – Existing at the same time or in the same place. *Coexistence* is often used to mean *peaceful coexistence,* as in *The goal of the Camp David Accords was the coexistence of Israel and Egypt.*

Cogent – Very convincing, logical.

> Most GMAT Critical Reasoning arguments are not terribly **cogent**—they depend on unspoken and unjustified assumptions.

Cognitive – Related to thinking. *Cognition* is the mental process of knowing (awareness, judgment, reasoning, etc.).

Collude – Conspire; cooperate for illegal or fraudulent purposes.

> After two competing software companies doubled their prices on the same day, leaving consumers no lower-priced alternative, the federal government investigated the companies for **collusion**.

Compliant – Obeying, submissive; following the requirements.

Those who are not **compliant** with the regulations will be put on probation and possibly expelled.

Compound – Add interest to the principal and accrued interest; increase or add to. When talking about substances, *compound* can also mean *mix, combine,* as in *to compound two chemicals.*

The town was greatly damaged by the hurricane—damage that was only **compounded** by the subsequent looting and even arson that took place in the chaos that followed.

Your success in studying for the GMAT can only be **compounded** by healthy sleep habits; in fact, the brain requires sleep in order to form new memories and thus solidify your knowledge.

Compromise – Reduce the quality or value of something. Of course, to *compromise* can be good in personal relationships, but often *compromise* means to give up something in a bad way, as in *to compromise one's morals.* So, if you say that the hull of your boat has been *compromised,* you mean that you are going to sink!

It is unacceptable that safety is being **compromised** in the name of profits.

Concede – Give in, admit, yield; acknowledge reluctantly; grant or give up (such as giving up land after losing a war).

The negotiations were pointless, with each side's representatives instructed by their home countries to make no **concessions** whatsoever.

Quebec was a French **concession** to Britain in the Treaty of Paris in 1763.

I suppose I will have to **concede** the argument now that you've looked up evidence on Wikipedia.

Condone – Overlook, tolerate, regard as harmless.

While underage drinking is illegal, at many universities, it is tacitly **condoned** by administrations that neglect to enforce anti-drinking policies.

Confer – Consult, compare views; bestow or give.

A Ph.D. **confers** upon a person the right to be addressed as Doctor as well as eligibility to pursue tenure-track professorship.

Excuse me for a moment to make a call—I can't buy this car until I **confer** with my spouse.

Consequently – As a result, therefore. (Don't confuse with *subsequently,* which means *afterwards.*)

The new medicine is not only a failure, but a dangerous one; **consequently**, drug trials were halted immediately.

Considerable – Large, significant.

Considerations – Factors to be considered in making a decision. Used in the singular, *consideration* can mean care for other people's feelings; high esteem or admiration; or a treatment or account, as in *The book began with a thorough consideration of the history of the debate.*

Consolidate – Unite, combine, solidify, make coherent.

She **consolidated** her student loans so she would only have to make one payment per month.

As group leader, Muriel will **consolidate** all of our research into a single report.

Contemplative – Contemplating, thoughtful, meditative.

Contend – Assert, make an argument in favor of; strive, compete, struggle. A *contention* is a claim, often a thesis or statement that will then be backed up with reasons. *Contentious* means controversial or argumentative, as in *The death penalty is a contentious issue.*

Contextualize – Place in context, such as by giving the background or circumstances.

Virginia Woolf's feminism is hard to truly understand unless **contextualized** within the customs of the highly restrained, upper-class English society of her time.

Contract – Shrink, pull together, and thus become smaller (used in this way, *contract* is the opposite of *expand*). You can also *contract* a disease or a debt, in which case *contract* means *get* or *acquire. To contract* can also simply mean to make a contract (to *contract* an agreement).

Conventional – Traditional, customary. This could be related to morals and culture (*Her family was surprised that she gave up a conventional wedding ceremony in favor of a bohemian ceremony on the beach)* or to technology, business methods, etc.—a *conventional* oven is simply a regular oven (without certain modern enhancements).

Converge – Move toward one another or toward a point; unite.

I know we're driving in to the wedding from different states, but our routes ought to **converge** when each of us hits I-95—maybe we could **converge** at a Cracker Barrel for lunch!

Conversely – In an opposite way; on the other hand.

I am not here to argue that lack of education causes poverty. **Conversely**, I am here to argue that poverty causes lack of education.

Convoluted – Twisted; very complicated.

Your argument is so **convoluted** that I'm not even able to understand it enough to start critiquing it.

To get from the hotel room to the pool requires following a **convoluted** path up two staircases and down two others—to get to someplace on the same floor we started on!

Copious –Plentiful, bountiful.

Although she took **copious** notes in class, she found that she was missing a big-picture understanding that would have tied all the information together.

Corresponding – Accompanying; having the same or almost the same relationship.

Our profit-sharing plan means that increases in profit will be matched by **corresponding** increases in employee compensation.

Corroborate – Support, add evidence to.

You're telling me you were 30 miles away riding a roller coaster when the school was vandalized? I have a hard time believing that—is there anyone who can **corroborate** your story?

Countenance – Approve or tolerate. *Countenance* can also serve as a noun, literally meaning face (*Her countenance was familiar—had I seen her before?).* The metaphorical meaning makes sense when you think about a similar expression: "I cannot *look you in the face* after what you did."

I saw you cheating off my paper, and I can't **countenance** cheating—either you turn yourself in or I'll report you.

Counterintuitive – Against what a person would intuitively expect.

Although it seems **counterintuitive**, for some extreme dieters, eating more can actually help them to lose weight, since the body is reassured that it is not facing a period of prolonged starvation.

Counterpoint – Contrasting item, opposite; the use of contrast or interplay in a work of art.

The play's lighthearted, witty narrator provides a welcome **counterpoint** to the seriousness and grief expressed by the other characters.

The hot peppers work in **counterpoint** to an otherwise sweet dish.

Counterproductive – Defeating the purpose; preventing the intended goal.

The candidate's attempt to win swing votes in Ohio was **counterproductive**—following his speech in Toledo, his poll numbers actually went *down* 5%.

Credibility – Believability, trustworthiness.

Many famous "experts" with "Dr." before their names are not medical doctors at all. Any television "doctor" who turns out to have a Ph.D. in a totally unrelated field, for instance, ought to suffer a serious drop in **credibility**.

Culminate – Reach the highest point or final stage.

A Ph.D. program generally **culminates** in a written dissertation and a defense of that dissertation to a committee.

Currency – Money; the act of being passed from person-to-person (*These old coins are no longer in currency*); general acceptance or a period of time during which something is accepted. *Cultural currency* refers to cultural knowledge that allows a person to feel "in the know."

The call center in Mumbai trained its workers in American slang and pop culture, giving them a **cultural currency** that, it was hoped, would help the workers relate to customers thousands of miles away.

Curtail – Cut short or reduce.

Cynical – Thinking the worst of others' motivations; bitterly pessimistic.

Debase – Degrade; lower in quality, value, rank, etc.; lower in moral quality.

Members of the mainstream church argued that the fringe sect was practicing a **debased** version of the religion, twisting around its beliefs and missing the point.

I can tell from the weight that this isn't pure gold, but rather some **debased** mixed metal.

You have **debased** yourself by accepting bribes.

Debilitating – Weakening, disabling.

Debunk – Expose, ridicule, or disprove false or exaggerated claims.

Galileo spent his last years under house arrest for **debunking** the widely held idea that the Sun revolved around the Earth.

The show MythBusters **debunks** pseudoscientific claims.

Decry – Condemn openly. The "cry" in *decry* means to cry out against, as in *The activist decried the destruction of the animals' habitat.*

Deem – Judge; consider.

> "You can take the black belt exam when I **deem** you ready, and not a moment before," said the karate instructor.

Deflect – Cause to curve; turn aside, especially from a straight course; avoid.

> The purpose of a shield is to **deflect** arrows or bullets from an enemy.

> Every time he was asked a difficult question, Senator Warrington **deflected** by changing the topic, saying he'd answer later, or even—insincerely, it seemed—calling for a moment of prayer.

Delimit – Fix, mark, or define the boundaries of.

> The role of an executive coach is **delimited** by our code of conduct—we may not counsel people for psychological conditions, for instance.

Denote – Be a name or symbol for. A *denotation* is the literal meaning of a word; a *connotation* is the feeling that accompanies that word.

> There's nothing in the **denotation** of "crotchety" (grumpy, having strong and irrational preferences) that indicates any particular group of people, but because of the expression "crotchety old man," the word **connotes**, for many people, an image of an especially unpleasant male senior citizen.

Deride – Mock, scoff at, laugh at contemptuously.

> The manager really thought that **deriding** his employees as "stupid" or "lazy" would motivate them to work harder; instead, it motivated them to hide his office supplies as an act of revenge.

Deterrent – Something that restrains or discourages.

> Some argue that the death penalty is a **deterrent** to crime—that is, the point is not just to punish the guilty, but to frighten other prospective criminals.

Dichotomy – Division into two parts or into two contradictory groups.

> There is a **dichotomy** in the sciences between theoretical or "pure" sciences, such as physics and chemistry, and the life sciences, which often deal more with classifying than with theorizing.

Disclosure – Revealing, exposing the truth; something that has been revealed. *Full disclosure* is an expression meaning to tell everything. In journalism, the expression is often used when a writer reveals a personal connection to the story. For instance, a news article might read, "MSNBC may have forced the departure of popular anchor Keith Olbermann (full disclosure: the author was employed as a fact-checker for MSNBC in 2004)."

Discount – Ignore, especially to ignore information because it is considered untrustworthy; to underestimate, minimize, regard with doubt. To *discount* an idea is to *not count* it as important.

> After staying up all night to finish the presentation, he was understandably unhappy that his boss **discounted** his contribution, implying that she had done most of the work herself.

Discredit – Injure the reputation of, destroy credibility of or confidence in.

> Congresswoman Huffman's opponent tried to use her friendship with a certain radical extremist to **discredit** her, even though the Congresswoman hadn't seen this so-called "extremist" since sixth-grade summer camp.

Discrepancy – Difference or inconsistency.

> When there is a **discrepancy** between a store's receipts and the amount of money in the register, the cashier's behavior is generally called into question.

Discrete – Separate, distinct, detached, existing as individual parts. This is NOT the same word as *discreet,* which means *subtle, secretive.*

> Be sure to use quotation marks and citations as appropriate in your paper in order to keep your ideas **discrete** from those of the experts you are quoting.

> The advertising agency pitched us not on one campaign, but on three **discrete** ideas.

Discretionary – Subject to someone's *discretion,* or judgment (generally good judgment). *Discretionary funds* can be spent on anything (for instance, a budget might contain a small amount for "extras"). *Begin at your discretion* means *Begin whenever you think is best.*

Discriminating – Judicious, discerning, having good judgment or insight. Many people automatically think of *discriminating* as bad, because they are thinking of racial discrimination. However, *discriminating* can also mean telling things apart and can be an important skill—it is important to *discriminate* legitimate colleges from fraudulent diploma mills, for instance.

> He is a man of **discriminating** tastes—all his suits are handmade in Italy, and I once saw him send back an entree when he complained that black truffle oil had been substituted for white. The chef was astounded that he could tell.

> You can tell a real Prada bag by the **discriminating** mark on the inside.

Disinterested – Unbiased, impartial; not interested. Don't confuse with *uninterested,* which means not interested, bored, apathetic.

> Let's settle this argument once and for all! We'll get a **disinterested** observer to judge who can sing the highest note!

Dismiss – Put aside or reject, especially after only a brief consideration; allow to disperse or leave; fire from a job. To *dismiss biases* (*biases* is the plural of *bias*) in science is to rule out possible prejudices that could have influenced results.

> "Before I **dismiss** class," said the teacher, "I want to remind you of the importance of **dismissing** biases in your research by ruling out or adjusting for factors that could have unintentionally affected your results."

Disparate – Distinct, different.

> He chose the college for two **disparate** reasons: the strength of the computer science program and the excellence of the hip-hop dance squad.

Dispatch – Speed, promptness (noun); send off or deal with in a speedy way (verb).

> So, you want to be a bike messenger? I need messengers who approach every delivery with alacrity, care, and **dispatch**—if the customers wanted their packages to arrive slowly, they'd use the post office.

> Acting with all possible **dispatch**, emergency services **dispatched** a rescue squad to the scene.

Disperse – Scatter, spread widely, cause to vanish. *Dispersal* is the noun form.

> Because the demonstrators didn't have a permit, the police showed up with megaphones, demanding loudly that the crowd **disperse**. The eventual **dispersal** of the crowd resulted in smaller protests at various points throughout the city.

Disseminate – Scatter, spread about, broadcast.

> In the 1760s, revolutionary ideas were **disseminated** in the Thirteen Colonies via pamphlets such as Thomas Paine's *Common Sense.*

Divest – Deprive or strip of a rank, title, etc., or of clothing or gear; to sell off holdings (opposite of *invest*).

> When she found out that the most profitable stock in her portfolio was that of a company that tested products on animals, she immediately **divested** by telling her broker to sell the stock.

> Once his deception was exposed, he was **divested** of his position on the Board.

Dovetail – Join or fit together.

When the neuroscientist married an exercise physiologist, neither thought they'd end up working together, but when Dr. Marion Ansel received a grant to study how exercise improves brain function and Dr. Jim Ansel was assigned to her team, the two found that their careers **dovetailed** nicely.

Dubious – Doubtful, questionable, suspect.

This applicant's résumé is filled with **dubious** qualifications—this is a marketing position and this résumé is mostly about whitewater rafting.

Echelon – A level, rank, or grade; the people at that level. A *stratum* is the same idea (*strata* is the plural, as in *rising through the upper strata/echelons of the firm*).

Obtaining a job on Wall Street doesn't guarantee access to the upper **echelon** of executives, where multi-million dollar bonuses are the norm.

I'm not sure I'm cut out to analyze poetry; I find it hard to dig beyond the most accessible **echelon** of meaning.

Eclectic – Selecting the best of everything or coming from many diverse sources.

Eclectic taste is helpful in being a DJ—crowds love to hear the latest hip-hop mixed with '80s classics and other unexpected genres of music.

Eclipse – 1) One thing covering up another, such as the sun hiding the moon or a person losing attention to a more famous or talented person; 2) To cover up, darken, or make less important.

Billy Ray Cyrus, who had a hit song, "Achy Breaky Heart," in the '90s, has long since found his fame **eclipsed** by that of his daughter, Miley.

Effectively – Of course, *effectively* can just mean *in a successful manner,* as in *He did the job effectively.* But it can also mean *in effect, but not officially.* For instance, when Woodrow Wilson was president of the United States, he was incapacitated by a stroke, and some people believe that Wilson's wife, Edith, *effectively* served as president. That doesn't necessarily mean that she did a good job. Rather, it means that she was doing the job of the president without officially being the president.

He went on a two-week vacation without asking for time off or even telling anyone he was leaving, thus **effectively** resigning from his position.

Efficacy – The quality of being able to produce the intended effect (often used in reference to medicines). Don't confuse *efficacy* with *efficiency*. Something *efficacious* gets the job done; something *efficient* gets the job done without wasting time or effort.

> Extensive trials will be necessary to determine whether the drug's **efficacy** outweighs the side effects.

Egalitarian – Related to belief in the equality of all people.

> It is very rare that someone turns down an offer to be knighted by the Queen of England; however, he was **egalitarian** enough to feel uncomfortable with the entire idea of titles and royalty.

Egregious – Extraordinarily or conspicuously bad; glaring.

> Your conduct is an **egregious** violation of our Honor Code—not only did you steal your roommate's paper off his computer and turn it in as your own, you also sold his work to a plagiarism website so other cheaters could purchase it!

Emancipate – Free from slavery or oppression. Lincoln's *Emancipation Proclamation* legally ended slavery in the United States. In law, to *emancipate* a minor is to declare the child (generally a teenager) no longer under the control of his or her parents.

Eminent – Prominent, distinguished, of high rank.

Emphasize – Give special force or attention to. This word often occurs in GMAT Reading Comprehension answer choices. Hint: While the purpose of a particular sentence could be to *emphasize* a point that came before, the main idea of an entire passage is never just to *emphasize* something.

Empirical – Coming from, based on, or able to be verified by experience or experimentation; not purely based on theory.

> The Ancient Greeks philosophized about the nature of matter (concluding, for instance, that everything was made of earth, water, air, and fire) without any **empirical** evidence—that is, the very idea of conducting experiments hadn't been invented yet.

> People always knew **empirically** that when you drop something, it falls to the ground; the theory of gravity later explained why.

Emulate – Copy in an attempt to equal or be better than.

> The ardent *Star Trek* fan **emulated** Captain Kirk in every way possible—his brash and confident leadership might have gotten him somewhere, but the women he tried to impress weren't so impressed.

Enigma – Puzzle, mystery, riddle; mysterious or contradictory person.

> The enormous rock sculptures in Stonehenge, Scotland, are truly an **enigma**—were they created as part of a religious observance, in deference to a great ruler, or for some other reason?

Enjoy – Of course, enjoy means "receive pleasure from," but it also means "benefit from." Thus, it is not true that only people and animals can *enjoy.* For instance:

> The college has long **enjoyed** the support of wealthy alumni.

Ensure vs. **Insure** – If you buy insurance for something, you have *insured* it. If you guarantee something, you have *ensured* it.

> If you go past this security checkpoint, I cannot **ensure** your safety.

Enumerate – Count or list; specify one-by-one.

> The Bill of Rights **enumerates** the basic rights held by every citizen of the United States.

Equitable – Fair, equal, just.

> As the university president was heavily biased toward the sciences, faculty members in the liberal arts felt they had to fight to get an **equitable** share of funding for their departments.

Equivalence – The state of being equal or essentially equal.

Equivocal or **Equivocate** – Use unclear language to deceive or avoid committing to a position.

> Not wanting to lose supporters, the politician **equivocated** on the issue, tossing out buzzwords related to each side while also claiming more study was needed.

Erratic – Inconsistent, wandering, having no fixed course.

> When someone engages in **erratic** behavior, family members often suspect drugs or mental illness. However, sometimes the person is just building a top-secret invention in the garage!

Erroneous – Mistaken, in error.

> Hilda was completely unable to assemble her new desk chair after the instructions **erroneously** instructed her to screw the left armrest onto a small lever on the bottom of the seat.

Erstwhile – Former, previous.

> A novelist and **erstwhile** insurance salesman, he told us his story of the long road to literary success, before he was able to quit his day job.

Escape velocity – The minimum velocity that an object must attain in order to completely escape a gravitational field.

Estimable – 1) Worthy of esteem, admirable; 2) Able to be estimated.

> As the first Black president of the Harvard Law Review, Barack Obama presented an **estimable** résumé when he ran for president in 2008.

> Riding a roller coaster is safer than driving on the highway, but there is still an **estimable** risk.

Ethos – The character, personality, or moral values specific to a person, group, time period, etc.

> At the prep school, the young man happily settled into an **ethos** of hard work and rigorous athletic competition.

Exacerbate – Make worse (more violent, severe, etc.), inflame.

> Hearing your band practicing in our garage has greatly **exacerbated** my headache.

Exacting – Very severe in making demands; requiring precise attention.

> The boxing coach was **exacting**, analyzing Joey's footwork down to the millimeter and forcing him to repeat movements hundreds of times until they were correct.

Execute – Put into effect, do, perform (to *execute* a process). *Execute* can also mean *enforce, make legal, carry out the terms of a legal agreement.* To *execute* a will is to sign it in the presence of witnesses. To *execute* the terms of a contract is to fulfill an obligation written in the contract.

Exhaustive – Comprehensive, thorough, exhausting a topic or subject, accounting for all possibilities; draining, tending to exhaust.

> The consultant's report was an **exhaustive** treatment of all possible options and their likely consequences. In fact, it was so **exhaustive** that the manager joked that he would need to hire another consultant to read the first consultant's report.

Exotic – Foreign, intriguingly unusual or strange.

Expansionist – Wanting to expand, such as by conquering other countries.

Expedient – Suitable, proper; effective (sometimes while sacrificing ethics).

> "I need this report by 2pm, and I don't care what you have to do to make that happen," said the boss. "I expect you to deal with it **expediently**."

> When invited to a wedding you cannot attend, it is **expedient** to send a gift.

Explicit – Direct, clear, fully revealed. *Explicit* in the context of movies, music, etc., means depicting or describing sex or nudity, but *explicit* can be used for anything (*explicit instructions* is a common phrase). The antonym of **explicit** is *implicit* or *tacit,* meaning hinted at or implied.

> The goal of my motivational talk is to make **explicit** the connection between staying in school and avoiding a life of crime.

Extraneous – Irrelevant; foreign, coming from without, not belonging.

> This essay would be stronger if you removed **extraneous** information; the paragraph about the author's life doesn't happen to be relevant to your thesis.

> Maize, which originated in the New World, is **extraneous** to Europe.

Extrapolate – Conjecture about an unknown by projecting information about something known; predict by projecting past experience. In math and science, to *extrapolate* is to infer values in an unobserved interval from values in an observed interval. For instance, from the points (1, 4) and (3, 8), you could *extrapolate* the point (5, 12), since it would be on the same line.

> No, I've never been to Bryn Mawr, but I've visited several small, private women's colleges in the Northeast, so I think I can **extrapolate**.

Facilitate – Make easier, help the progress of.

> A good meeting **facilitator** lets everyone be heard while still keeping the meeting focused.

> As a midwife, my goal is simply to **facilitate** a natural process.

Faction – A group (especially an exclusive group with strong beliefs, self-interest, bias, etc.) within a larger organization. This word is usually meant in a negative way (once people have joined *factions,* they are no longer willing to hear the issues and debate or compromise).

> The opposition movement was once large enough to have a chance at succeeding, but it has since broken into numerous, squabbling **factions**, each too small to have much impact.

Faculty – An ability, often a mental ability. Most often used in the plural, as in *A stroke can often deprive a person of important mental faculties.* (Of course, *faculty* can also mean the teachers or professors of an institution of learning.)

Fading – Declining.

> In the face of **fading** public support for national health care, the Senator withdrew his support for the bill.

Fashion – Manner or way.

The watchmaker works in a meticulous **fashion**, paying incredible attention to detail.

Fathom – Understand deeply.

I cannot even remotely **fathom** how you interpreted an invitation to sleep on my couch as permission to take my car on a six-hour joyride!

Finding – *The finding* (or *the findings*) refers to a discovery, report, result of an experiment, etc.

When the attorneys received the results of the DNA report, they were shocked by **the finding** that John Doe could not have committed the crime.

Fishy – Suspicious, unlikely, questionable, as in *a fishy story.* This expression probably arose because fish smell very bad when they start to spoil.

Fledgling – New or inexperienced. A fledgling is also a young bird that cannot fly yet.

The Society of Engineers is available for career day presentations in elementary schools, where we hope to encourage **fledgling** talents in the applied sciences.

Fleeting – Passing quickly, transitory.

I had assumed our summer romance would be **fleeting**, so I was very surprised when you proposed marriage!

Foreshadow – Indicate or suggest beforehand.

The children's ghost story around the campfire was meant to **foreshadow** the horrible things that would happen to the same kids years later as teenagers at a motel in the middle of the woods.

Forestall – Delay, hinder, prevent by taking action beforehand.

Our research has been **forestalled** by a lack of funding; we're all just biding our time while we wait for the university to approve our grant proposal.

Glacial – Slow, cold, icy, unsympathetic. *Glacial* can also just mean related to glaciers.

Progress happened, but at a **glacial** pace everyone found frustrating.

He had wanted to appear on the reality singing competition his whole young life, but he was not encouraged by the judges' **glacial** response to his audition.

Grade, Gradation – A *gradation* is a progression or process taking place gradually, in stages; to *grade* is to slant (the road *grades* steeply) or to blend (the dress's fabric *grades* from blue to green).

> The hill's **gradation** was so gradual that even those on crutches were able to enjoy the nature trail.
>
> The marshland **grades** into the water so gradually that it is difficult to tell the land from the bay.

Graft – Join together plant parts or skin so that two living things grow together (for instance, a *skin graft* for a burn victim); the act of acquiring money or other benefits through illegal means, especially by abusing one's power.

> The part of the book describing the financial crisis is good, but the "What You Can Do" section seems **grafted** on, almost as though written by a different author.
>
> It's not cool for your boss to pressure you into buying Girl Scout cookies from his daughter. If she were selling something larger, we'd call that **graft**.

Grandstand – Perform showily in an attempt to impress onlookers.

> I was really passionate about the candidate when he spoke at our school, but now that I think about it, he was just **grandstanding**. I mean, who could disagree that young people are the future? And doing a cheer for the environment doesn't actually signify a commitment to changing any public policies about it.

Guesswork – A set of guesses or estimates; work based on guesses or estimates.

Guile – Clever deceit, cunning, craftiness.

> The game of poker is all about **guile**, manipulating your own body language and conversation to lead other players to erroneous conclusions about the cards you're holding.

Hallmark – A mark of indication of quality, purity, genuineness, etc.; any distinguishing characteristic.

> Fast-paced rhymes, an angry tenor, and personal attacks on celebrities are **hallmarks** of Eminem's music.

Hallucination – A delusion, a false or mistaken idea; seeing, sensing, or hearing things that aren't there, such as from a mental disorder.

Handpick – To pick by hand, to personally select.

> The retiring CEO **handpicked** his successor.

Hardly – *Hardly* can mean *barely* or *probably not,* or *not at all.* The sentence *I can hardly see you* means *I can see you only a little bit.* In the following sentence, *hardly* means *not:*

> The news could **hardly** have come at a worse time. (The meaning is *The news came at the worst possible time.*)

Hardy – Bold, brave, capable of withstanding hardship, fatigue, cold, etc.

> While the entire family enjoyed the trip to South America, only the **hardier** members even attempted to hike to the top of Ecuador's tallest volcano.

Hearken or **Hark** – Listen, pay attention to. The expression *hearken back* or *hark back* means to turn back to something earlier or return to a source.

> The simple lifestyle and anachronistic dress of the Amish **hearken** back to an earlier era.

> The nation's first change of leadership in decades is causing the people to **hearken** closely to what is happening in government.

Hedge – Avoid commitment by leaving provisions for withdrawal or changing one's mind; protect a bet by also betting on the other side.

> When the professor called on him to take a stand on the issue, he **hedged** for fear of offending her: "Well, there are valid points on both sides," he said.

Hegemony – Domination, authority; influence by one country over others socially, culturally, economically, etc.

> The discovery of oil by a previously poor nation disrupted the larger, richer nation's **hegemony** in the region—suddenly, the **hegemon** had a competitor.

Heterogeneous – Different in type, incongruous; composed of different types of elements. *Homogeneous* (of the same kind) is the opposite of *heterogeneous.*

> Rather than build the wall with plain brick, we used a **heterogeneous** mixture of stones—they are not only different colors, but a variety of sizes as well.

Hierarchy – A ranked series; a classification of people according to rank, ability, etc.; a ruling body.

> The Eco-Action Coalition was led by a strict **hierarchy**—members followed orders from district leaders, district leaders from regional leaders, and regional leaders from the national head.

Holdings – Property, such as land, capital, and stock. *The company liquidated its holdings* means that the company sold off everything. Of course, the word *hold* has many meanings. *In a holding pattern* is an expression that means *staying still, not changing.*

Host – A large amount. *A host of problems* means a lot of problems.

Hyperbole – Deliberate exaggeration for effect.

> Oh, come on. Saying "That movie was so bad it made me puke" was surely **hyperbole**. I strongly doubt that you actually vomited during or following *The Back-up Plan.*

Iconoclast – Attacker of cherished beliefs or institutions.

> A lifelong **iconoclast**, Ayn Rand wrote a controversial book entitled, *The Virtue of Selfishness.*

Imminent – Ready to occur, impending.

> In the face of **imminent** bankruptcy, the company immediately slashed all unnecessary spending.

Immunity – The state of not being susceptible to disease; exemption from a duty or liability; exemption from legal punishment. *Diplomatic immunity* is an example of *immunity* meaning *exemption from legal punishment.* For instance, every year, New York City loses millions of dollars from U.N. diplomats parking illegally and then not paying their parking tickets, since the diplomats are not subject to U.S. laws.

Impair – Make worse, weaken.

> Playing in a rock band without earplugs will almost certainly **impair** your hearing over time.

Impartial – Unbiased, fair. *Disinterested, dispassionate,* and *nonpartisan* are all related to being fair and not having a bias or personal stake.

> Judge Gonzales removed himself from the case because, having a personal connection to the accountant accused of embezzlement, he did not think he could be appropriately **impartial**.

Impasse – Position or road from which there is no escape; deadlock, gridlock.

> If the union won't budge on its demands and the transit authority won't raise salaries, then we are at an **impasse**.

Impede – Hold back, obstruct the progress of.

> I didn't realize business school would be entirely group work—sadly, there's always at least one person in every group who **impedes** the group's progress more than helps it.

Impinge on – Trespass on, violate.

> Civil liberties experts argued that a school system's regulation of what its students do on Facebook outside of school is an **impingement** of their right to free speech.

Implode – Burst inward. Metaphorically, to collapse or break down.

The startup struggled for years before it **imploded**—the management team broke into factions, all of the clients were scared off, and employees who hadn't been paid in weeks began taking the office computers home with them in retribution.

Imply – Hint at, suggest.

Impute – Credit, attribute; lay blame or responsibility for.

The ineffectual CEO was nevertheless a master of public relations—he made sure that all successes were **imputed** to him, and all failures were **imputed** to others.

Inadvertently – Accidentally, carelessly, as a side effect.

In attempting to perfect his science project, he **inadvertently** blew a fuse and plunged his family's home into darkness.

Inasmuch – Since, because. Usually *inasmuch as*.

Inasmuch as a whale is not a fish, it will not be covered in this biology course specifically about fish.

Incentive – Something that encourages greater action or effort, such as a reward.

A controversial program in a failing school system uses cash payments as an **incentive** for students to stay in school.

Incidentally – Not intentionally, accidentally. *Incidentally* can also mean *by the way* and is used to introduce information that is only slightly related. *Incidentals* can refer to expenses that are "on the side" (*The company gives us $100 a day for meals and incidentals*).

The environmental protection law was **incidentally** injurious to the rubber industry.

I think we should rent the new office space. **Incidentally**, there's a great Mexican restaurant opening up right across the street from it.

Incinerate – Burn, reduce to ashes, cremate.

Inconsequential – Insignificant, unimportant. The sense here is that the thing is so small that it doesn't even have consequences.

You wrote a best-selling book and got a stellar review in the *New York Times*—the fact that your cousin didn't like it is simply **inconsequential**.

Incorporate – Combine, unite; form a legal corporation; embody, give physical form to.

When a business **incorporates**, it becomes a separate legal entity—for instance, the business can declare bankruptcy without the owners doing so.

Local legend has it that ghosts can **incorporate** on one night of the year and walk among the living.

Indeterminate – Not fixed or determined, indefinite; vague.

The results of the drug trial were **indeterminate**; further trials will be needed to ascertain whether the drug can be released.

The lottery can have an **indeterminate** number of winners—the prize is simply divided among them.

Indicative – Indicating, suggestive of. Usually used as *indicative of.*

Your symptoms are **indicative** of the common cold.

Induce – Persuade or influence (a person to do something); bring about, cause to happen (to *induce labor* when a birth is not proceeding quickly enough).

Inert – Inactive; having little or no power to move.

All of the missiles at the military museum are **inert**—they're not going blow up.

When she saw her father's **inert** body on the floor, she thought the worst, but fortunately, he was just practicing very slow yoga.

Inevitable – Not able to be avoided or escaped; certain.

Benjamin Franklin famously said that only two things in life are **inevitable**: death and taxes.

Inexplicable – Not able to be explained.

Inextricably – In a way such that one cannot untangle or escape something. If you are *inextricably tied* to something (such as your family), then you have so many different obligations and deep relationships that you could never leave, disobey, etc.

Infer – Conclude from evidence or premises. Remember, on the GMAT, *infer* means *draw a* definitely true *conclusion.* It does NOT mean to assume!

Inform – Inspire, animate; give substance, essence, or context to; be the characteristic quality of. *Inform* most commonly means to impart knowledge to someone; thus, many students are confused when they see the word used in other ways on the GMAT.

> Her work as an art historian is **informed** by a background in drama; where others see a static tableau, she sees a protagonist, a conflict, a denouement.

Ingenuity – Inventive skill, imagination, cleverness, especially in design.

Ingrained – Deep-rooted, forming part of the very essence; worked into the fiber.

> Religious observance had been **ingrained** in him since birth; he could not remember a time when he didn't pray five times a day.

Inherent – Existing as a permanent, essential quality; intrinsic. (See the similar *intrinsic* in this list.)

> New research seems to support the idea that humans have an **inherent** sense of justice—even babies become upset at puppet shows depicting unfairness.

Initial – First, at the beginning. An *initial deposit* might be the money you put down to open a new bank account.

Inordinate – Excessive, not within proper limits, unrestrained.

> Students taking practice computer-adaptive tests at home often take an **inordinate** number of breaks—remember, on the real thing, you can't stop just because you're tired or hungry.

Instrumental – Serving as a means of doing something. Just as you might call a weapon an *instrument of war,* saying *He was instrumental in the restructuring* has the sense that the person was used as an *instrument* of getting something done.

Insular – Pertaining to an island; detached, standing alone; narrow-minded (like the stereotype of people from small towns or places).

> The young actress couldn't wait to escape the **insularity** of her small town, where life revolved around high school football and Taco Bell was considered exotic international cuisine.

Interplay – Interaction, reciprocal relationship or influence.

> Bilingual readers will enjoy the **interplay** of English and Spanish in many of the poems in this anthology of the work of Mexican-American poets.

Intractable – Difficult to control, manage, or manipulate; hard to cure; stubborn.

That student is positively **intractable**! Last week, we talked about the importance of staying in your seat during the lesson—this week, she not only got up mid-class, but she actually scrambled on top of a bookcase and refused to come down!

Back injuries often result in **intractable** pain; despite treatment, patients never feel fully cured.

Intrepid – Fearless, brave, enduring in the face of adversity.

Intrepid explorers Lewis and Clark led the first U.S. expedition to the West Coast, facing bitter winters and rough terrain.

Intrinsic – Belonging to the essential nature of a thing. (See the similar *inherent* in this list.)

Despite all this high-tech safety equipment, skydiving is an **intrinsically** dangerous proposition.

Communication is **intrinsic to** a healthy relationship.

Inundate – Flood, cover with water, overwhelm.

As the city was **inundated** with water, the mayor feared that many evacuees would have nowhere to go.

I can't go out—I am **inundated** with homework!

Invaluable – Priceless; so valuable that the value cannot be measured.

Investiture – Investing; formally giving someone a right or title.

The former dean had her academic robes dry cleaned in preparation for her **investiture** as university president.

Involved – Complicated, intricate; confused or tangled.

The story is quite **involved**—are you sure you have time for it?

Invulnerable – Immune to attack; not vulnerable; impossible to damage, injure, etc.

Jettison – Discard, cast off; throw items overboard in order to lighten a ship in an emergency.

We got so tired while hiking the Appalachian Trail that we **jettisoned** some of our fancy camping supplies just so we could keep going.

Sadly, when school budgets are slashed, the first thing **jettisoned** is usually an art or music program.

Jumbo – Unusually large, supersized.

Juncture – Critical point in time, such as a crisis or a time when a decision is necessary; a place where two things are joined together.

> We are at a critical **juncture** in the history of this organization: either we can remain a non-profit or we can register as a political action committee and try to expand our influence.

> The little canoe started to sink when it split at the **juncture** between the old wood and the new material used to repair it.

Juxtapose – Place side-by-side (either physically or in a metaphorical way, such as to make a comparison). If a Reading Comprehension answer choice says something like "Juxtapose two theories," ask yourself if the main purpose of the entire passage was to *compare* two theories.

> Making a decision between two engagement rings from two different stores was difficult, he noted—it would be much easier if he could **juxtapose** them to compare them directly.

Kinetic – Pertaining to motion.

> Marisa told her mother what she had learned in science class: a ball sitting on a table has potential energy, but a ball falling toward the ground has **kinetic** energy.

Lackluster – Not shiny; dull, mediocre; lacking brilliance or vitality.

> Many young people today are so accustomed to being praised by parents and adults that they are shocked when a **lackluster** effort in the workplace receives the indifference or mild disapproval it deserves.

Landmark – Object (such as a building) that stands out and can be used to navigate by; a very important place, event, etc.

> The Civil Rights Act of 1964 was a **landmark** in the battle for equality in the United States.

> In Lebanon, many roads are unmarked, and people navigate by **landmarks**—for instance, "third house down from the water tower."

Latent – Potential; existing but not visible or active. A similar word is *dormant.*

> Certain experts believe that some people have a genetic propensity for addiction; however, if such a person never comes into contact with drugs, the propensity for addiction can remain **latent** for life.

Lateral – Sideways, related to or located at the side. A *lateral move* in a career is taking a new job at the same level.

Lax – Not strict; careless, loose, slack.

> My parents were really **lax** about homework—they never checked to see if I did it or not. Sadly, this legacy of **laxity** is not serving me well while studying for the GMAT.

Laypeople – Regular people, non-specialists.

> The doctor's books were so successful because he was able to explain complicated medical concepts in easy-to-understand language for the **layperson**.

Levy – Collect tax from or wage war on; act of collecting tax or amount owed, or the drafting of troops into military service.

> When England **levied** yet another tax on the colonists, the colonists were pushed one further step toward **levying** war. Soon, the worried British began to **levy** troops.

Liberal – Favorable to progress or reform; believing in maximum possible individual freedom; tolerant, open-minded; generous. (*Liberal* in modern American politics isn't quite the same as the dictionary definition. For instance, *liberal* Democrats tend to favor social programs that require a larger government to administer, while some conservatives say that *liberalism* means having the smallest government possible in order to maximize freedom.)

> Split pea soup benefits from a **liberal** application of pepper.

> **Liberal** reformers in Egypt pushed for freedom of speech, freedom of the press, and freedom of assembly.

Lift – Remove (such as a restriction); improve or lighten (such as a person's mood).

> If the city government **lifts** the water rationing restrictions, we'll be able to hold a car wash.

Likewise – Also, in addition to; similarly, in the same way. In conversation, **likewise** can mean "Me, too." ("Nice to meet you." "Likewise.")

> Chip was baffled by all the silverware set before him, so when his host began eating salad with the smallest, leftmost fork, Chip did **likewise**.

Log – Keep a record of, write down; travel for or at a certain distance or speed; a written record.

> Lawyers who bill by the hour have to be sure to **log** all the time they spend on every client's case.

> You cannot get your pilot's license until you have **logged** 40 hours of flight time.

Machination or **machinations** – Crafty schemes or plots.

It's cute to think that teen idols became famous because their talent was simply so great that the music industry reached out to them, but usually, any teen idol is the product of intense coaching and parental **machinations**.

Magnate – Very important or influential person, especially in business.

Many students pursue MBAs in hopes of becoming wealthy and powerful **magnates**; some students never quite make it there, instead spending their careers staring at spreadsheets and taking orders from **magnates**.

Makeshift – Improvised, relating to a temporary substitute. The expressions *thrown together* or *slapped together* express a similar idea of *making do* with the resources on hand. Similarly, to *jury rig* something is to assemble it quickly with whatever materials you have available.

Lost in the woods for more than 24 hours, the children were eventually found sleeping under a **makeshift** tent made from branches and old plastic bags.

Malleable – Able to be bent, shaped, or adapted. *Tractable*, *pliable,* and *plastic* can also mean physically bendable, or metaphorically bendable, as in easily influenced or shaped by others. *Mutable* means changeable.

The more **malleable** the material, the easier it is to bend into jewelry—and the easier it is to damage that jewelry.

My mother is a little too **malleable**—she said she liked all the things her first husband liked, and now she says she likes all the things her second husband likes.

Manifest – Obvious, apparent, perceptible to the eye (adj.), or to become obvious, apparent, perceptible to the eye (verb). Also to show, make clear, or prove (verb). As a noun, a *manifest* is a list of people or goods aboard a plane, ship, train, etc. A *manifestation* is often when something "under the surface" breaks out or becomes apparent.

Lupus is difficult to diagnose, but sometimes **manifests** as muscular weakness or joint pain.

The protest was a **manifestation** of a long-brewing discontent.

Max out – Take to the limit (in a good or a bad way). To *max out* your credit cards is to incur as much debt as is permitted; to *max out* your productivity is to achieve maximum productivity.

Maxim – A general truth or fundamental principle, especially expressed as a proverb or saying.

My favorite **maxim** is "Seize the day!" How much would it cost to get that on a tattoo? How much more for "Curiosity killed the cat"?

Mediated by – Brought about by means of; assisted as an intermediary. To *mediate* a dispute is to bring about a resolution, but *mediated* in science also has the idea of being in the middle. For instance, a study might show that poverty leads to inattentiveness in school. But how? Research might reveal that poverty leads to inattentiveness, *mediated by* poor nutrition. That is, poverty causes poor nutrition, which causes inattentiveness (because the kids are hungry). *Mediation* can help make sense of what seems like an indirect correlation.

Mercurial – Quickly and unpredictably changing moods; fickle, flighty.

> It's tough being married to someone so **mercurial**. I do pretty much the same thing every day—some days, she thinks I'm great, and other days, the exact same behaviors make her inexplicably angry.

Militarism – Glorification of the military; government in which the military has a lot of power or in which the military is the top priority.

Mired – Stuck, entangled (in something, like a swamp or muddy area), soiled. *Morass* and *quagmire* are also words (often used metaphorically) for soft, swampy ground that a person can sink into. The Vietnam War was famously called a *quagmire.* The expression *muck and mire* means, literally, animal waste and mud and can be used metaphorically. To *muck up* is to mess up or get dirty, and to *muck about* or *around* is to waste time.

> **Mired** in her predecessor's mess and mistakes, the new CEO found it difficult to take the company in a new direction.

> The federal prosecutor spent weeks wading through the **muck and mire** of the scandal—every uncovered document showed that the corruption was deeper and worse than previously thought.

Modest – Humble; simple rather than showy; decent (especially in terms of dress); small, limited.

> The reporter was surprised that the celebrity lived in such a **modest** house, one that looked just like every other plain, two-story house on the block.

> Her first job out of college was a rude awakening—her **modest** salary was barely enough for rent, much less going out and having fun.

Moreover – In addition to what has been said, for instance; besides.

> His actions cost us the job; **moreover**, he seriously offended our client.

Mores – Customs, manners, or morals of a particular group. Pronounce this word as two syllables (rhymes with "more ways").

> A Westerner in Saudi Arabia should study the culture beforehand so as to avoid violating conservative cultural **mores**.

Municipal – Relating to local self-government. A *municipality* is a city, town, etc.

Narrative – Story, report, narrated account.

Nebula – A cloud of gas and dust in space. A *nebula* can also be a cloudy spot on a person's eye, and *nebulous* can mean cloudy, unclear.

Net – Remaining after expenses or other factors have been deducted; ultimate; to bring in as profit; to catch, as in a net.

> In one day of trading, my portfolio went up $10,000 and down $8,000, for a **net** gain of $2,000.

> All those weeks of working weekends and playing golf with the boss ought to **net** her a promotion.

Nevertheless or **nonetheless** – However, even so, despite that. Note that both *nevertheless* and *nonetheless* are single words—the GMAT has tested this on Sentence Correction ("none the less" is NOT an expression in English and cannot be substituted for "no less").

> While losing the P&G account was a serious blow, we **nevertheless** were able to achieve a new sales goal this month because of the tireless efforts of the sales team in bringing in three new clients.

> I really can't stand working with you. **Nonetheless**, we're stuck on this project together and we're going to have to get along.

Nontrivial – Important or big enough to matter.

> The chief of staff told the assembled doctors, "We all make mistakes. But this mistake was **nontrivial**, and there is going to be an investigation."

Normative – Implying or attempting to establish a norm; expressing value judgments or telling people what to do (rather than merely describing that which is happening).

> The reason we are not understanding each other in this argument about grammar is that you are arguing **normatively**, telling me how people *should* talk, and I am simply reporting how people *actually* talk.

Nostalgia – Longing for the past.

> The retail store Urban Outfitters uses **nostalgia** as a marketing strategy, branding many products with cartoon characters popular 10–20 years ago. Sure enough, many adult women do want to buy Jem or Spongebob t-shirts and lip balm.

Nuances – Subtle differences in tone, meaning, expression, etc.

> It can be difficult to understand the **nuances** of non-literal speech. For instance, "You can come if you want to, but it's really going to be mostly family" really means that you shouldn't try to come.

Nucleus – Structure within a cell containing the cell's hereditary material; any central or essential part; core, kernel.

> As a member of the president's cabinet, he found himself in the **nucleus** of power.

Offhand – Casual, informal; done without preparation or forethought; rude in a short way, brusque.

> I was pretty happy with my salary until my coworker Deena mentioned **offhandedly** that she was thinking about buying a house now that she made six figures.

Offset – Counteract, compensate for. *Offset* is usually a verb, but can also be a noun: My company provided me with *an offset* against moving expenses.

> Property taxes did go up this year, but we didn't really suffer because the hit to our finances was **offset** by a reduction in fees paid to our homeowners association.

Oligarchy – Government by the few, especially by a class or a small group or clique.

Omit – Remove, delete, take out.

Operative – Operating; having influence, force, or effect; effective, key, significant. The expression *operative word* refers to the one most meaningful word within a larger phrase. An *operative* can be a worker or a detective or spy.

> In the doctor's prescription of daily cardio exercise, the **operative** word is "daily."

Optimal – Best, most desirable or favorable. To *optimize* is to make perfect, such as by "maxing out" or striking just the right balance.

> Many believe that the U.S. Constitution's genius lies in its striking an **optimal** balance between freedom and order.

Oral narratives – Stories told verbally, especially by people who are not literate or whose cultures do not have writing (or didn't at the time). An *oral tradition* is a practice of passing down a culture's history verbally.

Outstrip – Surpass, exceed; be larger or better than; leave behind.

> Our sales figures this quarter have **outstripped** those of any other quarter in the company's history.

Paradigm – Model or pattern; worldview; set of shared assumptions, values, etc.

Far from being atypically bawdy, this limerick is a **paradigm** of the form—nearly all of them rely on off-color jokes.

Paradox – Contradiction, or seeming contradiction that is actually true.

Kayla was always bothering the youth minister with her **paradoxes,** such as "If God is all-powerful, can He make a burrito so big He can't eat it?"

Paragon – Model of excellence, perfect example.

Unlike his sister, he was a **paragon** of responsibility, taking in her three children when she went to jail, and even switching jobs so he could be there to pick them up from school.

Partial – Biased, prejudiced, favoring one over others; having a special liking for something or someone (usually *partial to*).

Although I grew up in New York, I've always been **partial** to country music.

His lawyers are appealing on the grounds that the judge was **partial** to the plaintiff, even playing golf with the plaintiff during the trial.

Patent – Obvious, apparent, plain to see (adj.); a letter from a government guaranteeing an inventor the rights to his or her invention (noun).

Her résumé was full of **patent** lies: anyone could check to see that she had never been president of UNICEF.

Peddle – Travel around while selling; sell illegally; give out or disseminate.

After an unsuccessful year spent **peddling** cutlery door-to-door, he turned to **peddling** drugs, thus landing himself in jail.

"I don't want these people **peddling** lies to our children," said Mrs. Hoffman, protesting an event in which fringe political candidates were invited to speak to kids.

Per – The most common use of *per* is for each, as in, *We will need one sandwich per child.* However, *per* may also mean by means of or according to, as in *I have delivered the package per your instructions.*

Periodic – Happening at regular intervals.

Perpetuate – Make perpetual, cause to continue.

Failing public schools in already distressed neighborhoods only **perpetuate** the cycle of poverty.

Physiological – Relating to the normal functioning of a living thing.

A rapid heart rate is a **physiological** response to fear.

Piggyback – Metaphorically riding on something bigger or more important. *Piggyback* literally refers to one person riding on the back of another (the way one sometimes carries a child). This word can be an adverb, adjective, or noun.

The jobs bill arrived **piggyback** on the urgent disaster relief bill—a pretty dirty trick, if you ask me.

Maybe we can **piggyback** this smaller design project onto the bigger one and end up saving some money with our web designers.

Pilot program (or project) – Program planned as a test or trial.

Before rolling out the program nationwide, a **pilot program** was launched in just three cities.

Plutocratic – Related to government by the wealthy.

Polarized – Divided into sharply opposed groups.

The school board was used to rationally discussing issues, but when it came to the teaching of evolution in schools, the board was **polarized**, immediately splitting into two camps, with the discussion devolving into a shouting match within minutes.

Polemic – Controversial argument, especially one attacking a specific idea.

Laura Kipnis's 2003 book *Against Love: A **Polemic*** has been called "shocking" and "scathing." Perhaps Kipnis used the word **polemic** in the title to indicate that she's making an extreme argument as a means of starting a debate. After all, who's really *against love?*

Postulate – Claim, assert; assume the truth or reality of in order to form an argument.

Before proceeding further, let us **postulate** that men and women have some fundamental differences. If we can accept that, we can talk about what type of policies should exist to ensure workplace equality.

Pragmatic – Practical; dealing with actual facts and reality.

The congresswomen personally believed in animal rights, but she knew she had to be **pragmatic**—if she proposed animal rights legislation, she probably wouldn't get reelected.

Predatory – Living by preying on other animals; given to plundering, exploiting, or destroying others for one's own benefit.

Many "check-cashing" outlets are actually **predatory** lenders who charge interest rates that would be illegal in many nations.

Predisposed – Having an inclination or tendency beforehand; susceptible. A *predisposition* is an inclination or tendency.

His defense attorney argued that his abusive childhood **predisposed** him to a life of crime.

Predominant – Having the greatest importance or influence; most common, main. A design might have a *predominant color*; a country might have a *predominant religion.* Sentence Correction problems have tested the fact that you need to use *predominant, NOT predominating,* in these situations.

Preempt – Prevent; take the place of, supplant; take before someone else can.

The speaker attempted to **preempt** an excessively long Q&A session by handing out a "Frequently Asked Questions" packet at the beginning of the seminar.

Premise – Proposition on which an argument is based. The functional parts of an argument other than the conclusion. Less commonly, *premise* is a verb, as in *The report is premised on (based on) this study.* For somewhat obscure reasons, *the premises* can also refer to a building and its surrounding land.

Prey – An animal that is hunted and eaten. *Predators* are animals that hunt and eat *prey.*

Priceless – Extremely valuable, so valuable that the worth cannot even be estimated.

Pristine – In an original, pure state; uncorrupted. A *pristine* forest has not been touched by humans. Sometimes *pristine* is used to mean very clean.

Progeny – Offspring, descendants.

The study showed that selective breeding could cause the **progeny** of wolves to become more like dogs in a small number of generations.

Prominent – Projecting outward, sticking out; very noticeable. A *prominent* nose might not be a desirable characteristic, according to some people, but a *prominent* citizen is generally a well-known and important person.

Pronounced – Distinct, strong, clearly indicated.

Aunt Shirley claimed we would never know that her secret recipe for brownies involved lots of healthy vegetables, but the brownies had a **pronounced** asparagus flavor.

Propagated – Breed, cause to multiply.

Some plants can be **propagated** from cuttings—my mother gave me a piece of her houseplant, and it grew roots after just a few days in water.

Prospective – Potential, aspiring. *Prospective students* have not yet been admitted; *prospective entrepreneurs* are people considering becoming entrepreneurs. This word is related to *prospect,* which can be both a noun (a good possibility) or a verb (to look for something good, such as to *prospect for gold*).

> A committee was formed to evaluate the new plan's **prospects**. As part of their analysis, members of the committee looked at the past performance of the **prospective** leader of the new division. One member remarked that the **prospect** of opening up a completely new division was exciting but might stretch the company too thin.

Proximity – Closeness, the state of being near.

Psyche – The spirit or soul; the mind (as discussed in psychology). Pronounce this word "SY-key."

Qualified – Modified, limited, conditional on something else. *Unqualified* can mean not limited or not restrained. If your boss gives *unqualified* approval for your plan, you can do whatever you want. Qualified can also be used in the sense of *qualified for the job.* Use context to determine which meaning is intended. A *qualified* person is suitable or well-prepared for the job; a *qualified* statement or feeling is held back or limited.

> The scientist gave her **qualified** endorsement to the book, pointing out that, while it posed a credible theory, more research was still needed before the theory could be applied.

Radiometric, radioactive, carbon, or radiocarbon dating – Methods for determining the approximate age of an ancient object by measuring the amount of radioactivity it contains.

Recalcitrant – Not obedient, resisting authority, hard to manage.

> The aspiring kindergarten teacher was not prepared for a roomful of 20 **recalcitrant** children who wouldn't even sit down, much less learn the words to "Holding Hands Around the World."

Recapitulate – Summarize, repeat in a concise way.

> I'm sorry I had to leave your presentation to take a call—I only have a minute, but can you **recapitulate** what you're proposing?

Receptive – Capable of or ready and willing to receive, as in *receptive to a new idea.*

Reconvene – Gather, come together again (or call together again), such as for a meeting, as in *Let's break for lunch and reconvene at 1pm.*

Redress – Setting something right after a misdeed, compensation or relief for injury or wrongdoing (noun); correct, set right, remedy (verb).

> My client was an innocent victim of medical malpractice. As would anyone who had the wrong leg amputated in surgery, he is seeking financial **redress**.

Refute – Prove to be false.

She's not a very valuable member of the debate team, actually—she loves making speeches, but she's not very good at **refuting** opponents' arguments.

Rehash – Discuss or bring up (an idea or topic) again without adding anything new.

We're not going to agree, so why **rehash** the issue?

Remedial – Providing a remedy, curative; correcting a deficient skill.

After harassment occurs in the workplace, it is important that the company take **remedial** action right away, warning or firing the offender as appropriate, and making sure the complainant's concerns are addressed.

For those who need **remedial** reading help, we offer a summer school program that aims to help students read at grade level.

Reminiscent – Looking back at the past, reminding of the past. A *reminiscent* person is remembering; an old-fashioned object could be *reminiscent of* an earlier time.

Render – Give, submit, surrender; translate; declare formally; cause to become. To *render harmless* is to make harmless.

When you **render** your past due payments, we will turn your phone back on.

Only in her second year of Japanese, she was unable to **render** the classic poem into English.

The judge **rendered** a verdict that **rendered** us speechless.

Repercussions – Consequences.

One of the worries about the financial industry is that irresponsible executives rarely suffer lasting **repercussions.**

Respectively – In the order given. This is a very useful word! The sentence "Smith and Jones wrote the books *7 Success Tips* and *Productivity Rocks*" is ambiguous—did they work together on both or did they each write one of the books? "Smith and Jones wrote the books *7 Success Tips* and *Productivity Rocks*, respectively" answers the question—Smith wrote *7 Success Tips* and Jones wrote *Productivity Rocks.* The word is typically used to match up two things to two other things, in the same order.

His poems "An Ode to the Blossoms of Sheffield" and "An Entreaty to Ladies All Too Prim" were written in 1756 and 1758, **respectively**.

Reticent – Not talking much; private (of a person), restrained, reserved.

She figured that, to rise to the top, it was best to be **reticent** about her personal life; thus, even her closest colleagues were left speculating at the water cooler about whether her growing belly actually indicated a pregnancy she simply declined to mention to anyone.

Returns – Profits.

Revamp – Renovate, redo, revise (verb); a restructuring, upgrade, etc. (noun). Similarly, *overhaul* means to repair or investigate for repairs.

I had decorated my whole room in *Twilight: Eclipse* paraphernalia. When *Breaking Dawn* came out, I had to **revamp** my décor.

Rife – Happening frequently, abundant, currently being reported.

Reports of financial corruption are **rife**.

Rudimentary – Elementary, relating to the basics; undeveloped, primitive.

My knowledge of Chinese is quite **rudimentary**—I get the idea of characters and I can order food, but I really can't read this document you've just given me.

Sanction – Permission or approval, or to give permission or approval OR a legal action by one or more countries against another country to get it to comply (or the act of placing those sanctions on another country). Whoa! Yes, that's right—*sanction* can mean two different things that are basically opposites. Use context to figure it out—if it's plural *(sanctions),* it's definitely the bad meaning.

Professional boxers may only fight in **sanctioned** matches—fighting outside the ring is prohibited.

The United States's past **sanctions** on Cuba meant that it was illegal for Americans to do business with Cuban companies.

Satire – Literary device in which foolishness or badness is attacked through humor, irony, or making fun of.

Save – But or except. As a verb, of course, *save* means *keep safe, store up, set aside.* But as a preposition or conjunction, *save* can be used as follows:

All of the divisions of the company are profitable **save** the movie-rental division. (This means that the movie-rental division was not profitable.)

He would have been elected president, **save** for the scandal that derailed his campaign at the last minute. (Here, *save* means *except.*)

Scant – Not enough or barely enough. *Scanty* is used in the same way (both are adjectives).

> The new intern was **scant** help at the conference—he disappeared all day to smoke and didn't seem to realize that he was there to assist his coworkers.

> The soldiers were always very hungry, complaining about their **scanty** rations.

Scarcely – Hardly, barely, by a small margin. Sometimes the adjective *scarce* is used where it sounds like the adverb *scarcely* is needed. This is an idiomatic usage:

> She lived a lavish lifestyle she could **scarce** (or **scarcely**) afford.

Scrutiny – Close, careful observation.

Seemingly – Apparently, outwardly appearing to be a certain way. If an author says that something is *seemingly X,* the author is probably about to say that it is *actually Y.* The word *seemingly* means that something *seems* a certain way (but maybe isn't really).

> He's a **seemingly** honest man—I'll need to get to know him better to say for sure.

Semantic – Relating to the different meanings of words or other symbols.

> Bob said plastic surgery should be covered under the health care plan and Marion said it shouldn't, but it turns out that their disagreement was purely **semantic**—what Bob meant was *reconstructive* surgery and what Marion meant was *cosmetic* surgery.

Settled – Fixed, established, concluded. Sediment can *settle* in water, people who marry can *settle down,* and a *settled judgment* is one that has been firmly decided.

Siphon – Tube for sucking liquid out of something (some people steal gasoline from other people's cars by *siphoning* it). To *siphon funds* is to steal money, perhaps in a continuous stream.

Skeptical – Doubting, especially in a scientific way (needing sufficient evidence before believing).

> Don't confuse **skeptical** and *cynical* (thinking the worst of others' motivations; bitterly pessimistic). In a GMAT Reading Comprehension passage, an author might be **skeptical** (a very appropriate attitude for a scientist, for instance), but would never be *cynical.*

Sketchy – Like a sketch: incomplete, imperfect, superficial.

Skirt – Border, lie along the edge of, go around; evade.

> Melissa spent all of Thanksgiving **skirting** the issue of who she was dating and when she might get married.

> The creek **skirts** our property on the west, so it's easy to tell where our farm ends.

Slew – A large number or quantity. *Slew* is also the past tense of *slay* (kill), so you could actually say *She slew him with a slew of bullets.*

As soon as we switched software packages, we encountered a whole **slew** of problems.

Slight – Small, not very important, slender or delicate; treat as though not very important; snub, ignore; a discourtesy.

She was very sensitive, always feeling **slighted** and holding a grudge against her coworkers for a variety of **slights**, both real and imagined.

Natalie Portman has always been **slight**, but she became even thinner to portray a ballerina in *Black Swan.*

Smelt – Fuse or melt ore in order to separate out metal.

Sparing – Holding back or being wise in the use of resources; deficient. Be *sparing* with the ketchup in order to make it last longer, but don't be *sparing* in praising your employees for a job well done.

Spate – Sudden outpouring or rush; flood.

After a brief **spate** of post-exam partying, Lola is ready for classes to begin again.

Spearhead – Be the leader of. A *spearhead* can, of course, be the sharp head of a spear. It can also be a person at the front of a military attack, or a leader of anything.

Lisa agreed to **spearhead** the "healthy office" initiative, and was instrumental in installing two treadmills and getting healthy food stocked in the vending machines.

Staggered – Starting and ending at different times, especially also occurring in overlapping intervals.

Employees who work on **staggered** schedules may only see each other for part of the day.

Static – Fixed, not moving or changing, lacking vitality. *Stasis* is the quality of being *static.*

The anthropologist studied a society in the Amazon that had been deliberately **static** for hundreds of years—the fiercely proud people disdained change and viewed all new ideas as inferior to the way of life they had always practiced.

Stratum – One of many layers (such as in a rock formation or in the classes of a society). The plural is *strata.*

From overhearing his rich and powerful passengers' conversations, the chauffeur grew to despise the upper **stratum** of society.

I love this dish—it's like a lasagna, but with **strata** made of bread, eggs, and pancetta! Oh, look at the menu—it's actually called a **strata**! That makes perfect sense.

Subjective – Existing in the mind or relating to one's own thoughts, opinions, emotions, etc.; personal, individual, based on feelings

> We can give names to colors, but we can never quite convey the **subjective** experience of them—what if my "red" is different from your "red"?

Subjugation – Conquering, domination, enslavement.

Subordinate – Having a lower order or rank, inferior, secondary.

Subset – A set that is contained within a larger set.

Subvert – Overthrow, corrupt, cause the downfall of.

Succeeding – Coming after or following. *The succeeding sentence* is the sentence that comes after the current one.

> After the sale of the company, you will receive 5% of the profits from the current year, and 1% in all **succeeding** years.

> In 1797, George Washington was **succeeded** by John Adams.

Suffrage – The right to vote. *Women's suffrage* was ensured at a national level in New Zealand in 1893, the first time a country gave all women the right to vote.

Suppress – Prohibit, curtail, force the end of. A repressive government might *suppress* dissent against its policies.

Surge – Sudden, transient increase (*power surge*), heavy swelling motion like that of waves. A *surge* of troops is sending a lot of soldiers at once. A *surge* in interest is sudden.

Surpass – Transcend, exceed, go beyond, as in *It's only August and we've already surpassed last year's sales.*

Synchronized – Happening at the same time, simultaneous, in unison.

Syntax – The rules governing grammar and how words join to make sentences (or how words and symbols join in writing computer code), the study of these rules, or any system or orderly arrangement.

> Now that my linguistics class is studying **syntax**, it makes a little more sense when my computer flashes "SYNTAX ERROR" at me.

> Anyone learning a language is bound to make **syntactical** mistakes—even if he or she knows the appropriate vocabulary, it is still difficult to assemble the words perfectly.

Synthesis – Combining of complex things to create a unified whole.

Table – In American English, *to table* something means to postpone discussion of it until later. In British English, to *table* a bill is the opposite—to submit it for consideration. Use context to help you determine the intended meaning.

> I see we're not going to agree on whether to scrap our entire curriculum and develop a new one, so let's **table** that discussion and move on to voting on the budget.

Tardy – Late, not on time.

Taxonomy – Science or technique of classification.

Temperament – Natural personality, as in *an angry temperament* or *a pleasant temperament.*

Temperance – Moderation, self-control, especially regarding alcohol or other desires or pleasures; total abstinence from alcohol. Relatedly, *temperate* means *moderate,* as in *a temperate climate.*

> After the end of the Civil War in the United States, economic change led to an increase in alcohol problems and the birth of the **Temperance** Movement, which ultimately led to a ban on alcohol sales.

> Grandma is a model of **temperance**—she drinks red wine every night, but only the one-third of a glass that she read was the minimum amount needed to help prevent heart attacks.

Terrestrial – Relating to the Earth or to land; worldly.

> Mr. and Mrs. Daruza were certain they had seen a UFO, plus aliens running around in the night. What they really saw was an especially dense flock of birds in the air, and some mundane, **terrestrial** animals on the ground.

Thenceforth – From that time forward.

> In 1956, Grace Kelly married Rainier III, Prince of Monaco, and was **thenceforth** known as Princess Grace.

Theoretically – In theory (but not necessarily in reality). People sometimes just say *theoretically* when talking about theories, but they also often say it when they mean that something will not work in real life.

> Theoretically, we should be able to meet the deadline; in reality, I think we will be two days late.

Thesis – Proposition supported by an argument.

Thorny – Controversial, full of difficulties. Literally, having thorns, prickly (as a rose bush).

Tides – Periodic rise and fall of the ocean about every 12 hours, caused by the attraction of the sun and the moon. Metaphorically, you can say *the tides of refugees,* for instance—implying the refugees are arriving periodically, in large groups.

Token – Sign, symbol, mark, badge; souvenir, memento; sample or person, thing, idea taken to represent an entire group. As an adjective, it means "not very important."

> I am starting to realize that this law firm hired me to be its **token** woman. There I am, smiling in all the ads—but I never actually get to work on important cases.
>
> Hollywood movies are often guilty of **tokenism**—many have exactly one black character (the **token** minority), often present to give advice to the (usually white) main characters.
>
> I am giving you this "Best Friends Forever" necklace as a **token** of our friendship.

Trajectory – The curved path of an object in flight, as in *the missile's trajectory.*

Transient – Moving around, not settled; temporary, not lasting.

> In the past decade, podcasting was thought to be the next big thing, but it turned out to be a largely **transient** phenomenon.

Transmute – Transform, change from one form to another.

Transplant – Move from one place to another. Certainly you have heard of a *heart transplant,* for instance. It can also be used metaphorically: a person who has just moved to a new state might refer to herself as a *transplant from Texas.*

Truce or **Armistice** – Suspension of fighting for a specified period because of mutual agreement; cease-fire.

> After the earthquake, the two warring nations agreed to a **truce** and sent their soldiers to help the quake's victims.

Undergird – Strengthen, support. To *undergird* an argument is to make it stronger—the opposite of *undermine.*

Undermine – Weaken, cause to collapse by digging away at the foundation (of a building or an argument); injure or attack in a secretive or underhanded way.

> Rather than searching impartially for the truth, these so-called scientists willfully ignored any evidence that **undermined** the conclusion they were being paid to produce.
>
> You are nice to my face, but you are **undermining** me behind my back, suggesting to others in the office that I am making mistakes in my work and that you have been fixing them!

Underpin – Strengthen, corroborate, support from below.

> Her argument was **underpinned** by the results of several recent studies.

Underscore – Emphasize (or, literally, to underline text).

"You're not going to mess with Joey anymore," said Joey. His new bodyguards stepped forward threateningly, as though to **underscore** Joey's point.

Undifferentiated – Not distinguished from one another, the same.

Unfettered – Free, liberated.

Unforeseeable – Not able to be predicted.

Our company had disaster insurance and a succession plan in case something happened to the president, but we had no plans for the **unforeseeable** circumstance that our office would be completely overtaken by rats.

Unprecedented – Never before known or seen, without having happened previously.

When Nixon resigned, American bravado was at an all-time low—the resignation of a sitting president was **unprecedented**.

Untempered – Not toned down; not moderated, controlled, or counterbalanced. Often *untempered by*.

I wouldn't call it "tough love"—his harshness is **untempered by** any kind of affection.

The report was an **untempered** condemnation of the company's practices—the investigators didn't have a single good thing to say.

Untenable – Not defendable (as an argument), not able to be lived in (as a house).

GMAT Critical Reasoning is full of **untenable** arguments that rest upon unproven assumptions.

Unwarranted – Not justified or authorized.

Utopian – Related to ideals of perfection; unrealistically idealistic.

Reducing homelessness to zero is a **utopian** goal, but our agency views reducing the street population by 25% and getting children off the streets as more practical aims.

Via – Through, by means of, by way of (by a route that goes through or touches). *Per* can also be used in this way.

We will be flying to Russia **via** Frankfurt.

Many of the students at our college got here **via** special programs that assist low-income students in preparing for college.

Wanting – Lacking, insufficient, or not good enough (as in, *The book was not good; I found it wanting*). This makes sense when you think about the fact that people generally *want* good things, of course—so if a person is *left wanting,* he or she did not get those good things. Conversely, a person who *wants for nothing* is someone who already has everything.

Warranted – Justified, authorized (*warrant* can mean to justify or a justification, but it can also mean to vouch for or guarantee).

> The pundit's comments don't even **warrant** a response from our organization—they were mere name-calling, not suitable for public discourse.
>
> Your criticism of Anne is **unwarranted**—as your assistant, she has done everything you've asked her to do.
>
> He doesn't have his documents with him, but I'll **warrant** that he is indeed a certified forklift operator.

Whereas – While, on the contrary, considering that.

> Mr. Katsoulas had always assumed his son would take over the family buiness, **whereas** his son had always assumed he would go away to college and never come back.
>
> **Whereas** squash and peppers are vegetables, a tomato is technically a fruit.

Whet – Stimulate, make keen or eager (especially of an appetite).

> Dinner will take another 20 minutes, but maybe this cheese plate can **whet** your appetite?

Wholesale – Sale of goods in quantity to resellers (opposite of *retail).* The word can also mean *extensive, in a large way.*

> Neckties have an enormous markup—a tie that sells for $50 often has a **wholesale** cost of less than $5.
>
> Pol Pot's war crimes included the **wholesale** slaughter of his people.

Winnow – Sift, analyze critically, separate the useful part from the worthless part.

> We got 120 résumés for one job—it's going to take me hours just to **winnow** this down to a reasonable stack of people we want to interview.

Yoke – A frame for attaching animals (such as oxen) to each other and to a plow or other equipment to be pulled, or a bar across a person's shoulders to help carry buckets of water, etc. Metaphorically, a *yoke* is a burden or something that oppresses. To *yoke* is to unite together or to burden. To *throw off the yoke of oppression* is to free oneself from oppression.

> The speaker argued that humanity had traded the **yoke** of servitude to kings and tyrants for the **yoke** of consumerism, which enslaves us just as much in the end.

Test out your newfound vocab skills with the following drills. If you see a word that you don't know, make sure to look it up. Consider making a flash card to help you memorize it.

Vocab Drill 16.1

Match each word on the left with one of the definitions on the right.

1. Whereas	(A) Also, in addition to, similarly
2. Save	(B) In addition to what has been said, for instance; besides
3. Nonetheless	(C) However, even so, despite that
4. Moreover	(D) On the contrary, considering that
5. Likewise	(E) But or except

Answers are on page 410.

Vocab Drill 16.2

For each question, circle the two words out of the five given that are synonyms (or near-synonyms).

1.	Checked	Debilitated	Tempered	Impinged	Warranted
2.	Underpin	Undergird	Underscore	Undermine	Unfetter
3.	Spearhead	Nebula	Stratum	Enigma	Echelon
4.	Patently	Kinetically	Laterally	Baldly	Paradigmatically
5.	Enumerate	Delimit	Extrapolate	Infer	Polarize

Answers are on page 410.

Vocab Drill 16.3

For each word, circle the nearest synonym below.

1. Partial
(A) biased
(B) pleased
(C) rude
(D) invaluable

2. Mores
(A) rights
(B) language parts
(C) customs
(D) decisions

3. Dubious
(A) troubled
(B) immoral
(C) pessimistic
(D) doubtful

4. Eclipse
(A) cover
(B) begin
(C) expose
(D) end

5. Discrete
(A) secretive
(B) equal
(C) special
(D) distinct

Answers are on page 410.

Vocab Drill 16.4

Select the most appropriate word for each blank.

1. This report about the changes in the American family structure and the decline of marriage is purely descriptive rather than ___________.

(A) delimited (B) normative (C) debased

2. While the rich get richer, the ranks of the poor are greatly expanding and the middle ________ is disappearing completely.

(A) hierarchy (B) stratum (C) gradation

3. Some believe that a propensity for addiction is genetic, but it lies _________ until "activated" through use of drugs or alcohol.

(A) wanting (B) lateral (C) latent

4. While the analysts have collected a great deal of data, there are still many unknowns, and thus our results are _______________.

(A) exhaustive (B) indeterminate (C) discretionary

5. This new device has a faster processor and twice as much memory, and is thus easily able to ___________ the performance of the previous version.

(A) outstrip (B) revamp (C) offset

Answers are on page 410.

Vocab Drill 16.5

For each question, circle the two words out of the five given that are synonyms (or near-synonyms).

1.	paradigm	impasse	gridlock	dovetail	maxim
2.	dichotomy	host	paradox	slew	paragon
3.	impartial	disinterested	eclectic	inert	fledgling
4.	debunk	aggravate	eclipse	fathom	exacerbate
5.	explicitly	baldly	dubiously	cynically	fadingly

Answers are on page 410.

RC Idioms for the GMAT

The following are expressions that are appropriate for use in the type of writing excerpted on the GMAT, and that often appear in writing about business, science, and history. To increase retention of this material, try to use these expressions in your own sentences. Soon, you will be talking like a dignified old professor!

The idioms are followed by a 20-question drill allowing you to test your understanding of these expressions when used in complex sentences.

". . ." – Quote marks can 1) indicate that the word or phrase is not to be taken literally, or 2) introduce a new, made-up word or phrase. So, some context is needed to understand the meaning.

> The factory employs several people who add defects and rough edges to its popular line of **"antique"** furniture. (The furniture is not really antique.)

The company has sent its top people to ethics training and courses on Aristotle in an attempt to build a **"philosophically correct"** business. (The idea of a "philosophically correct" business is really weird, perhaps something that the company itself came up with.)

Accorded to – Given or granted to. (Sometimes *accorded* is used without *to,* as in *I was surprised by the adulation accorded the elderly author at the high school assembly.*)

Account for – 1) Take into consideration or make adjustments based on; 2) Cause. This is not the same as *give an account of,* which just means *explain.*

I **accounted for** the fact that Joe is always late by telling him to meet us at 1:30 when the event is really at 2. (Here, *accounted for* means *made adjustments to compensate for.*)

I did get us the meeting, but Ellen's hard work **accounted for** the rest of our success. (Here, *accounted for* means *caused.)*

A given – The use of *a given* as a noun is different from the use of *given* alone. For instance, a person's *given name* is the one *given* by his or her parents (a "first name" in the United States), and you might also say, "The truth differs from the *given* explanation." Here, *given explanation* just means *the explanation that someone gave.* However, *a given* means something taken for granted, something assumed, or something that does not require proof.

When I was planning my wedding, it was **a given** that my parents would invite anyone they wanted, since they were paying for everything.

It's **a given** that everyone here is against human trafficking—what we disagree about is the best way to fight it.

Albatross or **albatross around the neck of** (a person or group) – A constant burden or worry; an obstacle. Literally, an albatross is a bird. The expression *an albatross around one's neck* creates the silly image of a person wearing a (dead?) bird—but that certainly sounds like a constant burden or worry! (This expression comes from *The Rime of the Ancient Mariner,* in which an old man had to wear an albatross around his neck as punishment for his sins.)

The city has done an admirable job rebuilding its infrastructure and marketing itself, but the crime rate continues to be an **albatross** around the city's neck in trying to attract tourists.

All but – Almost definitely. *The bill's passage is all but assured* means that the bill will almost certainly pass.

Your objections have arrived too late; the proposal is **all but** approved.

And yet – A stronger way of saying *yet.* The expression *and yet* seems ungrammatical (two conjunctions right next to each other is very strange—you don't say *and but*), but it is an idiom used for emphasis. It indicates a surprising twist, an ironic realization, etc. It is often used at the beginning of a sentence for emphasis, and can even be used on its own, although this usage is casual.

The company was lauded for its commitment to the environment. **And yet** its employees regularly fly in private jets, creating carbon footprints that would embarrass any true environmentalist.

Arms race – Competition between two countries to build up the best and largest supply of weapons. This term is often associated with the Cold War between the United States and the Soviet Union. Metaphorically, an arms race is a competition that implies a sort of "More, more, more!" mentality and may not be entirely rational.

Analysts carefully watched stock prices as the two Internet giants competed in an **arms race**, expanding rapidly by buying up smaller companies with little due diligence.

Aside from – In addition to, not even counting.

Aside from the obvious financial benefits of investing in a socially responsible fund, you can rest assured that your money is used to maximize social good.

(Adjective) as it is, . . . – This pattern is used to contrast the part after the comma with the part before. For instance, *Charming as she is, I just don't want to be friends with her anymore.*

As pleased as we are to see more minorities on the board than ever before, discrimination in hiring and promotion is still a serious problem.

As well as – Sometimes, *as well as* just means *and,* as in *I had ramen for lunch, as well as a hot dog.* But *as well as* can also be used to mention one thing as a way to contrast with or emphasize another.

You know what I discovered? My French teacher speaks Chinese, **as well as** French! (Here, the point of the sentence is that it is amazing that the French teacher also speaks Chinese. Of course, everyone already knows that the French teacher speaks French—that part is only mentioned to highlight how amazing it is that the teacher knows *another,* unrelated language.)

Therefore, vitamins may protect against emotional instability, **as well as** physical deficiencies. (If this were the conclusion to a Critical Reasoning argument, it would be good to realize that the *physical deficiency* part is not relevant. Everyone knows that vitamins protect against physical deficiency, so that part is only included to contrast with or emphasize the *amazing* fact that maybe vitamins also counteract emotional instability.)

At best – At the most, interpreted in the most favorable way. *The seminar drew 20 people at best* means that 20 or fewer people attended.

My college algebra teacher can barely factor a polynomial! He is qualified to teach elementary school math, **at best**.

At fault – Guilty.

The insurance company is investigating who is **at fault** for the collision.

At loggerheads – In conflict, at a standstill.

The strike is not likely to end soon—the transit authority and the union representatives have been **at loggerheads** for weeks.

At odds – In conflict.

The teachers' union and the state government are always **at odds**.

At once – 1) Immediately; 2) At the same time.

Once the hurricane veered near the coast, the governor ordered that we evacuate **at once**. (Here, *at once* means *now.*)

We've received three proposals that are all quite different, but we can evaluate them all **at once**. (Here, *at once* means *at the same time.*)

The better part – The largest or longest part. *The better part* does NOT have to be good! The word *better* is a bit confusing here.

For **the better part** of human history, slavery has been a reality. (The speaker is NOT saying that slavery is good. The speaker is saying that, for most of human history, slavery has existed.)

When the oil magnate died, he left **the better part** of his fortune to his third wife, and only a small sliver to his children.

Beside the point – Irrelevant, off-topic.

Bite the hand the feeds you – This expression means exactly what it sounds like (think of a mean and not very smart dog). Although informal sounding, this expression has appeared in business writing.

The music industry **bites the hand that feeds it** when it penalizes consumers who share (and therefore publicize) their favorite songs with friends.

(Adjective) but (adjective) – This pattern is used for two adjectives that provide a contrast. They can be opposites, or one good and one bad, etc. For instance, *a boring but lucrative job.*

The food available in such neighborhoods is inexpensive but unhealthy.

By no means – Not at all. The use of *means* here is similar to its use in "The ends justify the means," a controversial expression meaning that, as long as the goals (the "ends") are good, it's acceptable to do anything (the "means") in order to achieve the goals. So, *means* can have the meaning of *ways of getting something done.* You can also say, *This scheduling software is the means by which we intend to manage the project.* So, the expression *by no means* indicates that there is no way, or *means,* to interpret something in the manner you are about to say.

This is **by no means** a new idea. (The idea is certainly not new.)

By the same token – This expression means that the speaker will then say something else based on the same evidence he or she just used to make a different point.

> As a libertarian, he wants to abolish the IRS. **By the same token**, he wants drugs legalized.

The case at issue – The matter at hand, the thing that is being discussed.

> Usually, raising prices results in a drop in demand, but in **the case at issue**, the price jump convinced consumers that the product was a luxury good, thus spurring demand from aspirational consumers.

Caught red-handed – Caught in the act of doing something wrong, so that the person cannot deny guilt. The expression refers to having blood on one's hands.

> The scientists on the company payroll could no longer claim that the fish in the river were all dying from natural causes once the company was **caught red-handed** dumping waste at the river's mouth.

Colored by – Influenced or prejudiced by.

> Her opinion about the prison system was **colored by** having grown up effectively an orphan while both her parents served sentences in separate prisons.

Couldn't have come at a better time – The same as *could hardly have come at a better time,* this expression means that something happened at the best possible time, such as at a very convenient moment or just in time to prevent disaster.

Curry favor – To try to gain favor (such as preferential treatment from a boss) through flattery or servile behavior. The expression is derived from French and is not related to *curry,* the food.

Cut bait – Give up, abandon an activity. Often part of the expression *fish or cut bait,* to *cut bait* is to stop fishing.

> As much as he wanted to be an entrepreneur, after a year of struggling, he **cut bait** and asked his former boss for his old job back.

Due diligence – Research or analysis done before taking action (such as investing); care that a reasonable person would take to prevent harm to others.

En masse – All together, in a group. This expression is from French and is related to the word *mass.* Like many foreign expressions, *en masse* is often written in italics.

> The protesters marched ***en masse*** to the palace.

Entrée into – Admittance, permission to enter. Most people in the United States think of an *entrée* as the main dish of a meal, but in French it means an appetizer—a dish that leads into the main course (the word is related to the word enter). A person who wants to rise in society might seek an *entrée* into a certain social group. (You can also say "seek *entrée*"—sometimes in that expression, the word *an* is omitted.)

> For disadvantaged young people, good public schools can provide an **entrée** into the middle class.

For all X, Y – This sentence pattern means, "Despite X, actually Y"—that is, X and Y will be opposites, or one will be good and one will be bad. The word "actually" (or a similar word) often appears in this pattern, but doesn't have to.

> **For** all its well-publicized "green" innovations, the company is one of the worst polluters in the state.

> **For** all the criticism she has received for her actions during the merger, she's actually a really nice person if you get to know her.

Former and latter – When two things are mentioned, the first one is the *former* and the second one is the *latter.*

> Your grades are slipping and you've been very secretive about your behavior—**the latter** worries your father and me the most.

> I intend to choose a business school based on reputation and cost, the **former** more so than the **latter**.

For show – For appearances only.

> The company was voted the best in the country for working mothers, but the women who work there report that it's all **for show**; for instance, the much-publicized free on-site daycare is tiny and has a three-year waiting list.

For years to come – For a long time. The negative version *the consequences won't affect us for years to come* means that they WILL affect us, but not for the next several years.

> My parents are only in their sixties and are healthy and active, so I am hopeful that my children will get to enjoy their grandparents **for years to come**.

Full throttle – With much speed and energy. On a related note, sometimes *juice* is used to mean *energy.*

> The plan was a good idea with little **juice** behind it; because it was never implemented with much gusto, it's hard to say whether it could have succeeded. We'll have to wait until another company goes **full throttle** with a similar idea to observe the outcome.

Garden-variety – Ordinary, common.

Gloss over, paper over, whitewash – These are all expressions for covering up a problem, insult, etc., rather than addressing it or fixing it. Think of a dirty floor that you just put a pretty rug on top of instead of cleaning. Because *gloss* is slippery (think of lip gloss), *gloss over* often has the sense of trying to smoothly and quickly move on to something else.

> He made a snide remark about short people and then tried to **gloss over** it when he realized his 5'2" boss had overheard.

> The journalist accused the officials of trying to **whitewash** the scandal by claiming that the cover-up was based on national security concerns.

Go down the tubes – Become much worse, fail. One theory is that this expression is about the plumbing attached to toilets.

Go sour – Think of milk going bad—that's the idea behind the expression *go sour.* A relationship *goes sour* before the couple breaks up. An economy *gone sour* can't be good. This is not the same as the expression *sour grapes,* which refers to pretending something you can't have wasn't any good anyway, as in, *Her hatred of the rich is just sour grapes—if she could afford luxury, she'd take all she could get.*

Hand-wringing – An excessive expression of concern, guilt, or distress.

> There has been much **hand-wringing** (or **wringing of hands**) over falling test scores, with so-called "experts" acting as if the world will end if students do 1% worse in math and science.

Hold the line vs. **toe the line** – *Hold the line* means *keep something the same.* It is a reference to (American) football, in which players want to prevent the opposing team from advancing down the field. To *toe the line* is to conform to a policy or way of thinking, or follow the rules. One theory about the origin of the expression is that, on ships, barefoot sailors were made to line up for inspection—that is, to put their toes on an actual line on the deck of the ship.

> My boss doesn't want to hear original ideas at all—he just wants me to **toe the line**.

> If colleges cannot **hold the line** on tuition costs, students will have to take on even more crippling loan burdens as tuition becomes even more expensive.

However much, as much as – Even though, no matter how much.

> **However much** people may agree that saving money is a virtue, the majority of Americans don't have sufficient funds for any kind of emergency.

> **As much as** I'd like to attend your wedding, I just can't afford a trip to Taiwan.

In contrast to – This phrase is important in Inference questions on Reading Comp. If a writer says *In contrast to X, Y is A*, you can draw the conclusion that *X is not A*.

> **In contrast to** our competitor's product, our product is made with organic materials. (This means that the competitor's product is NOT made with organic materials, which very well could be the answer to a question about what you can infer from the passage.)

Just cause – *Just* as an adjective means *justified, legal, fair. Just cause* means a legally sufficient reason. In some legal codes, an employer must show *just cause* for firing an employee.

Legions or **is legion** – *Legions* are large military units, generally consisting of a few thousand soldiers. Saying that a group is *legion* is saying that it is large.

> Surely, the developers could have foreseen that **legions** of Mac users would protest when news emerged that the new version of the software would not be Mac compatible.

> The former governor has been called a demagogue by many commentators who nevertheless must grudgingly admit that her supporters **are legion**, populating rallies in every state.

No X OR Y vs. no X AND Y – When you are talking about having two things, saying "salt AND pepper" is very different from saying "salt OR pepper." However, when you are talking about a lack of two things, *and* and *or* can often be used to express the same idea. The following two sentences have the same meaning:

> Pioneer towns were characterized by little access to the outside world **and** few public institutions.

> Pioneer towns had almost no access to the outside world **or** public institutions.

Not (adjective) – Of course, putting *not* before an adjective indicates the opposite. However, sometimes it indicates a softer or more polite way to say something. If someone asks if you like the meal he cooked or the outfit he is wearing, and you know him well enough to be honest, you might say, *It's not my favorite.* Or, sometimes, you say something like *not irrelevant* instead of simply *relevant* in order to indicate that you are correcting someone else's misconception.

> Concern about foreign debt is **not misplaced**. (Here, this means that you should be concerned! The phrase also may be implying that others incorrectly think you should *not* be concerned.)

Not only X but also Y – This is a two-part expression, introducing the first part before adding on the second, more extreme or surprising part.

> The executive was **not only** fired, **but also** indicted for fraud.

> He **not only** bought his girlfriend an iPhone for her birthday, **but also** took her entire family on a vacation to the Catskills.

Not X, let alone Y – The meaning is *Not X and definitely not this even more extreme thing, Y.*

Our remaining funds are **not** enough to get us through the week, **let alone** pay next month's payroll. (Here, getting through the week is less expensive than next month's payroll, so if you can't afford the cheaper thing, you *definitely* can't afford the more expensive thing.)

No worse than – Equal to or better than.

Although exotic, this illness is really **no worse than** the common flu.

On face – At first appearance, superficially. If someone says *on face,* you can expect that later on, the person will give the "real story." In a Reading Comprehension passage, seeing *on face* is a good clue that the author's main idea will probably be the opposite of what *seems* true at first glance.

On its face, the donation seems like a selfless act of philanthropy. However, the wealthy donor mainly made the donation for the tax benefits.

On face, the theory seems sound. However, new research has uncovered serious flaws.

Only looks (adjective) – Appears (some certain way) but isn't really.

She **only looks** homeless—she is actually a famous and wealthy artist who lives eccentrically.

On par with – Sometimes *on a par with,* this expression comes from golf and means *about equal to* or *equivalent to.*

Opening salvo – A *salvo* is a simultaneous firing of guns or release of bombs. Metaphorically, an *opening salvo* is something that starts a fight.

The introduction of Bill H.R. 2, given the inflammatory name "Repealing the Job-Killing Health Care Law Act," was seen by some as an **opening salvo** by the opposition party.

Outside of the home – Working *outside of the home* means having a regular job, such as in an office. However, working *out of your home* is actually working at home. If that's hard to understand, think of the expression *living out of your car,* which actually means living *in* your car—the idea is that you leave the car to go "out" but return back to the car as your base, just as someone who works *out of their home* leaves the home to go to meetings, for example, but uses the home as a central point.

The study compared incomes of women who had worked **outside of the home** to incomes of women who worked **out of their homes** as freelancers or owners of small businesses.

Per se – In itself, by itself, intrinsically. From Latin, often written in italics. *Per se* is often used to indicate that while something isn't *naturally* or *the same as* something else, it still has the same effect.

The policy isn't sexist, ***per se***, but it has had a disproportionate impact on women that deserves further study.

Press for – Argue in favor of. Think of *pushing people* toward what you want them to do.

> The advocates **pressed for** greater regulation of child care providers.

Rabid – Rabies is a disease that some animals (dogs, raccoons, etc.) contract and that causes the animal to become insane and violent. Thus, the word *rabid* (having rabies) is used metaphorically to mean *zealous* or *excessively or angrily passionate.* One symptom of rabies is *foaming at the mouth,* which is also an expression for being extremely (and violently or irrationally) angry.

> One debater called himself a "peace activist" and his opponent a "**rabid** right-wing gun nut." His opponent called herself a "champion of the American way" and her opponent a "**rabid** anti-American zealot."

Ranks of – The people in a group other than the leaders. Many people know the word *rank* as a level or grade, as in *A general has a higher rank than a sergeant.* The other use of *ranks* is also originally related to the military: the *ranks* or sometimes the *rank and file* means all the regular soldiers (not the officers). *Ranks* also refers to soldiers standing in a particular formation, so the expression *to break rank* means to rebel, disobey, disagree, or disrupt a situation in which everyone is doing the same thing.

> Among the **ranks** of our alumni are two senators and many famous authors.

> The author **broke rank** with her colleagues in the field of personal development by suggesting that "positive thinking" may be doing more damage than good.

Reap and **sow** – These are metaphors related to farming, and specifically the idea that the seeds that you plant (or *sow*) determine what you will later harvest (or *reap*). *Sow* is pronounced the same as *so,* and the past tense is *sown,* as in *Having sown the love of knowledge in the minds of children, the teacher's influence extended well past her own lifetime.* A common expression is *You reap what you sow.*

> He worked night and day in the strange new country, never stopping to rest, for he knew he would **reap** his reward when his family greeted him as a hero for all the money he had sent back home.

Red flag – Warning sign or something alarming.

> Bernie Madoff's sustained, ultrahigh returns should have been a **red flag** for the banks with which he did business.

Red herring – Something irrelevant that distracts from the real issue. A herring is a fish. One theory for the origin of the expression is that criminals trying to escape the police would sometimes rub a smelly fish across their trail as they ran away, in order to mislead the dogs used to track them down.

> Johnson's new Maserati turned out to be a **red herring** in investigating where the stolen funds had gone—it turns out, Johnson's wife bought the car with her inheritance, and the real culprit behind the theft was the mild-mannered junior accountant no one had suspected.

Reign vs. **reins** – These two words are pronounced the same as *rain* and *rains,* but the meanings are different. *Reign* means rule, as in *Conditions have improved under the king's reign.* Using this word metaphorically, such as for a CEO, implies that the leader is a bit like a king. *Reins* are leather straps used by a rider to control a horse. Metaphorically, you might say *Since the new CEO took the reins of this organization . . . .*

> In an era of near-total transparency, some would say that the media now **hold the reins** in our society in a manner formerly reserved for the government.

Ridden (adjective) or (adjective)**-ridden** – Dominated, burdened, or afflicted by (adjective). In the phrase *disease-ridden slum,* it's pretty obvious that the meaning is bad, but actually, adding *-ridden* to anything makes the meaning bad. If someone said *an equality-ridden society,* that person is actually against equality! *Ridden* can also be used alone, as in *The neighborhood was ridden with crime.*

School of thought – A group of people with similar beliefs or perspective on things, or the beliefs themselves. If a GMAT writer says *One school of thought argues X,* it is probably the case that the author is about to say the opposite (calling something a *school of thought* can emphasize that it's not the only way to think about the issue).

> One **school of thought** says that companies don't need to "give back" to communities, since the companies make profits from voluntarily trading with others; **a competing school of thought** says that companies benefit from a nation's infrastructure, the school systems that educate their employees, etc., and thus have responsibilities similar to those of citizens.

Sight vs. **Site** vs. **Cite** – To **sight** is to see, or discover by looking. A **site** is a location. To **cite** is to reference or to give credit to.

> The sailors had nearly given up hope when the finally **sighted** land. When they reached the shore, they planted a flag on the **site** of their landing.

> A good research report **cites** relevant studies.

So much as – Typically used in the negative, as in *My teacher is so awful that she won't so much as answer a question.* In other words, the teacher won't *even* answer questions.

> After her husband decided to take up day trading and lost $100,000 in one day, she wouldn't **so much as** look at him. (She wouldn't even look at him.)

Sound the depths – Explore, investigate, or look into something really deeply. This expression is a metaphor based on the idea of a sounding line, which is a rope with a weight on the bottom that you drop to the ocean floor to see how deep the ocean is.

> Other books have dealt with the topic in a superficial way, but this is the first book to really **sound the depths** of the response of the British lower class to the American Revolution.

Steeped in – Immersed in, saturated with. A teabag *steeps* in hot water. A person *steeped in* classic literature probably thinks about almost everything in terms of old, famous books.

> The Met's new campaign seeks to answer affirmatively the question of whether music lovers **steeped in** hip-hop and pop can learn to love opera.

Stem from – Grow out of, be caused by. This is related to the idea of a plant's *stem.*

> The psychologist believed that his neurosis **stemmed from** events in his childhood.

Sway or **hold sway over** – Persuade, influence.

> The lawyer attempted to **sway** the jury with an emotional account of the defendant's tough childhood.

> Repressive governments are suspicious of individuals who **hold sway** over the people, and often imprison or execute such people.

Take umbrage – Become offended.

> With 15 years of experience on all kinds of campaigns, she **took umbrage** to her sexist coworker's suggestion that she was only qualified to develop advertising for "women's products."

Tracks with – Is consistent with, makes sense in relation to. Think of *train tracks* running parallel to each other—if two ideas *track,* that means they are going in the same direction. You can say that information *tracks with* something you already know when you want to say that what you are hearing sounds like it *could be* true (although you don't know for sure).

Trappings – Accessories, the characteristic items, products, etc., that come with or are associated with something. Think of the side dishes or condiments that come with a meal. The *trappings* of fame include invites to fancy parties and free items from companies.

> Mr. and Mrs. Seguro moved to the United States because they wanted a better education for their children. The children, however, were soon decked out in the **trappings** of American teenage life—cell phones, iPods, and fashionable clothes—with little care for studying.

Vanguard and **avant-garde** – The *avant-garde* (French for *in front of the guard*) were the leading soldiers at the front of an army. *Vanguard* is derived from *avant-garde* and means the same thing. Metaphorically, the *avant-garde* (noun or adjective) or *vanguard* (noun) are innovators, those at the forefront of any movement or those who are ahead of their time.

> While Google has won the search engine wars, in 1994, Yahoo was on the **vanguard** of search technology.

> She arrived at the mixer in a dress that was a little ***avant-garde*** for the otherwise conservative Yale Club—she would have looked more appropriate at an art gallery or Lady Gaga concert.

The very idea (or *the very notion,* etc.) – This expression is used to express a strong contrast.

> The author conjures up a drifting yet haunting word picture that challenges **the very idea** of what constitutes a story. (This means that the author's strange "word picture" story goes against the most basic things that you think must be true about stories.)

With a grain of salt – To take something (a statement, claim, etc.) *with a grain of salt* is to maintain a small amount of skepticism. The origin of this expression is related to an old belief that a small amount of salt could help protect against poison.

> Take the consultant's advice **with a grain of salt**—the software he's recommending is produced by a company that is also a client of his.

With respect to, in some respects – These expressions are not really about giving respect. *With respect to* (or *in respect to)* just means *about.* The expression *in some respects* just means *in some ways.*

> **With respect to** your request for a raise, I'm afraid no one is getting one this year. This year is, **in some respects**, the worst year we've ever had.

Wreak havoc – Cause destruction. The past tense of *wreak* is *wrought.*

> Unsurprisingly, a combination of heroin abuse and living on the streets can really **wreak havoc** on a person's health.

Drill 16.6 — Decoding Idioms

Pick the multiple-choice answer that best expresses the meaning of the original sentence.

Complete this quiz "open book"—feel free to go back and look up anything you want in this book, and to use any online dictionary (such as dictionary.com). You will gain much more from the process of looking things up and decoding the statements than you would by merely testing yourself in the usual manner.

1. In contrast to the Swedish social welfare system, Ireland's does not provide paid paternity leave.

    (A) Ireland's social welfare system does not provide paid paternity leave and Sweden's does.
    (B) The Swedish and Irish social welfare systems are different in many ways, and Ireland's does not provide paid paternity leave.
    (C) Both the Swedish and Irish social welfare systems provide paid paternity leave.

2. He can hardly be called a liberal, for his voting record belies the beliefs he professes to hold.

   (A) He is not really a liberal because he votes in a way that goes against liberalism.
   (B) He is a very strong liberal and always supports liberal beliefs with his vote.
   (C) He is slightly liberal, and his voting record goes along with his beliefs.

3. However much the committee may be deadlocked now, the progress made to this point has been nontrivial.

   (A) The committee is now committed to one course of action and is making progress.
   (B) The committee members are fighting with one another, but have made progress on one point they were discussing.
   (C) Although it is true that the committee is stuck and not moving forward, it has already made significant progress.

4. Although the book has addressed the issue of educational equity head on, it has sidestepped the thorny question of school vouchers.

   (A) The book talked about owning stock in education, but it has talked in an indirect way about the painful issue of school vouchers.
   (B) The book talked directly about equality in education, but it avoided talking about the controversial issue of school vouchers.
   (C) The book talked in a smart way about fairness in education, but it only gave an overview of the controversial issue of school vouchers.

5. Her appointment to the office is all but assured.

   (A) She has a meeting at the office, but the time is not set.
   (B) She will almost certainly be given a new job or leadership role.
   (C) She may be promoted, but it is not likely.

6. You discount the consultant's prescription at your peril.

   (A) You may put yourself in danger by dismissing the consultant's recommendations.
   (B) Paying less for the consultant's advice is not a wise idea.
   (C) You have gotten a good deal on a dangerous medicine.

7. Davis seemingly spearheaded the project and has taken credit for its success. Nonetheless, those in the know are aware of his patent appropriation of the ideas of others.

   (A) Davis seems to have led the project, and he took credit for it. However, those who know the real situation know that he openly stole other people's ideas.
   (B) Davis was the leader of the project and got the credit, and those who know about what happened know that he used the intellectual property of other people in an appropriate way.
   (C) Davis seems to have damaged the project, but took credit for its success. However, those who know the real situation know that he used other people's ideas.

8. The experiment only looks like a success.

   (A) It is not possible to see the experiment as anything but a success.
   (B) The experiment seems successful, but we don't know for sure.
   (C) The experiment has the appearance of a success, but really is a failure.

9. On its face, the dispute is about the study's integrity. But in actuality, the lead scientist will brook no opposition to his own theories.

   (A) The dispute is directly about the honesty of the study. But really, the lead scientist will not "go with the flow" of opposition to his own theories.
   (B) The dispute at first seems to be about the study's honesty. But really, the lead scientist will not tolerate opposition to his own theories.
   (C) The dispute is directly about the honesty of the study. But really, the lead scientist will not encourage opposition to his own theories.

10. We will not likely reconcile the apparent discrepancy for years to come.

   (A) It will probably take us many years to show that what looks like a contradiction really isn't.
   (B) We do not want to work out a difference of opinion in the coming years.
   (C) Over the next several years, we will probably not attempt to work out what seems like an error.

11. The dictator had long sown discontent, and as dissident thinkers began to hold sway over the populace, no one could be surprised when the regime was subverted.

    (A) The dictator was dissatisfied, and as rebellious thinkers began to have policial power over the people, it was not surprising when the government became corrupt.
    (B) The dictator had been planting seeds of unhappiness that were destined to grow, and as thinkers who disagreed with the government began to influence regular people, it was not surprising when the dictator was overthrown.
    (C) The dictator had been more and more dissatisfied over time, and as thinkers whose ideas went against the government began to influence the people, it was not surprising when the dictator lost his power.

12. A variable-rate mortgage is no worse in this respect than a fixed-rate one.

    (A) There is something bad about a fixed-rate mortgage, and that same quality is either equally bad or somewhat better in a variable-rate mortgage.
    (B) A variable-rate mortgage does not indicate less respect than a fixed-rate mortgage.
    (C) If you look at it a certain way, a fixed-rate mortgage is the same or better than a variable-rate one.

13. As to whether Dr. Stuttgart is a token academic on a board of otherwise mercenary executives, you need look only at the board's response to the latest crisis, when Dr. Stuttgart was at once turned to for counsel and granted discretionary power over the board's funds.

    (A) If there is a question about whether the main reason Dr. Stuttgart is on the board is so the executives who only care about money can look good, then the only way to answer that question is to look at the board's response to the latest crisis, when Dr. Stuttgart was put in charge and given power over the board's money.
    (B) If you want to know whether Dr. Stuttgart is really an academic even though he is on a board of executives who will do anything to win, then the best place to look for an answer is at the board's response to the latest crisis, when Dr. Stuttgart was asked for his advice and allowed to secretly control the board's money.
    (C) If you are questioning whether the main reason Dr. Stuttgart is on the board is so the executives who only care about money can look good, then you can easily answer that question by looking at the board's response to the latest crisis, when the board asked for Dr. Stuttgart's advice while at the same time giving him power to spend the board's money on whatever he thought was best.

14. The author is seemingly a garden-variety Marxist.

    (A) The author seems to be a Marxist who has a lot of diversity in his or her opinions.
    (B) The author is a Marxist who is concerned with many different Marxist issues.
    (C) It seems as though the author is a typical Marxist, but that may not really be true.

15. The windfall could hardly have come at a better time: payment was due on a large tax bill that he had inadvertently triggered by agreeing to a company restructuring he didn't fully understand.

    (A) The disaster happened at a very bad time, because he had also just agreed to a company reorganization that he didn't understand and that improperly caused a large tax bill to come due.
    (B) The money he received came at a very convenient time, because he had just agreed to a company reorganization that he didn't understand and thus the situation had accidentally led to a large tax bill.
    (C) The good fortune could have happened at a better time, because he had also just agreed to a company reorganization that he didn't understand and that prompted a large tax bill.

16. Which of the following, if true, best reconciles the apparent discrepancy?

    (A) Which of the following is true and shows that a contradiction does not really exist?
    (B) Which of the following, if it happened to be true, would show that what looks like a contradiction really isn't?
    (C) Which of the following, if it happened to be true, would help us accept a contradiction?

17. The evidence has been taken as supporting Fujimura's conclusion.

    (A) Other people have interpreted the evidence in a way that makes it seem to support Fujimura's conclusion.
    (B) The evidence definitely supports Fujimura's conclusion.
    (C) The evidence has been deeply understood by others in a way that allows them to effectively support Fujimura's conclusion.

18. Hardly a debased example, this shifty, hedging, practically unreadable document is paradigmatic of corporate memos.

    (A) This memo switches positions often, holds back information, and is very hard to read. It is a very poor example of corporate memos.
    (B) Although this memo refuses to take a stand, tries to reduce the writer's risk, and is very hard to read, it is a poor example of corporate memos and should not be judged to be representative.
    (C) This memo is evasive or tricky, avoids taking a stand so as not to risk being wrong or offending anyone, and is almost unreadable. However, this is not an especially bad example of a corporate memo—they are all this bad.

19. Which of the following best underscores the argument that a failure to enforce the regulation is on par with publicly condoning illegal dumping?

    (A) Which of the following most weakens the argument that a failure to enforce the regulation is just as bad as publicly tolerating illegal dumping?
    (B) Which of the following most strengthens the argument that a failure to enforce the regulation is just as bad as publicly tolerating illegal dumping?
    (C) Which of the following most emphasizes the argument that a failure to enforce the regulation is worse than publicly tolerating illegal dumping?

20. The central idea is juxtaposed with the results of a study that seemingly corroborates a long-derided school of thought.

    (A) The central idea is placed next to and contrasted with evidence that seems to support the ideas of a group of people whose ideas have been looked down on or made fun of for a long time.
    (B) The central idea is judged to be better than evidence that seems to support the ideas of a group of people whose ideas have been looked down on or made fun of for a long time.
    (C) The central idea is placed next to and contrasted with evidence that supports the ideas of a group of people whose ideas used to be looked down on or made fun of.

Answers are on pages 411–413.

Answers to Drill Sets

Vocab Drill 16.1

1. Whereas	**(D)** On the contrary, considering that
2. Save	**(E)** But or except
3. Nonetheless	**(C)** However, even so, despite that
4. Moreover	**(B)** In addition to what has been said, for instance; besides
5. Likewise	**(A)** Also, in addition to, similarly

Vocab Drill 16.2

1. *Checked* and *Tempered* both mean limited, held back.
2. *Underpin* and *Undergird* both mean strengthen or support (an argument).
3. *Stratum* and *Echelon* both mean a layer of something.
4. *Patently* and *Baldly* both mean explicitly, openly.
5. *Extrapolate* and *Infer* both mean to draw a conclusion from available data.

Vocab Drill 16.3

1. **(A)**
2. **(C)**
3. **(D)**
4. **(A)**
5. **(D)**

Vocab Drill 16.4

1. **(B)**
2. **(B)**
3. **(C)**
4. **(B)**
5. **(A)**

Vocab Drill 16.5

1. *Impasse* and *gridlock* both mean a standstill.
2. *Host* and *slew* both mean a large number.
3. *Impartial* and *disinterested* both mean unbiased.
4. *Aggravate* and *exacerbate* both mean make worse.
5. *Explicitly* and *baldly* both mean bluntly, in a straightforward or obvious way.

Answers to Drill 16.6 — Decoding Idioms

1. **(A).** The original sentence and correct answer (A) both indicate that Ireland's system does not provide paid paternity leave and the Swedish system does. Choice (B) does not specifically indicate that Sweden's system does provide paid paternity leave; it indicates only that the two systems are different in *many* ways. Choice (C) says that Ireland does provide paid paternity leave; this contradicts the original sentence.

2. **(A).** Both the original sentence and correct answer choice (A) say that his voting record goes against the beliefs that he says he holds. Answers (B) and (C) do not include this contrast.

3. **(C).** The original sentence and choice (C) state that the committee is stuck now, but that it did make good progress before becoming stuck. Choice (A) does not indicate that the committee is stuck, or deadlocked. Choice (B) does not go far enough: the committee has made *nontrivial*, or relatively significant, progress, not progress on just one point. (The word *point* is a trap. *To this point* means up until now. *On one point* refers to just one particular issue or question.)

4. **(B).** The original sentence and answer (B) both say that the book directly addresses one issue (educational equality), but does not address another (school vouchers). Choice (A) substitutes *owning stock* for *educational equity* (in this case, *equity* refers to equality, not equity as in owning stock!). Choice (C) mischaracterizes the treatment of school vouchers. The book does not address this issue at all.

5. **(B).** The original sentence and answer (B) both indicate that she is almost certainly going to be appointed to the new role. Choice (A) mixes up *appointment* with *meeting*; in the original sentence, *appointment* refers to someone being appointed to a role. Choice (C) has the wrong meaning; *all but assured* means that something will almost certainly happen.

6. **(A).** In the original sentence and answer (A), the consultant has advised something; if you don't listen, then you may find yourself in a bad position. Choices (B) and (C) mix up *discount* with the idea of *paying less for* or getting *a good deal on* something; in the original sentence, *discount* is a synonym for disregard or ignore. Choice (C) mixes up *prescription* with the idea of a medication. In the original sentence, *prescription* is a synonym for advice.

7. **(A).** The original sentence and answer (A) both indicate that Davis only appeared to have been responsible for the success of the project; in fact, he stole ideas from other people. Answer (B) is not entirely correct: according to the original sentence, Davis was only *seemingly* the leader of the project, not necessarily the actual leader of the project. In addition, stealing ideas from others is definitely not appropriate! Choice (C) says that the project was damaged; the original sentence does not say this.

8. **(C).** Both the original sentence and answer (C) imply that the experiment actually was not a success. Incorrect answers (A) and (B) convey the opposite meaning.

9. **(B).** The original sentences and answer (B) indicate that, on the surface, the dispute is about one thing (integrity), but it is actually about something else (the scientist won't allow others to disagree

with him). Choices (A) and (C) both mistakenly indicate that the dispute really is about the honesty, or integrity, of the study.

10. **(A).** The original sentence and correct answer (A) both indicate that something seems like a discrepancy but really isn't; further, they imply that it will take a while to show or prove that this is true. Choices (B) and (C) focus on the desire to fix a disagreement; this is not in the original sentence.

11. **(B).** Both the original sentence and correct answer (B) indicate that the populace was already unhappy with the dictator when others started to gain influence, so it really wasn't that surprising that the dictator's regime eventually fell. Choices (A) and (C) mix up *discontent* with *dissatisfied*. To *sow discontent* is to make other people dissatisfied, not yourself.

12. **(A).** The original sentence is confusing! A variable-rate mortgage is *no worse than* a fixed-rate one? This means that the variable-rate mortgage is the same as or better than the fixed-rate one. Answer (A) matches this meaning. Answer (C) gets the relationship backwards. Answer (B) mixes up *in this respect* with *less respect*; the former means in this way or in one way, while the latter has to do with the level of respect people have for this product.

13. **(C).** The original sentence first asks a question: Is Dr. Stuttgart a *token academic*, or a person included on the board just to make the board look good? In order to answer that question, look at what happened in the latest crisis: the board asked for Dr. Stuttgart's advice and gave him money to help fix the problem. Answer (C) matches this meaning. Answer (A) is close but misses the mark by indicating that the *only* way to answer the question is to look at the latest crisis. Answer (B) questions whether Dr. Stuttgart is an academic at all; this is not the question in the original sentence. Nor was the control given to Dr. Stuttgart *secret*.

14. **(C).** The original sentence and correct answer (C) both indicate that the author only *seems* to be a typical Marxist; in reality, he might not be. Choice (A) mixes up *garden-variety* with *diverse*. *Garden-variety* means typical; *diversity in . . . opinions* means having a lot of different opinions. Choice (B) makes the same type of error, in addition to mistakenly indicating that the author definitely is a Marxist.

15. **(B).** The original sentence first says that a good thing happened at the best possible time. Why? Because he had just inadvertently triggered a large tax bill (by making a decision that he didn't really understand). Answer (B) matches this meaning. Choice (A) refers to the *windfall* as a *disaster*, but a *windfall* is a good thing (often a big sum of money). In addition, *improperly* (not correctly, morally, or legally done) does not mean the same thing as *inadvertently* (by mistake). Choice (C) mixes up the meaning of *could hardly have come at a better time*. This means that it could not have come at a better time; it came at the best possible time.

16. **(B).** The original question and correct answer (B) both ask you to find an answer that, if true, will fix a discrepancy that is not really a discrepancy. Choice (A) says *is true*, rather than *if true*. Choice (C) talks about accepting an actual contradiction; the original question talks about explaining something that really is not a contradiction.

17. **(A).** Both the original sentence and correct answer (A) indicate that certain evidence may support the conclusion, but not everyone necessarily agrees that it definitely does support the conclusion. Choice (B) contradicts this idea. Answer (C) is close but misses the idea that some people think this evidence directly supports the conclusion (vs. *allowing* these people to *effectively support* the conclusion).

18. **(C).** The original sentence starts with a confusing idiom: *hardly a debased example.* First, this means it is *not* a debased (or poor) example. Rather, this really badly written document is actually typical of corporate memos. Answer (C) matches this meaning. The first part of both incorrect answers (A) and (B) is accurate, but the memo is not a poor example; it is a typical example.

19. **(B).** *Underscore* is a synonym for *strengthen*, so both the original question and correct answer (B) ask you to strengthen the idea that failing to enforce the regulation is basically the same as *condoning* (or accepting) the actions of the law-breakers. Choice (A) asks the opposite question (*weaken*). Choice (C) asks the wrong question (*emphasizes* vs. *strengthens*) and mixes up the meaning of *on par with* (as bad as, not worse).

20. **(A).** The original sentence and correct answer (A) state that a main idea is compared to or contrasted with a study that appears to support something that has long been considered ridiculous or without value. Choice (B) incorrectly calls the main idea *better than* the other. Choice (C) is close but drops the meaning of *seemingly*: it *seems* to support the school of thought, but it may not actually do so. In addition, the *long-derided school of thought* is still viewed that way today in the original sentence.

Appendix A

Helpful Hints for Indian Speakers of English

In This Chapter...

Helpful Hints for Indian Speakers of English

Helpful Hints for Indian Speakers of English

This article was written by Manhattan Prep instructor Jen Dziura.

Many, many Indian and Indian-American students have come through the doors of Manhattan Prep.

As such, we've heard our Indian students say all kinds of things that are different from the equivalent expressions in American English. For instance, Americans do not *prepone* meetings, although we have to agree that the idea makes perfect sense (we usually say "move a meeting up," based on the idea that earlier times are higher up on a printed schedule). In the United States, a store has "hours," not "timings," and a handsome movie star might be called a "leading man," but not a "hero."

All of this is very interesting, but not particularly relevant to the GMAT.

However, there are a few differences between Indian and American English that are indeed relevant to the exam, and we will discuss those here.

We want to be clear that our purpose is not to say that Indian English—or any other dialect of English—is wrong. Americans can hardly claim that their form of the language is the "right" one when, of course, the English were speaking their own language long before the United States was even a country. In some ways, Indian English is closer to the "original" (British English) than American English is. So our purpose here is simply to help speakers of other dialects master a few nuances of American English.

In 2010, I traveled to India, noting language used in local newspapers, in advertisements, and by people I spoke to. I was a bit surprised when a Citibank ATM said, "Your transaction is getting done." (An American version would probably say, "Your transaction is being processed.") I was amused to learn that a "non-veg" joke is a dirty one. But more importantly, I collected much of the information appearing in this appendix.

We are fully aware that there are many regional differences in how English is spoken in India, and that some usages below are only prevalent among Hindi speakers, for instance, or are casual and wouldn't be used in business writing even in India.

The Progressive Tense

Some speakers of Hindi have a tendency to overuse the progressive tense in English. For instance, "I am knowing how to do it" (incorrect) instead of "I know how to do it."

A less obvious example is, perhaps, "I am living on Broad Street." Most Americans would say this if they mean to refer to a time period—for instance, "I am living on Broad Street *these days*." However, if you simply mean to tell someone where you live, just say, "I live on Broad Street."

INCORRECT: He *is wanting* to apply to Stanford.

CORRECT: He *wants* to apply to Stanford.

Here are some situations in which you *should* use the progressive:

CORRECT: She *is writing* a letter and does not want to be disturbed.

CORRECT: He *is going* to the store.

CORRECT: The professor *is talking* about derivatives.

What is different about these last three examples? Or, in other words, how can you tell when you can use the "is (verb)ing" construction? One guideline is that you: only use the progressive for things you can physically see people doing:

CORRECT: He is waiting.

INCORRECT: He is needing the report.

This guideline won't work every time, though. "He is thinking" is fine, but "He is desiring" is not. One other guideline might also help you: don't use a complicated verb tense when a simple one will do.

The Subjunctive

Sentences in the command subjunctive take this pattern:

CORRECT: The CEO demanded that we be on time.

CORRECT: I suggest that you run faster.

Some Indian speakers tend to say things like:

INCORRECT: I request you to do it.

This does not match the pattern above. You need the word *that,* and the word *to* is incorrect:

CORRECT: I request *that* you do it.

"Could" and "Would"

INCORRECT: I *could be able* to attend the meeting.

CORRECT: I *am able* to attend the meeting.

CORRECT: I *could* attend the meeting *if you gave me a ride.*

Could is used for things that are not certain to happen—in the last case, the speaker is only able to attend the meeting IF a condition is met. *Could* is also the past tense of *can* (*Back in 1985, I could speak German*). *Could have* is used for actions a person had the ability to do but did not (*I could have married a very rich man, but instead I married for love*).

In real life, people often say things like, "Sure, I *could* get that done by Tuesday." By itself, this is not entirely grammatical—rather, it is a way to avoid responsibility. It is implied that there is some unspoken "if"—as in, *If I feel like doing it and everything goes perfectly, sure, it's possible that it could be done by Tuesday.*

A stronger statement would be, "I can get that done by Tuesday." A person who was really committing to do the job would say, I will get that done by Tuesday."

Now that we've discussed *could,* let's discuss *would:*

INCORRECT: Six of us *would* be attending the conference.

CORRECT: Six of us *will* be attending the conference.

CORRECT: Our company *would* have paid for our lunch *if we had kept the receipt.*

Don't use *would* in place of *will.* If something is definitely happening or has been planned, use *will.* Use *would* for imagined situations (*I would love to be a rock star*), as the past tense of *will* and *won't* (*He said he would do it*), or for conditionals (as in the example above with *if we had kept the receipt*).

The Past Perfect

INCORRECT: The company had gone bankrupt.

CORRECT: The company went bankrupt.

Don't use complicated past tenses (the *past perfect*) when the regular past tense will do. As you learned in the chapter on verbs (specifically pages 47–57), only use a "had" verb when expressing an action that happened prior to another action also in the past:

CORRECT: The company had been on the brink of bankruptcy until it was saved by an investor.

Here, *had been* is correct, as the company was first *on the brink of bankruptcy* and later *was saved.*

"As" after "Called" or "Consider" (Etc.)

INCORRECT: Aretha Franklin is called *as* "The Queen of Soul."

CORRECT: Aretha Franklin is called "The Queen of Soul."

INCORRECT: I consider you *as* a friend.

CORRECT: I consider you a friend.

Do not use *as* after consider, called, etc.

"To" After Comparisons

INCORRECT: She is more experienced *to* the other candidates.

CORRECT: She is more experienced *than* the other candidates.

Follow comparatives by *than: taller than, smarter than, more intelligent than . . .*

Countable vs. Non-countable Nouns

Pay attention to which nouns are pluralized and which are not. For instance, *suggestion* can be pluralized—I could give you three *suggestions,* for instance. However, *advice* cannot be pluralized. I cannot give you "*three advices.*" Instead, I would give you "a lot of advice" or "three *pieces* of advice." (Also, *advice* is a noun. The related verb is *advise.*)

Adverbs (or the Lack Thereof)

There is a definite lack of adverbs in some Indian English. For instance, many street signs say "Go Slow." (Since *slow* modifies a verb, it should be *slowly.*) Watch out to make sure you do not modify verbs with adjectives.

In India, *timely* is used as an adverb, as in *Please do it timely.* In American English, this is NOT correct. While *timely* ends in "*-ly*," it is actually an adjective, so *Please do it timely* is incorrect, just as *Please do it quick* and *Please do it cheerful* are wrong. Instead, say *Please do it in a timely manner.*

Usage Issues Related to GMAT Math

There should not be any language differences that affect your ability to answer GMAT math problems.

However, if you attended school in India and then attend an American-English GMAT class, or try to read an American-English test prep book, you may run into a few small differences that we can clear up right now.

It may help avoid confusion to know that, in American English, "2 into 10" equals 5, not 20. (The wording "into" is quite casual and will not appear on the GMAT itself, but it is something that an American GMAT instructor might say while teaching.)

Americans use "into" as a short version of "divided into" and "by" as a short version of "multiplied by." For instance:

6 into 12 = 2

5 by 10 = 50

Again, these phrases are informal and often spoken out loud, but not written in textbooks or used on exams such as the GMAT. It would be very common for someone to say that he lived in a "10 by 12 bedroom," meaning a bedroom with dimensions of 10 and 12 feet and an area of 120 square feet. Such a usage is very common in construction, real estate, carpet purchasing, etc. The real GMAT, though, will not use such casual language.

A few other issues: Undoubtedly, you have already familiarized yourself with the different use of separators in the American numbering system—for example the number twelve million, four hundred thousand, two hundred nine:

Indian:	1,24,00,209
American:	12,400,209

Numbers of this size just don't occur that often on the GMAT, and in cases such as 5,600,000 (or 56,00,000), it is often best to put the number in scientific notation anyway: 5.6×10^6.

Americans tend to say every number in a series even when there are repeats. For instance, the phone number 229–3334 is spoken *two, two, nine, three, three, three, four*. Of course, anyone will understand you when you say *double two, nine, triple three, four*, but it might throw the person off enough that he or she has trouble writing down the number and needs to ask you to repeat it.

Finally—and I'm not sure what language or cultural difference is causing this confusion—I have seen many students incorrectly interpret this question:

What is the average of $a + b + c + d$ and 7?

Many students write $\frac{(a+b+c+d+7)}{5}$. This is incorrect! My best guess as to the confusion is that you might be mixing up the summation (represented by the plus sign, +) with the *and* that is used to list the two numbers to take the average of. If you routinely think of 5 + 2 as "five and two," you might make this mistake. In American English, 5 + 2 would typically be read as "five *plus* two."

If the GMAT intended the variables as individual items, it would have separated *a*, *b*, *c*, and *d* with commas. As is, "$a + b + c + d$" is all one item. Use the commas to count items! For instance, "the average of $a + b$, 2, and $c + d$" means that there are three items being averaged (two commas separating three items). To recap:

The average of $a + b + c + d$ and 7 is written as $\frac{(a+b+c+d+7)}{2}$.

The average of *a*, *b*, *c*, *d* and 7 is written as $\frac{(a+b+c+d+7)}{5}$.

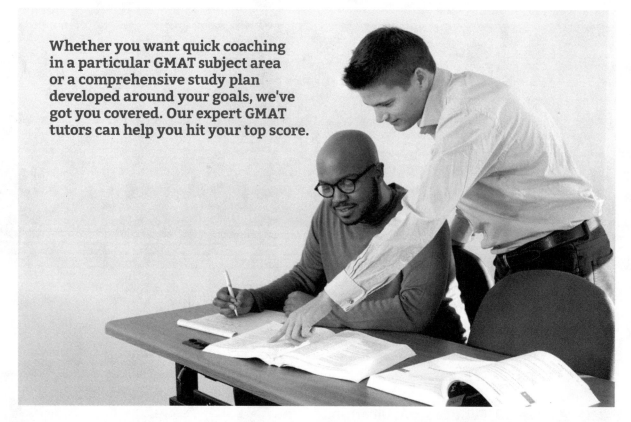